COMPARATIVE PERSPECTIVES ON

SOCIAL
PSYCHOLOGY

COMPARATIVE PERSPECTIVES ON

SOCIAL PSYCHOLOGY

Edited and with Introduction by

WILLIAM WILSON LAMBERT
and RITA WEISBROD

Cornell University

LITTLE, BROWN AND COMPANY Boston

LIBRARY OF CONGRESS CATALOG CARD NO. 73-142334

FIRST PRINTING

Printed simultaneously in Canada by
Little, Brown & Company (Canada) Limited

PRINTED IN THE UNITED STATES OF AMERICA

TABLE OF CONTENTS

v

COMPARATIVE PERSPECTIVES ON

SOCIAL
PSYCHOLOGY

I

Introduction

WILLIAM WILSON LAMBERT
AND RITA WEISBROD

We want to do several things in this Introduction: first, say something about what social psychology is, and then what a comparative perspective on social psychology is; second, summarize briefly the development of the comparative perspective in social psychology, indicating the methodological and substantive status of comparative research, and suggesting some courses for future development; and finally, provide guidance to this book.

Social psychology is a fast-growing field to which psychologists, sociologists, anthropologists, and others have made important contributions. Because their field combines these disciplines, social psychologists disagree on how to define its exact subject matter. Probably all would agree that social psychologists attempt to discover and test hypotheses about "human nature" and human interaction. They borrow (or develop) models of processes that occur within and between people. Their models are borrowed from psychology, sociology, or even mathematics or physics. The

1

major activity of social psychologists is providing the evidence for their selection of the models with which they explain an observed social phenomenon or social process. Social psychologists test specific hypotheses stemming from these models. The evidence comes from laboratory experiments, field studies, sample surveys, tests and questionnaires, and systematic observations.

The present body of knowledge in social psychology, it is apparent, is scattered; most of its theories pertain only to particular areas of study. The theories are specific to human *cognition* (the input and storing of information), to *social learning* or development, to *behavior in social interaction*, to *personality* as a summary description of an individual, to *group effects on the individual* and the individual's adjustment to group demands, or to *the individual within society as a whole.*

Most of social psychology grew up (and remained until recently) in the United States and Europe. During the forties and fifties, a revolution in methods placed emphasis on an inward-turning laboratory method, where the investigator cut the problem down to manageable size and emphasized "internal validity" rather than "external validity" in his work. That is, the investigator knew what he was doing with the subjects he was studying, under controlled conditions, but he gave up (temporarily at least) his worry about fitting the findings to the world outside the laboratory (external validity).

Just as this emphasis on the laboratory and its analytic tools was paying off, another revolution, emphasizing external validity, was in the offing. This newer development did not deny the importance of the laboratory method or internal validity, but stemmed from an acceptance of it and a desire to go beyond it. The "revolution" involved a booming interest in testing hypotheses in natural settings, especially where a social process could be examined both at home and in some other culture. It also involved submitting conclusions already reached in the laboratory to testing in settings having cross-cultural diversity. In large part, this comparative development in social psychology might be dubbed "Fulbright's revolution," since it was the Fulbright program (along with help from foundations and increased availability of sabbatical leaves) that permitted a number of social psychologists to go to one another's countries. They discovered that it was fascinating and challenging to test old findings in new places, and they discovered what our colleagues in anthropology have talked about so long. Moving into a new culture leads to "culture shock" and a respect for the possible relativism of many social phenomena. It was natural to question social psychological conclusions that seemed final, and to test them again in a new setting. Much to their chagrin, some social psychologists discovered that if they were to study a social process in a new culture or society, they must be prepared to study it in a different way. One laboratory technique (or one way of asking a question) may be understood differently in any two cultures studied (Schachter, 1954 and Rommetveit and Israel, 1954). Even more disturbing, they occasionally found that a conclusion held to be true about a social process when studied in the laboratory or in a natural setting at home did not hold up under cross-cultural testing. Apparently this finding was dependent on conditions which were not considered related in the earlier study, but which were operating differently in the new setting (Schachter, 1954). This evidence of a need for different methods as well as an accumulation of sometimes divergent and sometimes convergent findings in different places presented a challenge.

Comparative social psychology presented this challenge to social psychology, and now is the focal point of response to it. The response has to be directed principally toward defining social psychological subject matter and social psychological variables in a more abstract manner. The comparative perspective in social psychology requires a movement toward more general models of social processes — models involving more abstract and less culturally specific variables, whose hypotheses have been confirmed in widely varied settings, giving the models a high degree of external *as well as* internal validity.

Just how do comparative social psychologists operate? Most social psychologists doing cross-cultural work are interested in cultural variations in the principles that guide social interaction. However, they are not interested in cultural variations as unique patterns. Cross-cultural work is undertaken because cultural variations are useful in providing individuals and groups falling along a range of values of a given variable (such as different group sizes) in order to study the effects of that variable upon another (such as aggressiveness). Cross-cultural work thus takes advantage of the variation in social attitudes and social responses being greater among all men than within any given culture of men. Comparative social psychologists find themselves turning to well-traveled anthropologists, economists, or sociologists and asking such questions as, "Where will I find the most restrictive norms against interpersonal aggression?" or, "Where will I find the most helpful people?" Alternatively, they seek out the Human Relations Area Files [1] and look at the descriptions ethnologists

---

[1] The Human Relations Area Files are available at twenty-four locations, as follows:

The University of Chicago; University of Colorado; Cornell University; Harvard University; University of Hawaii; University of Illinois; Indiana University; University of Iowa; University of Michigan; City University of New York; State University of New York at Buffalo; University of North Carolina; University of

have provided of aggression or helpfulness in various cultures. They then choose to study cultures that they believe will vary substantially in their handling of aggression or helpfulness. They might study such things as group size or frequency of interaction in these selected cultures, testing the hypothesis that it is either variations in group size or interaction rates that explain the observed (and also studied) methods of handling aggression or level of helpfulness.

The point of cross-cultural work is to examine a hypothesis about a social process in a number of settings, natural or experimentally manipulated, so our confidence in the resulting finding may be increased. If a finding holds everywhere it has been tested, we feel we have attained a generalization about human nature that holds universally. If a finding holds in some settings but not in others, we know we must keep looking for conditions that affect the generalization that we have made. Here we see that one strength of the cross-cultural approach, as indicated by Fred Strodtbeck (1964), is in the *discovery* of hypotheses. Testing a hypothesis in a number of settings can provide clues to those conditions that may affect the generalization, thus expanding our understanding of the social processes involved.

Most social psychologists doing cross-cultural work are therefore interested in cultural variations because they lead us to a broader testing of generalizations about human universals. As we will see, a number of lines of comparative research have resulted in convergence on a similar set of universal dimensions in the explanation of values, the meaning of terms, and the character of universal behavior. Such research, ultimately identifying human universals, is directly relevant to *comparative* social psychology in the psychologists' or ethologists' sense of "comparative" — making comparisons across species. Truly comparative social psychology in this sense, where comparisons in the social behavior of man and other animals are examined, is still in the speculative stage, but it constitutes a new frontier in comparative social psychology. By its very character, research of this kind requires cross-cultural testing in the broadest sense.

We have spoken of comparative social psychology in its general out-

---

Oklahoma; University of Pennsylvania; University of Pittsburgh; Princeton University; Smithsonian Institution, Washington, D.C.; University of South Carolina; Southern Illinois University; University of Utah; University of Washington; Yale University; Kyoto University, Japan; École Pratique des Hautes Etudes and Maison des Sciences de l'Homme, Paris, France.

In addition, a microfilm edition of the Files is available at one hundred and forty sites and through University Microfilms, Inc., Ann Arbor, Michigan.

For information about the Files, see Clellan S. Ford, "Human Relations Area Files 1949–1969: A Twenty Year Report," *Behavior Science Notes*, 1970, 5:1, or write to The Human Relations Area Files, Box 2054 Yale Station, New Haven, Connecticut 06520.

lines with an eye to where it is going. We have characterized it as a "revolution" in social psychology, aimed at external validity of generalizations. Generally speaking, just how far has this "comparative revolution" gone? The answer from many points of view must be "not very far." We are only at the beginning. To be sure, two new journals now publish comparative studies,[2] and other journals have accommodated themselves in one way or another to the publication of these new materials. A newsletter has appeared to help keep track of travelers' whereabouts and fields of study.[3] Yet, at the same time, the authors of one of the major texts in the field decided to leave out most of this material, suggesting that comparative social psychology was a new and different science. It would be neater to describe the revolution as "merely the addition of a new dimension to the study of social psychological phenomena"; but it is more radical, affecting the basic character of research and theory in social psychology. It is therefore more accurate to speak of "the comparative perspective in social psychology" than of "comparative social psychology," since the former emphasizes the character of comparative work as basic to social psychology rather than as an adjunct to it.

Some people have also viewed cross-cultural and cross-societal studies solely in *practical* terms, dismissing them only as aids in translating the tools of social psychology to help developing nations solve problems. Certainly, social psychologists doing comparative studies often *do* prove to be very useful people, but their interests and work have theoretical, as well as practical, implications.

In this Introduction, we promised to provide a summary of the methodological and substantive status of research in comparative social psychology. In doing so, we will first highlight the central features and then make some critical remarks that illustrate the limitations of the comparative revolution to date. In closing, we will make some recommendations for the future.

1. THE METHODOLOGICAL FOCUS

The emphasis in comparative social psychology to date has been primarily methodological. New research tools, mostly quantitative measures, have

[2] The *International Journal of Psychology* initiated publication in 1966. It is published by Dunod (92, rue Bonaparte, Paris 6e, France) for the International Union of Psychological Science (G. Montmollin, editor, 28, rue Serpente, Paris 6e, France). The *Journal of Cross-Cultural Psychology* began publication in 1970 (Department of Psychology, Western Washington State College, Bellingham, Washington 98225).

[3] The *Cross-Cultural Social Psychology Newsletter*, Yasumasa Tanaka, editor, Department of Political Science, Gakushuin (Peers') University, Mejiro, Toshima-ku, Tokyo, Japan.

been developed that are relatively objective in cross-cultural use. Let us illustrate this trend with a brief recounting of one of the major successful lines of development.

For years Charles Morris, the philosopher and behavioral scientist, had worked on the development of a test for personal values. With the help of Lyle Jones, Morris subjected his test to one form of cross-cultural testing (see pages 255–273). This "ways of life" test was a crystallization of Morris' many years of comparative scholarly study of human ethical and religious systems. Samples of college students from several countries were given the test, choosing for themselves their favorite "paths of life." National and cultural differences in the average choice of these lifeways were obvious as Morris went from country to country. When the sets of answers were factor-analyzed, however, a fairly common underlying structure emerged. We can use the measurement of rooms as an appropriate analogy: the sizes of rooms vary as one goes from house to house, just as the individual (or group) averages vary for choices of preferred ways to live. Underlying these varying choices, however, lie *dimensions* analogous to the height, width, and depth of rooms. Superficially there are great (and very important) differences between societies; at a "deeper level," however, the clustering of choices reveals a similar structure of dimensions of values, providing the quantitative basis for systematic cross-cultural comparison.

Additional researchers have sought and achieved this same pattern of discovery. When Charles Osgood and his colleagues, for example, had discovered that three "dimensions" seemed to underlie affective meaning measurements taken in the United States, it was quite natural for them to see if these dimensions underlay affective meaning judgments in other cultures as well. Thus was born the most ambitious cross-cultural study and the most practically useful set of tools that comparative social psychology has to offer: the growing family of "differentials," the first of which was the "semantic differential." Osgood repeated his study in eighteen countries and language groups, developing methods that help to minimize the mysterious influences of translating from one language to another (as Przeworski and Teune (1966) have also done by formalizing the criteria for equivalence in cross-national research). Semantic differentials stand among the most tried and tested tools in social science, and many important theoretical and practical studies now refer to the basic dimensions of affective meaning as "evaluation," "potency," and "activity," again analogous to the height, width, and depth of rooms.

One of the most useful tools that has spun-off from the cross-cultural semantic differential is the forthcoming cross-cultural *Atlas of Affective Meanings*, a collection of actual judgments of many concepts made by people in a large number of cultures. The potentialities of these data can be seen in Jakobovits' report (see pages 164–174). This expendable looseleaf book will include the judgments of the evaluation, potency, and activeness of five hundred concepts, including measures of the level of social agreement on these concepts' affective meaning in each of the society samples. These dimensions of evaluation, potency, and activeness (continuing our spatial analogy to measuring rooms) are referred to as "semantic space," and the placement given to various concepts in this space is very revealing, as Jakobovits demonstrates.

The spin-off from semantic differentials and semantic space has hardly begun. "Job differentials" for obtaining comparative data on perceptions or judgments of jobs were quickly developed, as was a similar tool for judging personalities. Triandis and his colleagues (see pages 185–213) have moved toward developing a cross-culturally useful "role differential." As Osgood, in developing the semantic differentials, reduced and ordered *adjectives* that could apply to people, objects, jobs, things, and ideas, Triandis has similarly begun to reduce and order *verbs and adverbs* in developing a "behavior differential," upon which the role differential is built. The role differential provides a description of the culturally unique and pan-culturally common dimensions "underlying" actions. It provides a common "role space" for comparing the behaviors that people in different cultures expect in their significant self-other relationships, or roles.

Of course, many other important developments in methods might be mentioned here. Quite a different line can be seen in the work of Barker, who with Herbert Wright has developed a new set of tools for systematic observation (see pages 16–32). Similarly, Longabaugh (1963) has developed a new category system for interpersonal observation. Many other new tools are in various stages of development. (W. Holtzman's new objective method with ink blots is among the many projective and self-report tests that are beginning to be tried and revalidated in many places in the world.)

2. THE SUBSTANTIVE CONTRIBUTIONS

A number of studies in widely different subject areas have converged on a very similar set of underlying dimensions of explanation. Although methodological developments have been the keynote of the "comparative revolution" we have discussed, the most important substantive or theoretical development has been the convergence on similar explanatory dimensions in a wide variety of specific subject areas. As outlined above, Morris and Jones analyzed their cross-cultural paths of life data on values, and Osgood and his colleagues analyzed their nineteen-nation data on the meaning of terms, arriving at very similar dimensions. Triandis and

Lambert (1958) have pointed out the great similarity between these dimensions and the axes along which facial expressions are judged cross-culturally. Quite independently, Longabaugh (1966) examined a whole range of behavioral tendencies or traits, stemming from the observation of children in the Six Culture Study. He finds either two or three cross-cultural dimensions underlying their interpersonal behavior, depending on whether he analyzes the rates of action or the proportion of a particular kind of action to total action. These dimensions have been found in more limited cultural contexts by a number of authors examining interpersonal behavior.

3. PROBLEMS OF SOCIAL PSYCHOLOGICAL RESEARCH HIGHLIGHTED BY CROSS-CULTURAL STUDIES

(a) *Problems in Interpreting the Data*

Most of the important work in obtaining comparative data in social psychology has been done by Americans and Western Europeans, and most of the studies have used exclusively Western European and American samples. This concentration of effort has greatly limited the extent to which cross-cultural work has been truly comparative. It has led to the accusation of international research imperialism, and, more fundamentally, it rules out the use of techniques that would aid in the interpretation of findings. This problem requires elaboration.

Let us say that we have a similar finding in structures or processes across cultures. This finding remains ambiguous when the studies are managed by people from (largely) one culture. How much of the order or similarity found across cultures is actually there, and how much is implanted by the scientists? For example, D'Andrade (1965) had American subjects judge the similarity of meaning of a number of trait adjectives. The Six Culture Study researchers (mostly Americans) had "discovered" a similarity of structure in the relationships among observed behavior traits of children in these cultures (Longabaugh, 1966). The structures obtained by D'Andrade and Longabaugh are the same. Why? Because the structure in the similarity of English meanings was somehow *imposed* by the English-speaking observers upon the behavior of the children in the six cultures, or because the same structure actually resides in both the language and in the behavior observed in the six different cultures?

Campbell (pages 121–141) insists that when we move from doing research in one language or cultural group to another, we must first show some similarity between our behavior and that of the new culture in order to prove that we have communicated. Only then can we systematically and convincingly document the differences in the behaviors. The only way to resolve the fundamental ambiguity in our findings, however, is patient, coordinated study by scientists from many cultures. Campbell proposes "triangulation" as a technique for clarifying our findings. Suppose we have Cultures C and D. We have scientists from two other cultures, A and B. Suppose a scientist from A does a study of each of these cultures C and D (reports 1 and 2), and a scientist from B does a study of each of these same cultures (reports 3 and 4). Under these ideal conditions, we can make at least some unambiguous decisions. We can attribute to Mr. A those things in his reports not shared with Mr. B in his reports. We can attribute to Mr. B those things in his reports not shared with Mr. A. Most important, the common attributes of the reports by Mr. A and Mr. B on Culture C that are not present in the two reports on Culture D can be attributed to Culture C as "objectively known." The same is true of those shared attributes on Culture D which are not present in reports on Culture C. However, attributes common to all four reports are still ambiguous. They may be shared biases of the scientists, or they may be genuinely shared features of the cultures studied.

The triangulation technique is of particular interest if we want to increase our confidence in the validity of descriptions of *particular* cultures and cultural variations. All social psychological data come from *particular* cultural settings and require interpretation by the investigator. What we need to develop in social psychology are methods of cross-checking the interpretations made by investigators from different cultural backgrounds. As an alternative means of assessing our interpretations of data and the cross-cultural findings based on them, Roberts and Sutton-Smith (1962) have proposed "subsystem validation" of cross-cultural findings. Irvin Child (1968) has given us an example from his own research. Bacon, Barry, and Child (1965) used data from a number of cultures to examine the hypothesis that "high levels of use of alcohol are in part motivated by a need to relieve frustration or conflicted dependency needs." Child indicates that his confidence in the cross-cultural finding is increased because the same hypothesis was independently used by other investigators to explain why individuals within United States society differ in their drinking habits. The Whitings (see pages 33–45) demonstrate such a double-method approach — the *cross*-cultural and *intra*-cultural (or "subsystem") examination of a relationship. Most of the workers on the Six Culture Study, on which the Whitings' paper is based, were from Western societies, but their field assistants were natives of the culture each was studying, thereby providing an opportunity for Western observers to check on their interpretation of the data collected.

The problem of interpreting data collected by social scientists whose cognitive structure may differ is often ignored or denied. More often understood, but equally disregarded, is the lack of sufficient sociological and anthropological context to make the data maximally meaningful. Viewed from the fierce standards of good anthropological field work, a handful of questionnaires or a small experiment, obtained from a few badly sampled informants on a short jetflight by an investigator who does not know the bigger picture, can look pretty silly. More extensive experience with the cultures studied or coordinated projects involving experts on other cultures can prevent misinterpretation and misapplication of findings. In addition, knowing more about the cultural context of the research permits the emergence of many new insights and hypotheses. Coordination of the tools and skills of all the social sciences can enhance the value of comparative studies in social psychology and make the results useful to a broader audience of theoretical *and* practical people.

The future of comparative social psychology depends on having active and equal participation by research workers in many cultures in order to resolve the ambiguity that arises in work or from investigators from one culture. Participation in the research by workers who know the cultural context is crucial also to a full understanding of cross-cultural findings. Campbell points out that when scientists come from the same culture, the replication of results becomes more a matter of reliability than validity. Many social psychologists argue that we do not have enough replication of results by our own culture-mates within our own culture. The task ahead is all the more vast by comparison. We must lure into the game brilliant and independently trained social psychologists from a wide variety of cultures and begin to work out shared facilities and interlocking relationships of great complexity if we are going to move toward social psychological generalizations having real external validity. Fortunately, comparative research is now beginning to come from Asia, Latin America, and Africa, done by people who grew up in those cultures.

(b) *Sampling Problems*

An important criticism of most cross-cultural studies is that they have been two-society affairs, reflecting the Fulbright grant or sabbatical leave syndrome. This is analogous in a sense to limiting research to a sample of two cases from a population (and a nonrandom sample at that). Although studies of this kind are useful as a start and often suggest important new hypotheses, the limitation of the sample makes it difficult to rule out a host of alternative explanations for the findings.

The best cross-cultural studies, like Osgood's nineteen-language study, tend to be large, with a large number of cultures involved. However, even when the number of studies is small, the value of the study could be much enhanced if these societies were selected on *systematic* grounds (for example, because they are known to differ in their treatment of inter-personal aggressiveness).

Apart from the problem of sampling cultures or societies, the sampling of individuals to be studied within these societies has been generally poor. This criticism is not mitigated by the fact that sampling of individuals has also been poor in studies confined to either the United States or Europe. Most of the samples are dependent on opportunity, employing school groups which have no perceptible ethnic ties or other homogeneous characteristics and which are taken up quickly by an investigator with little time or money to do better. Some studies are exceptions to this criticism, of course, and the sampling issue cannot be made an important consideration. However, cultures are entities that are very complex in their human, behavioral, valuing, and structural complexion, and more attention to proper sampling is an important desideratum in future work.

Sampling considerations are even more important in cross-cultural work because an extra spin-off from basic research may otherwise get lost. Opportunity is provided in cross-cultural work for consideration of both the usual scientific analytic generalizations, and the kinds of propositions Barker calls "ecological" ones. If, for example, we are testing to see if the number of frustrations a child has received has an effect on his aggression, it is easy (if we have sampled adequately for settings of action and for children) to compare cultures on how frequently each day a child is frustrated or acts aggressively. We see here, therefore, an extra motivation to sample more carefully.

(c) *Lack of Coordination with Past and Present Work*

With the notable exception we have discussed above, cross-cultural studies have not been cumulative in their findings. The possibility of *coordinated* studies has also not been realized. One man goes off to Hoobagooba country and studies a particular topic and a group of subjects with a particular method. The next man comes to the same place and studies a different topic with different individuals. We forget that a bit more co-ordination could provide an interesting spin-off — how the same people behave with regard to both topics, or with regard to two different methods. Why can't we cooperate to repeat studies with different topics, methods, and measures on the same people?

(d) *Frequent Lack of Methodological Precautions*

Finally, many tools are used without an adequate check on their reliability and validity when applied to new groups of people. Although the biggest developments in comparative social psychology have been methodological, much remains to be done with tools we have.

We have come full circle in our discussion of the "comparative revolution," and what we have said here is critical of most social psychological, as well as comparative, work. In looking to the future of comparative social psychology, we want to conclude with a proposal. *Bold and imaginative international planning and research activity should be developed if comparative social psychology is to realize its potential as a tool of behavioral science.* It could make the work more cumulative and less imperialistic in its financing and direction, help solve the ambiguities in social science research by systematic triangulation procedures, and bring the inherent wisdom of people from other cultures to bear on the questions to be asked and the criteria to be accepted for methods of proof. External validity of findings is a problem in social science, and in the long run only cooperative effort on the part of social scientists from many cultures will permit abstract theories and valid findings to emerge in their full generality. "Human nature" can best be known through an objective social science if all men and all human cultures have some probability of observing it and being observed.

The selections we have included are designed to provide an introductory student in social psychology with a sampling of the major categories of knowledge and theory in the field and to demonstrate the major methods of collecting and treating data. Unfortunately, not all traditions and categories of theory in the field have produced comparative work, and some methods of collecting data have not been adapted for cross-cultural use, limiting the extent to which these goals could be realized. The selections have been kept readable for underclassmen who are prepared to use the dictionary and who command some understanding of statistics and the basic concepts of social psychology. As a result, many good comparative studies had to be excluded because they were too technical or too lengthy. However, to the extent that readability and space permitted, we present work which is especially significant in the development of comparative social psychology, or which provides a sampling of what seems to be an important new direction.

A number of the most ambitious studies of cross-cultural design are presented. Two articles draw upon the Six Culture Study (Lambert and the Whitings). The massive work of Osgood and his colleagues is represented by Jakobovits' paper, and the extensive work of McClelland on need achievement is summarized in his article. The work of Bronfenbrenner, Devereux, and colleagues in several cultures is represented by one study. Siegel, Campbell, and Herskovits' work on environmental conditions for visual illusions is presented in a summary paper by Campbell.

We have placed articles within five broad problem areas of general interest to social psychologists. Some assignments to these categories are arbitrary, and the vigilant instructor or student will notice that for some purposes recategorizing would be useful.

The first problem area contains comparative studies of socialization, one of the most active and diversified research areas in comparative social psychology. We have included studies of the impact of different behavior settings on individual motivation and on the apparent effects of task assignment on socializing boys toward responsible behavior. We have included a cross-cultural study relating child-rearing practices to romantic love, which treats a large number of cultures methodologically as if they were independent individuals. The paper by Barker compares the behavior setting complex in two cultures. The paper by the Whitings mixes the strategy of cross-cultural study with that of subsystem validation, as discussed earlier.

The second problem area involves cross-cultural studies of personality, a potentially huge and growing area of research, related to the studies on socialization. We have provided papers that deal with the study of the general background conditions for personality development (Lambert), and a number of papers that deal with limited strands of personality, such as the ability to delay gratification, the development of Machiavellianism and of authoritarianism, and the effects of self-esteem in competitive choice behavior. The papers reflect a number of designs and techniques, including the comparative use of controlled experimental manipulations. Many other papers in the reader deal with personality issues. Irvin Child (1968) has provided an extensive discussion of cross-cultural studies of personality that should be consulted by readers with a special interest in this subject.

Our third area includes cross-cultural studies of cognition, with special emphasis on processes of categorizing and communicating. Here we have placed studies on differences in perception and in the development of cognitive skills, stereotypes, affective meanings, and reaction to different languages, and on the cognitive aspects of the concept of kindness. Some of these studies are cross-cultural experiments, whereas others result from various kinds of interviews or questionnaires.

The fourth problem deals with social roles and interaction, presenting new tools for the study of role perceptions, intentions, and behaviors, on cultural differences in response to peer as compared with adult pressures, differences in group behavior resulting from different kinds of leaders, field experiments of palpable honesty in different large cities, and class differences in communication, creativity, and problem-solving.

Finally, Section Six focuses on comparative studies of man and modern society. In content, these papers deal with values, individual motives and their effect on economic development, and happiness. Methodologically, the findings rest upon techniques of behavioral science, ranging from the use of standardized tests and systematic sample surveys to field and laboratory experiments.

Generally speaking, we have included papers with substantial intrinsic interest coupled with competent design and method, illustrative of the various strategies being pursued and the kinds of statistical treatment of data presently being used. We have also selected papers that are easy to read for people with varying backgrounds and training. This reader clearly reflects that contributions to comparative social psychology have come from both the psychological and sociological sides of the discipline. Also, many cross-cultural social psychologists have been trained and advised by those anthropologists who have been transforming the study of the relations between psychology and anthropology. The influence of some of the leaders in this endeavor — the Whitings, John Roberts, Robert LeVine, and others — can be found here.

Although this reader will be useful in several courses, we hope that it will be particularly helpful in warding off the parochial presentation of social psychology as limited to data collected in only a few Western countries. More important, we hope it prevents the parochialism of presenting the field as limited to particular bodies of knowledge and theory, or particular research traditions and strategies. By presenting social psychology in comparative perspective, we want to highlight the diversity of theory and method in the field and to emphasize its direction as a generalizing science that develops knowledge of those principles of human social life that are *shared* — by some men or by all men. Social psychology ultimately seeks an organized and coherent body of knowledge encompassing cognition and learning, attitudes and behavior, and the principles of interaction and group functioning. The very distance we must go to reach these goals is one of the fascinations and challenges of the field.

References

Bacon, Margaret K., H. Barry III & I. L. Child. A cross-cultural study of drinking. *Quart. J. Stud. Alcohol*, 1965, Suppl. No. 3, 29–48.

Child, I. L. Personality in culture. *In* Borgatta, E. and W. W. Lambert, *Handbook of Personality Theory and Research*. Chicago: Rand McNally and Co., 1968.

D'Andrade, R. G. Trait psychology and componential analysis. *Amer. Anthrop.*, October 1965, 67:5, Part 2, 215–228.

Longabaugh, Richard. A category system for coding interpersonal behavior. *Sociometry*, September 1963, 26:3, 319–344.

Longabaugh, Richard. The structure of interpersonal behavior. *Sociometry*, December 1966, 29:4, 441–460.

Osgood, Charles and others. *The Atlas of Affective Meanings*. Urbana: The University of Illinois Press, forthcoming 1972.

Przeworski, Adam and Henry Teune. Equivalence in cross-national research. *Public Opinion Quarterly*, Winter 1966–67, 30, 551–568.

Roberts, J. M. and B. Sutton-Smith. Child training and game involvement. *Ethnology*, 1962, 1, 166–185.

Rommetveit, Ragnar and Joachim Israel. Notes on the standardization of experimental manipulations and measurements in cross-national research. *Journal of Social Issues*, 1954, 10:4, 61–68.

Schachter, Stanley. Interpretive and methodological problems of replicated research. *Journal of Social Issues*, 1954, 10:4, 52–60.

Strodtbeck, F. L. Considerations of meta-method in cross-cultural studies. *Amer. Anthrop.*, June 1964, 66:3, Part 2, 223–229.

Triandis, H. C. and W. W. Lambert. A restatement of Schlosberg's theory of emotion with two kinds of subjects from Greece. *J. Abnorm. Soc. Psychology*, May 1958, 56:3, 321–328.

II

Comparative Studies
of Socialization

1   ROGER G. BARKER

*Individual Motivation and the Behavior
Setting Claim*

THEORY OF BEHAVIOR SETTINGS

. . . Field studies in which I and my associates have been engaged, of
the behavior of children in their natural habitats, have brought us to the
hypothesis that under certain precisely defined and frequently occurring
conditions, people stand in the relationship of media to behavior settings;
and that under certain other less common conditions people stand in the

Abridged from Roger G. Barker, "Ecology and Motivation," *Nebraska Symposium on Motivation 1960*, Copyright 1960, The University of Nebraska Press
and published by permission.
The research reported here was supported by grants from the Carnegie Cor-

relationship of things to behavior settings, imposing certain absolute constraints upon them. This hypothesis brings some order into data upon American-English differences in the behavior of children and adults, into data upon differences in the behavior of individuals in settings of different sizes, and into data concerning the behavioral consequences of physical disability. The wide ramifications of these simple ideas suggest that they may have a basic significance for psychology, and particularly for the psychology of motivation, as we shall see.

The story of these field studies is too long to give here in detail, but I shall try to present enough of it to make our line of thinking clear.

It is first necessary to describe behavior settings. When a mother writes, "There is a baseball game in progress on the playground across the street," she does not refer to any individual's behavior, but to the behavior of children en masse. The same is true of a newspaper item which reports, "The annual fete held in the St. Ambrose Church garden was a great success."

These are behavior settings. They are highly visible behavior phenomena; laymen mention them in conversation and in writing as frequently as they do individual persons (Barker & Wright, 1955). Here are the ten behavior settings of Midwest, Kansas and Yoredale, Yorkshire in which the residents of the towns spend the greatest amount of time, with the person-hours spent per year in each setting (Table 1). Behavior settings such as these are phenomenal entities with as precisely identifiable features and boundaries as organisms, mountain ranges, or gas jets. These features of behavior settings will not be described here, as this has been done elsewhere (Barker & Wright, 1955). Of special relevance in the present connection, however, are the following characteristics of settings:

1. Behavior settings involve ongoing patterns of extraindividual behavior whose identity and functioning are independent of the participation of particular persons.

2. A behavior setting has a circumjacent soma of physical objects: of walls, doors, fences, chairs, dishes, typewriters, ad infinitum, arranged in a characteristic spatial pattern, at a particular temporal and physical locus.

3. Behavior settings are homeostatic systems; they normally persist, often for years, at a relatively stable, characteristic level.

Although behavior settings involve the behavior of people and are easily perceived phenomenal units, they are preperceptual and ecological;

---

poration of New York and the National Institutes of Mental Health, as well as pursuant to a contract with the United States Office of Education, Department of Health, Education and Welfare.

TABLE 1. TEN BEHAVIOR SETTINGS WITH LARGEST POPULATIONS

Behavior settings	Hours/year	Percentage of time in all settings
Midwest		
Streets and sidewalks	77,544	8.3
Kane's Grocery	24,780	2.6
Clifford's Drug Store	20,855	2.2
Gwyn Cafe	17,000	1.8
Pearl Cafe	16,821	1.8
Midwest State Bank	14,719	1.6
7th grade, school class	14,705	1.6
Cabell's Dep't Store	13,911	1.5
Denton's Drug Store	13,871	1.5
Midwest Post Office	13,602	1.4
Yoredale		
Streets and sidewalks	300,000	19.3
Yoredale market day	44,000	2.8
Yoredale R.R. Station	29,585	1.9
Express Dairy	28,830	1.8
Supreme Cinema	28,704	1.8
Marble's Garage	27,565	1.8
Upper jrs., school class	26,694	1.7
Church, builder and funeral director	26,325	1.7
Lower jrs., school class	26,082	1.7
Castle Cinema	22,880	1.5

Data refer to year September, 1954 through August, 1955.

they exist "out there" independently of their apprehension by anyone. Even the persons whose behavior is essential for the occurrence of a setting, who construct their own private worlds within the setting, and who are themselves influenced by the setting need not be aware of the setting per se. Indeed people within a setting are sometimes able to see it less clearly than those on the outside. A person struggling from the street into a New York Subway at 4:45 P.M. may be aware only of the succession of individuals he must avoid, pass, dodge, make way for, shove, and resist. Still, he behaves according to the requirements of the setting, New York City Trafficway. But an onlooker atop a neighboring skyscraper, a different setting, has clearly spread before him the whole pattern and boundaries of this setting; it is he who perceives it as a total extraindividual behavior unit.

A behavior setting is a behavior entity, but its laws of operation are not the laws of individual psychology. In the functioning of the Pearl Cafe in Midwest, for example, the availability and the price of food, the season of the year, the prevailing temperature, the size, lighting, and ventilation of the building, the state laws concerning hygienic practices, the customers, and the employees are all involved. We have only the beginning of an understanding of how these incommensurate phenomena are combined into the reliable, nonerratic entity known so well to Midwest residents. . . .

For our purposes, the self-regulatory characteristic of behavior settings is crucial and must be considered further [see Figure 1]; it is this, indeed, which gives behavior settings, under certain conditions, the position of things which impose their own patterns on the people within them, who have the position of media. . . .

FIGURE 1. Pattern of Forces Maintaining Homeostatic Level of Behavior Settings

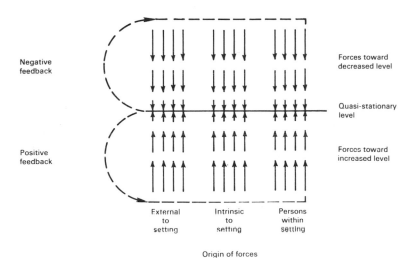

Origin of forces

BEHAVIOR SETTINGS: LOCUS OF OPPORTUNITIES AND OBLIGATIONS

It will be of value now to change our viewpoint from behavior settings per se to the individual inhabitants of behavior settings.

A behavior setting is a place where most of the inhabitants can satisfy a number of personal motives, where they can achieve multiple satisfactions. In other words, a behavior setting contains opportunities. Furthermore, different people achieve a different cluster of satisfactions in the same setting. The unity of a behavior setting does not arise from similarity in the motives of the occupants. In the behavior setting Football Game, for example, the quarterback will experience a complex system of social-physical satisfactions, depending upon what kind of a person he is; his mother in the bleachers will at the same time have quite a different set of satisfactions; and the coach will have still others. But unless these and other inhabitants of a football game are at least minimally satisfied, they will leave, or will not return on another occasion, and the setting will cease. In other words, a setting exists only when it provides its occupants with the particular psychological conditions their own unique natures require. Heterogeneity in the personal motives of the individual inhabitants of a setting contributes to the stability of the setting.

Behavior settings impose obligations upon their occupants, too. These obligations are consequences of the intrinsic structure of behavior settings. If the inhabitants of a setting are to continue to attain the goals which bring them satisfactions, the setting must continue to function at a level which each occupant defines for himself in terms of his own satisfactions. Every occupant of a setting is, therefore, faced with two routes: one is the immediate, direct route to his goals; and the other route is directed toward maintaining the setting in such condition that the goals, and the routes to them, will remain intact.

The strengths of these sets of forces are controlled by feedback from the setting's quasi-stationary level of functioning. When an occupant of a behavior setting sees that this level *threatens* to decline, and thereby to reduce the valence of the goals it provides him, or to increase the resistance of the paths to these goals, an increase in the forces along the routes which maintain the setting occurs. The amount and direction of the increase depend upon the degree of the perceived threat, and upon the person's perception of its sources and the most promising ways of countering the threat.

It is the resultant of such adjustment circuits which keeps a setting on a quasi-stationary level, or moving toward a more satisfying level for the inhabitants. Sometimes, of course, the forces along the maintenance routes are too weak, and the setting deteriorates.

This constitutes an amplification of the theory of behavior settings to include a particular circular relation whereby a behavior setting, as the external thing, constrains the people within it, as media, and they in turn counterconstrain the behavior setting, as part of their external environment. We are interested in discovering the details of these circuits; this is an empirical problem, like tracing the wiring of an electrical system.

THE INTERFACE OF BEHAVIOR SETTINGS AND LIFE SPACE

. . . From the general relations between thing and medium discussed above,* we would expect certain modifications to occur in both individuals and behavior settings when the population of a setting is reduced below the optimum. We can derive the nature of these modifications in this particular case from the characteristics of behavior settings we have considered. The property of homeostatic level means that behavior settings

---

* [Ed. note: See the original paper for the full discussion.]

are strongly self-determined, that they therefore provide a coercive environment for their interior elements, that they stand as clear-cut things to the media within them. The optimal population requirement of each homeostatic level means that there are feedback circuits which connect the *number* of people in a setting with the state of the setting. The opportunities and obligations of behavior settings refer to details of the couplings by means of which particular individuals are constrained by the setting; it is this that particularly concerns us here.

We can subsume opportunities and obligations under the concept of behavior setting *claim*, meaning thereby all the forces acting upon individual members of a setting to enter and participate in its operation in particular ways. Let us see how behavior setting claim operates in the particular case in which we are interested, namely, when the differentiation of the internal medium of the setting is reduced below optimum, i.e., when the number of people is less than optimum for the level upon which the setting functions.

The homeostatic mechanism of the setting insures that a reduction in personnel, within certain ranges, does not change the absolute number of opportunities or obligations the setting contains. The opportunities and the obligations are therefore shared by fewer people. The consequence is clear: the average valence-per-person is greater and also the average obligation-per-person is greater along both the direct and the maintenance routes of the setting. In general, then, the claim of the setting upon its inhabitants increases in strength. This amounts to a further amplification of the theory of thing and medium as it applies to behavior settings, namely, the media of behavior settings (people) are of a sort which are able to compensate via increased energy for decreased parts. Our first conclusion is that one consequence of reduction in personnel of a setting below its optimal level is increased behavior setting claim upon the remaining persons. . . .

EVIDENCE AND APPLICATIONS

It is time to turn to the data which have led us to this line of thought. First, however, let me point out that the aspect of the ecological environment to which we have directed attention appears to be especially relevant to motivation, to the energetics of behavior. . . . If our argument is correct, it means that behavior settings with less than optimal personnel to serve as media for the functioning of the setting constitute ecological situations with respect to which laws can be stated that are more than probability laws recapitulating empirical observations. We predict that the members in undermanned settings (as defined)* *have* to be more

* [Ed. note: See the full discussion for more details.]

energetic, more versatile, more insecure than members of a setting with optimal population. . . .

I will turn first to evidence that the claim of a behavior setting varies as proposed. I have no experimental evidence to present to you. However, there is a small amount of data in the literature of industrial psychology bearing upon this issue, and we have assembled some other field data. The question upon which these data bear is this: Is there any relationship between the size of behavior settings and their coercive power over their members? . . .

. . . As evidence of the coercive power of settings, we have taken all data that indicate the frequency with which members participate in them. These are in most cases attendance records. According to our theory, attendance at small settings should be higher than at large settings, when stated in terms of per cent of total membership.

In some cases the data available are for entire institutions; in this case it is assumed that the settings within the institutions have on the average the same relative populations as the institutions.

For a number of years industrial psychologists have reported data which show that absenteeism is less in small than in large industrial establishments. When this was first observed it was interpreted as an artifact due to contamination of the data by urban-rural differences, by differences in management policy, or by differences in type of work. Recently, however, the size factor has been taken seriously, and more adequate data have confirmed the association between size and attendance of employees. Some representative data from three investigations in the United States and England are shown in Figure 2 (Acton Society Trust, 1953; Baumgartel & Sobel, 1959; Hewitt & Parfit, 1953).

We have extended this analysis to Rotary Club attendance in Eastern Kansas, Figure 3. Again size of setting is negatively correlated with per cent attendance. Here one may suspect that urban-rural differences confuse the picture. Data relevant to this issue are found in the attendance at urban Rotary Clubs. Such data are given in Figure 4. All clubs here are city clubs. Those clubs with 300–399 members have been separated from those with 400 or more members.

In Figure 5 data of a somewhat different sort are presented, namely, data on church membership and Sunday school enrollment. Sunday school size is widely considered by churchmen to be an indication of the claim of a church upon an important sector of its clientele. It is largely a voluntary activity at both the member and the teacher level, and enrollment requires much more active attendance and participation than does church membership. In Figure 5 the relationship between church and Sunday school size among the Presbyterian churches of Eastern Kansas is shown.

FIGURE 2. Mean Rate of Industrial Absenteeism and Size of Unit

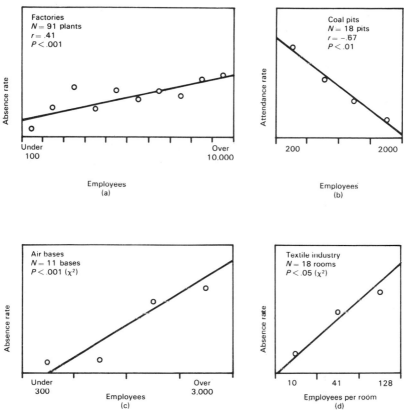

Sources: *a* and *b*, Acton Society Trust, 1953; *c*, Baumgartel and Sobel, 1959; *d*, Hewitt and Parfit, 1963.

FIGURE 3. Rotary Club Attendance and Size of Club, Mean Attendance Rate for the 32 Clubs of District 571 for 20 Months. Months selected randomly from the 96 months, 1950–1958.

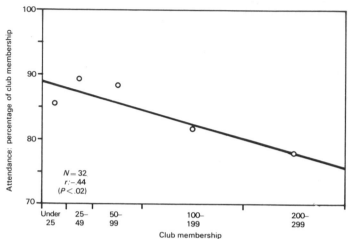

Source: Governor's Monthly Letter, Rotary District 571

FIGURE 4. Rotary Club Attendance and Size of Club. Mean Attendance Rate of Urban Clubs of Two Size Ranges

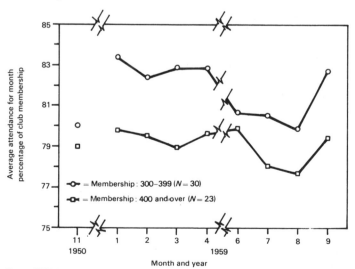

Source: USCB Attendance Contest monthly reports, issued by Rotary International, Evanston, Illinois.

FIGURE 5. Church Membership and Sunday School Enrollment, Churches of Topeka Highland, Wichita, and Soloman Presbyteries in Kansas, and Kansas City, Missouri

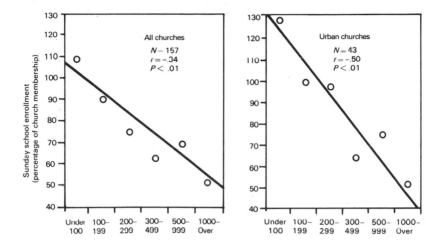

Source: Minutes of the General Assembly of the United Presbyterian Church of the United States of America, 1959.

Again, a substantial negative relation between church size and its claim upon its potential Sunday school members is found. It will be seen that this holds too for the urban churches.

This is somewhat surprising in view of the fact that the largest churches have professional religious education staffs, and very often elaborate buildings and facilities which the small churches do not have.

We have assembled data on participation in district music festivals by students of high schools of different sizes. (Figure 6.) Again a significant negative correlation between school size and proportion of participating students is found. We have data which show that the same negative correlations occur between school size and participation in debating, dramatics, and athletics.

This long course of thought began with our study of the life of children in an American and an English town. Let me try . . . to get back to our starting place and tell you what we think this means for culture differences.

One of the striking differences we discovered between Midwest, Kansas and Yoredale, Yorkshire is this: Yoredale has, in proportion to its population, half as many behavior settings as Midwest; Yoredale, with a population of 1300 people, has 494 settings, and Midwest, with a population of 715, has 587 settings. At first we viewed this as an interesting but

FIGURE 6. Music Festival Attendance and Size of High School. Schools of Eastern Kansas in 1958–1959

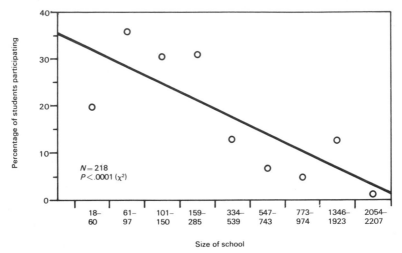

Source: Kansas High School Activities Association

isolated fact, along with many others. But now, in view of the ideas I have discussed here, we look upon it as a fundamental difference in the ecological environment of Americans and Englishmen, and one that is at the root of a basic motivational difference in the people of the two countries.

The behavior settings of Midwest and Yoredale are predominantly of the same varieties; most of them could be transposed between the towns with little disruption in their operations. Their temporal occurrence and their durations are approximately the same too. There are some important differences in the patterns of behavior of equivalent settings, some differences in emphasis, and some differences in the characteristics of the people who inhabit equivalent settings. But the overriding difference is that the settings of Midwest have only half the number of inhabitants as those of Yoredale to serve as "inside" media for their functioning. Relative to Yoredale, and to their own homeostatic levels, Midwest's behavior settings are relatively deficient in personnel. They should have, therefore, very strong claims upon their members and potential members, and in view of the theory of behavior settings we have proposed, differences in the behavior of Midwest and Yoredale residents are to be expected. Relative to Yoredale citizens, Midwesterners in general should be busier, be more versatile, be more important within the town's settings, have broader social contacts, undertake more difficult tasks, be less evaluative of themselves and others, have less highly perfected skills, have more responsibilities, and be more insecure. In fact one can simply read off the list of predictions concerning the consequences for the occupants of undermanned behavior settings. Our observations indicate that these predictions are, in fact, true for Midwest and Yoredale. Here I shall present data bearing upon participation, responsibility, versatility, and breadth of social contact.

The basic data with respect to people, behavior settings, and responsible positions in the two towns are given in Table 2. These data make it clear that Midwest and Yoredale differ greatly in their arrangements with respect to behavior settings and people. Midwest has half the number of people per setting that Yoredale does. In interpreting this, one must bear in mind that the behavior settings of the two towns are of the same sorts: school classes, grocery stores, football games, church services, etc. On the average the "same" setting in Midwest has half as many people to maintain it as it does in Yoredale.

TABLE 2. POPULATION, NUMBER OF BEHAVIOR SETTINGS, AND NUMBER OF RESPONSIBLE POSITIONS IN MIDWEST AND YOREDALE

	Midwest	*Yoredale*	*MW/YD*
Number of people	721	1300	0.55
Number of behavior settings	579	494	1.18
Number of people per setting	1.25	2.63	0.47
Number of responsible positions	5093	3044	1.67
Responsible positions per setting	8.8	6.2	1.42
Responsible positions per person	7.1	2.3	3.09

Data refer to year September, 1954 through August, 1955.

Does this mean, as our theory of behavior settings predicts, that Midwest settings have a greater claim upon Midwest citizens than do Yoredale settings? Are there more opportunities and obligations in Midwest? Data on this issue, in general, are given in the bottom panel of Table 2. *Responsible position*, as used in this table, means a position in a setting that is essential to the effective functioning of the setting: it refers to presidents and secretaries of societies; to proprietors and clerks of stores; to chairmen and soloists at entertainments. It does *not* refer to customers, members of audiences, spectators.

We find that while Midwest has 18% more settings than Yoredale, the settings of Midwest contain 67% more responsible positions. In other words, Midwest's small settings have even more responsible people per setting than Yoredale's large settings. In a year's time Midwest provides and requires more than three times as many responsibilities of each of its residents as Yoredale requires.

More detailed data on participation and responsibility are given in Table 3. In the first section, data are presented for all residents of each town. Here we find that Midwest residents participate in the town's settings about 2.5 hours per week more on the average than Yoredale residents, and the data on this much greater involvement in responsible positions are repeated. When we look at the age subgroups in the following sections of this table, we see that more frequent responsible participation by Midwest citizens occurs at each of these ages. However, the greatest difference between the towns in this respect is in the adolescent age group. On the average, adolescents in Midwest fill 3.5 times as many responsible positions in community settings during a year as do Yoredale adolescents. On the average, every Midwest adolescent acts in a play, works in a store, teaches a Sunday school class, plays in a basketball league game every three weeks; Yoredale adolescents occupy such positions every eleven weeks, on the average.

TABLE 3. PARTICIPATION AND RESPONSIBILITY IN
BEHAVIOR SETTINGS

	Midwest	Yoredale	MW/YD
All residents			
Hours per person per week as BS occupants	25.0	22.6	1.11
No. of responsible positions filled per person	7.1	2.3	3.09
Children under 12 years of age			
Hours per person per week as BS occupants	20.5	19.8	1.03
No. of responsible positions filled per person	8.4	2.7	3.11
Percent of town's responsible positions			
filled per child	0.18	0.09	2.00
Adolescents, 12 to 17:11 years old			
Hours per person per week as BS occupants	53.7	41.9	1.28
No. of responsible positions filled per person	16.6	4.7	3.53
Percent of town's responsible positions			
filled per adolescent	0.34	0.19	1.79
Adults and aged persons			
Hours per person per week as BS occupants	23.6	22.3	1.06
No. of responsible positions filled per person	5.9	2.0	2.95
Percent of town's responsible positions			
filled per person	0.13	0.11	1.18

Data refer to year September, 1954 through August, 1955.

These data mean, as we see it, and as the theory of behavior setting predicts, that the relatively undermanned settings of Midwest "claim" more of the citizen's time, more of his energy, and elicit from him greater versatility of behavior than the Yoredale settings with a greater number of inhabitants. The greater versatility is implied by the more frequent participation in responsible positions in Midwest. In towns the size of Midwest and Yoredale there are not many chances to repeat the same kind of performance in different settings, so the 7.1 responsibilities per person in Midwest necessitate taking a variety of roles and engaging in a range of skills. Another side of versatility is exhibited in Table 4, which shows that in over half the settings of Midwest all age groups (from infants, under two years of age, to old people, over 65 years of age) are regular occupants. This is true of 23% of Yoredale's settings. Midwest residents must be more practiced than Yoredale residents in dealing with all ages of humanity. This is true too to a lesser degree of social-class contacts.

TABLE 4. BREADTH OF SOCIAL CONTACT WITHIN BEHAVIOR
SETTING IN MIDWEST AND YOREDALE

	Midwest	*Yoredale*	*MW/YD*
Percent of all behavior settings completely unsegregated:			
with respect to age	52	23	2.26
with respect to social class	92	76	1.21
with respect to sex	86	83	1.04

Data refer to year September, 1954 through August, 1955.

More than this, these data mean that people are functionally more important in the Midwest system than in the Yoredale system. The last item in the three lower panels of Table 3 presents what we have christened the Pied Piper Index. It is the average loss which would occur to the town with the piping away of any citizen. This loss is measured here in terms of the proportion of the town's responsible jobs which the citizen performs, and which therefore have to be "made up" by someone if the town is to continue to function at the same level, i.e., if homeostasis is to be maintained. It is a measure of the average contribution to the town's essential functioning of the average person in each designated age group. According to this measure, Midwest citizens in each age category are, on the average, functionally more important within the town than Yoredale citizens.

The same type of information is given in another way in Table 5. Here we find, for example, that 7.8% of all of Midwest settings and 2% of all Yoredale settings would be seriously crippled in their operations without

TABLE 5. BEHAVIOR SETTINGS WHICH DEPEND UPON CHILDREN
AND ADOLESCENTS TO FILL RESPONSIBLE POSITIONS
(PERCENTAGE OF ALL SETTINGS) IN MIDWEST AND YOREDALE

	Midwest	*Yoredale*	*MW/YD*
Depend upon children	2.9	0.8	3.6
Depend upon adolescents	7.8	2.0	3.9

Data refer to year September, 1954 through August, 1955.

adolescents to carry out the necessary tasks; this does not include settings, such as school settings, where adolescents are in the position of members and customers. By this measure too Midwest adolescents and children have a greater importance within the framework of the town than they do in Yoredale.

The converse side of the picture is given in Table 6. Here Midwest settings are shown to exclude children and adolescents less frequently than Yoredale settings.

TABLE 6. BEHAVIOR SETTINGS WHICH EXCLUDE CHILDREN AND ADOLESCENTS (PERCENTAGE OF ALL SETTINGS) IN MIDWEST AND YOREDALE

	Midwest	Yoredale	MW/YD
Exclude children	12.8	28.5	0.45
Exclude adolescents	8.6	18.2	0.47

Data refer to year September, 1954 through August, 1955.

We judge that these differences in the participation, responsibility, importance, and breadth of social contacts of Midwest and Yoredale residents are neither capricious nor the consequence of individual choices, but that they are a necessary consequence of the behavior setting arrangement within the ecological environments of the two towns. People in Midwest *have* to participate to a greater degree than in Yoredale. We predict that Englishmen imported to Midwest would *have* to participate also, and that this would occur immediately with no learning period involved. The reverse occurs when an American settles in Yoredale, as I have dramatically experienced.

The Midwest and Yoredale systems for educating children are congruent with these facts about the settings of the communities. According to the Midwest theory of education, children are prepared for adulthood by participating to the maximum of their abilities in the regular behavior settings of the town along with adults; it is of particular value to children to undertake important and responsible roles even before they can discharge them with complete adequacy. This is exactly what Midwest behavior settings require: personnel to discharge important and responsible functions, even if this is done with considerably less than perfection. School behavior settings are considered important in Midwest education, but they are thought to function best along with regular community settings.

According to the Yoredale theory of education, children are prepared for adulthood by removing them from the community settings and placing them in special, reserved school settings under the direction of experts who, over a period of time, are able to prepare children for entrance to the normal life of the town's behavior settings. School settings are the unique and almost complete means of educating children, and it is one of their particular values that when they are in school behavior settings, children do not disturb community settings until the requisite skills and responsibility have been imparted to them so they can take their parts smoothly. This again is exactly what Yoredale behavior settings are able to require: protection from incompetent personnel, who may disturb the desired smoothness of operation.

It would be extremely difficult to exchange the educational systems of the two towns. Many Midwest community settings which would be crippled by the *removal* of children would in Yoredale be disrupted by their presence. In fact it appears that the towns could not tolerate such a shift without a major transformation in the whole community system.

The ideas I have presented to you have relevance for a current social issue of great concern in many quarters. The so-called population explosion is usually considered in connection with economic, industrial, nutritional, and political problems. I would suggest that it has equally important psychological implications, particularly motivational implications, rooted in the ecological environment it produces. The population explosion means that underpopulated behavior settings of all sorts are becoming more infrequent and overpopulated settings more common.

The United States, for complicated reasons that are revealed by our history, has been a culture of underpopulated behavior settings. We have been called a people shaped by the free frontier, a people of plenty, an affluent society, the land of opportunity. These designations all imply something psychologically fundamental, I think, namely, a shortage of human media for the demands of our behavior settings. There has always been too much to do, and there have been claims upon people elsewhere when they have not been needed in the settled areas. The homesteads were called claims, and they claimed the settlers, in our terms, as strongly as they were claimed, in a legal sense, by the settlers.

Underpopulated settings have had a profound effect upon American character. The predictions made earlier in this paper about behavior in settings with deficient human media are in fact a catalogue of American character traits.

But now things are changing. We are becoming a nation of overpopulated settings. It is likely that in the Midwests of the U.S.A. underpopulated settings are making their last stand.

The meaning of this change for American society is too vast to be considered here. But let me mention a single one of its facets. Behavior settings with less than optimal people for their homeostatic levels are self-disciplining settings. The opportunities within them are matched by the obligations they contain. When we list their consequences, we use the words of a good disciplinarian: effort, difficult tasks, responsibility, toleration, self-identity, success and failure, social pressure. We have made a nation's ideal of the fact that these are not *imposed* controls in American culture. We sometimes call them self-discipline. In reality they are controls built into the structure and the dynamics of the setting, into the ecological environment. . . .

References

Acton Society Trust. *Size and Morale*. London: 1953.

Barker, R. G. and H. F. Wright. *Midwest and its Children*. Evanston, Ill.: Row Peterson, 1955.

Baumgartel, H. and R. Sobol. Background and organizational factors in absenteeism. *Personnel Psychology*, 1959, 12, 431–443.

Hewitt, D. and J. Parfit. A note on working morale and size of group. *Occupational Psychology*, 1953, 27, 38–42.

For further elaboration of the ideas presented in this paper, and for more confirming data, see:

Barker, Roger G. and P. V. Gump. *Big School, Small School*. Stanford: Stanford University Press, 1964.

Barker, Roger G. *Ecological Psychology*. Stanford: Stanford University Press, 1968.

Wicker, Allan W. Size of church membership and members' support of church behavior settings. *Journal of Personality and Social Psychology*, November 1969, 13:3, 278–288.

Baird, L. L. Big school, small school: A critical examination of the hypothesis. *The Journal of Educational Psychology*, 1969, 60, 253–260.

2

BEATRICE B. WHITING AND
JOHN W. M. WHITING

Task Assignment and Personality: A Consideration of the Effect of Herding on Boys

Parents around the world assign chores to their children. Some do so because they are overworked and genuinely need their help; others, especially modern urban mothers, because they hope to teach their children to be responsible and concerned with the welfare of the family, a concern that they feel may not be transmitted in school. What effect, if any, does the performance of chores have on the personality development of children? Does the type of work affect, for example, the degree to which a child behaves in a responsible fashion and assumes responsibility when he encounters a situation that calls for such behavior? What about children who go to school and cannot spend much time helping with the family economy — are they more or less responsible than their peers who do not attend school?

To find an answer to these questions we have scrutinized materials from two sources. First, an intensive study of child rearing practices and children's behavior in six cultures carried out in 1954-1955 under the direction of Whiting, Child, and Lambert; and second, an extensive study by Bacon, Barry, and Child (1959) of child rearing practices derived from the ethnographic descriptions of this topic in one hundred and eleven societies. The six cultures on which the intensive study was carried out and the field teams who did the research are as follows:

(1) Taira   A village in northern Okinawa. Thomas and Hatsumi Maretzki.

(2) Tarong   A community in northern Luzon, Philippines. William and Corinne Nydegger.

This is a modified version of a chapter for a forthcoming monograph *Children of Six Cultures: Egoism and Alterism*, in progress. This paper was presented at the University of East Africa Social Science Conference, Dar-es-Salaam, January 1968.

(3) Juxtlahuaca   A barrio in the state of Oaxaca, Mexico. A. Kimball and Romaine Romney.

(4) Khalapur   A local segment of the Rajput caste in a town in Uttar Pradesh, India. Leigh Minturn and John Hitchcock.

(5) Nyansongo   A localized sub-clan of the Abagusii in the Nyanza Province of Kenya. Robert and Barbara LeVine.

(6) Orchard Town   A community in a suburban town in New England, U.S.A. John and Ann Fischer.

As can be seen, a man and a woman field worker were involved in each study. They spent approximately a year in each of the above communities using standard ethnographic techniques combined with an intensive study of a sub-sample of twenty-four children (twelve girls and twelve boys, between the ages of three and ten, each from a different family). A general description of child rearing in these six cultures has already been published (B. Whiting, 1963). This paper will draw particularly upon a set of standardized observations of the social interactions of the sample of children observed over a period of six months to a year in a variety of natural settings. These observations have been classified into seven major categories of social behavior:

(1) Succorance   asking for help and comfort.

(2) Nurturance   giving or offering help and comfort.

(3) Sociability   engaging in friendly interaction.

(4) Aggression   assaulting and insulting.

(5) Arrogance   boasting and calling attention to self.

(6) Dominance   attempting to influence others for purposes of self-interest or self-aggrandisement.

(7) Responsibility   making responsible suggestions, enforcing rules.

In this paper we will present some evidence relating to the effects of herding as an assigned task upon the personality of boys as measured by their social behavior. We will also discuss briefly schooling as a contrasting task.

The basic theoretical assumptions underlying the analysis to be presented are as follows: first, it is assumed that the tasks assigned to and performed by boys and girls during their childhood have an important effect upon their style of social behavior. The more important the task as perceived by the parents, the greater is this effect. Assuming that on the basis of instruction, punishment for negligence, reward for diligence, and the intrinsic reinforcement from a sense of competence, the task becomes well-learned and an important part of the child's habit system, it should influence his behavior in other contexts. Thus, a task that involves interaction with live and active animals requires the learning of quite a different set of skills than the manipulation of inert symbols, and it is our assumption that this learning will be transferred to and manifested in a child's interaction with his peers and siblings.

It is further assumed that a child not only learns to perform the task assigned, but also, incidentally by the process of identification, he learns the role of the parent or other socializing agent who assigns the task and supervises its performance. Again the degree to which he learns this task is a function of the importance attached to the task by the parent or other socializing agent. The greater the perceived importance of the task the more severe the punishment for negligence and the more powerful the task assigner and supervisor seems to the child. According to a recent theory of learning by identification (J. Whiting, 1960), this state of affairs should lead the child to envy the status and covertly practice the role of the task assigner and supervisor. This learning by identification should also transfer to other contexts and influence a child's style of social interaction.

It is our specific thesis in this paper that boys who are assigned the task of caring for the family herds learn responsibility or pro-social dominance from performing this duty, and that their scores on this type of behavior will be higher than those of children who are assigned other tasks, such as performing routine household chores or attending school.

A herd boy must be able to manage animals that are bigger and stronger than he. He must beat and drive them if they are not docile and hence is required to make and execute commands. He must not lose control of the animals through fear. If he does not anticipate their moves, he will make extra work for himself. He must be alert and skilled to handle them without damage to himself, the animals, or the environment. He demands obedience and compliance not only from the animals but from younger siblings who may tag along to help him herd. If he fails in his job, he knows that he has committed a serious offense, the consequences of which will affect his entire family, and the immediate and severe punishment he is likely to receive is clearly connected with his negligence. The rules for task performance are clear, and the punishment for non-compliance is not arbitrary. Furthermore, the job assigned is important, and a herd boy may well feel that he is a contributor to the economic welfare of his family. If he does his job well, he has a sense of competence and personal pride.

The task of going to school and learning a set of seemingly arbitrary symbols is in sharp contrast to that of herding. To be punished for letting the cattle in his charge get into the maize field seems just and reasonable to the herd boy, but the schoolboy who is berated for saying that two plus two equals five must sometimes wonder. Not only are the standards of performance in the classroom arbitrary, but the relationship of the tasks assigned to basic needs are ambiguous and tenuous. The schoolboy must take on faith the need to study, but the herd boy knows that his task is directly related to the food supply.

The timing of rewards and punishments offers another sharp contrast between herding and schooling. For the former they are usually immediate; for the latter they may be delayed — often for years until examinations are passed or failed. When one set of exams is passed, new goals are set and the final goal recedes into the future — from primary school diplomas, to secondary school, to college, to postgraduate degrees. The schoolboy can seldom feel the sense of completion and accomplishment that the herd boy experiences when his charges are safely shut in the corral in the evening.

In addition, the schoolboy seldom gets the individual attention from the teacher that the herd boy gets from his parents. Instructions are usually to the class as a whole and general enough so that considerable delay in compliance is often not apparent. Not so with the herd boy. Parental commands are explicit and disobedience apparent.

Finally, tasks associated with animal husbandry and agriculture are for the benefit of the family as a whole, but school tasks are focused on the individual. Although an educated man or woman may eventually contribute to the economic well-being of the entire family, this eventuality is not apt to be immediately clear to a young child. In the classroom each individual is out for himself and his goal is individual achievement.

As for the influence of the role model, it is assumed that the parent as supervisor of herding is seen to be a much more important and powerful figure than the teacher. As the provider of food, shelter, and love, the former occupies a much more envied status than the latter. The teacher operates with secondary authority and has limited sanctions under his control. The right of physical punishment is denied him or her in many societies and the other punishments and rewards that he has the right to exercise are trivial as compared to those the parents can employ. Thus, the covert learning of an adult role should be much greater for the herd boy than for the schoolboy.

In sum, herd boys are taught to be responsible and dominant. They receive direct commands, are expected to be obedient, and to dominate others in carrying out their responsibilities. Schoolboys are expected to strive individually to achieve future goals. They are expected to learn to work by themselves, without constant guidance. Finally, the herd boys identify with adult role behavior more strongly than schoolboys.

Habits learned in the context of these contrasting types of chores will result in a contrast of personality as judged by profiles of behavior. Per-centage-wise, herd boys will be observed to behave more responsibly and to give more pro-social commands than schoolboys. In contrast, school-boys will exhibit more egotistic, achievement-oriented behavior.

Since responsibility is one of the major concerns of this paper, it will be useful to explain in detail what is meant by it. Children observed sug-gesting to others that they perform their duties, reprimanding them for failing to do so, or scolding them for breaking accepted rules were scored as acting responsibly.

Of the sample boys five and over, all but one of the Nyansongo boys in the Kenya sample was observed taking care of cattle, sheep, and goats, his father having no animals at the time the study was done. Furthermore, since at the time of the study none of these boys attended school, they spent the greater part of the day tending the cattle. Five, or fifty-five per cent of the sample boys in Khalapur, India spent some time herding but unlike the Nyansongo boys in Kenya, three of the five Rajput boys also attended school. However, since the school was casual, and attendance, especially during the afternoon session, was erratic, it is difficult to esti-mate accurately what per cent of their time these boys spent in animal care.

In Taira, Okinawa and Orchard Town, U.S.A., none of the families had large animals that required herding. Although most of the families in Tarong, Philippines had a carabao that was used as a draft animal, the boy's responsibility for it was limited. When not being used, the family animal was tethered, and the only herding activity was driving it to one of the wells morning and evening to be watered and washed. Although Tarong boys participated in this activity, they were usually accompanied by their fathers and only rarely were observed carrying out this task with-out an adult being present. In contrast the boys of our Indian and Kenyan samples usually carried out their herding duties without the aid of adults. Although the Tarong boys sometimes changed the tethers of the animals, all the older boys regularly attended school, so this duty was performed occasionally rather than as a regular chore.

Only one of the sample families in Juxtlahuaca, Mexico owned cattle. The seven year old boy in the family attended school, but on Saturday and Sunday drove the animals out of town to pasturage and stayed with them all day. Three of the families owned burros and the sons six and over were expected to curry and feed these animals if their fathers were too busy to do so. Thus only one Mexican boy in our sample was assigned the task of herding as we have defined it and even in this case it was a weekend activity.

In sum, then, herding is a salient task for most of the older boys in the Indian and Kenyan samples. Although some care of animals is expected of some of the boys in the remaining cultures, it was so minimal that herding cannot be considered as a salient task for boys.

Let us now consider the hypothesis that the experience of herding increases a boy's score in responsibility of pro-social dominance. Table 1 shows the comparison of boys in the two herding societies with those in the other four societies. It can be seen that the hypothesis is supported. Boys in the two herding societies made responsible suggestions and reprimanded their peers and siblings two to three times more frequently than did boys in the non-herding cultures. Furthermore, the score of the Nyansongo boys was higher than the boys of Khalapur, which is in line with their relative degree of involvement in herding chores.

Although Table 1 represents the scores of over fifty boys, only six cultures are involved. Our results are therefore not as convincing as they might seem. Two procedures for further testing the hypothesis suggest themselves. First is a more intensive analysis of the data available on the six cultures, and second, a more extensive analysis involving data from a larger sample of cultures.

TABLE 1. THE MEDIAN "PERCENTAGE RESPONSIBILITY" SCORES FOR BOYS BETWEEN FIVE AND ELEVEN IN EACH OF SIX SOCIETIES GROUPED ON THE BASIS OF THE IMPORTANCE OF HERDING AS A TASK ASSIGNED TO BOYS OF THIS AGE

	Median percentage responsibility
Herding unimportant	
Juxtlahuaca	10 (n = 9)
Orchard Town	11 (n = 9)
Taira	11 (n = 10)
Tarong	11 (n = 8)
Herding important	
Khalapur	19 (n = 9)
Nyansongo	31 (n = 6)

The appropriate within-culture test of the effect of herding can only be made in the two herding societies since there is no contrast in the other four. This limits the sample to the ten older boys in our Indian and Kenyan samples. The median score for per cent responsibility of the six boys who were observed to herd was 27.5 per cent. The four boys who were not observed to herd during the period of field work had a median score of 26 per cent. This difference, although in the expected direction, is far from reaching statistical significance. It may be that there is such a high cultural value on the type of behavior that would make a good herdsman that the boys who do not herd learn it. This is suggested by the fact that the score of the four non-herders in the herding societies was considerably higher than the average for the boys in any of the non-herding societies. It is impossible, however, to decide this question on the basis of such a small sample.

The fact that boys are not assigned the task of herding until they are five or six years old makes another test of our hypothesis possible. If herding is important in developing pro-social dominance in children, the difference between boys from herding and non-herding societies should appear only after the former have had some practice in herding. Table 2 shows this to be the case. The difference in the median responsibility scores for the younger boys is only three percentage points, which is not statistically significant. The older boys in the herding cultures, on the other hand, have a median score more than double the magnitude of the older boys of the non-herding cultures — a difference that is significant at the .005 level of confidence.

In order to test the relationship between herding and responsibility on a larger sample of societies, we turned to the work of Bacon, Barry, and Child. In 1959 they published a paper relating subsistence economy to child training practices. Their study was based on an analysis of the ethnographic accounts of one hundred and eleven societies distributed throughout the world. On the basis of the published data, raters made judgments about the types of pressures parents and other socializing agents exerted on boys and girls to be responsible, nurturant or helpful, obedient, self-reliant, independent, and achievement oriented. They then related these scores to the type of basic economy as classified by G. P. Murdock

TABLE 2. THE MEDIAN PERCENTAGE RESPONSIBILITY SCORES FOR YOUNGER AND OLDER BOYS IN SOCIETIES GROUPED ON THE BASIS OF THE IMPORTANCE OF HERDING

| | Age of boys | |
	3 - 6	7 - 11
Herding	%	%
Important	11 (*n* = 10)	24.5 (*n* = 10)
Unimportant	8 (*n* = 23)	12 (*n* = 23)
Difference	+3	+12.5
P Value (Fischer exact test)	ns.	<.005

in his article on a "World Ethnographic Sample" (1957). The societies were categorized as to whether the major food supply was obtained by hunting, gathering or fishing, animal husbandry, horticulture, or agriculture. They found that the pressure for responsible behavior in their children exerted by parents and other socializers was greatest in those societies with animal husbandry and least in those societies whose major economic activity was hunting and gathering, societies whose subsistence economy was primarily agricultural being intermediate on this score.

There has been some criticism of the Bacon, Barry, and Child findings based upon the bias of their sample (see J. Whiting, in press). Since the majority of herding societies in their sample fell in sub-Saharan Africa, it could be argued that their findings represent a culture area bias. A general African cultural value for responsibility might account for their findings. It was determined therefore to recalculate their results separating Africa from the rest of the world. Furthermore, since in a number of instances two closely related societies were included in the original Bacon, Barry, and Child sample, it was decided to eliminate such duplication by selecting at random one society whenever two or more occurred in the same cluster as defined in the *Ethnographic Atlas* (Murdock, 1967). This yielded a sample of twenty societies in sub-Saharan Africa and fifty-four for the rest of the world.

The importance of herding in the economy was also derived from the *Ethnographic Atlas*. A score of 2 or above on column 10, indicating 16 per cent or more dependence upon animal husbandry as a means of subsistence, was taken as an indication that herding was of sufficient importance that it might be assigned as a task to the older boys of the culture. As can be seen from Table 3, over 80 per cent of the societies in which animal husbandry was of appreciable importance to the economy were above average with respect to the pressure exerted upon boys for being responsible, whereas in societies such as those in the tropical rain forest areas where herding is unimportant or absent, only 12.5 per cent of the societies were above the median on pressure toward responsibility.

Since only nine of the fifty-four societies representing the rest of the world reached our criterion of importance of animal husbandry, it is questionable whether an appropriate test of our hypothesis can be made on such a skewed sample. Six of these nine cases were, however, above the world median on the pressure toward responsibility score. From these data, then, it seems that the relation between responsibility and herding has a generality greater than the six cultures previously reported on.

It is argued by Bacon, Barry, and Child that the relation between animal husbandry and pressure toward responsibility is due to an accumulated capital in the form of livestock, and that children must be trained to be

TABLE 3. THE RELATION BETWEEN THE PERCENTAGE OF
SUBSISTENCE BASED UPON ANIMAL HUSBANDRY AND THE AMOUNT
OF PRESSURE TOWARD RESPONSIBILITY EXERTED UPON BOYS BY
SOCIALIZING AGENTS.[a]

Pressure toward responsibility	Proportion of subsistence from animal husbandry			
	Less than 15%		15% or more	
High			Masai	13
			Turkana	13
			Fon	12
			Nyakyusa	12
			Swazi	12
			Nuer	11
			Tswana	11
			Kikuyu	10
			Tallensi	10
Median	Oyo Yoruba	11	Thonga	09
	Ashanti	09	Mbundu	08
	Azande	09	Bena	07
Low	Chewa	09		
	Ganda	09		
	Lamba	08		
	Kongo	08		
	Tiv	06		

p < .005

[a]The numbers following the name of each society represent its score on pressure toward responsibility.

responsible so they will maintain this capital as adults. Although this is a plausible argument, the alternative explanation (that it is a direct consequence of the nature of herding as a task) seems more plausible. For the latter interpretation to be valid, it must be determined whether or not boys are indeed assigned the task of herding in those societies where animals are important in the economy. We are now engaged in a cross-cultural study of task assignment. Although we have not gone far enough to report conclusively, only one of the fourteen herding societies in our work sample reports that boys do not help care for the animals.

Bacon, Barry, and Child also report that parents in societies that engage in animal husbandry or agriculture exert more pressure on their sons to be obedient than do parents whose economy is based on hunting, fishing, and gathering. They also report that there is a strong positive relationship between obedience pressure and pressure for responsibility. Unfortunately, this relationship cannot be directly checked on the data available from the Six Culture Study since there are no scores on parental pressure toward obedience. There are, however, two scores available that bear upon the variable of obedience. First, we have a rating of the type of punishment that mothers reported they used when their children were disobedient, and, second, we have a score derived from the observation of the children of the rate at which they were given commands and suggestions by their mothers and the proportion of such commands that they obeyed.

An analysis of the type of punishment for disobedience reported by mothers of herd boys as contrasted with non-herd boys is presented in Table 4. It will be seen that physical punishment defined as slapping, beating, or switching is reported more frequently by the former than by the latter. Seventy-two per cent of the mothers of herd boys five years of age and over report the use of physical punishment for disobedience, in contrast to twenty-seven per cent of mothers of boys who do not herd. The difference is statistically significant at the .01 level of confidence. Assuming that physical punishment for disobedience represents a stronger pressure than less expressive forms of punishment, this finding confirms the cross-cultural results that herd boys are under strong demands to be obedient.

TABLE 4. MOTHERS' REPORTS ON THE USE OF PHYSICAL PUNISHMENT FOR DISOBEDIENCE AS IT RELATES TO PRESENCE OR ABSENCE OF HERDING AMONG BOYS FIVE TO ELEVEN YEARS OF AGE

Reported use of physical punishment	Boys who herd	Boys who do not herd
Present	18	8
Absent	7	13
	p < .01	

Herd boys are also issued more commands and suggestions by their mothers than other boys of the same age. As Table 5 shows, 60 per cent of the mothers of the former group were above the median on issuing orders to their herd boy sons, whereas 30 per cent of the mothers of boys not assigned the task of herding gave commands to their sons as frequently. This difference is statistically significant at the .025 level of confidence.

It should not be supposed, however, that because herd boys are so frequently told what to do and are so dramatically punished for disobedience

TABLE 5. RELATIONSHIP OF OBSERVED RATE OF COMMANDS BY MOTHER AS IT RELATES TO THE PRESENCE OR ABSENCE OF HERDING AMONG BOYS FIVE TO ELEVEN YEARS OF AGE

Rate of commands	Boys who herd	Boys who do not herd
Above median	12	6
Below median	8	14
	p < .025	

they are more obedient than others. In fact, quite the contrary is true. This inverse relationship previously reported by Imamura (1965) from a study of the interaction between blind children and their mothers is shown in Table 6 replicated on the basis of the six culture data. Only one-third of the mothers whose rate of commanding was one or more commands per five minutes can expect above average obedience from their children, but over two-thirds of those mothers who issue commands at a slower rate can expect obedience this often.

TABLE 6. RELATIONSHIP OF NUMBER OF COMMANDS BY MOTHER
PER FIVE MINUTES OBSERVATION PERIOD TO PERCENT
OBEDIENCE FOR BOYS FIVE TO ELEVEN YEARS OF AGE

Rate of commands by mother	Percentage obedience to commands	
	Below median	Above median
Above median	13	5
Below median	6	10

$p < .05$

Thus the profile of the herd boy is one to whom commands are frequently issued, who often ignores these commands and is beaten for it, and who in turn frequently issues commands and responsible suggestions to others. Since the rules governing herding are explicit and strongly sanctioned in the interests of the family, the herd boy is neither an individualist nor an innovator.

To make an equally detailed analysis of the effect of the assignment of tasks other than herding such as gardening, marketing, baby tending, and the like is beyond the scope of this paper. In many parts of the world and particularly in East Africa, the primary task assigned to boys is rapidly shifting from herding and other economic tasks to schooling. We would like, however, to make a few comments on some features of going to school that contrast with caring for cattle.

It was suggested at the beginning of this paper that schooling emphasized individual achievement rather than responsibility for maintaining group norms. The children of the Six Culture Study were scored on the proportion of their behavior that was labeled "arrogance." This consisted of calling attention to oneself and boasting. Both the boys and girls over six years of age who attended school exhibited significantly more of this type of behavior than their peers who did not attend school.

It was also assumed that in contrast to herding the task of learning in the classroom involved a considerable delay of rewards and punishments. Although there is no evidence from the Six Culture Study bearing on this point, a cross-cultural study reported by one of the authors (B. Whiting, 1961) showed that societies having formal school systems are more likely to believe that the gods punish wrong-doing in the future life, whereas in herding cultures punishment from the gods is believed to be immediate.

Other features could doubtless be found that would contrast the herd-boy and the schoolboy, but enough has been presented to permit us to speculate on some of the changes that are now taking place in East Africa.

It has been said by some educators that, comparatively speaking, the East African schoolboy shows relatively little initiative or creativity in his work. Coming from a culture where for generations a boy's main task is to help in the herding, this is hardly surprising. For a boy to try out new ideas about herding is neither expected nor admired. Even if the school-boy himself has had little or no experience in herding, the majority of East African school children today have parents who were brought up on a farm in which livestock and their care were highly valued and have fathers who learned as herd boys the importance of following the rules and the dangers of innovation and individual initiative. Such parents believe that a child should do what he is told, respect authority, and value the welfare of the family above his own selfish needs. Furthermore, children brought up in such families expect to be supervised and commanded. They expect tasks to be clearly defined and the rewards and punishments predictable and immediate.

Also, the vast majority of teachers, especially in primary school, have been brought up with herding values. It is not surprising that they expect obedience, feel comfortable with "rote" methods of teaching, and do not reward individual initiative.

It is interesting, with the rapid changes in the life of a child, to speculate how many generations it will take for East African values to change from responsibility to individual achievement, from bossing to boasting.

References

Barry, Herbert III, Margaret K. Bacon, and Irvin L. Child. A cross cultural survey of some sex differences in socialization. *Journal of Abnormal and Social Psychology*, 1957, 55, 327–332.

Barry, Herbert III, Irvin L. Child, and Margaret K. Bacon. Relation of child training to subsistence economy. *American Anthropologist*, 1959, 61, 51–63. See also Ford, C. S. (ed.). *Cross Cultural Approaches — Readings in Comparative Research*. HRAF. New Haven: 1967, 246–258.

Imamura, Sadako. *Mother and Blind Child: the Influence of Child Rearing Practices on the Behavior of Preschool Blind Children*. New York: American Foundation for the Blind, 1965.

Minturn, Leigh and William W. Lambert. *Mothers of Six Cultures — Antecedents of Child Rearing.* New York: John Wiley and Sons, 1964.

Murdock, George Peter. World ethnographic sample. *American Anthropologist,* 1957, 59, 664–87.

———. Ethnographic atlas: A summary. *Ethnology,* 1967, VI, No. 2, and Pittsburgh: University of Pittsburgh Press, 1967.

Whiting, Beatrice B. (ed.). *Six Cultures — Studies of Child Rearing.* New York: John Wiley and Sons, Inc., 1963.

———. "Task Assignment and Character Development." Unpublished paper presented 1961.

Whiting, John W. M. Resource mediation and learning by identification. In *Personality Development in Children,* I. Iscoe and M. Stevenson (eds.). Austin, Texas: University of Texas Press, 1960.

———. Methods and Problems in Cross-Cultural Research. G. Lindzey and Elliot Aronson (eds.). *Handbook of Social Psychology,* Vol. 2, pp. 693–728. Reading, Massachusetts: Addison Wesley, 1968.

3   PAUL C. ROSENBLATT

A Cross-Cultural Study of Child Rearing and Romantic Love

In the classic cross-cultural study of Whiting and Child (1953) considerable evidence was presented in support of the Freudian hypothesis of negative fixation: Frustration of a need in childhood is correlated with expression of the need in adult behavior. Evidence for positive fixation, overindulgence in a behavior system producing a surplus of adult concern and interest in the area of behavior, was much weaker. The differential evidence for the two kinds of fixation could be due to differences in op-

Paul C. Rosenblatt, "A Cross-cultural Study of Child Rearing and Romantic Love," *Journal of Personality and Social Psychology,* Vol. 4, No. 3, 1966, pp. 336–338. Copyright (1966) by the American Psychological Association, and reproduced by permission.

Supported by a grant from the Graduate School Research Council of the University of Missouri. Robert E. Cowan and John Stuart Garrity made the extracts and ratings of importance of romantic love.

portunities for their development — frustrating environments perhaps being more common and more consistent than indulgent environments — or in opportunities for their prevention through subsequent learning — frustration-based motives being more difficult to unlearn than indulgence-based motives (Lawrence & Festinger, 1962). One expectation that can be derived from the differential evidence for positive and negative fixation in the Whiting and Child data is that negative fixation is more likely to occur than positive fixation in cross-cultural comparisons where either could occur.

Perhaps because of their interest in measures that could be used with a variety of behavior systems, Whiting and Child did not test directly one of the most important specific predictions that can be made from Freudian fixation theory. It is a prediction that can be made on the assumption that negative fixation is far more common than positive and one that has important implications for human social behavior: Early frustration of oral and dependency needs, needs which are most closely related to affection, is reflected in adult concern for affection. It is the purpose of the present paper to report a cross-cultural test of the hypothesis, using ratings by Whiting and Child of initial satisfaction of oral and dependency needs and subsequent severity of oral and dependence socialization as measures of infancy and childhood experiences. The measure of adult concern for affection used is importance of romantic love as a basis for choice of marital partner. Before the specific methods are reported, a problem of difference between the Whiting and Child data on oral socialization and their data on dependence socialization must be mentioned.

Whereas Whiting and Child's ratings of initial indulgence and later severity of socialization in the area of oral behavior correlate strongly, the two kinds of ratings do not correlate significantly in the area of dependence behavior. They report the former correlation to be −.60, which with 37 cases is significantly different from .00 beyond the .001 level, and the latter to be −.18, which with 27 cases is not significantly different from .00 (Whiting & Child, 1953, p. 108). Thus, across cultures, oral socialization from infancy into childhood is rather consistent, while dependence socialization is not. The difference in consistency seems reasonable in that postinfancy dependence-independence socialization has been shown to respond strongly to demands of technology (Barry, Child, & Bacon, 1959), while postinfancy oral socialization appears to be much more free to respond to the same factors as infant socialization. An obvious implication of the difference in developmental consistency between oral socialization and dependence socialization is that if prolonged frustrative experiences are necessary for negative fixation to occur, stronger support for a negative-fixation hypothesis would come from cross-cultural data on oral socialization than from data on dependence socialization.

METHOD

The initial sample consisted of 21 societies which had been rated by Whiting and Child on at least one of the four oral or dependence socialization variables, this information being available from the Human Relations Area File microcards at the University of Missouri library. Of these 21 societies, 2, Malekula and Marquesan, were dropped because the information available on importance of romantic love as a basis for marriage was inadequate. The number of cases involved in each of the correlations performed was reduced further because Whiting and Child were unable to rate confidently each aspect of socialization of interest in the present study for one or more of the 19 remaining societies in our sample.

For the rating of importance of romantic love as a basis for marriage, extracts were made of ethnographic materials in categories 581 (Basis of Marriage) and 831 (Sexuality) of the Human Relations Area File microcards. Two raters independently rated the extracts on an 11-point scale, the end points being "0 — active avoidance of marital unions based on romantic love; virtually no unions based on romantic love" and "10 — virtually all unions based on romantic love; romantic love extremely important in the culture." The major criteria for judging the presence of romantic love were ethnographers' specific statements about romantic love, presence of nonarranged marriage or frequent elopement where marriages are traditionally arranged, idealization of those characteristics of members of the opposite sex which are not directly relevant to subsistence activities such as cooking or planting, and belief in predestination for marriage partners.

The ratings of the two judges, which correlated .72 ($p < .001$) for the 19 societies which could be rated on importance of romantic love, were added together, giving scores on importance of romantic love as a basis for marriage [1] that could range from 0 to 20.

RESULTS AND DISCUSSION

Importance of romantic love as a basis for marriage was rather strongly related to the two measures of oral frustration. In the case of initial oral indulgence, the rank correlation was −.54, which with 18 societies is significantly different from .00 beyond the .05 level. In the case of later severity of socialization the rank correlation was .37, which with 16 societies is different from .00 at the .08 level (one-tailed test), not significant

---

[1] The combined ratings of importance of romantic love as a basis of marriage were as follows: Abipón, 2; Alorese, 11; Andamanese, 11; Azande, 6; Chagga, 17; Ifugao, 4; Jivaro, 13; Kurtatchi, 2; Lepcha, 4; Manuans, 1; Marshallese, 10; Murngin, 4; Papago, 7; Pukapukans, 15; Rwala, 17; Samoans, 13; Tikopia, 14; Trobrianders, 18; Wogeo, 15.

but nearly so. Both of these correlations fit the negative-fixation hypothesis. However, for the two measures of dependence frustration, the correlations with importance of romantic love as a basis for marriage are virtually zero. In the case of initial dependence indulgence, the correlation is .07 $(N = 18)$; in the case of later severity of socialization, the correlation is .10 $(N = 16)$.

Although the correlations for oral frustration fit the negative-fixation hypothesis, the ones for dependence frustration do not. Since, as was mentioned above, oral socialization practices in infancy and early childhood are consistent, while dependence socialization practices are not, the fact that the correlations with romantic love were strong for oral frustration but not for dependence frustration may be interpreted as reflecting the importance of prolonged frustration in producing negative fixation.

References

Barry, H., III, I. L. Child, and M. K. Bacon. Relation of child training to subsistence economy. *American Anthropologist*, 1959, *61*, 51–63.

Lawrence, D. H., and L. Festinger. *Deterrents and Reinforcement*. Stanford: Stanford University Press, 1962.

Whiting, J. W. M., and I. L. Child. *Child Training and Personality*. New Haven: Yale University Press, 1953.

III

Comparative Studies
of Personality

4   WILLIAM WILSON LAMBERT

Cross-Cultural Backgrounds to Personality
Development and the Socialization of
Aggression: Findings from the Six Culture Study

In this paper we report findings from what has become known as the Six Culture Project. This study was co-directed by J. W. M. Whiting, Irvin Child, and myself and began more than ten years ago when field teams

Earlier versions of this paper were presented to various groups, including the opening session of Midwestern Association for the Education of Young Children, Milwaukee, May, 1967, and the international meeting of the World Organization for Early Childhood Education (O.M.E.P.), UNESCO Building, Paris, July 1966 and published in the Proceedings of that meeting. Its preparation was aided by a Special Fellowship from NIMH.

49

went off to six communities in widely spaced areas of the world: to a village caste group in northern India, an Indian village in Mexico, an American Baptist community, a Gusii village in Kenya, a barrio in northern Luzon, Philippine Islands, and to a village in Okinawa.[1] These six communities were selected because they were relatively *homogeneous* within themselves: our Indian families were all Hindus of the Rajput caste; our Americans shared a middle class way of life and a common special form of Protestant religion; and so on. Although none of these communities are urban, we feel that similar groups can be found in all large cities. All of our present six cultural groups are *rural*; but much of the world is rural, still living on farms and in villages, in the country or in the suburbs. Further, much of man's daily life is still spent in relatively homogeneous, local groupings within which marriages and other practices occur by long-lasting rules, as in our six communities.

STUDYING CHILD TRAINING PRACTICES IN THE SIX CULTURE STUDY

In each community a sample of mothers was interviewed on the same questions in order to discover how they and their child's father behaved toward the child. It was possible to factor-analyze into "clusters" or groups the mothers' answers to many of the questions. These factors collect together the practices and emphases that vary together. This method permits us to reduce these clusters to manageable small numbers that are independent of each other. We can also give each family in each culture a "factor score" that represents its relative standing on the cluster.

Peer Aggression: an Example of Cultural Differences [2]

One of our "clusters" of practices dealt with how the parents handle occurrences of peer aggression, as when children fight or scold one another, and also with how the parents handle obedience to parental orders. Families with a high score on this "peer aggression factor" tend to punish a child more intensely for fighting back when he is picked on by his age-mates; they also tend to have more consistent rules against aggression, and they tend to be more consistent in following through on demands for

---

[1] The Ford Foundation aided in the costs of the field work. Since that time, the analysis of the data has been aided by funds and patience from U.S. National Institutes of Mental Health. See Whiting, B. B. (ed.), *Six Cultures* (New York: John Wiley and Sons, Inc., 1962); and Whiting, J. W. M., I. L. Child, W. W. Lambert (and others), *Field Guide for a Study of Socialization: Six Culture Series*, Volume I (New York: John Wiley and Sons, Inc., 1966).

[2] The general source for these findings is L. Minturn, W. W. Lambert, and others, *Mothers of Six Cultures* (New York: John Wiley and Sons, 1964). Discussion of peer aggression will be found in chapter 8, with a relevant table on p. 151.

obedience. These are the practices that *cluster* together and *vary* together when all the families from all the cultures are considered as one large group. *Low* scoring families generally tend in the opposite direction on this cluster. That is, they reward a child for fighting back, they have less consistent rules regarding fighting, and they do not follow through on situational demands for obedience.

Now, consider how the six communities differ on this factor of punishment for peer-directed aggression. The Mexican Indian group stands out as particularly *high* on this factor; the American New England group stands out as particularly *low*; in between are the Okinawan, the north Indian, the African, and the Philippine groups. Such ordering of cultural groups is intrinsically interesting, but the next questions arise immediately: *Why* are Mexican Indians so firm in punishing when fights develop between children? *Why* are the New Englanders so relatively lax on the same issue? One partial answer seems to rely on how many close relatives live nearby and, probably, on how interdependent these families of close relatives are. That is, "I cannot permit my son to fight with the child next door in the Mexican town, because he is my brother's child, and if our children don't get along, then my brother and I may come to a parting of the ways, and that may lead to great problems." In the American town, where almost no relatives live nearby, the child can fight anyone he wishes without getting in the parents' way. Besides, as one American mother put it: "If he can't get along with one child, he can always play with someone else. There are many children around to choose from." The Mexican child has no such freedom; the "other children around" will usually be related also. Thus, his *family* must try to control his fighting, or at least they must adopt an attitude that publicly displays their opposition to peer fighting. In a seventh culture, Formosa, Margery Wolf has documented [3] that it is a wise child who sees that related families are caught in this important difficulty. If, in Formosa, a child has hurt some other child, all the hurt child need do is report to the other's mother and the latter will get a public whipping!

Two methods are available to check further on this general hypothesis that cultures where relatives live nearby have stricter rules against peer fighting. We can turn to the broad resources of data on many cultures as reported in extant ethnographies or in the Human Relations Area Files. When we checked the HRAF files, our hypothesis was generally supported.[4]

[3] Margery Wolf, "Child training and the Chinese family," in Maurice Freedman, *Family and Kinship in Chinese Society* (Stanford: Stanford University Press, 1970), p. 55.

[4] See L. Minturn, W. W. Lambert, and others, *Mothers of Six Cultures, op. cit.*, chapter 9.

However, another and independent testing method is available with which we can test our general hypotheses *within* each of the cultural groups. We can, for example, see if the particular families *within* the Mexican community, who have more relatives close at hand in a common courtyard, have stricter rules and practices regarding peer aggression than do those who have *fewer* close, courtyard relatives. This procedure can be repeated within each cultural group, and statistical tests of general cross-cultural trends can be made. This has been my own favorite method for testing pan-cultural hypotheses in the Six Culture Study, and in this paper I shall limit myself to reporting just such *cross-culturally common trends* in parent-child relationships.

One of our most reliably clear findings is the positive relationship between the number of children in a basic family and the strictness of the rules regarding peer aggression. If a family has more children than the average for their cultural group, then they will be more punitive toward fights that occur among peers. This prediction holds a significant trend across the six cultures.[5]

Mother-Directed Aggression: Another Example

Now consider the cultural ordering on the cluster of items that represents how firm the parents are with *aggression that is directed at the mother herself*.[6] The most important items that define this cluster are: first, how negative or punitive the mother is when the child becomes angry when scolded, and second, how aggressive the mother is when, for any reason, the child is angry or aggressive toward *her*. How much the mother emphasizes immediate obedience, and her overall use of physical punishment, also enter into this cluster. The Gusii mothers of Kenya are the most punishing toward this kind of child aggression, and the Philippine mothers are second, followed by the Mexicans. The Okinawan and New England mothers are in the middle. The northern Indian mothers are by far the *least* punitive when aggression is directed at them.

To what family and community antecedent conditions is *this* cultural ordering related? It does not serve merely to consider the African mothers as innately more prideful and therefore more angry when a child hits them. What in the *pan-cultural human condition* is probably responsible? At present, there are several suggestions. Pan-culturally, the personally aggression-sensitive mothers are those in houses where there are extra adults present.[7] The punitiveness may arise from the reasonable fear that

[5] Ibid., p. 277.
[6] Ibid., chapter 7.
[7] Ibid., pp. 272–273.

an aggressive child may also aggress against the *other* adults in the house. "Would it be wise to let my son develop a habit of hitting *me* if there is a chance that he will *then* hit his grandfather? Particularly if his grandfather owns the house I live in?"

The lack of punitiveness of the Indian mother may, in addition, reflect her general low family status when she is the newly married young woman brought from out of town into the family. Generally, also, the mothers who make an independent contribution to the family economy expect their children to be more responsible and therefore to be *obedient* to their mother who (particularly in the African group) must get her children to be helpful in chores and other duties early in life so that she can take charge of the work in the fields.[8]

General "Determinants" of Parent-Child Relationships

The story of the correlates of these two factors is repeated in all the other factors. There are always pan-cultural correlates, and they tend to be of this ultimately practical sort. In fact, my own general impression is that some, at least, of the very basic building blocks of parent-child relations are best seen as being fashioned out of a series of difficult (and often heartrending) decisions on how the parent can *best utilize his or her limited resources of energy, attention, and affection*. Note how the theme of limited resources recurs as I list some of our other cross-cultural generalizations: [9]

1. The child is more frequently called upon to do more chores and more *kinds* of chores where his mother is more involved in making an independent contribution to the economics of the family. He also does more chores where there are more *younger* siblings to take care of (not the total number of siblings in this case), and where he happens to be the *oldest child*.

2. The mother does *less* of the caretaking of her baby when the immediate family includes other adults or more siblings. Her baby care duties are also less when related adults live in the nearby courtyard. She does less of the caretaking of her older child when other female adults and more older siblings are at home, and apparently, when the mother's mother lives closer at hand.

3. Let us now look at what many of us would consider the most important of our child training factors, *maternal warmth*.[10] The mothers

---

[8] Ibid., pp. 269–271.
[9] Ibid., chapter 17.
[10] Ibid., chapters 2 and 17.

who score high on this factor display a high degree of general warmth in dealing with their children, show a low degree of general hostility in their relationships, tend to use a relatively large amount of praise, and use physical punishment rarely and with relatively low intensity. Now, under what conditions does a mother act toward her child in this warm and positive way?

A child receives more *maternal warmth* (and is thereby handled with a strategy that includes an emphasis on reward rather than punishment) when there are other adults in the house, when there are fewer siblings around, when the child is the youngest or only child, and when he has fewer courtyard cousins whose presence would generally restrain his mother from pridefully rewarding his good behavior in public.

4. We have also studied the degree of a mother's *emotional stability*,[11] rated by her tendency toward "blowing hot or cold" for no apparent reason. The emotional stability of a child's mother is *lower* when there are fewer adults around to help and when there are more of her own children around to handle.

This, then, is part of the picture of how, and possibly *why*, parents relate in particular ways to their children in these "other places" in the world where they are left to make use of traditional, limited resources as best they can. We are not surprised at these results. We *are* surprised somewhat, however, at the clarity of the empirical *pan-cultural* force of these simple issues of exchange of scarce resources.

Some Cross-Cultural Generalizations Regarding "Significant Others" as Scarce Resources

Let us now generalize at a somewhat higher level of abstraction. The child training practices that we have studied are affected by, and possibly even determined by, a number of people who surround the work of the parents and their child, either in the larger household or the immediate community. I suggest that most of our findings relate to three basic kinds of such people and that we can summarize our cross-cultural findings simply in terms of these three kinds of "significant others" — surrogates, competitors, and targets, named according to their function.

1. The importance of parental surrogates. First let us consider the people we will call surrogates for the mother and for the father. These are people who can be trusted to serve as temporary replacements. Further, they must serve as replacements at relatively low cost in terms of expected reciprocation, and here such costs as money, services, and expressions of love and gratitude must all be considered. Surrogates exist, of

[11] Ibid., chapters 3 and 17.

course, in varying degrees both within and between our communities in the Six Culture Study.

I find two things very interesting about these surrogates. First, they are highly *selected* from among the older children and adults in the community, and *it appears that kinship is very important in deciding who can be an acceptable replacement,* as is a rational consideration of the cost of reciprocating such aid. The second thing that interests me is that *where acceptable surrogates are available,* their service tends to be used.

The presence or absence of surrogates is the only cross-cultural correlate of the two child training factors that have to do with amount of baby care and child care done by the mother.[12] Cross-culturally, then, *the more these acceptable, low cost surrogates are available, the lower is the proportion of the total child care and baby care that is done by the mother herself.* The issue of surrogates also enters into both the emotional stability of the mother and the warmth of her treatment of her child.[13] *The more the available surrogates, the more stable and warm is the mother.* However, it is important that these surrogates in our data are a very limited group, consisting solely of other adults who are already in the household. It is possible that their effectiveness in relation to such deeply stylistic matters as maternal warmth and emotional stability is related both to the low additional cost of reciprocation involved, and to their *constant* presence to help in handling the finer texture of life problems inside the home. This is perhaps our most important finding. It suggests that the mental health, or at least the style of emotional life, of both the mother and her child are enhanced by the availability of acceptable surrogates. This matter deserves careful consideration and more detailed research.

2. The importance of competitors. The second kind of "significant other" in this picture encompasses the people whom I shall call *role competitors.* These are people who compete with our sample child for the limited attention, energy, and affection of the parent. They too are highly selected. Their presence, in the form of "too many" siblings or "many" courtyard cousins have a marked and significant *negative* effect on the stability and warmth of the mother. It is easy to see why having many children of her own would deplete her reserves of warmth and stability. The reason that her child's courtyard *cousins* enter the picture is probably because *any given mother must help provide for the care of these related children as one of the reciprocity costs that must be paid to get help from surrogates.*[14]

The presence of competitors is also related to the *responsibility training*

[12] Ibid., pp. 266–267.
[13] Ibid., p. 263.
[14] Ibid., p. 259.

the sample child receives.[15] Where economic activities compete for the
mother's energy, she will call upon her available children, particularly the
older ones, to take on more chores, and she will tend to demand less
parent-directed aggression and more obedience from *all* of her children.
After all, she must, under these stresses, become a boss, or a work supervisor, toward her useful children!

3. The importance of target people. It is also with regard to responsibility training that the importance of our third kind of "significant other"
begins to show up. I shall call these *target people*, though they can easily
be divided into those people who provide "extra opportunities" or "extra
temptations" to our sample child. The more such target people are present,
in the form, for example, of younger siblings who provide an opportunity
for, and reward for, the practice of responsibility, then the more will a
given child in our sample receive general training in responsibility.

Target people also function as temptations, and in this sense they enter
very centrally into the pattern of aggression control. *The more people who
may serve as tempting targets for aggression are present, the more firm is
the punitiveness for aggression.* In the case of peer aggression, the important targets appear to be several siblings, or the presence of economically important grandparents, as in the stem family. In the case of
mother-directed aggression, the sternness here is a function of adult targets
to whom authority-directed aggression might generalize.[16] That is, as a
parent, I will try to stamp out or control with punishment any fighting
among my children whenever I have a large *number* of children to control, or when my child's fighting habits may carry over toward other
adults who live with me. I will also punish any anger shown toward me if
there is any chance that such anger may be carried over toward my own
father, mother, or brothers who live with me.

STUDYING "OBSERVED PERSONALITY" IN THE SIX CULTURE STUDY

In addition to analyzing parental responses to questions about their practices in child rearing, we have recently been engaged in the analysis of the
child behavior itself.

The focus of our new analysis is on laying out the various possible
causes of individual differences in the observed rates of behavior of our
children. In each community we obtained verbatim records of timed
samplings of interpersonal behavior for each sample child. Each theoretically relevant act was given its own IBM card, and the card was filled with

[15] Ibid., pp. 269–270.
[16] Ibid., pp. 271–278.

information regarding the child, the apparent instigation (if any) to the specific act of the child, and the group and setting conditions preceding and following the specific act. These cards permit us to study the relationship between the child training practices and the child's behavior, as well as the effects of sex and age of the child, and of the instigating agents, the family structure, and the structure of the courtyard, as conditions that cause the particular kinds and levels of behavior rates of the child.

Although the analysis of these cards is still incomplete, I can now see some of the major findings.[17]

Pan-Cultural Sources of Personality Differences in Asking for Help and Giving Help

What correlates (summing, again, the within-community correlations across communities) with the individual differences in rates of *asking for help?* I was surprised at the empirical answer: Children who do a great deal of asking for help tend to live in nuclear families with few adults around, rather than in families where there are many adults to turn to. This form of dependent, "succorant" behavior emerges from the very conditions where its reward is most partial: from the limited resources of the nuclear (mother-child, father) family rather than the more rich and diversified resources of the stem or extended family.

Further, "asking for help" rates are much higher, across cultures, for *only* children and for children low in the birth order. The courtyard factors are not involved in this kind of behavior, so high help-seeking is a prerogative of the child who has low responsibility demands placed on him, who has been given permissiveness in being aggressive toward the mother, and who has an emotionally stable mother. We are now analyzing for the effects on these rates of the finer texture of the immediate situation in which each act occurs, and I feel certain that pan-cultural factors will emerge in this realm that will help to determine the occurrence of these dependent behaviors. We will also seek to discover whether the child training effects are independent of the family structure effects, and look for interaction among these as well.

It is also informative to look at some of the correlates of the rates of *giving* help that our children display. The clearest cross-cultural correlate (and possible determinant) of *giving help* is the presence of a large number of cousins and older people in the courtyard. It is also related to being

---

[17] The remaining findings discussed in this paper are not yet published. Most of them will appear in the forthcoming volume, *Children of Six Cultures,* by Whiting, J. W. M., B. Whiting, R. Longabaugh, W. W. Lambert, and others.

an oldest child whose father has been present more than usual, and to having been required to do more chores than usual. Giving help is more frequent in the behavior of girls in all cultures. The high helper, then, is a child who has the oldest child's role and who has been rewarded for responsibility. She has nobody above her among her family siblings, and she has a large number of cousins in the courtyard who serve as targets for her help-giving, along with adult relatives around the community who can check up on her *general* responsibility, and, of course, on her helpfulness in particular.

Pan-Cultural Sources of Personality Differences in Aggression

Earlier in this paper I discussed what enters into the factors, or clusters, which describe *parental training practices* which deal with peer aggression, and with mother-directed aggression. I have also outlined some of the family and community structures that relate to the severity of the parents' discipline for these problems. We also have assembled data on children's *observed aggressive behaviors.* Now I want to report on our findings relating parental practices to observed aggressive behaviors.

Our first finding is that we *cannot* directly predict a child's overall *rate* or *proportion* of aggressive behavior from either the way peer aggression has been reportedly handled, or the way parent-directed aggression has been handled. No reliable relation has been discovered so far, either *within* any culture, or *across* the cultures.

I therefore wish to suggest here that parental disciplinary practices related to aggression are best viewed as *effects*, or as symptoms of problems of resource mediation, rather than as *direct and potent causes* of aggressive behavior traits in the children's personalities.

The second interesting finding I wish to report is that socially active children in a society appear to display *in their behavior* the cultural values regarding aggression that parents are attempting to inculcate. Recall that the Mexican Indian mothers are the most negative toward peer aggression of all our mothers, and that the United States mothers were by far the most permissive. When we correlate a child's *aggressive score* with a measure of his *total rate* of *all* social behavior, this correlation reflects the values of the mothers: in Mexico the correlation is *negative*; in the United States it is highly *positive*. This means that in Mexico, the more active child (who may well be a peer leader) tends to be *less* aggressive than the less lively child, whereas in New England the lively child tends to be an *aggressive* one. Furthermore, the size of this correlation between aggression and liveliness is itself correlated with the *cultural average* of the parents on *peer aggression permissiveness*, when all cultures are included.

How, then, did the *socially active children* in each culture come to reflect the average family values on aggression, when children in general do not directly reflect the results of their *own families' particular* attempts to shape them in this realm?

One way to begin an answer to this question is by looking at the antecedents of a child's *total social action rate.* That is, what in a child's history is correlated with his being a "lively one"? I will simplify the picture here a bit to make my major point. The extent to which a child is cared for, when a *baby*, by only his mother, is positively related to his total rate of social interaction per minute!

These facts have led us to develop a theory regarding the socialization of aggression that we are now testing.

A Two-Phase Theory of Aggression Control

Simply stated, this theory suggests that the shaping of aggressive traits is achieved in two stages. First, parental care, and more particularly maternal caretaking of babies, provides the basis, probably in the form of self-confidence, that makes a child a high social interactor. Second, the positive or negative response of peers to the child's aggressive behavior shapes the high social interactor more quickly than the low interactor.[18] In addition, parents get across to the Mexican child, for example, that retaliatory aggression is *not* valued, and to the American child that it is, under certain conditions, *permitted* or *valued*. In Mexico peers will shun him if he is aggressive; in the United States, he will be valued and made a leader.

Some facets of this theory seem to be upheld by the data. We know that the high social interactors do, in fact, receive a higher total number of reactions from peers (and others) when they engage in *any form* of *aggressive* behavior than do the low interactors (though the percentage of reactions remains the same). It is also clear that most of the reactions the sample children received to their own aggressions come from other children rather than from adults. We are now checking to see whether these reactions received by active children are more *supportive of aggression* in New England, and more *discouraging* in Mexico. We are also checking whether peers in the *other* four cultures are giving *supportive* or *discouraging* feedback in the correct proportion that their parents' modal cultural values would call for.

It is interesting that this theory, if it is correct, may apply *best* to exactly the kinds of communities that we selected for the Six Culture Study in the first place: communities that achieve homogeneity through

---

[18] This version of the two-phase theory is an elaboration of results of discussion with Richard Longabaugh, Patricia Licuanen, and Arthur Wolf.

their smallness. The parents tend to agree with one another, and, as a result, peers tend to cognize acceptable aggressive behavior in the same ways. It is interesting that this theory assumes that, on the average at least, children learn early in life (through imitative or observational learning processes) to recognize in others the valued and unvalued behaviors, and they learn to act toward peers on the basis of such recognition even before they have fully internalized these value discriminations into their own behavior patterns. Under such conditions, it does not matter so much that parental discipline has little direct effect: the peers, and others, can take on part of the task, and the community-wide process will *still* converge toward common standards.

A Social Engineering Interpretation: Limitations in Natural Communities

What would these findings suggest to us if we were social engineers? *Suppose* all our discovered antecedents to child training practices are equally causative. *Suppose* we had the power to vary these correlates of the child training practices, and *suppose* we knew how to do the varying. Suppose we attempted to reconstruct a community so that, for example, we could have mothers with *high emotional stability* and that *high maternal warmth could also be the rule*. We would, then, provide (in the service of both these aims) a stem family or other extended family structure that provides more adults as surrogates. Both these aims would also be served by making sure that nuclear family size was kept small. But then we run into trouble: in order to get maternal warmth as high as possible, we would have to keep down the number of courtyard cousins. But how could we do this and still provide the extra adults? Having extra adults normally means having extra children, and therefore more courtyard cousins, whose presence will tend to restrain the mother's style from one of warmth to one of coldness and to serve as a reciprocal cost for surrogate aid. This is merely a random example of how difficult in principle it is to engineer these determining conditions toward some agreed-upon pattern of excellence. As we add more restrictions or requirements, the inconsistencies and difficulties increase. In the West we have tended to see the role of the parent in the life of the child from one of two basic perspectives. The parent has often been seen as constructing this role for himself out of his unconscious wishes and drives. Equally often we have, perhaps out of our hope and our good intentions, viewed the parent as one who is constructing his role toward his child out of a tendentious plan for molding the child into something ideal and close to his own desire or ideals of the culture.

Regardless of differences in definitions of what kind of behavior or personality may be "best," we find that there do not exist within most cultures sufficient resources of surrogates, competitors, and targets to mold the personalities and the capacities of children to any maximum pattern. Furthermore, our Six Culture data demonstrate that the parental behavior that impinges upon a child is a result of *the limited resources of energy, attention and affection that are at the parents' disposal*. All too many of the specific factors determining how particular resources will be allocated are well beyond the *control* of the parent, of the family, and certainly of the child. These causes rest in the very structure of the community and in the complex social and psychological interplay that results from the activity of these community structures.

Although our basic knowledge on these large issues is still very scanty, our study shows that some of the determiners of child behavior and personality are among the tough and unyielding parameters of the human condition. Few parents can control, as yet, their family's size, the availability of surrogates, or the residence patterns and housing conditions that, in turn, control the availability of targets and competitors.

It follows that maximal conditions for childhood development are very rare in natural communities and are very difficult to arrange or to create in such places. These community systems, like our six groups, cannot remain closed systems, sufficient unto themselves, and *at the same time* provide any particular set of maximal conditions. New ideas, new organizations, new sources of energy, of attention, and even of affection must enter the system from outside if human personality is to have an opportunity for its fullest development.

It also follows, it seems to me, that no cultural group existing in the world at present provides the maximal conditions for *all* the child training factors that even our small Six Culture Study has uncovered. Given a personal choice, I'd like to grow up in Okinawa, and certainly if I were a mother that would be my preferred place to rear my children. There is help available for baby and child care, and maternal warmth and emotional stability are high. But even in Okinawa certain aspects of the responsibility training tend to be low, and there is at least a medium level of punitiveness used to quell aggression.

But another and more positive fact also follows from these considerations. Since no one culture has managed to achieve a monopoly of all the "good" or "bad" conditions for parent-child relations, then we are going to be delighted as we travel about the world. We are always going to find some facet of human personality or of personality organization which glows with a serene excellence that we have never met before. And lying below the fact of that fresh, though partial and perhaps even fleeting, excellence, is new knowledge about how to make some future generation (and its parents) better, more happy, or more free.

Father-Absence and Delay of Gratification: Cross-Cultural Comparisons

The dual purpose of this study is to investigate the effect of father-absence in the home on children's ability to delay gratification, as measured by their preference for immediate, smaller reinforcement (ImR) over delayed, larger reinforcement (DelR); and test hypotheses based on ethnographic data concerning cross-cultural and intracultural differences in preferences for ImR or DelR. Opportunities to study systematically the effect of father-absence on the child's behavior, in this case on his delaying the immediately available but relatively trivial for the sake of later but larger outcomes, are rare. Either fathers are not absent for long periods or other conditions tend to be so deviant that generalizations to less extreme cases must be most tentative. The possible effect of prolonged absence of a parent is nevertheless of such import for any theory of identification and personality development that data are much needed. For example, Whiting (1959) is persistently concerned with developmental and identification differences between children reared in mother-child and children reared in nuclear (father-present) households.

The present research, based on investigations in the southern Caribbean, presents data on a large number of father-present and father-absent boys and girls, sampled from a variety of settings, and differing sufficiently in age so that the role of the latter can be tested. Father-presence or absence is related in this study to the individual's choice preference for ImR or DelR. Such choice preferences are fairly easily elicited and

Walter Mischel, "Father Absence and Delay of Gratification," *Journal of Abnormal and Social Psychology*, Vol. 63, No. 1, 1961, pp. 116–124. Copyright (1961) by the American Psychological Association, and reproduced by permission.

This study was carried out under the partial support of a grant from the Laboratory of Social Relations, Harvard University, and Grant M-2557 (A) from the National Institute of Mental Health. Grateful acknowledgment is made to the Education Office of the Government of Trinidad and Tobago, and of the Government of Grenada, and to their officials for kind cooperation in testing within the school systems.

provide lifelike behavior which is readily quantified and some of whose empirical correlates have been explored independently. Namely, preference for DelR (as opposed to ImR) has been related positively to accuracy in time statements and to social responsibility (Mischel, 1961b). The latter was measured by an independently validated scale (Harris, 1957) and found to correlate substantially with other measures of personal and social adjustment and maturity. Preference for DelR has also been negatively related to delinquency, positively to strength of n Achievement, and negatively to acquiescence or "yeasaying" (as opposed to "naysaying") tendencies (Mischel, 1961a). The preference for DelR-ImR distinction may thus be thought of as delineating two empirically-elaborated clusters, associated with significant differences in "maturity," responsibility, delay over time, long-term goal direction, and autonomy.

Singer and his associates (e.g., Singer, Wilensky, & McCraven, 1956) have investigated "delaying capacity," primarily as inferred from the frequency of human movement (M) in Rorschach responses, and have pointed to relevant correlates of delaying which overlap to some degree with those just indicated. Conceptually, the empirical correlates of preference for DelR and ImR are related to Freud's (1922) distinction between functioning on the pleasure principle as opposed to the reality principle and are relevant to Mowrer and Ullman's (1945) position. The latter maintain that the inability to delay gratification is an important factor in immature, neurotic, and criminal behavior.

The data on preference for DelR or ImR from the previous studies in this program all come from the same general culture area outside the United States and are based on West Indian children's responses, tested in comparable settings and with techniques similar to those used in the present study. Thus a network of correlates associated with the two reinforcement preference patterns with respect to delay has begun to be established. The findings of this study on choice behavior of father-absent and father-present children become meaningful in that context. In an earlier exploratory study (Mischel, 1958), using a small sample of Trinidadian rural children aged 7–9, a significant relationship was found between father-absence and preference for ImR. Further, Negro subjects were found to show greater ImR preference when compared with East Indian subjects in the same cultural setting, the differences between the two groups seemingly being due to greater father-absence in the Negro sample. The present study is in part directed at replicating this relationship and testing its generality by sampling male and female children from a large variety of settings.

More important, however, is the attempt to test also the effect of father-absence on older children. Thus far investigations on the effects of father-absense (Bach, 1946; Lynn & Sawrey, 1959; Sears, Pintler, & Sears, 1946; Tiller, 1958) have all been based on samples of children under age 10. Lynn and Sawrey (1959) summarized these findings. Their own research included hypotheses of greater immaturity and poorer peer adjustment on the part of father-absent boys as compared to father-absent girls and a control group of father-present boys. These (and other) hypotheses were generally supported by data based on Norwegian boys and girls, ranging in age from 8 years to 9 years 6 months. The present study offers data for this age group (ages 8 and 9) as well as for a second, older group, aged 11–14. Lynn and Sawrey rightly point out that the findings of the earlier studies are limited by the fact that the father-absence with which they were concerned was a temporary state of affairs during wartime. In contrast, Lynn and Sawrey's subjects came from Norwegian sailor families where the father is often away from home for periods of 2 years or more with only infrequent visits. These authors recognize that "unknown cultural factors specific to the samples may be operating instead of or in addition to the variable of father-absence. Women who marry sailors may, for example, be such a select group that the variable 'sailor wife' may be the crucial one" (p. 259). The present data on father-absence from the Caribbean have the additional advantage of coming from a culture in which father-absence is a common and widely accepted pattern. Common-law marriage is extremely popular and according to some estimates a permanent father or father-figure is prolongedly absent in over one-third of all households.

The general hypothesis here expects an inverse relationship between father-absence and preference for DelR. Father-absent children should show relatively less preference for DelR and relatively more preference for ImR in choice situations, when compared with comparable father-present children. This relationship is expected to reflect the relatively greater immaturity and other correlates of preference for ImR which, it is anticipated, should characterize the father-absent group more than the father-present group.

The second aim of the study is to test experimentally an anthropological hypothesis concerning gross personality (or "national character") differences with respect to preference for DelR or ImR existing between the populations of two islands, Trinidad and Grenada, both in the southern Caribbean. The two islands may be thought of as subcultures within the same larger culture of the West Indies. The significance of this second aim lies in the application of quantitative, experimental techniques for testing a cross-cultural hypothesis, in this case a hypothesis dealing with an important psychological dimension that has been used frequently to make global but largely untested characterizations of groups and societies. This requires some explication of the cultural contexts within which the anthropological hypothesis was formulated.

On the basis of anthropological observation, a major personality difference between the Negro groups of the two islands was noted. This difference, as expressed by many informants with experience in both subcultures, is that the Trinidadian tends to be more impulsive, indulges himself, and settles for relatively little if he can get it right away. He is described as not working or waiting for larger rewards in the future, but tending instead to prefer immediately available relatively trivial gratifications. In contrast to this, the Grenadian, although on the whole poorer, is said to be more willing and able to postpone immediate gains and gratifications for the sake of larger rewards and returns in the future.[1] These observed personality or "national character" differences are supported by the further observations that the Trinidadian's savings (e.g., for the education of children) tend to be less than the Grenadian's of equally poor or even poorer circumstances.

Such differences between the islands may be related historically to the fact that the Grenadian, in contrast to the Trinidadian, has tended to hold on to his own land from generation to generation, and has been able to develop a much more autonomous role with respect to dependence on non-Negroes and colonials in government, in the professions, and in all forms of business.

The observed distinction between Trinidadians and Grenadians may be thought of as reflecting differences with respect to preference for ImR as opposed to DelR in choice situations, with the Trinidadian preferring the former more and the latter less than the Grenadian. This difference between individuals from the two islands may be conceptualized, at least in part, as related to differences in "trust" experiences with respect to the actual anticipated occurrence of delayed reward.

Indeed, in accord with Rotter's (1954) social learning theory we have conceptualized earlier (Mischel, 1958) that the person's choice of an immediate, smaller or delayed, larger reward in a choice situation is, at least to some extent. a function of his expectation that the reward will actually occur and the reward value, or preference value, of the particular reinforcement. Mahrer (1956) has already shown that the person's expectancy that reinforcement would follow from the social agent making the promise, even after time delay, is an important variable in such choice behavior. In common sense terms, this kind of behavior may be thought

[1] The distinction in this respect between Trinidadians and Grenadians has been made previously to differentiate the Negro and East Indian subgroups within Trinidad (Mischel, 1958), and will be referred to again, with replicating data, later in this paper.

of as "trust" or the belief that the agent promising delayed reinforcement will actually supply it.

The Grenadian may be thought of as having had a longer history of actual reward occurrence in delay situations (e.g., in the form of long-term gratifications accruing from land ownership) and as living in a cultural situation in which there is a good deal of trust with respect to promise-keeping and with respect to other means through which reward delay may be mediated, (i.e., long-term "payoff"). Certainly direct observation suggests the Grenadian to be far less suspicious and skeptical in his relations to strangers as well as to his own peers than is the Trinidadian. In sum, the former may be thought of as having long experiences in a relatively stable "delayed reward culture" (at least in its economic aspects) within which he himself has had a relatively autonomous and "trusted" role; in contrast, the Trinidadian may be thought of as participating in a relatively "immediate reward culture" within which he has had a highly dependent and "untrusted" role. These differences should, in turn, be reflected in the expectations with respect to reward delay transmitted to the children within the two cultures. The prediction follows that there would be greater preference for ImR than DelR on the part of Trinidadian as compared to Grenadian children of comparable age and socioeconomic background.

Lastly, a hypothesis concerning differences between the Negro and East Indian populations of the same island, Trinidad, on the same dimension of preference for ImR or DelR is tested. Ethnographic observation suggested differences between these two intra-island groups similar to those noted between Trinidadians and Grenadians (where reference is made only to the Negro populations of both islands). Namely, when compared to Trinidadian Negroes, the East Indian group of Trinidad appears to show clearly greater preference for DelR in daily behavior. As previously indicated, this observation has been made and supported in earlier research (Mischel, 1958). Here, an attempt is made to replicate these findings, taking into account any possible differences in extent of father-absence in the samples tested.[2] This also permits comparisons of intra-island differences between large groups on the dimension of concern.

---

[2] With respect to household structure in the three samples studied, the following tentative observations were made. Trinidad and Grenada are alike in the household structure of lower class and lower middle class Negro families. In both islands common-law marriage is extensive and accepted, fathers are frequently prolongedly or permanently absent, and the mother-child relationship is the family nucleus. The child usually knows who his natural father is or was, although the mother's partner may change at irregular intervals. In contrast, in East Indian Trinidadian families the father tends to be permanent and common-law marriage is rare.

METHOD

Subjects

A total of 68 Trinidadian Negro children (30 boys and 38 girls), and of 69 Grenadian Negro children (36 boys and 33 girls), all in the age group 8 through 9 were tested. The Trinidadian subjects came from two schools, both on the outskirts of the capital city. The Grenadian subjects similarly came from two schools, both located on the outskirts of Grenada's capital city. Care was taken to select all schools so that subjects of roughly comparable socioeconomic backgrounds (all lower middle and lower class) would be obtained. This selection was guided by impressions formed on the basis of inspection of a variety of schools, participant observation in both cultures, and the counsel of local school officials. Inspection of the father's occupation reported by father-present subjects in all samples reveals no striking differences. Over 90% of the responses seemed classifiable as "unskilled workers."

Further data were collected on two samples of Trinidadian East Indian subjects aged 8 through 9 from the same Trinidadian schools. The first sample consisted of 22 boys and 15 girls; the second of 20 boys and 23 girls. In addition to these young subjects, similar data were collected from a total of 112 older Trinidadian Negro subjects (68 boys and 44 girls) aged 11 through 14 at one of the Trinidadian schools indicated above, and on 75 Negro subjects (40 boys and 35 girls) in the same age range, coming from the second Trinidadian school.[3]

Task and Measures

The reinforcements used with the younger group were selected through pretesting with a random sample of 20 boys and girls, aged 8 and 9, tested at another government school on the outskirts of the capital city in Trinidad. In these pre-experimental sessions subjects were seen in individual sessions and their preferences for specific reinforcements, all candy, were elicited. As a result, two candy reinforcements, varying markedly in price, size, and packaging (i.e., a $.02 and a $.10 candy bar) were selected. These met the desired requirements inasmuch as the larger reinforcement was uniformly preferred in a straight choice situation ("which *one* of these two would you like to take?"), but when the choice was "you can have this one (the smaller) today *or* this one (the larger) in one week," approximately 50% of the group chose the former and approximately 50% the latter. The purpose of this procedure was to select a reinforce-

[3] The 112 older subjects were also administered other measures, the results of which have been previously reported (Mischel, 1961a).

ment pair which would, as closely as possible, dichotomize the choices of subjects in one of the two ethnic groups being compared supplying an approximate 50-50 split in the Trinidadian sample which could be used as the criterion for comparison with the Grenadian data.

With the older subjects, a different reinforcement pair, namely, a $.10 and a $.25 candy bar were used on the basis of the procedure reported earlier (Mischel, 1961b). In addition, two verbal items, to which the subject was to respond with "yes" or "no," one inserted near the beginning of the total procedure and the other in the middle, were included with the older subjects. The items were:

1. I would rather get ten dollars right now than have to wait a whole month and get thirty dollars then.

2. I would rather wait to get a much larger gift much later than get a smaller one now.

The behavioral choice (candy) of preference for ImR as opposed to DelR was given as the last item of the total battery. Previous research (Mischel, 1961b) has shown that the use of these three measures in combination is more fruitful than the use of single items.

Although there are no formal data available on the comparative subjective value of the candy bars in the two cultures to be compared, direct observation, confirmed by those with intimate knowledge of both cultures, indicated that in both Grenada and Trinidad the particular candies used were of similar appeal and availability. In both cultures such candies are sold in virtually every corner store and are popular with, and commonly consumed by, middle and lower class children alike. Candy allowances in the two cultures appear to be essentially the same.

The measure of father-absence or presence consisted of the response ("yes" or "no") to the question: "Does your father live at home with you?" Twenty-eight out of 30 such responses, randomly selected, were in agreement with the child's mother's response to the question, "Does his (specifying the child's name) father live at home with you?" asked in subsequent interviews with mothers of subjects in the older Trinidadian sample.

Procedure

The same experimenter was used in all testing. He was introduced as an American from a college in the United States interested in gathering information on the children in the various schools of the island. To help with this, subjects were asked to answer a number of simple questions, e.g., name, age. The details of this procedure have been described previously (Mischel, 1958).

Upon completion of the questions, the experimenter expressed his wish to thank the group for their cooperation. He displayed the two kinds of reinforcement and said: "I would like to give each of you a piece of candy, but I don't have enough of these (indicating the larger, more preferred reinforcement) with me today. So you can either get this one (indicating the smaller, less preferred reinforcement) right now, today, or, if you want to, you can wait for this one (indicating) which I will bring back next Friday (one week delay interval)." These instructions were repeated in rephrased form to insure clarity and both reinforcements were carefully displayed. It was stressed that getting the (smaller) candy today precluded getting the (larger) one next week and vice versa. Subjects were asked to indicate their choice by writing T (today) or F (Friday, next week) on their questionnaires. The response made here was the measure of preference for ImR or DelR. Subjects were seated sufficiently far apart from each other to insure reasonably that their choices were made independently. All testing was done in group settings, and conducted on the same weekday (but in different weeks) and at similar times of day, within each of the schools in large classrooms.

RESULTS AND DISCUSSION

The data from the present study were analyzed in terms of differential preference for ImR as opposed to DelR in relationship to cultural group (Trinidad as compared to Grenada), and in relationship to presence or absence of the father within the home in each culture. In addition, the relationship between the experimental choice of preference for ImR as opposed to DelR and presence or absence of the father in the home was examined in data from the group of older Trinidadian subjects, for whom a Grenadian comparison group is not available. All statistical analyses were made with the chi square test.

Careful examination of possible sex differences with respect to either extent of father-absence or preference on the experimental choice, within each of the subsamples and in combination, revealed no differences approaching statistical significance. Indeed, no consistent sex trends were observed in examining all reported relationships separately for each sex. Consequently, the male and female data were combined for all subsequent statistical analyses. The similar choice preferences with respect to delay of father-absent boys and girls in this Caribbean sample is of interest in view of Lynn and Sawrey's (1959) Norwegian data, in which differential effects of father-absence on the sexes were found.

The data used for relating the experimental choice with cultural groups are given in Table 1, which shows the number of Negro subjects (ages 8 through 9) within each of the schools, in Trinidad as compared to in

TABLE 1. NUMBER OF FATHER-PRESENT (Fa+) AND
FATHER-ABSENT (Fa-) SUBJECTS CHOOSING IMMEDIATE,
SMALLER OR DELAYED, LARGER REINFORCEMENT[a]

| Reinforcement preference | Grenada (Negro) | | | | | | Trinidad (Negro) | | | | | |
| | School 1 | | School 2 | | Total[b] | | School 3 | | School 4 | | Total[c] | |
	Fa+	Fa-	Fa+	Fa-	Fa+	Fa-	Fa+	Fa-	Fa+	Fa-	Fa+	Fa-
Immediate, smaller	5	4	4	4	9	8	11	10	8	7	19	17
Delayed, larger	16	6	26	4	42	10	16	6	10	0	26	6

Note. Grenada versus Trinidad X Reinforcement Preference: $\chi^2 = 10.40$, $p < .01$ (corrected for continuity).
[a]Subjects are aged 8 and 9.
[b]$\chi^2 = 5.15$, $.05 > p > .02$; $\chi^2 = 3.80$, $.10 > p > .05$, if corrected for continuity.
[c]$\chi^2 = 4.93$, $.05 > p > .02$ (corrected for continuity).

Grenada, preferring ImR or DelR. Comparison of the number of subjects preferring ImR or DelR *within* each of the two cultures (i.e., comparing School 1 with School 2 in Grenada and School 3 with School 4 in Trinidad) results in no chi square which reaches significant probability levels, and consequently the data from the two schools within each culture can be combined for further comparisons. This combination, namely, a comparison of the total number of Negro Trinidadian subjects preferring ImR or DelR with the total number of Negro Grenadian subjects preferring ImR or DelR, results in a chi square (using Yates' correction for continuity) of 10.40, with $p < .01$. As predicted by the cultural hypothesis, a significantly larger proportion of the Trinidadian subjects, as compared to the Grenadian subjects, chose ImR rather than DelR.

The data used for relating father-absence and the experimental choice, in Trinidad and in Grenada, are also presented in Table 1. The chi square test applied to the relevant data yields uncorrected chi square values of 6.14 for Trinidad and of 5.15 for Grenada. These values are significant ($p < .02$ and $p < .05$, respectively) and indicate a greater proportion of father-absent subjects, as compared to father-present subjects choose ImR rather than DelR in each culture. If extreme caution is used and the Yates correction is employed on all fourfold contingency tables (in spite of the fact that all expected and marginal frequencies are relatively large) the chi square value for Trinidad becomes 4.93 ($p < .05$) and for Grenada 3.80. A value of 3.84 is required for $p < .05$ when $df = 1$.

In view of this support for the relationship between father-absence and preference for ImR, it becomes important to examine the differences between the two cultures with respect to degree of father-absence. Table 1 shows the number of father-absent and father-present subjects within each of the samples from the two cultures. Among the Grenadians, 18 of the 69 subjects reported father-absence; among the Trinidadians, 23 of the 68 subjects reported father-absence. Application of the chi square test to these data results in no p values approaching statistical significance, and suggests that the difference between the two cultures on the experimental choice cannot be attributed to differential father-absence, although within each culture father-absence is related to the choice behavior.

This finding is of special interest in view of the finding obtained earlier (Mischel, 1958) in a comparison of Negro and East Indian subjects, both within the Trinidadian culture, on preference for delayed reinforcement. Although the two Trinidadian subgroups differed significantly in the choice behavior (the Negro subjects more frequently preferring the immediate, smaller reinforcement), the differences appeared attributable to differences in father-absence (the Indian subjects being characterized by more father-present households). The present data permit an attempt to replicate this relationship. The new data for Trinidadian East Indian subjects aged 8 through 9 were as follows. Among the Indians, 26 chose the ImR and 54 the DelR. Only 4 subjects in the Indian group were father-absent, 2 of these choosing ImR and 2 DelR. Comparing the Indians with the Trinidadian Negro subjects on preference for ImR as opposed to DelR results in a corrected chi square of 5.50 ($p < .02$). As was found earlier, the East Indian group again shows greater preference for DelR as opposed to ImR relative to the preferences of the Trinidadian Negro group. Note that there are no significant differences in reinforcement preference with respect to delay between the Trinidadian Indian group and the Grenadian group, although the latter shows significantly greater father-absence (chi square $= 11.47$, $df = 1$, $p < .001$). Comparison of the Trinidadian Indian group with the Trinidadian Negro group on extent of father-absence results in a corrected chi square of 18.5 ($df = 1$, $p < .01$); clearly the latter show significantly greater father-absence than the former. If *only* father-present subjects from the two groups (Trinidadian Indian and Trinidadian Negro) are compared on preference for ImR or DelR, no significant relationship holds. In contrast, comparison of only father-present Trinidadian Negroes with Grenadian father-present subjects on reinforcement preference still yields a corrected chi square of 5.85 ($p < .02$), the Grenadians showing greater DelR preference. Thus the intra-island observed differences between the two Trinidadian groups appear to be largely related to differential father-absence between the two groups. However, the Trinidadian-Grenadian Negro differences with respect to reinforcement preference cannot be attributed to differential father-absence.

Summarizing the results thus far, the following relationships, condensed in Table 2, should be noted. Grenadian Negro children showed significantly greater preference for DelR as opposed to ImR when compared with Trinidadian Negro subjects. This difference cannot be attributed to differential father-absence since the two groups show no significant

TABLE 2. SUMMARY OF RELATIONSHIPS BETWEEN ETHNIC
GROUP,[a] SUBJECTS WITH FATHER-PRESENT (Fa+) OR FATHER-
ABSENT (Fa–), AND PREFERENCE FOR DELAYED, LARGER (DelR)
AS OPPOSED TO IMMEDIATE, SMALLER (ImR) REWARDS

Comparison	Greater DelR preference	p value[b]
Trinidadian Negro vs. Grenadian Negro (Fa+ and Fa–)	Grenadian	< .01
Trinidadian Negro vs. Grenadian Negro (Fa+ only)	Grenadian	< .02
Trinidadian Negro vs. Grenadian Negro (Fa– only)	–	ns
Trinidadian Negro Fa+ vs. Fa–	Fa+	< .05
Grenadian Negro Fa+ vs. Fa–	Fa+	< .07
Trinidadian East Indian vs. Trinidadian Negro (Fa+ and Fa–)	East Indian	< .02
Trinidadian East Indian vs. Trinidadian Negro (Fa+ only)	–	ns
Trinidadian East Indian vs. Grenadian Negro (Fa+ and Fa–)	–	ns
Trinidadian East Indian vs. Grenadian Negro (Fa+ only)	–	ns

Note. Comparisons with East Indian subjects on father-absence in relation to other variables
cannot be made in view of the small N (4) of such father-absent subjects. Trinidadian Negro
subjects, as well as Grenadian Negroes, show significantly greater father-absence ($p < .01$) than
Trinidadian East Indian subjects, but the difference between the two Negro groups in extent of
father-absence is ns.
[a]Using Trinidadian Negro, Trinidadian East Indian, and Grenadian Negro subjects, all aged 8
and 9.
[b]Based on chi square comparisons, corrected for continuity; ns = p value > .10

difference with respect to that variable, and since the difference in DelR-
ImR preference holds even when only father-present subjects from the
two islands are compared. In contrast, comparisons between Trinidadian
Negro subjects and Trinidadian East Indian subjects reveal that the difference between these two, namely, the relatively greater DelR preference on
the part of the East Indian group, does appear attributable to differential
father-absence. This seems the case since the Trinidadian Negro subjects
show significantly greater father-absence than do the East Indian subjects,
and since the latter's relatively greater DelR preference does not hold
when this differential father-absence is taken into account, i.e., when
comparisons are based only on father-present subjects. Also note that Negro subjects from Trinidad and Grenada do not differ in their choice behavior *if* only father-*absent* Negro subjects from the two islands are
compared (see data in Table 1). The small N of father-absent East Indian
subjects prevents their being compared with other father-absent groups.
Finally, the Trinidadian East Indian group and the Grenadian Negro
group are not significantly different in their reinforcement preferences,
although the latter show significantly greater father-absence.

The present results thus suggest that the difference between the Trinidadian and Grenadian subjects on the experimental choice must be
sought in sources other than family constellation with respect to father-
absence or father-presence. This illustrates a situation commonly encoun-

tered in cross-cultural research. In spite of overlapping rearing conditions, not merely in terms of the father in the family constellation but also in terms of numerous patterns that link the two cultures and make them homogeneous in many ways, other unspecified sources of variance must account for gross observed differences, in this case differences in the delay of gratification patterns. The writer is inclined to focus on some of the cultural and economic differences, especially differences in autonomy and independence, as indicated earlier. The lack of a significant difference between father-*absent* Trinidadian and Grenadian Negro subjects in preference for DelR as opposed to ImR (Table 2) also suggests the possible argument that when fathers are absent differences in cultural values are less likely to be internalized by the children, since fathers may be needed to transmit such cultural values.

We turn next to the data on the relationship between father-absence and reinforcement preference obtained from the 112 older (ages 11 through 14) Trinidadian subjects. Here, as previously described, three measures of reinforcement preference with respect to delay were available. Application of the chi square test resulted in no p value less than .30. This lack of relationship was obtained in comparisons using the candy choice alone, as well as all possible combinations of preferences over the three measures. To inquire further into this failure of the anticipated relationship for older subjects, the same experimental procedure was repeated on another sample of 75 Trinidadian subjects of the same age range, tested in another but highly similar Government school, comparably located, and with subjects of similar socioeconomic and ethnic backgrounds. Again, no relationship between the experimental choice and presence or absence of the father in the home was obtained that reached or approached significant probability levels. Thus although the expected relationship was repeatedly obtained at the younger age levels, the null hypothesis cannot be rejected for seemingly similar subjects at older age levels.

The possibility exists that the instructions for the experimental choice, specifically the phrase "but I don't have enough of these (DelR) with me today," may have partially confounded the results by producing a conflict in older subjects, eager for the DelR yet reluctant to make the experimenter return. However, this seems extremely unlikely. First, during the administration, that phrase, used only as an introduction to make the choice plausible, was probably overshadowed by the frequent repetitions of the actual choice conflict and the implication that the experimenter would *definitely* return next week to hand out the DelR to those in the group who chose it. Second, and more definitive, in over 20 pre-experimental sessions with other comparable subjects from the same culture, used to select the particular reinforcements sets, postchoice inquiries into reasons for the choices yielded nothing remotely suggestive of such an "obliging response."

It is tempting to argue that for older subjects the measures of preference for ImR as opposed to DelR is meaningless or invalid, and consequently relations with father-absence should not be expected. It must be recalled, however, that the same measures used with Caribbean subjects of this age, and indeed including subjects from the present older sample, have yielded significant correlations with conceptually relevant variables (social responsibility, need for achievement, nonacquiescence), all of the above being positively correlated with preference for DelR (Mischel, 1961a, 1961b). In this context, it should also be noted that no relationships approaching statistical significance were obtained in attempts to relate father-absence with these correlates of preference for DelR. This suggests that father-absence at older age levels may not have some of the effects (e.g., "immaturity," poorer adjustment) apparently associated with it at the earlier age levels (e.g., Lynn & Sawrey, 1959). The question cannot be answered at present in view of the lack of research on father-absence with older children. Of course, the present data are seriously hampered in the gross measure of father-absence or presence used, which gives no information on the extent or duration of the father's absence or presence. Nevertheless, the same gross measure did yield the expected results with the younger subjects, and excellent agreement between older subjects' reports of father-absence and mother's reports on the same question was obtained.

The *post hoc* interpretation being suggested for these findings is that as the individual develops and matures, he begins to participate in an environment that extends beyond the immediate family and consequently his expectations with respect to promise-keeping, his "trust," and his choice behavior with respect to delay of gratification become contingent upon numerous factors and experiences other than those within the household itself. Similarly, at least in southern Caribbean cultures, sources of influence outside the immediate family may become important determinants of other variables correlated with ImR-DelR preferences, such as "social responsibility" and need for achievement, at relatively early periods in the person's life.[4]

[4] It should be noted that in the cultures studied, the individual becomes independent of the family and autonomous, e.g., vocationally, relatively early in life. For example, official "student-teachers" in public schools are often 13 years old. In all three samples, the child from age 10 or 11 on becomes increasingly free to move about, visiting with other relatives (e.g., uncles, grandparents, etc.) who may or may not be living in the immediate neighborhood, and whom he may visit for a day or longer periods.

Although this interpretation is clearly tentative, pending further and more controlled research, the data illustrate the complexity of some of the conditions that may influence such choice behavior. In spite of these complexities, significant support was obtained for the anthropological hypothesis concerning cross-cultural differences between Trinidad and Grenada with respect to delay of gratification. Earlier findings of differences with respect to ethnic groups on the same variable were replicated. It is recognized, of course, that the findings are necessarily limited by sampling problems which make any generalizations tentative. Nevertheless, the findings are construed as illustrative of the possibilities of applying quantitative simple experimental techniques for testing cross-cultural differences on important psychological dimensions.

SUMMARY

This study tested an anthropological hypothesis concerning differences in preference for immediate, smaller (ImR) as opposed to delayed, larger reinforcement (DelR) between two subcultures (Trinidad and Grenada) within the West Indies. The data, in the form of choice preferences for ImR or DelR elicited from children in both islands, supported the cultural hypothesis. Further, a significant relationship between absence of the father within the home and greater preference for ImR as compared to DelR was found in both cultures, using subjects aged 8–9. However, this relationship was not found for older subjects (aged 11–14). These results were discussed in terms of increased sources of variance relevant to the formation of trust behavior and expectancies outside the household with increasing age. Data replicating previously obtained differences with respect to preference for ImR as opposed to DelR between two ethnic groups (Indian and Negro) within the island of Trinidad were also presented.

References

Bach, G. R. Father-fantasies and father-typing in father-separated children. *Child Develpm.*, 1946, 17, 63–80.

Freud, S. *Beyond the Pleasure Principle.* New York: Boni & Livewright, 1922.

Harris, D. B. A scale for measuring attitudes of social responsibility in children. *J. abnorm. soc. Psychol.*, 1957, 55, 322–326.

Lynn, D. B. and W. L. Sawrey. The effects of father-absence on Norwegian boys and girls. *J. abnorm. soc. Psychol.*, 1959, 59, 258–262.

Mahrer, A. R. The role of expectancy in delayed reinforcement. *J. exp. Psychol.*, 1956, 52, 101–105.

Mischel, W. Preference for delayed reinforcement: An experimental study of a cultural observation. *J. abnorm. soc. Psychol.*, 1958, 56, 57–61.

Mischel, W. Delay of gratification, need for achievement, and acquiescence in another culture. *J. abnorm. soc. Psychol.*, 1961, 62, 543–552. (a)

Mischel, W. Preference for delayed reinforcement and social responsibility. *J. abnorm. soc. Psychol.*, 1961, 62, 1–7. (b)

Mowrer, O. H. and A. D. Ullman. Time as a determinant in integrative learning. *Psychol. Rev.*, 1945, 52, 61–90.

Rotter, J. B. *Social Learning and Clinical Psychology.* New York: Prentice-Hall, 1954.

Sears, R. R., Margaret H. Pintler and Pauline S. Sears. Effect of father separation on preschool children's doll play aggression. *Child Develpm.*, 1946, 17, 219–243.

Singer, J. L., H. Wilensky and Vivian G. McCraven. Delaying capacity, fantasy and planning ability: A factorial study of some basic ego functions. *J. consult. Psychol.*, 1956, 20, 375–383.

Tiller, P. O. Father absence and personality development of children in sailor families. *Nord. psykol. Monogr.*, 1958, Ser. No. 9.

Whiting, J. W. Sorcery, sin, and the superego. In M. R. Jones (ed.). *Nebraska Symposium on Motivation: 1959.* Lincoln: Univer. Nebraska Press, 1959, 174–195.

6   ALBERT PEPITONE, CLAUDE FAUCHEUX, SERGE MOSCOVICI, MARCELLO CESA-BIANCHI, GRAZIA MAGISTRETTI, GUSTAVO IACONO, A.M. ASPREA AND GUILIA VILLONE

The Role of Self-Esteem in Competitive Choice Behavior

This paper is a preliminary report of a cross-national experimental research program which is concerned with the determinants of competitive and cooperative choice behavior. The general objective of the program is to

Reprinted from the *International Journal of Psychology – Journal International de Psychologie*, 1967, Vol. 2, No. 3, pp. 147–159. By permission of IUPS and Dunod, Publisher, Paris.

Versions of the papers contained in this report were read at the First Conference on Experimental Studies of Competitiveness and Productivity, held at

make experimental tests of hypotheses in different national settings. Secondarily, descriptive cross-national data are of interest because of the insight they provide into cultural forces that shape the personality in the socialization process. We shall first sketch the methodological and substantive backgrounds of our research, and then present some findings and tentative conclusions reached by some preliminary experiments.

In recent years, social psychology has shown considerable interest in experimental games as a means of studying interpersonal choice behavior. The Prisoner's Dilemma game is of special interest because it involves for each of the two decision-makers psychological considerations that go beyond rational strategy of the sort found in applications of game theory to economic and business decisions. The 2×2 payoff matrix of the Prisoner's Dilemma game (see Luce and Raiffa, 1957) specifies the rewards to each player that are contingent upon each of the four possible joint choices. The basic problem for each player in this type of game is that if he consistently chooses the alternative with the maximum possible payoff, he gains less, or loses more, than if he chooses the alternative with less than the maximum possible payoff, that is, the alternative which would result in the largest *mutual* reward. But to pursue a strategy of mutually rewarding, but not individually maximizing, choices, each player must trust that the other will not try to gain as much as possible by well timed defections from such cooperative arrangements. Although there is no unique, rational strategy solution to the Prisoner's Dilemma, the underlying assumption in game theory is that players in the long run are exclusively motivated to maximize the possible gains. In other words, were he not constrained by the equivocal property of the matrix, each player would always choose the alternative which would bring him the highest possible reward.

The social psychologist makes no such assumption in advance about an exclusive human motivation. Indeed, if he assumes anything, it is that there certainly are motivations other than reward-maximization which govern choice behavior. The experiments to be reported in this paper are concerned with one such non-maximizing drive: a tendency to seek rewards in amounts that are judged to be deserved, equitable, or valid, and not necessarily the *maximum* amount that is obtainable. Observations of interpersonal relationships in the real world suggest a particular application of this equity principle: people compete for rewards in proportion

---

Gavirate, Italy (May 23–27, 1966). The support of this conference on basic research and group processes by the US Office of Naval Research is gratefully acknowledged. The assistance of F. Berger and A. Harris for the USA study, M. Plon for the French study, and A. Beretta for the Milanese study is gratefully acknowledged.

to what they think they as persons are worth. In other words, the individual's self-evaluation serves as a standard for determining his level of aspiration and the effort he puts into achieving it. Thus, in a Prisoner's Dilemma game with given maximizing possibilities, the player who has a low self-esteem would be expected to choose the more profitable alternative less often than the player who has a relatively high self-esteem.

Theoretically, the hypothesized tendency to obtain an equitable share of rewards is closely related to the tendency to seek and maintain valid interpersonal and self-evaluations (Pepitone, 1964). From the individual's point of view, both the equity of rewards he and others receive and the validity of his evaluations of them and himself are optimal conditions of adjustment to the social, and physical, environment. Moreover, valid evaluations of himself and others represent criteria for the equitable distribution of rewards, while at the same time, the tendency to distribute rewards equitably confirms the validity of social and self-evaluations.

The hypothesis that individuals compete in proportion to what they believe they are worth is difficult to put to an unequivocal test. There are several alternative interpretations of positive findings which must be rendered relatively implausible. One experimental control for this purpose is to induce experimentally the self-esteem of the players. If the theoretical prediction is confirmed when the self-esteem of randomly selected players has been manipulated, it could not be argued that the more competitive and profitable choices of those with high self-esteem are due to the habitual standard of achievement in those individuals. Nor, for that matter, could it be claimed that some personality factor associated with self-esteem is responsible. Other features of the experimental design which deal with alternative interpretations will be discussed after the presentation of the findings.

THE TWO-PERSON DECISION-MAKING SITUATION

Two preliminary experiments were done with pairs of American undergraduate females between 19 and 21 years of age, mostly from middle and upper middle socio-economic backgrounds. With the exception of one detail, the experimental procedures were identical in the two studies.

Procedure

Two subjects were selected at random from a pool of volunteers (Introductory Psychology students) who had been requested by their professors to serve in experiments. They were phoned and told to come to the Social Psychology Laboratory room at a designated hour. After it was determined that the girls did not know each other, one was chosen at random to receive the high self-esteem induction, and the other, the low self-esteem induction. The experimenter, in the first study a female, in the second, a male, described a test of "Inverse Creativity" which measured an extremely important and hitherto neglected personality characteristic and capacity. The test was described as having exceptional reliability and validity. To show that he had no interest in the outcome of the test, E made it clear to the Ss that it was not his idea to give it. He said that the Chairman of the Department wanted information about students who volunteer for psychology experiments. Then the Ss were separated and E tested them one at a time. The S inspected fifteen cards on each of which were four drawings of people, landscapes, objects, etc. With each card, E supplied a word and the S's task was to select — in the first experiment — the drawing whose meaning was most similar to the meaning of the word, or — in the second experiment — the drawing most dissimilar in meaning. Following the test, E scored each S's performance on the basis of an official table of norms representing college undergraduates. One S was told that she had done very well with a score that placed her above the 97th percentile. The other was told she had done rather poorly with a score at the 60th percentile.

Then, a set of twenty personality self-rating scales, each representing eight degrees of a personality characteristic or trait (*e.g.*, creativity, maturity, intelligence, etc.), was administered to each S, also under the pretext of getting information for the Chairman. Actually, the evaluation the S made of her personality on the twenty scales was used to obtain independent evidence on whether the induction of high and low self-esteem was effective.

After putting the materials away with a show of indifference as to their purpose, E expressed his real interest in studying the social interaction patterns revealed by choice behavior. He gave examples of various human relationships in which the individuals jointly determine the amount of reward each receives. Then, each S of the pair was shown the table of rewards (Figure 1).

FIGURE 1. Table of Rewards

	Subject A: Red	Subject A: Green
Subject B: Red	1 , 1	0 , 2
Subject B: Green	2 , 0	0 , 0

It was carefully explained that on each of fifty trials, the Ss would simultaneously choose Red or Green. If both A and B chose Red, each would receive a 1 point reward; if both chose Green, each would receive zero points. If B chose Green and A chose Red, B would get 2 points and A nothing. If B chose Red and A chose Green, A would get 2 points and B nothing. It was pointed out that Green was a "competitive" choice in that it could maximize her points and minimize the other S's. Red, on the other hand, was a "cooperative" choice in that it could provide a modest reward to both players equally. It was emphasized that the pattern of choices which the S decided to make was entirely up to her and depended essentially on how many points she wanted.

Although from the S's point of view the points that she received from E after each trial depended upon the choice of the other combined with her own choice, the choices thought to be made by her partner were actually based on a standard pre-arranged sequence of Reds and Greens. In this program of choices, ostensibly being made by the other S, there were 31, or 62%, Reds, distributed approximately evenly throughout the fifty trials. In other words, the Ss came to perceive each other as highly co-operative. Accordingly, they came to see that it was fairly easy to maximize the point rewards.

Results

An examination of the self-ratings of personality attractiveness confirms the effectiveness of the experimental induction. In each experiment, the mean rating of the assorted traits was found to be higher for Ss who had been given the high self-esteem treatment than for the low Ss. There is evidence, then, that the Ss' self-evaluation in the general sphere of personality was altered by the manipulation, at least temporarily.

The variable of central interest in the studies is the competitive choice behavior displayed by the two Ss. In this respect the results of the two experiments also seem clear cut: Ss in whom a high self-evaluation was induced tend to make more Green, competitive choices than the Low Ss. Table 1 shows that the mean number of Green choices differs between

TABLE 1. MEAN NUMBER OF COMPETITIVE (GREEN) CHOICES BY
AMERICAN SUBJECTS UNDER HIGH AND LOW SELF-ESTEEM
CONDITIONS

	High SE		Low SE		t	p[a]
	N	M	N	M		
Exp. 1a	17	30.5	12	26.2	1.32	ns
Exp. 1b	10	31.1	7	21.3	3.00	< .005
Combined		30.7		24.5	2.63	< .01

[a]Two-tail tests of hypothesis

two levels of self-esteem in both experiments despite the small number of cases.

When the mean number of Green choices is examined for each of the five, 10-trial blocks, it is evident that the High group is consistently more competitive during the entire fifty trials. As can be seen in Figures 2 and 3, there is no overlap between the groups in either experiment.

The results are thus consistent with the hypothesis stated earlier: Ss compete for rewards to a degree depending on their level of self-esteem, in accordance with what they think they are worth. It must be quickly conceded, however, that the data allow for alternative interpretations and we now turn our attention to an analysis of some specific possibilities.

Insecurity of Status or Self-Esteem

For example, it often appears that individuals compete strenuously in order to enhance or defend their self-esteem and status. Underlying the contest over various external rewards such as grades, money, points, and the like, are powerful status and self-esteem drives. In the present setting, the individual who seeks status and self-esteem should presumably try to win the maximum number of points in absolute terms or relative to the other individual. The literature on the effects of ego-involvement suggests that the essential condition for arousing these drives is a threat or

FIGURE 2. Mean Number of Competitive (Green) Choices by American Ss (Exp. Ia)

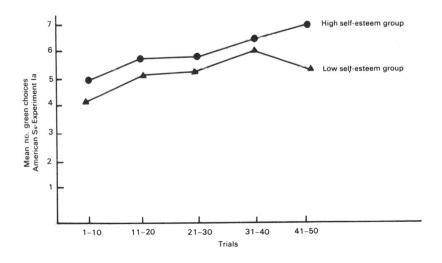

FIGURE 3. Mean Number of Competitive (Green) Choices by American Ss (Exp. Ib)

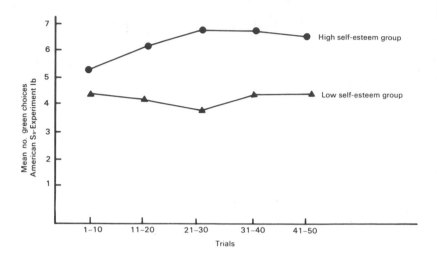

an insecurity about one's relative status position or worth. According to this view, the greater competitiveness of a high self-esteem S would be explained by insecurity as to whether she is really superior, and an accompanying fear of losing status and esteem. Frequent choices of the competitive alternative would be regarded as a means of allaying this status- and self-insecurity. There are difficulties in applying this theoretical interpretation to the experimental results just described. The more formidable one is that there is no reason to believe that the Ss were insecure or uncertain about their worth. The fictional ability of inverse creativity was deliberately chosen so that the authoritative induction by E would be accepted uncritically. The fact that the self-ratings on twenty heterogeneous personality traits were strongly affected by the induction cannot be regarded as a sign of insecurity over self-evaluation.

It should also be noted that, for the self-esteem-insecurity interpretation to accord with the data, it would have to be assumed that the insecurity of the Low group was less (*i.e.* that Ss who were given Low self-esteem treatment felt less threatened about their worth) than the High Ss. Intuitively, this view is not altogether plausible; it is easier to conceive that the induction of low Inverse Creativity would cause the greater threat to S's status and self-esteem. A somewhat different analysis leads to the same prediction. Thus, one might assume that Ss with low self-evaluation have a greater hunger for self and status rewards. But neither the insecurity nor "hunger" theory can satisfactorily handle the obtained results.

Self-Confidence in Ability to Compete

The role of the self as a perceived capacity to deal with and master the physical and social environment is obviously relevant to an individual's competitiveness. If the person is confident of victory in a contest, he can be expected to compete more than if he lacks confidence. Assuming the experimental situation was interpreted as a risky contest, the self-confidence interpretation would imply that Ss in whom high creativity was induced perceived they had greater ability than the Low Ss to maximize points. Two features of the experiment argue against such an interpretation. First, if the S understood the matrix she would have perceived that on any trial her optimum choice is Green regardless of which alternative her partner selects. If her partner chooses Green, she would lose no more by not choosing Green herself; she would receive zero points whether she chose Green or Red. And if the partner's choice is Red, then it is more profitable for her to choose Green, for Green would result in two points whereas Red would bring in only one point. Secondly, if she attended the outcomes of the trials, she would have perceived that the partner had an overweening tendency to choose Red (six out of ten trials). Thus, whatever her induced level of self-esteem, the contest, if it was so construed, was a fairly easy one. Where it is so easy to accumulate a maximum number of points, any differences in self-confidence associated with high and low Inverse Creativity are not likely to have been functional.

A second weakness in the perceived self-capacity interpretation is that it assumes a specific transfer from inverse creativity to the skills perceived necessary to achieve a competitive success. For the S who didn't understand the matrix and thought she was playing a risky game of skill there are two related talents likely to be seen by her as important: predicting when the adversary is going to choose Red so as to play Green on that trial, and actually influencing the adversary to choose Red on a given trial. The assumption that a high self-evaluation in the area of inverse creativity generalizes to high confidence with respect to one or both of these abilities does not seem compelling.

Despite their weaknesses, however, the two alternative interpretations of the data cannot be unequivocally ruled out. Moreover, with respect to the proposed hypothesis that Ss compete for rewards in proportion to how much they think they equitably deserve, there is no uniquely affirmative evidence. Experimental steps are therefore necessary to weaken further the alternative interpretations and to strengthen the hypothesis affirmatively.

THE NONSOCIAL CHOICE SITUATION

The view that the greater frequency of competitive choices by High Self-Esteem Ss is based on their higher confidence in overcoming the adversary would become less tenable if S's choices cannot influence the choices of the other S. For, without an opportunity to determine the partner's choice of Red or Green on any given trial, or to determine the pattern of his choices, no differential in the perceived ability to achieve victory can plausibly exist. Following this line of reasoning, Faucheux and Moscovici (1968) designed an experiment in which each S interacted with file cards or playing cards instead of another S.

Procedure

The Ss chose from a set of thirty-one Red and nineteen Black cards (or, in the Nature condition to be described below, thirty-one Y and nineteen Z cards). The ordering of the fifty cards paralleled exactly the sequence of Red and Green choices ostensibly being made by the partner in the original pair of experiments described above. The table of rewards which specified the points to each player contingent upon the four possible joint choices was exactly the same. The instructions regarding the two possible strategies, as well as the indifference of E as to which the S should pursue, were the same. The purpose and sponsorship of the Inverse Creativity test, the test procedure, and the high or low feedback of information on the level of the Ss creativity, all duplicated the original experiments. Finally, the set of personality-trait rating scales used to assess the effectiveness of the experimental manipulation of self-esteem was identical. In fact, the only difference from the previous experiments was that the single S played with a stack of cards instead of a human partner. Procedurally, the S made his choice of Red or Black (Y or Z) and then turned the top card face up.

In addition to High or Low Self-esteem the variable "partner identity" was manipulated in order to induce a set in the S concerning the way the cards were prepared — the strategy of the imaginary partner. In one condition the S was told he was playing against Chance (in French, *basard*) to create the image of an adversary who tries to deceive or even to hurt and who, in any case, is unpredictable. In a second condition, the S was told he was playing against Nature in order to create the image of a neutral or even benevolent partner whose actions are systematic and orderly. To reinforce these images, in the Chance condition regular playing cards were used. In the Nature condition, a stack of ordinary file cards was used. After the matrix was explained to the S, several questions were asked in order to define his initial level of expectation in comparison with his partner or other Ss. The Ss were males selected from among registrants of a student employment agency. They were paid from ten to twelve francs for their services.

Results

An examination of the rating scale data showed that the self-esteem manipulation was entirely successful in creating two distinct groups of Ss, one High in self-attractiveness, the other Low, in terms of a variety of personality traits.

The average number of exploitative (Black or A) choices in each of the self-evaluation and partner identity groups is given in Table 2.

TABLE 2. MEAN NUMBER OF COMPETITIVE CHOICES BY FRENCH Ss UNDER H OR L SELF-ESTEEM CONDITIONS[a]

Self-esteem		Partner identity	
		Chance (Black)	Nature (Z)
High		34.3	39.6
Low		28.8	34.6
	Self-esteem	4.83	$p < .05$
F	Partner identity	5.42	$p < .05$
	Interaction		ns

[a]N = 12 in each condition.

It is clear that whether playing with a Chance or Nature partner, Ss with high self-esteem tend to be more competitive than Ss with low self-esteem. Secondly, the frequency of these exploitative choices is greater when the partner is Nature than when the partner is Chance. Indeed, in Nature, low self-esteem Ss choose the exploitative alternative as frequently as high self-esteem Ss in Chance. Both main effects are significant by analysis of variance.

Since S knew that his choices could not affect the order in which the cards turned up, it is difficult to argue that differential confidence in the ability to influence the partner could have been responsible for the difference in the performance of the two self-esteem groups. The fact that Nature elicits more exploitative behavior than Chance appears to affirm the existence of a set according to which the cards are arranged by Nature in a relatively helpful way, while Chance arranges her cards haphazardly, to trick or even harm the individual. The S who has Chance as a partner plays with greater restraint, as if not to antagonize her.

Another result lends support to the equitable reward-seeking hypothesis and weakens the self-confidence hypothesis. If the induction of high creativity creates higher confidence in playing a winning game, then one should expect a more optimistic estimate on the part of the High Ss. On the other hand, if self-esteem determines the level of reward that is considered equitable, it could be supposed that Ss who seek a higher level would estimate beforehand that it would be more difficult to obtain. Ss were asked to estimate if they expected to gain more, as many, or fewer points than Chance (or Nature). It was found that there are (in Chance and Nature combined) relatively more Ss in the High self-esteem group who expect to gain the same or less than in the Low group. In the latter, on the other hand, more Ss expect to gain more points ($x^2 = 4.33$, $p < .05$).

Although the data are consistent with the hypothesis that competitiveness is a reflection of an equity-maintenance or self-validating tendency, we are far from being satisfied that we understand the details of these processes. The question may be asked, for example: Does the differential competitiveness or exploitativeness reflect conformity to E's expectations? That is, rather than compete for rewards which are consistent with their self-esteem, could it be that the Ss behave in line with how they think the E evaluates them? Could those who are told by E that they possess high Inverse Creativity suppose that he thinks they have generally attractive personalities, and, further, that he "authorizes" them to compete at a high level? There are two considerations that make this interpretation unlikely. 1) E explicitly dissociated himself from the Inverse Creativity test procedure. He made clear he was not responsible for the test and maintained a disinterested, objective attitude in feeding back to the Ss information about their performance. It would be difficult to assume that the Ss perceived that E personally evaluated them in line with their high or low creativity, much less cared one way or another. 2) E explicitly stated that he was indifferent as to whether the S chose a competitive or cooperative strategy. Consequently, to assume that the Ss in the High group thought that E wanted them to choose the more rewarding alternative would be gratuitous.

To argue that the results are not likely to be such obvious experimenter effects is not to say that the competitiveness of High and Low Ss is independent of the evaluation given in the situation. It is well to emphasize that prior to the induction procedure, Inverse Creativity did not exist in the S's mind. That is, it is safe to assume that S had never made any evaluation of himself in this specific area. Therefore, it is wholly correct to say that the self-esteem with which competition tends to be consistent is situational. The important theoretical point is that the situationally-derived self-esteem was *accepted* by the average individual. Although acceptance of the evaluation need not, and most probably does not, last for any protracted period of time, there is evidence that the estimates of Inverse Creativity were regarded as valid.

Of course, not every S accepted the induction. Despite the purported validity of the Inverse Creativity test and the credibility of E's interpretation of S's performance on it, some Ss undoubtedly rejected the information that would have classified them as low or high in Inverse Creativity. Other Ss were undoubtedly threatened by the possibility that it might be true (in the case of Low Ss) or untrue (in the case of High Ss). Additional experiments indicate that when the induction is not accepted, Ss in the Low treatment condition compete more vigorously than Ss in the High treatment. Moreover, when Ss are assigned to High or Low self-esteem conditions according to their self-ratings on the personality scales exclusively, that is, where no experimental induction procedure is used, selected Low self-esteem Ss tend to be more competitive than selected High Ss. These studies may be briefly described.

ATTEMPTED REPLICATIONS

Italian Two-Person Choice Studies

Two independent experiments were carried out at the University of Milan and the University of Naples, employing male and female student paid volunteers drawn from various faculties. The procedures followed by the female E at Naples and the male and female Es at Milan followed exactly those used in the two earlier American studies. The same instructions were used, the same table of rewards, the same objective role of E, etc. There was one deviation: because of time pressure, personality self-rating scales were not administered to the Naples sample. Everything else in form and content was standardized. Table 3 presents the basic data on competitive choices under the two experimental conditions.

It can be seen that in both studies, Ss in the Low self-esteem conditions tend to be more competitive, a result exactly opposite to the findings based on American and French Ss, reported previously. In the Naples sample the differences between conditions are considerably stronger when variance due to sex of subject is parceled out. For male Ss the difference,

TABLE 3. MEAN NUMBER OF COMPETITIVE CHOICES BY ITALIAN Ss UNDER H AND L SELF-ESTEEM CONDITIONS

	Self-esteem			
Sample	High	Low	t	p
Milan	26.4	35.2	1.31	.21
	(N = 11)	(N = 11)		
Naples	29.3	32.7	1.81	< .08
	N = 30	N = 30		

Combined probability with 4 df, $\chi^2 = 13.24$, $p < .02$[a]

[a]Since each probability corresponds to $\chi^2 = -2 \log e$, p (for 2 df), we may obtain a composite χ^2 value by adding the logarithmic transformations (Lindquist, 1940).

although in the same direction, is negligible; for female Ss, the difference is highly significant. In the case of the Milan study, the sample was too small to allow for a meaningful breakdown of data according to sex of Ss or Es. As seen in Figure 4, the Naples Ss who received the Low self-esteem treatment are persistently more competitive than those in the High self-esteem treatment. The mean number of Green choices in each of the five, ten-trial blocks is higher for the Low group. There is no overlap.

FIGURE 4. Mean Number of Competitive Choices by Italian Ss during Course of Game

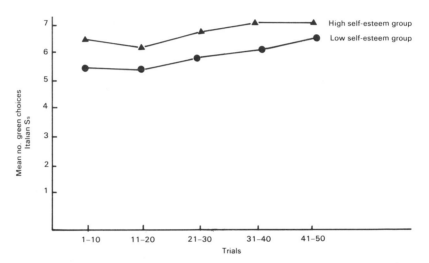

It needs to be said straightaway that we do not fully understand what caused these apparent reversals. We do know that the experimental induction of Inverse Creativity was utterly ineffective in the Milan sample: there was no difference between the High and Low treatment group. Furthermore, the self-ratings on the twenty personality scales were low compared with the American and French samples, and observations of the Ss during the Inverse Creativity test and the feedback of scores revealed considerable resistance to the induction. Males, especially in the Low treatment, voiced doubts that their creativity had been correctly assessed. The failure of the manipulation to have effects on the personality ratings plus these observations seem to constitute the symptoms of a self-defensive process in the Ss who received the Low self-esteem treatment. It appears that the Low Ss not only resist the negative information about Inverse Creativity but make additional "compensatory" efforts to deny inferiority such as striving for relatively high rewards.

Why this defensive, compensatory pattern characterizes the two independent Italian samples is not clear. As already indicated, the induction of Inverse Creativity and the instructions regarding the table of rewards were the same as in the American and French studies. It is possible, of course, that the manner in which the Italian experiments were conducted somehow stimulated the compensatory reward-seeking in the Low Ss. For example, through nonverbal, expressive cues, E might have urged the Low Ss to compete and make up for their deficit in Inverse Creativity. However, it seems unlikely that such a factor would operate in two different experiments in which several Es were involved. Perhaps we are dealing with a sampling difference. It is possible that the sample of Italian students contained a larger percentage of defensive personality types than the American and French samples. Indeed, concerning this possibility there is evidence that students who have chronic attitudes of inferiority about themselves display the defensive, compensatory pattern of competitiveness.

Selected French Subjects in a Nonsocial
Choice Situation

Faucheux and Moscovici (1968) conducted an experiment which in every respect but one followed the procedures used in the first French study reported above. But instead of trying experimentally to induce Inverse Creativity, Ss at both extremes of self-esteem were selected in terms of their personality ratings on the standard set of twenty scales. Two such selected groups were constituted from the 70 volunteers who filled out the personality scales: 16 subjects who had the highest self-esteem and 16 subjects with the lowest self-esteem. Three weeks after they made these ratings each S from the sample of university students participated in a game with either Nature or Chance as a partner. It will be recalled that the choices of these partners were arranged in a deck of playing or file cards. The S made his choice, then overturned the first card in the deck. The payoffs, in points, were in terms of the standard table of rewards used in all of the other experiments. Table 4 shows the number of competitive choices (Black in Chance and Z in Nature) made by the two selected groups.

As in the first French experiment where self-esteem was experimentally induced, the greater exploitativeness by Ss who interact with Nature is noted in this study based on a selected sample. But unlike the first study, Table 4 shows a general tendency for chronically Low self-esteem Ss to be more exploitative than the chronically Highs. An examination of the choices by the two selected groups of Ss over the fifty trials in five, 10-trial blocks shows that in the Nature condition Low Ss make more ex-

TABLE 4. MEAN NUMBER OF COMPETITIVE CHOICES MADE BY
FRENCH Ss WITH CHRONIC H AND L SELF-ESTEEM[a]

Self-esteem	Partner identity		
	Chance		Nature
High	29.8		37.0
Low	31.5		41.6
Self-esteem		1.87	ns
F Partner identity		13.9	< .01
Interaction		.37	ns

[a]N = 8 in each condition.

ploitative choices at each of the five points; there is no overlap. Under Chance, Low Ss are more competitive only in the last three blocks. As Faucheux and Moscovici point out, the compensatory behavior on the part of the chronically Low Ss is more understandable in Nature, for that partner is regarded as highly benevolent. In other words, there is a greater opportunity for the S to achieve the rewards he needs to compensate for his inferiority. In Chance, when the partners are perceived to be less benevolent, it takes time before each S realizes that the other is not choosing at random.

DISCUSSION AND CONCLUSIONS

The research thus far indicates that competitive or exploitative choice behavior of subjects who are dependent on each other for rewards is determined by 1) an equity-seeking tendency and 2) a self-compensatory or defensive tendency. More specifically, the data suggest that individuals who accept the experimental induction of High or Low self-esteem relative to each other perceive a correspondingly high or low level of reward as equitable. Accordingly, the tendency to make lucrative choices, i.e., the tendency to compete for such equitable rewards, varies as a direct function of the individual's self-esteem. On the other hand, individuals who do not accept the self-esteem induction, particularly those who are told their performance is poor, appear to become threatened with a loss of self-esteem. In order to defend against such a loss these individuals strive to obtain more rewards than do their partners. There is also evidence that compensatory behavior to defend the self is characteristic of those individuals who have chronically low self-esteem.

We do not know if there is a common factor in French students selected for their high and low chronic self-esteem and the samples of Italian students in whom an attempt was made to induce high and low Inverse Creativity. Perhaps there are two independent sets of conditions which are responsible for the compensatory or defensive pattern of competitiveness observed in these studies. However, since this pattern was demonstrated by Ss who did not receive an experimental treatment as well as by Ss who did receive it, the induction itself appears not to have been a decisive factor in producing the phenomenon. It can also be said that since the defensive pattern of competitiveness occurred in both French and Italian samples, no exclusively cultural basis can be claimed for this category of response.

According to the self-ratings on personality it appears that American students have higher levels of self-esteem than either of the two European samples. Before this even approaches being a firm conclusion, however, samples of students from the various national groups must be more extensively and carefully matched on relevant background characteristics. Furthermore, it is possible that the difference is a linguistic one based on different meanings and intensity values of personality trait words, or that American students have a response bias on the self-evaluation rating scales which spuriously gives the impression of higher self-evaluation.

References

Faucheux, C. and S. Moscovici. Self-esteem and exploitative behavior in a game against chance and nature. *Journal of Personality and Social Psychology,* January 1968, 8:1, part 1, 83–88.

Lindquist, E. F. *Statistical Analysis in Educational Research.* Boston: Houghton Mifflin, 1940.

Luce, R. D. and H. Raiffa. *Games and Decisions.* New York: John Wiley, 1957.

Pepitone, A. *Attraction and Hostility.* New York: Atherton, 1964.

LOIS OKSENBERG

Machiavellianism in Traditional and Westernized Chinese Students

A common stereotype among Americans is that Chinese are sly and deceitful (Katz and Braly, 1933). They are reputedly masters of the art of saying yes and meaning no. Since these adjectives could be used to describe the Machiavellian as well, the stereotypic view of Chinese character would lead one to hypothesize that Chinese are relatively Machiavellian.

Other considerations lead to the view that Chinese might be less Machiavellian than Westerners. Chinese culture has traditionally emphasized conformity to role expectations and social rules. This is particularly pronounced within the family where duties and the proper forms of behavior between family members are defined in specific detail. In short, in interpersonal behavior, Chinese seem to be guided by expectations and rules more than by individual inclination, compared with members of Western societies. The more one's behavior is determined by role requirements, the less room he has for the maneuvering hypothetically required for Machiavellian behavior. This would lead one to hypothesize that Chinese would be correspondingly less Machiavellian.

If this reasoning is correct, why is it that the Chinese apparently appear Machiavellian to Westerners? This misperception could be due to a cultural misunderstanding. The rules and expectations governing interpersonal behavior are different in Chinese and Western societies. For instance, in Chinese culture it is apparently considered improper to give a person a flat "no" in response to a request. The Chinese may present considerations which he hopes will lead the person to withdraw his request. Or, he may say "yes" and then not carry through, presenting reasons afterward why it was impossible for him to oblige. In this way no one loses face and no one has reason to be dissatisfied. When this happens to a Westerner, he may feel manipulated. In this case, behavior considered polite by the Chinese appears devious to the Westerner. Thus, behavior appearing Machiavellian to a Westerner may have a different meaning in the Chinese context.

Are the Chinese really Machiavellian, as the stereotype implies, or are they relatively un-Machiavellian, as follows from the argument about behavioral expectations? To shed light on this problem, a study involving the Mach Scale was carried out in Hong Kong.

AIMS OF THE STUDY

The Hong Kong study had several goals. One was to obtain a Chinese translation of the Mach IV Scale. The second was to gather data on Machiavellianism among Chinese subjects. Rather than compare a sample of Chinese subjects with, say, American subjects, it was decided to compare Chinese subjects who had received a relatively traditional Chinese education with those who had received a relatively Westernized education. What should be the effect of Westernization within the Chinese cultural context? In comparison with a traditional society such as the Chinese, a Westernized society is hypothesized to have less rigid role expectations and therefore more personal choice in behavior. Presumably, where there is more room for individual initiative in interpersonal behavior, Machiavellian behavior is more likely to occur. In line with this, then, one would expect relatively traditional Chinese to be *less* Machiavellian than Chinese who are relatively Westernized. Alternatively, the accumulated folklore expressed in the popular Western stereotype would indicate that the relatively traditional Chinese are actually *more* Machiavellian than those who are more Westernized. Thus, theoretical considerations pull in one direction, whereas popular belief pulls in the opposite.

PROCEDURE

Subjects

The subjects were 213 male and female secondary school students in Hong Kong. They averaged approximately 17 years of age. A school with a local reputation of holding Confucian values and of teaching a comparatively traditional curriculum provided the Traditional subjects. The language of instruction in this school was the local Chinese dialect, Cantonese. The Westernized subjects came from a school with Western sponsorship and many Western teachers. The language of instruction was English, and a "Western" curriculum was taught. There was no significant difference between the two schools in the percentage of subjects who were not born in Hong Kong (and thus most probably were born in mainland China). Although students from the Westernized school appeared to represent a higher socio-economic level than those from the Traditional school, difficulties in determining the socio-economic level of the subjects prevented its measurement.

Materials and Testing

The 20 item version of the Mach IV Scale (Christie and Geis, 1970) and a set of background questions were administered to all subjects.

The scale and the background questions were translated into Chinese by a professional translator. The translations were then discussed and altered slightly by a group of ten psychology students from the University of Hong Kong. The background questions were translated solely by these students. Both the original English version and the Chinese version were used in the study.

The Mach Scale and background questions were administered to all subjects during regular class time. All groups first heard a short introduction in Cantonese. All Traditional subjects received the Chinese language version of the scales. The English and Chinese versions were distributed randomly among the Westernized subjects. Thus, there were three separate groups: Traditional-Chinese Version, Westernized-English Version, and Westernized-Chinese Version.

RESULTS AND DISCUSSION

Traditionality versus Westernization

The major aim of the study was to compare respondents representing traditional Chinese culture with other Chinese respondents from a more Westernized environment on endorsement of Machiavellian precepts. The Chinese stereotype in America would lead to the prediction that Traditional Chinese should be more Machiavellian than Westernized Chinese. If, however, the hypothesized relationship between lack of highly formal role relationships and Machiavellianism is valid, the Westernized Chinese should have the higher Mach scores.

Table 1 presents the Mach Scale means and variances for the Traditional and Westernized respondents, broken down by sex and language version of the scale they answered. An analysis of variance on the four groups of Mach scores using only the Chinese version data had been planned to assess differences between schools and between sexes. A Bart-

TABLE 1. TRADITIONAL VS. WESTERNIZED MACH MEANS AND VARIANCES

School	Male			Female		
	Mean	Variance	N	Mean	Variance	N
Traditional Chinese	91.88	233.26	41	88.69	125.74	26
Westernized Chinese	100.70	322.75	27	95.31	169.40	45
English	101.93	271.21	29	97.64	136.73	45

lett's test indicated that the assumption of homogeneity of variance was tenable at the conventional level of significance ($x^2 = 6.65$, $p > .05$). Therefore an analysis of variance for the case of unequal cell frequencies was performed. The results shown in Table 2 indicate that there was a significant difference in Mach Scale mean scores between Traditional and Westernized subjects. The Traditional subjects had significantly *lower* mean Mach scores than the Westernized subjects ($F = 9.30$, $p < .01$). The effect of sex was not significant ($F = 2.92$, $p > .05$).

TABLE 2. ANOVA OF TRADITIONAL VS. WESTERNIZED MACH MEANS (CHINESE VERSION)

Source	df	MS	F	p <
School (A)	1	1950.07	9.30	0.01
Sex (B)	1	612.32	2.92	n.s.
A x B	1	39.88	0.19	n.s.
Within	135	209.77		

The validity of this analysis of variance may be questionable. Although the *p*-value of the Bartlett's test was greater than .05, it was only slightly greater. Accordingly, the data were also tested with Scheffé's (1959, p. 362–363) approximation procedure. According to Scheffé, if the results are sufficiently conclusive, further analysis may be dispensed with.

The results of this analysis (Table 3) were similar to the above. Traditional subjects had lower mean Mach scores than Westernized subjects ($F = 9.31$, $p < .005$). The sex difference was not significant ($F = 2.41$, $p > .05$). It seems safe to conclude that Traditional subjects had lower Mach scores than Westernized subjects.

TABLE 3. ANOVA BY SCHEFFÉ'S METHOD OF TRADITIONAL VS. WESTERNIZED MACH MEANS (CHINESE VERSION)

Source	df	MS	F	p <
School	1	59.60	9.31	0.005
Sex	1	15.44	2.41	n.s.
Within	135	6.40		

Several questions were included on the background data sheet in an attempt to assess whether the respondents labeled "Traditional" and "Westernized" actually represented the cultural milieu implied by the label. In response to a question about religion, it was expected that the Traditional subjects would tend to claim to be Buddhists or to have no religion, whereas more Westernized subjects would claim to be Christians. The distribution of the responses of all subjects responding to the question is consistent with this expectation (Table 4). The difference between

TABLE 4. RELIGION OF THE SUBJECTS[a]

School	None	Buddhist	Protestant or Catholic	Other	Total
Traditional	49	4	10	0	63
Westernized	56	4	83	1	144

$\chi^2 = 31.97$, p $<$ .001, two-tailed

[a]Tables 4-6 are based on only those subjects who replied to the particular item for that table.

the two groups of subjects is highly significant ($\chi^2 = 31.97$, $p < .001$, two-tailed test).

In response to a question concerning newspaper preference, Westernized subjects were expected to prefer English language newspapers to a greater extent than Traditional subjects. This expectation is also borne out (Table 5). However, it is clear that the extent to which this is true depends on whether the subject responded to the English or Chinese version. A contributing factor may have been the up-down format of the Chinese version. Although Chinese is often written left to right, and thus could easily be written in the blank on the English version, English is never written in an up-down fashion, and therefore the Chinese version would have to be turned sideways in order to write in an English name. Thus, the format of the Chinese version may have encouraged replies in Chinese characters. In view of these considerations, it was decided to test the significance of the tendency to prefer English newspapers for the Westernized subjects by using only the results from the Chinese version of the questionnaire. As planned initially, all subjects preferring a Chinese Communist newspaper were eliminated from the analysis because of a lack of a hypothesis as to whether Chinese Communist sympathies indicated traditionality, Westernization, or neither. When two newspapers, one Chinese and one English, were preferred, each was given a weight of one-half. Even under this more stringent test, the tendency for Westernized subjects to prefer English papers more than the Traditional subjects was highly significant ($\chi^2 = 15.63$, $p < .001$, two-tailed test).

Two questions were included in an attempt to measure how strictly the

TABLE 5. NEWSPAPER PREFERENCE

School	English	Chinese (non-Communist)	Chinese (Communist)	Total
Traditional				
Chinese	0	61	1	62
Westernized (total)	53	62	2	117
Chinese	13	44	1	58
English	40	18	1	59

traditional behavioral roles and relationships were followed among the subject's own families and relatives. The first question, dealing with the strictness of "family rules", did not differentiate the two groups (Table 6A). A question concerning the strictness of "etiquette among relatives" was successful, however (Table 6B). As expected, of those who responded to the question, Westernized subjects claimed that the etiquette among their relatives was less strict than did the Traditional subjects ($x^2 = 7.03$, $p < .05$, two-tailed test). In this test, the results for the Chinese and English versions were combined for Westernized subjects since they were found not to differ significantly. When a corresponding analysis was performed using the Chinese version data only, the two groups differed in the expected manner, but the difference did not reach significance.

The results for the two questions concerning family rules and etiquette among relatives fit the original expectations fairly well. Chinese informants felt that the question concerning strictness of family rules was poorly worded in both the Chinese and English versions. It was intended to determine how strictly the subjects thought their families followed the traditional behavioral roles, but unfortunately no concise Chinese phrase expressing this was available. The informants felt that in both versions the question would be interpreted inappropriately, to refer to things such as curfews and dating. In contrast, the informants felt that both the Chinese and English versions of the question dealing with etiquette among relatives would be understood in the intended way.

The Equivalence of the Chinese and English Versions of the Mach Scale

A second purpose of the study was to obtain a Chinese translation of the Mach Scale. Since the difference between the Traditional and Westernized subjects was expected, the equivalence of the two versions of the

TABLE 6.

School	Very strict	Moderately strict	Not strict	Total
A. Strictness of family rules				
Traditional	6	51	10	67
Westernized	11	116	16	143
B. Strictness of etiquette among relatives				
Traditional	10	52	5	67
Westernized	18	89	31	138

$x^2 = 7.03$, $p < .05$, two-tailed

Mach Scale can only be tested with the Westernized subjects, where the two versions were distributed randomly. An analysis of variance of the data from the four Westernized groups (shown in Table 1) had been planned, but a Bartlett's test indicated that the assumption of equality of variance was untenable ($x^2 = 8.15$, $p < .05$). Individual F tests indicated that within each version, scores for males had a higher variance than those for females (Chinese version: $F = 1.91$, $p < .05$; English version : $F = 1.98$, $p < .05$). Between version differences in variance did not reach significance.

Because of the unequal cell frequencies and inequality of variances, the Scheffé approximation method described above was also carried out. The appropriate analysis is presented in Table 7. The lack of a significant difference in mean scores between the English and Chinese versions is quite clear ($F = .53$). The F ratio for a difference in mean Mach scores for the two sexes just misses significance ($F = 3.90$, $p > .05$). In view of the nature of the method used, it would be unwise to come to a definite conclusion as to the effect of sex on Mach scores. The possibility of a true difference related to sex is consistent with a similar trend among the Traditional subjects, and with sex differences found in the United States.

Another approach to assessing the equivalence of the two versions is the comparison of their reliabilities. All reliabilities are split-half reliabilities corrected by the Spearman-Brown formula. Again, comparisons among the Westernized subjects are most appropriate. The reliabilities of the two versions of the Mach Scale for the males hardly differ (.79, Chinese Version and .72, English Version), whereas the females' difference is greater (.57, Chinese Version and .39, English Version). The reliability of the Chinese version for the Traditional males was .74, whereas that for the females was .61.

TABLE 7. ANOVA BY SCHEFFÉ'S METHOD OF MACH MEANS OF ENGLISH AND CHINESE VERSIONS (WESTERNIZED SUBJECTS)

Source	df	MS	F	p <
Version	1	3.168	0.53	n.s.
Sex	1	23.426	3.90	<.05
Within	142	6.014		

In summary, no significant differences in mean Mach scores or variances were found between the two versions among the Westernized subjects. The reliabilities were quite comparable for males, while the English version reliability was lower than that of the Chinese version for females. Though in general the evidence supports the equivalence of the scales, the evidence is in the form of group means rather than individual scores.

To test the equivalence further, it would be desirable to have the same subjects reply to both versions of the scale and to compare the scores.

CONCLUSION

The evidence does not support the popular stereotype of Chinese character. Instead, it supports the argument about the greater importance of social roles and standards of behavior in traditional Chinese society. It appears that Westernization, in the Chinese context, implies an increase in Machiavellianism. If the reasoning presented above is correct, this reflects the weakening of constricting behavioral expectations.

References

Christie, R. and F. Geis. *Studies in Machiavellianism.* New York: Academic Press, 1970.
Katz, D. and K. W. Braly. Racial stereotypes of 100 college students. *Journal of Abnormal and Social Psychology,* 1933, 28, 280–290.
Scheffé, H. *The Analysis of Variance.* New York: Wiley, 1959.

8   ROBERT D. MEADE
      AND JAMES O. WHITTAKER

A Cross-Cultural Study of Authoritarianism

INTRODUCTION

Adorno *et al.* (1950) report that the personality dimension which they have labeled authoritarianism is closely related to family and cultural

Reprinted from *The Journal of Social Psychology,* 1967, Vol. 72, pp. 3–7. Copyright (1967) by The Journal Press, 2 Commercial Street, Provincetown, Mass.

This investigation was inaugurated while the senior author was visiting Fulbright Professor at Balwant Rajput College, Agra University, Agra, Uttar Pradesh, India.

conditioning of the individual. In the development of the California F Scale designed to measure this personality factor, quite different results were obtained between various subgroups within the American culture. Later, studies by Christie and Garcia (1951) and Courtney et al. (1951), which investigated various other subcultures in America, also reported significant differences. Minkowich and Shaked (1962) have found considerable variation in authoritarian tendencies in various subcultures in Israel.

Since these studies have found differences between various ethnic and social groups within the confines of a single nation, it is to be expected that still greater differences in authoritarianism would be found in cultures which show an even greater divergence from any one national standard that may be assumed. The few empirical studies that have been undertaken outside the United States reveal that such is the case. Prothro and Melikian (1953) and Melikian (1956, 1959) report a significantly higher level of authoritarianism in college students from various Arabian cultures than is found among a comparable student group in the United States. This effect is reported for both Christian as well as Moslem respondents. Caladarci (1959), on the other hand, reports no differences in authoritarianism between Japanese and Americans who are involved in the field of education.

A strict comparison between the results of these different studies is rendered difficult if not impossible because of confounding by many factors other than those that are strictly cultural. Differences in ages, education, and occupation are notable among these factors. For this reason and also because of a general paucity of data from cultural groups outside America, the present study was undertaken.

METHOD

Five groups of respondents known on general grounds to be culturally disparate were chosen purposefully for making comparison with a sixth group from the United States. Within each cultural group, specific rather than random samples were investigated. These groups were all college students and are comparable with groups found to be exercising an increasing role in leadership functions in the societies of which they are members. Selection of this type of respondent also circumvented the problem of illiteracy prevalent in some of the cultures chosen for study. The groups consisted of three from Asia and one each from Africa, South America, and the United States.

The African group was made up of 50 males and 23 females from the Mashona people whose traditional home is what is now Rhodesia. These people until recently lived under a tribal system in which elders made nearly all decisions and where the tribal council and chief were responsible for general policy. Most of the respondents had attended missionary schools and some had adopted the Christian religion.

The first Asian group was made up of 40 males and 19 females from the Near Eastern Arabian countries of Jordan, Lebanon, Egypt, and Sudan. This culture is characterized by strong leadership from the male members of the group, as well as strong adherence to religious traditions. Nearly all were Moslems, but a few were Christians.

The second Asian group was from the Gangetic Plain of Uttar Pradesh in northern India and was made up of 30 males and 24 females. All but three, who were from the Sikh religion, were Hindus and there was a representation from each of the four major castes.

The third Asian group was made up of Chinese who live in the New Territories of Hong Kong. This group was comprised of 16 males and 46 females. Most belonged to the Taoist religion, some were Buddhists, and there were a few Christians. Many were refugees from the Chinese mainland.

The South American group lived in Brazil. The background of these 24 male and 46 female respondents was primarily Portuguese with some native Indian mixture of several generations longstanding. Nearly all were members of the Roman Catholic faith.

The American cultural group consisting of 41 males and 44 females was from both public and private colleges in New England and the Pacific Northwest. Seventy six per cent were Protestant and 24 per cent were Roman Catholic.

All respondents in these six cultures were regularly enrolled students attending college on a full-time basis. They were given the California F Scale printed in the language used for instruction in their respective colleges. English was used for Americans, Arabs, Chinese, and Africans; Hindi for the Indian students; and Portuguese for the Brazilians. Subjects were instructed to complete the questionnaire by using a seven-point scale for each item which ranged from strong agreement to strong disagreement. The questionnaires were administered by a member of the faculty of the institution the students were attending and hence the study could not be attributed to an American investigator.

RESULTS AND DISCUSSION

None of the mean scores for male and female respondents in the six groups differed significantly, and therefore they were combined for purposes of comparison with other groups in Table 1. The most striking result is that all five cultures, when compared with American students, show a significantly higher degree of authoritarianism. This conclusion is sup-

TABLE 1. MEAN F-SCALE SCORES FOR SIX CULTURAL GROUPS

Culture	Institution	N	Mean	SD
U.S.A.	Trinity College, Connecticut; and Western Washington State College	85	3.16	.57
India	Agra College, Agra, U.P.	54	5.06	.57
Rhodesia	Umtali College, Umtali; and University College, Salisbury	73	4.91	.62
Brazil	Sao Paulo University, Sao Paulo	70	4.02	.90
Arabia	American University, Beirut	59	4.45	.63
Hong Kong	Chung Chi College, Chung Chi	62	4.61	.54

ported statistically when the American data are compared with those from each of the other cultures. These results are found in Table 2. All of the values comparing Americans with other cultural groups shown in Table 2 justify rejection of the null hypothesis well beyond the .01 level of confidence.

TABLE 2. STATISTICAL COMPARISON OF SIX CULTURAL GROUPS USING t-TEST

Culture	U.S.A.	Brazil	Arabia	Hong Kong	Rhodesia
Brazil	6.62[a]				
Arabia	12.90[a]	3.07[a]			
Hong Kong	16.11[a]	4.45[a]	1.45		
Rhodesia	19.44[a]	6.85[a]	4.18[a]	2.00[b]	
India	19.00[a]	7.43[a]	5.55[a]	4.09[a]	1.35

[a] $p < .01$.
[b] $p < .05 > .01$.

Secondly, Brazilian students, while significantly higher in authoritarianism than American students, are significantly lower than each of the other cultural groups.

Listed in order of increasing authoritarianism, the cultural groups are United States, Brazil, Arabia, Hong Kong, Rhodesia, and India. Each of these groups, however, does not have a significantly higher score than the one preceding it. It is quite clear that, while Indians and Rhodesians do not differ from each other significantly, taken together they are more authoritarian than all other cultures tested. Students from Hong Kong and Arabia appear to constitute a higher intermediate degree of authoritarianism and do not differ significantly from each other, while at the same time they differ from the other groups.

It should be noted that the conclusions concerning the relative degree of authoritarianism in Americans and Arabians corroborates the earlier findings of Prothro and Melikian (1953).

No attempt can be made here to analyze how one cultural group has come to be more authoritarian than any of the others. Differences in religion, family structure, child-rearing practices, education, and type of government, working singly or in interaction with others, may provide an explanation. The cultural groups which are represented here quite obviously differ with respect to all of these factors and many more as well. Further research is needed before specific factors contributing to authoritarianism or lack of it in each culture studied are isolated. Respondents tested in this investigation, moreover, were all college students, and it seems reasonable to expect that they represented the more liberal elements of the cultural groups to which they belong. It is quite likely that testing other educational strata of these cultures would reveal an even higher degree of authoritarianism. Indeed, it is also reasonable to expect significant variation among the various subcultures which comprise the broader national groups. Such differences suggest the need to investigate the role played by authoritarianism in the social relations of these cultures and subcultures.

SUMMARY

The personality dimension, authoritarianism, was investigated in six culturally disparate groups of college students: Americans, Arabs, Rhodesian Africans (Mashona), Chinese, Indians, and Brazilians. Mean scores on the California F Scale were significantly lower for Americans than for any of the other groups. Brazilians scored significantly lower than all except Americans. Arabians and Chinese showed no difference and together constituted the next highest level of authoritarianism. Rhodesians and Indians exhibited no differences and together were highest in authoritarianism. Implications for further research in personality, leadership, and social relations employing this parameter of personality are discussed.

References

Adorno, T., E. Frenkel-Brunswik, D. Levinson, and R. Sanford. *The Authoritarian Personality*. New York: Harper & Row, 1950.

Caladarci, A. The measurement of authoritarianism in Japanese educators. *Calif. J. Educ. Res.*, 1959, *10*, 137–141.

Christie, R. and J. Garcia. Subcultural variation in authoritarian personality. *J. Abn. & Soc. Psychol.*, 1951, *46*, 457–469.

Courtney, D., F. Green, and J. Masling. "Leadership identification and acceptance." Report No. 1, Institute for Research in Human Relations, Philadelphia, Pennsylvania, 1951.

Melikian, L. Some correlates of authoritarianism in two cultural groups. *J. of Psychol.*, 1956, *42*, 237–248.

————. Authoritarianism and its correlates in Egyptian culture and in the United States. *J. Soc. Issues*, 1959, *15*, 58–68.

Minkowich, A. and A. Shaked. Haishiyut hasamkhutit (The authoritarian personality). *Megamot*, 1962, *12*, 24–47.
Prothro, E. and L. Melikian. The California Public Opinion Scale in an authoritarian culture. *Public Opin. Quart.*, 1953, *17*, 353–362.
———. Generalized ethnic attitudes in Arab Near East. *Sociol. & Soc. Res.*, 1953, *37*, 375–379.
Sanford, F. *Authoritarianism and Leadership*. Philadelphia, Pa.: Inst. Res. Hum. Rel., 1950.

IV

Comparative Studies of Cognition: Categorizing and Communicating

9   JACQUELINE J. GOODNOW

Cultural Variations in Cognitive Skills

In recent years there has been a considerable increase in studies conducted with children who are not from the same cultural background as our usual middle-class subjects. The backgrounds have varied, sometimes

Reprinted from *Cognitive Studies*, Vol. 1, in press, published by Brunner/Mazel, Inc., 80 East 11th Street, New York, N.Y. 10003. A substantial part of this paper was presented at the meetings of the American Psychological Association, September, 1967. The preparation was partially supported by PHS Grant 1 KO3 HD 36971.

being pre-literate societies, sometimes cultures that are literate but still of
a village type, and sometimes milieus that are urban and educated but not
Anglo-Saxon in tradition or style.

My aim is not to provide an extensive review of these studies. Rather, I
hope to use some illustrative studies as a way of asking some general questions, questions about the nature of cross-cultural variations and their implications for ideas about how intelligence develops, and how differences
in skills arise.

We may start with the question: Why be interested in children from
other cultures? It is often said that different cultures provide some ready-
made variations in environment that would be impossible to produce in
the laboratory or in a planned experiment. This is true, but it is also true
that we are not as yet skilled in specifying the critical points of difference
between one environment and another, critical, that is, for the performance we have in mind. As a result, it is often difficult to interpret results
in any fine way, to know what the environmental conditions are that give
rise to the similarities and differences we find. How much of a problem
this represents depends, of course, on the state of our knowledge. There
are times when we have so little data that all is grist to the mill, and times
when we need data of a particular type in order to advance. At our present state of knowledge, however, the problem is large enough to give a
special point to questions about what one can learn from cross-cultural
studies that cannot be learned in other ways.

In a broad sense, each cross-cultural study provides a piece for a developmental puzzle. The puzzle lies in accounting for the fact that we
change as we grow older, that at 2, 5, 20, and 40 we are not identical
when it comes to remembering, classifying, or problem-solving. The fact
that we change with age is easy to observe. What is difficult is answering
those perennial questions: Just what is the difference? And how does it
come about?

For this general puzzle, cross-cultural studies can supply pieces we did
not have before, variations in method we did not think were possible or
significant, upsets in relationships we had come to think of as constant. As
in all puzzles, of course, the pieces are not all equally valuable at any one
time, and on occasion we have to set a piece aside until we reach a point
where it can be fitted in.

From the puzzle point of view, the biggest difficulty with cross-cultural
studies has been the lack of overlap between pieces: each study a new culture, and, very often, a new task. Now we are a long way from being able
to plan for critical points of overlap between cultures; i.e., we do not
know as yet how to match culture X and culture Y on the features that
affect performance Z, or on all the features save one. Overlaps between

tasks, however, can be planned, and such overlaps are much to the fore in a number of recent cultural studies. Some examples are:

1. Segall, Campbell, and Herskovits (1966) have gathered results from a wide variety of cultures, using the same visual perception tasks throughout. Their results have been so intriguing that other psychologists, like Jahoda (1966), have been taking the same tasks to still more cultural groups, trying to pin down just what produces the variations in performance.

2. A group with a Harvard core has used the same classification task with children from several settings: Boston, Senegal, Alaska, urban and rural Mexico. This is the work of Olver and Hornsby, Greenfield, Reich, Maccoby and Modiano, all branching out from the Harvard Center of Cognitive Studies (Bruner, Olver, & Greenfield, 1966).

3. Vernon (1965, 1966) has used the same extensive battery of tasks with several samples of 11-year-old boys: English, West Indian, Canadian Indian, and Eskimo. In a rare step, he has as well made ratings on a number of environmental variables and is attempting a set of direct relationships between the environmental differences and the patterns of test performance.

4. Lesser, Fifer, and Clark (1965) have given the same tasks to lower and middle class American children with varying ethnic backgrounds: Chinese, Negro, Jewish, and Puerto Rican. Class variations, it turned out, lowered the level of performance but not the pattern of abilities; ethnic differences varied the pattern.

The last example is a group of people who have come to overlap through no deliberate intent on their part, but through a shared interest in tasks developed by Piaget and his colleagues. It is this group I shall emphasize. It offers some nice overlaps in several respects: in the sample of tasks, the sample of Ss, the environmental variable, and happiest of all, in some of the results.

The group of studies has the following points in common:

1. Two or more tasks have been used. This similarity is critical, since what is often most informative for the developmental puzzle is not the absolute level of performance so much as the relationships among performances.

2. Some of the tasks have been the same. In particular, at least one of the tasks has been a Genevan conservation task; i.e., a task where a change is made in the perceptual appearance of an object and the child is asked whether there has been a change in some invariant quality like weight or length.

3. On the environmental side, the studies have all been strongly concerned with variations in the amount and quality of schooling.

To run through the list quickly, the set of studies includes three where the children have had no formal schooling or practically none: studies by Siegel and Mermelstein (1965) with Negro children in Prince Edward County, Virginia; by Magali Bovet [1] with Algerian children; and by myself in Hong Kong. In addition, there are two studies by psychologists primarily interested in the difference between types of schooling: by Peluffo (1962, 1964, and personal communication), working in Italy with children coming up to the urban North from southern villages, and by Vernon (1965) comparing English schoolboys with West Indian schoolboys.

What has come out of these overlapping pieces?

1. As we move away from a technological society there is not any overall lag or retardation across tasks, but rather what Vernon has called a series of "peaks and troughs." Some tasks shift their difficulty level more than others.

2. Fortunately, there is some consistency to the tasks that stand up well throughout. If we list tasks in terms of the extent to which performance changes as we shift away from our traditional S, some of the conservation tasks appear at the top of the list as showing either no change or the least degree of change. Only some of the conservation tasks are sturdy in this sense, namely the tasks for amount, weight, volume, and surface, but not tasks for the conservation of length (Vernon, 1965) or time and speed (Bovet).

3. Again fortunately, there is the beginning of consistency in the tasks not handled so well outside the traditional group. This consistency is harder to define, but in a rough fashion they seem to be predominantly tasks where the child has to transform an event in his head, has to shift or shuffle things around by some kind of visualizing or imaging rather than by carrying out an overt series of changes. The spatial or perceptual aspect of these tasks comes as something of a surprise. It used to be thought that "disadvantaged" groups would be most handicapped on verbal or abstractive tasks and that imaging or spatial-type tasks would be the fairest. This seems not to be so, and a division of tasks into "verbal" and "non-verbal" seems not to be the most fruitful that could be made.

The three results warrant some special attention. They provide a set of focal points for looking at cross-cultural variations, both in terms of the

---

[1] All references to the work of Magali Bovet are based on personal communication.

way they parallel the results of other studies and in terms of the problems and implications they bring with them.

The first result — no overall lag but a differential shift — has its parallels in several studies. To span a time range, Nissen, Machover and Kinder pointed out in 1935 that children in French Guinea gave varying performances on a number of tasks. They were, for instance, much closer to Western norms in reproducing a sequence of moves made by a tester (touching a set of cubes) than in reproducing designs. Recently, this kind of effect has been taken further by results showing that differential patterns of skill are more likely to occur among children of similar formal schooling with differences in ethnic background than with differences in class (Lesser, Fifer, and Clark, 1965), and more likely to occur with major differences in schooling than with differences of class or ethnic background (Goodnow, 1962), or differences in intelligence (Goodnow & Bethon, 1966).

Whenever such differential shifts are found, they challenge assumptions we may hold about general factors underlying performance. It is easy to assume that tasks with the same difficulty level, especially if they have some surface similarity, are based on the same abilities and processes, or on a general and unitary intelligence. This assumption requires a closer look when we find the tasks we work from do not necessarily hang together. From the particular set of studies cited, for example, one would become cautious about assuming "conservation" to be a skill more general than it is content-specific. Equally, the closer look may need to be at some of our global descriptions of environments. In recent years, for example, there has been a great deal of interest in "amounts of stimulation," in searching for an "optimal amount" that will neither "under-stimulate" nor "over stimulate." To this pattern of search, differential shifts are a reminder that "stimulation" is a variable constantly in need of definition and specification, in terms of kind as well as amount. The critical factors may equally well turn out to be some specific experiences.

The second and third results — areas of agreement on the skills that unite and divide children from different backgrounds — are the ones that help most toward specifying what kind of experience leads to what kind of skill. They are the points from which we can start a sharper analysis of just what it is that a task demands and a society provides. These analyses are, for me, the heart of cross-cultural studies, and some examples of them form the major body of this paper.

PINNING DOWN DIFFERENCES IN SKILLS

Matches between the features of a task and the features of an environment may well start from an analysis of tasks, either by asking what it is that some tasks have in common or what it is that gives rise to uneven performances. Typically, the focus is either on the content of the task or on the operation that is to be carried out. One may start, for example, from the fact that the scores of Negro children on a number of intelligence tests are by and large lower than those of middle-class white children, and set up the hypothesis that the difficulty stems from the content, from varying degrees of familiarity with the words used and the objects portrayed. Alternatively, one may look not so much to features of the material as to what the child has to do with the material, the operation he is asked to carry out. This is the direction taken in the suggestion that poorly schooled children have particular difficulty with tasks calling for some kind of imaged change in material. And finally, one may look for the solution in some interaction between content and operation: children from a particular background may well be able to carry out a particular operation with one kind of material but not with another.

From any direction, it is never easy to specify and prove just what it is about a task that makes it easier for children of some cultures than for others. But the effort is critical if we are to make any meaningful connections between skills and experiences. For a particular example, I would like to turn to the data that suggest the importance of "imaged transformations." I have suggested that children with little schooling may be especially handicapped on tasks calling for imaged changes, for transformations that have to be carried out in the head. In stressing this kind of difference among groups, I am not alone. Vernon (1965, 1966) has suggested a similar kind of task area in his stress on an "imaging" factor, affecting performance on a number of perceptual-spatial tasks. Vernon looks to an environmental variable other than schooling, namely the extent that the background is, for boys, purposeful, planful, and male-oriented. For the moment, the important thing is the stress on a common area as highly vulnerable to group differences, whatever its source. Despite the common stress, however, neither "imaging" nor "imaged transformations" nor "mental shuffling" is a definitive description of what underlies the vulnerable tasks, and I would be the first to admit that these identifications of the vulnerable area are tentative.

To give a closer look at an identification in terms of "imaged changes," I shall take two sets of results. The first set comes from a combination of some Hong Kong data with some American data gathered by Gloria Bethon and myself. The second set is drawn from Vernon's work with West Indians. From these results and the nature of the tasks they are based on, others may draw hypotheses different from the one presented here. Whatever the hypotheses, the overlap in results is striking enough and rare enough to call for some detailed attention.

Figure 1 presents data adapted from Goodnow and Bethon (1966). There are three groups of boys, all 11 years old. One group is Chinese with little or no schooling. The other two are American schoolboys with known levels on an intelligence test, the California Test of Mental Maturity. The median for the group labelled "dull" is 81, with a top of 88; the median for the group labelled "average" is 111, with a top of 120.

FIGURE 1. Patterns of Task Difficulty for Ss Varying in Nationality, Schooling and Intelligence (adapted from Goodnow & Bethon, 1966)

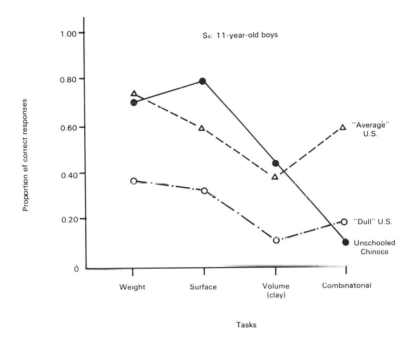

The interesting features in these results are:

1. First, the pattern or order of difficulty is the same for the dull and the average American groups. We can eliminate the possibility that any change in pattern with a non-schooled group is the result of a simple drop in general intelligence.

2. On the first three tasks, there is very little difference between the Chinese group and the average American group. These tasks are all conservation tasks. The first is the well-known task for conservation of

weight, with two pieces of clay. The second — conservation of surface — is perhaps less well-known. The child starts with two equal pieces of green paper, each one a grassy field with a cow on it. The child agrees that one cow has as much to eat as the other, and then the experimenter starts putting down 12 houses on each field, one on each field at a time. In the end the two fields look quite different with the houses on one arranged in two rows of six, and the houses on the other scattered widely. Again the child is asked if one cow has as much to eat as the other. The fourth task is conservation of volume, with displacement of water. (Two balls of clay are shown to displace equal amounts of water. Then, with one ball changed to a pancake-shape, comes the question: What about now? Do both push the water up by the same amount, or does one push the water up more than the other?

3. The only task on which the Chinese boys fall below the "average" Americans is the Genevan task of combinatorial reasoning. The child has to make pairs of colors, repeating no pairs and omitting none. He starts off with practice on three colors, then on four colors, and he is helped to get all pairs. Finally, he is asked to work with six colors. The heart of the request is that he figure out something in advance. He is asked to try to figure out a trick or a system that will make the task easy, will help him to repeat none and omit none. The task is scored for the presence of a systematic approach to the problem, and this is what the unschooled group had trouble with. A number of them ended with 15 pairs, and some of them became aware that they had to have the same number of each color, but they relied a great deal on moving the pieces around physically, shifting them from here to there in actual movements and then looking at the moved-around pairs.

My first hypothesis for these results (Goodnow, 1962) was that there might be something special to conservation tasks in general. But that hypothesis is set aside by Vernon's (1965) results with conservation of length, and by Magali Bovet's results with conservation of time: both conservation tasks, but both poorly handled in contrast with conservation of amount. For the combinatorial task, I had the feeling that the trouble was in the request to work it out in advance, in the head, so to speak; but one task provided a poor basis to work from. The result in itself seemed a stable enough one, in that Peluffo (1964) also found the combinatorial task harder than conservation of volume for rural but not for urban school children in Sardinia.

A much wider base was offered by Vernon's (1965) results. I have taken out some of his West Indian results to illustrate again a pattern of strengths and weaknesses, and to show how they raise again a theme of mental rather than physical shuffling of material. Figure 2 shows the material selected.

FIGURE 2. Patterns of Task Difficulty for English and West Indian Schoolboys (adapted from Vernon, 1965)

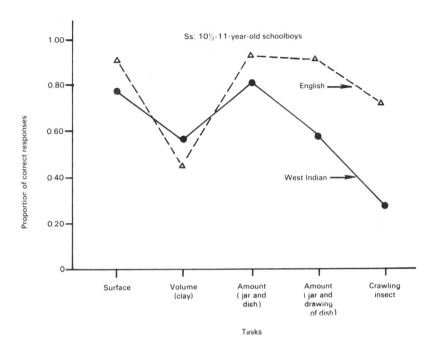

In one of those happy overlaps, Vernon was also working with boys around 11. In his case the Ss were schoolboys aged 10½ to 11, one group Jamaican, the other English. And he had used some of the same tasks as were given in Hong Kong: conservation of surface, with the cows in the fields, and conservation of volume with water displaced by two balls of clay. On neither of these tasks, as Figure 2 shows, was there a difference between the two groups. What is more, the absolute levels of performance on these two tasks by all four groups of boys (American, English, Chinese, and Jamaican) do not vary widely. All the scores on the volume task, for example, are between 40 per cent correct and 60 per cent correct at this age level.

Both the third and fourth tasks selected from Vernon (1965) ask about conservation of amount with liquids. The third task starts with two transparent jars, half filled with water. The child adjusts them until they are equal. Then the experimenter presents a small dish and says, "Now I'll pour mine into this dish. Have we the same, or have you more, or less than me?" On this task, the two groups were equal. On the fourth task, however, the Indian group falls well below the English group, even though the task seems to involve only a minor change. The tester now uses one tall jar and the drawing of a dish, and asks: "If I poured the water from this bottle into this dish, would there be more water in the dish than in the bottle, or less, or the same?"

The difference between the two forms of the amount task may be simply a difference in content. It has often been said that children from less technological societies have trouble with drawings and diagrams. The difficulty could also be a combination of content and operation. The child not only has to cope with a drawing rather than an object — a difference that should not faze schoolboys too greatly — but he must also imagine the water transferred from bottle to dish without the benefit of first adjusting for himself the level in two jars or of seeing the experimenter actually pour all the water from the jar to the dish.

That the difficulty may lie in the operation as much as in the content is suggested by some other tasks used by Vernon. One of these is shown in Figure 2 — the task of the crawling insect. Vernon showed the child a circle 2½ inches in diameter and said, "Here's a drawing of a jar on its side. I'm going to draw a little insect on top." The drawing shows a clear head and tail, with the head pointing left. "Now," says Vernon, "the insect starts walking around the outside edge, like this. You draw for me what he would look like when he gets round to here." "Here" is a dot on the bottom rim of the circle. If we ask how many Ss draw the insect with his head pointed correctly, the answer is 71 per cent of the English group and 28 per cent of the West Indians.

Again the task seems to have two parts to it. The child must attend to direction or orientation as a critical part of a drawing, and he must make a transformation in his head. Orientation in a drawing does appear to be a feature that is made salient by learning. McFie (1961), for example, points out that student nurses and boys entering high school in Uganda were very different from English Ss in their attitude towards orientation in copying designs or on the Kohs Block Test, so that on the first encounter with the tasks inversions and rotations were common.

Paying inadequate attention to direction may be part of the Jamaicans' difficulty. There is as well, however, the need to image the reversal in position, and it seems to be this part of the task that links it with the poorer Jamaican performance on two further tasks. On one of these, the child is shown a string of cards, each containing a number, so that what he sees is 3 2 5, or 2 8 4 9 3. He is asked, "What is the biggest number you could make with these?" He is not allowed to shift the cards around by hand. On this task, the English and the Jamaican schoolboys are again widely apart: 86 per cent and 58 per cent respectively with three numbers, 73 per cent and 32 per cent with five numbers. The two groups are equally apart on a last task, where they have to think through some left-right relationships. The tester places a pencil, a penny, and an eraser in a line, and asks such questions as: "Is the rubber to the left of the penny or to the right? Is the rubber to the left of the pencil or to the right?" With six questions like these 61 per cent of the English schoolboys make no errors, but only 30 per cent of the West Indians.

No one of these tasks is conclusive in itself, but taken together they suggest that one of the sharpest differences among cultural groups may lie in tasks where the child has to carry out some spatial shuffling or transforming, in his head, without the benefit of actually moving the stimulus material around. This suggestion, we may add, is in line with a recurring comment on a difference in task approach among groups with varying degrees of formal schooling in the Western sense. Ss with less formal schooling often impress their highly educated observers as making greater use, even excessive use, of action and direct manipulation of material. This kind of comment has been made for non-Western groups by Maistriaux (1955), McFie (1961), and Richelle (1966), and for Western adults by Hanfmann (1941).

I have looked at the role of "transformations in the head" in some detail for several reasons. There is a need for working hypotheses in comparing cultural groups, and differences in "imaging" or "imaged transformations" have now appeared often enough and with enough specificity to qualify as a promising working hypothesis (cf. Vernon, 1965, 1966; Goodnow & Bethon, 1966; Goodnow, 1968). And as we come closer to such specific skills, we may begin to ask more sharply whether there are experimental differences that might match the differences in skill. I do not wish to suggest, however, that the picture is in any way final. Very recently to hand, for example, is the first major statement of Vernon's results with Canadian Indians and Eskimos (Vernon, 1966). Both groups were surprisingly weak on conservation tasks, perhaps, as Vernon suggests (1966, p. 192), because of linguistic factors. (Vernon's Ss were all tested in English, a language more familiar to the Jamaican than to the Canadian Ss; Goodnow's Chinese Ss were tested, through an interpreter, in their own dialect.) Whatever the explanation for the poor conservation performance, the surprise still remains of a good performance, by the Eskimos especially, on most of the perceptual-spatial tasks. On these, the Eskimos were close to the English norms. This kind of result means that good spatial or imaging performances occur without high-level schooling, a result that sharpens and spices considerably the question of what kinds of experience help in producing particular kinds of skill.

MATCHING SKILLS TO EXPERIENCE

Suppose for a moment that varying degrees of skill in mental shuffling or in imaging transformations do account for the recurring performance differences we have noted among several cultural groups. This would represent one of the two aims in cross-cultural research: pinning down the nature of a difference in skill. The other aim is to tie the difference in skill to a difference in experience. How could it come about that the children in our usual samples have developed some kinds of imaging skills more fully than the children in some other groups have? And how is it that there is so much less variation in performance on tasks like the conservation of amount?

At this point, we must lean to some extent on conjecture, and on some general points in the literature on spatial skills. To start with, we may note that "spatial" skills — often imaging skills — seem to be a highly variable area of performance in general. Piaget, for example, rarely comments on a great deal of variability in the age at which a child can master a task, but it is for a spatial task (predicting the flat shape of a folded or rolled piece of paper) that he notes a considerable effect from specific experiences: "The child who is familiar with folding and unfolding paper shapes through his work at school is two or three years in advance of children who lack this experience" (Piaget & Inhelder, p. 276). And Sherman (1967) has recently argued that many of the sex differences on cognitive tasks stem from the stress on spatial visualization in the tasks, visualization that girls, because of sex-typed activities, are poorly prepared for. It seems unlikely, then, that there will be any simple or single explanation of how differences arise in skills at mental shuffling or transforming. In a broad sense, the explanations that have been suggested can be placed into two groups, one emphasizing the role of general attitudes, the other stressing more specific experiences.

An example of a general factor is Vernon's argument for a relationship between performance on perceptual-spatial skills and the degree of purposefulness and planning shown in the home (cf. Vernon, 1966). Vernon points out that the relationship is yet to be fully tested. It seems quite reasonable, however, to expect that a general readiness to stop and plan ahead would make a considerable difference in tasks where premature action can lead to difficulties that are hard to undo (as in many mazes), or where there is a premium on a systematic approach to a task (as in the Genevan task of combinatorial reasoning). In fact, Richelle (1966) considers the reluctance to "inhibit action" as the chief cause of poor scores by a large group of Congolese children on many of Rey's performance tasks.

Even if a child has the readiness, however, to stop and think ahead, he needs the tools to do so. It is here that specific experiences would appear to be most critical. Such experiences have often been pointed to. Vernon (1966), for example, mentions the training that Indian and Eskimo children have in tracking and in locating objects spatially. Porteus (1931) felt that tracking helped some primitive peoples achieve a better performance on his mazes, and Havighurst, Gunther and Pratt (1946) considered that experience in drawing and painting played a similar role for the Draw-a-Man task. These identifications of critical experience are highly plausible, but two things are needed. One is some *a priori* identification; the other is some clear demonstration of a difference in skill between two groups selected to vary in terms of some specific experience.

Price-Williams' (1968) recent study of conservation of amount is a case in point. From the Mexican town of Tlaquepaque he selected boys with two kinds of family background. One group came from pottery-making families; the other from non-pottery-making families of a similar social class. Out of several conservation tasks, the former group is significantly better on only one: conservation of amount with clay. Price-Williams is currently conducting a replication of this kind of study. Whatever its outcome, his study is a nice example of the kind of research needed to make explicit and testable any matches between experiences and skills.

Even given demonstrated matches between experiences and skills, we shall still have to ask how the specific experiences can give rise to the skill we have in mind. How, for example, do certain past actions or experiences lead to skill in thinking a problem through in one's head, without benefit of some reminding or testing action? One of the general effects of repeated and varied actions may be an atmosphere in which magical explanations do not easily survive. Beyond this, past actions may provide an "action model," a pragmatic model that serves as a landmark, reference point, or mnemonic device for pinning down a relationship and holding it in mind. An example of this comes from a Chinese boy explaining conservation of weight. He pointed out that sometimes when he bought rice it came in a [wide, shallow bag] and sometimes it came in a [tall, narrow bag], but it was always the same weight: he knew because he had carried them.

Another function actions may have is to provide the opportunity for translating a problem into terms other than actions. For a translation from actions to some map of relationships, we may simply need a fair amount of practice. This is, for example, the argument Mandler (1954) makes for maze-learning. Ss at first find their way through a maze mostly by feel and in terms of a sequence of actions. With more and more practice, however, they begin to have some kind of mental map of how the maze might be laid out. The same sort of learning seems to occur in mastering the layout of a new city. It takes a considerable amount of actually going to places and actually consulting a map before we have some independent picture of how things are arranged, clear enough to realize that such and such a street ought to be able to provide a detour if a familiar path is blocked. I am not suggesting that this translation into units that can be mentally shuffled around takes place automatically. Part of it must depend upon a certain amount of general practice in "mapping things out," a certain amount of learning to drop unessential details out of the mapping.

That translation with "maps" does not take place automatically is suggested by some actual maps — drawn maps — gathered by Dart and Pradhan (1967) from Nepalese children. Even for a familiar route, these children gave maps that marked places by pictures rather than points, where the path reflected more the sequence of actions than a set of relationships. They were, comment Dart and Pradhan, essentially "like a string of beads, list(ing) in correct sequence the places we should pass through without giving any clues as to distance, trail intersections, changes of direction, and so on" (1967, p. 653). One can find such directions outside of Nepal, but at least we are usually aware that there is another kind of map, and by and large the difference between cultures is not in complete presence and complete absence, but in frequencies of occurrence and in the content to which an idea or a principle is applied.

I have suggested so far that in order to move from a physical to a mental shuffling of objects and events, we may need practice with actually moving the objects around, or seeing them move, and we may need general practice in mental shuffling and mapping. To close the argument, we may turn back briefly to the shared and unshared skills described earlier.

For the argument to be reasonable, we would have to argue that most cultures provide the practice and the pragmatic models needed for judgments of properties like amount, weight, surface and displacement of water . . . or at least that practice for these judgments is more widespread among cultures than is practice for judging properties like length or time. That seems feasible. Amount and weight especially seem to be areas that meet Price-Williams' criteria (1961, 1962) for good task performance: a variety of actions for practice and a high value placed on the accuracy of judgment.

We would also have to argue that cultures differ more among themselves in the practice they provide in mental as against physical shuffling. That also seems feasible. There are almost certainly culture and class differences in attitudes towards impulsive or unnecessary action, in the number of times that a child is told: "You didn't have to do it that way, or you didn't have to ask me that; you could have worked it out." Formal schooling is very likely to be another source of differences in restraints on unnecessary or impulsive action, and of differences in amount of time spent constructing things, putting them together and taking them apart, or matching a drawn shape — often schematic — against the memory of an object. There is a world of difference, as McFie (1961) points out, between the American or British middle-class child who has played with "shapies" and jig-saw puzzles, and the child who has few construction toys, or toys at all, and who sees few diagrams or schematic representations of things. The Nepalese children referred to, for example, "use no other kind of map; they do not use drawings or spatial representations at all (except for records of land ownership, which does not change very frequently), and the lack of spatial models may be very natural" (Dart and Pradhan, 1967, p. 653). Vernon's Eskimo boys, however, are a reminder that "familiarity with the spatial products of white civilization" (1966, p. 193) is not a necessary condition for developing spatial skills and that the road to a set of nicely specific ties between skills and experiences is likely to be a long one.

One last remark about ties between skills and experiences: If the ties are likely to be so specific, how is it that so often one cultural group is poorer than another on a large number of tasks? And is the overall goal to be simply a long list of specific ties? For such questions, Ferguson (1954, 1956) offers a provocative argument. There is, he argues, considerable transfer among skills, and the lack of one which normally opens the road to developing several others can easily create a picture of generally lower performance. If we can ever identify such cornerstone skills, or firm hierarchies of skills, then the task of describing how differences in skill develop is likely to become much easier.

References

Bruner, J. S., R. Olver and P. M. Greenfield. *Studies in Cognitive Growth.* New York: Wiley, 1966.

Dart, F. E. and P. L. Pradhan. Cross-cultural teaching of science. *Science,* 1967, *155,* 649–656.

Ferguson, G. On learning and human ability. *Canadian Journal of Psychology,* 1954, *8,* 95–112.

————. On transfer and the abilities of man. *Canadian Journal of Psychology.* 1956, *10,* 121–131.

Goodnow, J. J. A test of milieu differences with some of Piaget's tasks. *Psychological Monographs,* 1962, *76,* No. 36 (Whole No. 555).

————. Problems in research on culture and thought. In D. Elkind and John H. Flavell (eds.). *Studies in Cognitive Development: Essays in honor of Jean Piaget.* New York: Oxford University Press, 1969.

———— and G. Bethon. Piaget's tasks: The effects of schooling and intelligence. *Child Development,* 1966, *37,* 573–582.

Hanfmann, E. A study of personal patterns in an intellectual performance. *Character & Personality*, 1941, 9, 315–325.

Havighurst, R. J., M. K. Gunther and I. E. Pratt. Environment and the Draw-a-Man Test: The performance of Indian children. *Journal of Abnormal and Social Psychology*, 1946, 41, 50–63.

Jahoda, G. Geometric illusions and environment: A study in Ghana. *British Journal of Psychology*, 1966, 57, 193–199.

Lesser, G. S., G. Fifer and D. H. Clark. Mental abilities of children from different social groups and cultural groups. *Monographs of the Society for Research in Child Development*, 1965, 30, Whole No. 102.

McFie, J. The effect of education on African performance on a group of intellectual tests. *British Journal of Educational Psychology*, 1961, 31, 232–240.

Maistriaux, R. La sous-évolution des noirs d'Afrique. Sa nature – ses causes – ses remèdes. *Revue de Psychologie des Peuples*, 1955, 10, 167–189, 397–456.

Mandler, G. Response factors in human learning. *Psychological Review*, 1954, 61, 235–244.

Nissen, H. W., S. Machover and E. F. Kinder. A study of performance tests given to a group of native African Negro children. *British Journal of Psychology*, 1935, 25, 308–355.

Peluffo, N. Les notions de conservation et de causalité chez les enfants prévenant de différents milieux physiques et socio-culturels. *Archives de Psychologie*, 1962, 38, 75–90.

————. La nozione di conservazione del volume e le operazioni di combinazione come indici di sviluppo del pensiero operatorio in soggetti appartenenti ad ambienti fisici e socioculturali diversi. *Rivista di Psicologia Sociale*, 1964, 11, 99–132.

Piaget, J. and B. Inhelder. *The Child's Conception of Space*. New York: Norton, 1967.

Porteus, S. D. *The Psychology of Primitive People*. New York: Longmans, Green, 1931.

Price-Williams, D. R. A study concerning concepts of conservation of quantities among primitive children. *Acta psychologica*, 1961, 18, 297–305.

————. Abstract and concrete modes of classification in a primitive society. *British Journal of Educational Psychology*, 1962, 32, 50–61.

———— and W. Gordon. "Manipulation and Conservation: A Study of Children from Pottery-Making Families in Mexico." Unpublished paper, 1968.

Richelle, M. Étude génétique de l'intelligence manipulatoire chez des enfants africains à l'aide des dispositifs de Rey. *International Journal of Psychology*, 1966, 1, 273–287.

Segall, M. H., D. T. Campbell and M. J. Herskovits. *The Influence of Culture on Visual Perception*. New York: Bobbs-Merrill, 1966.

Siegel, I. E. and E. Mermelstein. Effects of nonschooling on Piagetian tasks of conservation. Paper presented at APA meeting, September, 1965.

Sherman, J. A. Problem of sex differences in space perception and aspects of intellectual functioning. *Psychological Review*, 1967, 4, 290–299.

Vernon, P. E. Environmental handicaps and intellectual development. *British Journal of Educational Psychology*, 1965, 35, 1–12, 117–126.

————. Educational and intellectual development among Canadian Indians and Eskimos. *British Journal of Educational Psychology*, 1966, 18, 79–91, 186–195.

On Cross-Cultural Studies of
Perceptual Differences

This paper has two goals: to report on the results of a cross-cultural comparison of susceptibility to optical illusion, and to discuss a problem in applied epistemology. . . . First I shall present evidence of substantial cultural differences in a basic psychological process. This evidence will be presented confidently, as though there were no methodological problems. And I do, in fact, believe these to be "real" differences, i.e., potentially demonstrable by a large variety of methods. Next I shall present the practical efforts which we took to ensure optimal communication of the task, and our means of sifting out instances where the task was misunderstood. With these concrete illustrations before us, I shall ask the more general question: How can we discriminate between misunderstanding and disagreement? How can we tell when we are communicating well enough to know that we see things differently?

ETHNIC DIFFERENCES IN OPTICAL ILLUSION

These are preliminary results from a wide-reaching cooperative effort started in 1956 [1] and soon to be presented in monographic detail elsewhere. [2] The study began as a debate between the late Professor Melville

Abridged and reprinted from "Distinguishing Differences of Perception from Failures of Communication in Cross-Cultural Studies," in *Cross-Cultural Understanding: Epistemology in Anthropology*, edited by F. S. C. Northrop and Helen H. Livingston. Copyright 1964 by the Wenner-Gren Foundation for Anthropological Research, Incorporated. Reprinted by permission of Harper & Row, Publishers.

The research reported in this paper has been supported by the Program of African Studies, Northwestern University, the late Melville J. Herskovits, Director.

[1] Herskovits, Melville J., Donald T. Campbell, and Marshall H. Segall, A *Cross-Cultural Study of Perception* (Evanston, Ill.: The Program of African Studies, Northwestern University, 1956). (Instruction manual and test items.)

[2] Segall, Marshall A., Donald T. Campbell, and Melville J. Herskovits, "Cultural differences in the perception of geometric illusions," *Science*, vol. 139, 1963, 769–771; *The Influence of Culture on Visual Perception* (Indianapolis: Bobbs-Merrill, 1966).

Herskovits and myself. Herskovits had long been an articulate advocate of cultural relativism.[3] While sympathetic to this perspective, I argued that cultural relativism presumed the biological homogeneity of culture-learning man, and that this biological homogeneity would include the basic perceptual and learning processes. On the basis of experience in Africa, Herskovits was quite sure we would find differences in visual perception. As it turned out, he was right, and fortunately so, for differences are more fun to report than samenesses.

There were, of course, good psychological as well as anthropological grounds for expecting differences. As we stated in the test manual:[4]

> Not only will the findings be of interest for those concerned with the comparative study of culture, [but] they will also contribute to the theory of perception, particularly with respect to the role of experience. Currently there are a number of lines of development in the theory of visual perception which create a new interest in the nativist-empiricist controversy. There is new evidence which emphasizes the role of early visual experience in setting the base for adult perceptual processes. Clearly relevant to this topic would be findings on perceptual illusions among peoples whose visual worlds are quite different from that of the European.
>
> If cross-cultural differences in extent of illusion are found, the initial explanatory effort would be focused on differences in the usual visual environment. For this reason, it is very important that details of the visual environment of each group be recorded on the form provided. Such details include the typical form of houses, the maximum distance at which objects are typically viewed, whether or not vistas over land or water occur, typical games, skills, artistic training, and other aspects of culture that might affect habits of inference from line drawings.
>
> Two cultural factors are apt to be of particular significance for this investigation. In the carpentered Western world such a great proportion of artifacts are rectangular that the habit of interpreting obtuse and acute angles as rectangular surfaces extended in space is a very useful one. Such an inference pattern would generate many of the line illusions here tested. In a culture where rectangles did not dominate, this habit might be absent. Similarly, elliptical retinal images are interpreted as circles extended in the third dimension. This in-

    [3] Herskovits, Melville J., *Man and His Works* (New York: Knopf, 1948), pp. 61–78; "Tender and tough-minded anthropology and the study of values in culture," *Southwestern Journal of Anthropology*, vol. 7, 1951, pp. 22–31; "Some further comments on cultural relativism," *American Anthropologist*, vol. 60, 1958, pp. 266–273.
    [4] Herskovits, Melville J., Donald T. Campbell, and Marshall H. Segall, A *Cross-Cultural Study of Perception, op. cit.*, note 1, pp. 2–3.

ference pattern might be absent where objects are truly elliptical in cross-section.

Another cultural factor which might be related to illusions is two-dimensional representation of three-dimensional objects. Perspective drawing is a most pervasive feature of Euroamerican culture. It is a substantial feature of the visual world from childhood on. Children in this culture from a very early age attempt to make representations of this kind themselves. The techniques or conventions involved may be related to the habits of inference which some illusions illustrate.

These and other considerations lie behind the inventory of the visual environment which is included with the respondents' record sheets.

Our test figures were assembled in a compact 5 by 7 inch booklet of 71 pages printed on washable Eastman paper. Professor Herskovits distributed these booklets and the accompanying record sheets to volunteer collaborators in Africa and elsewhere. Over the past six years some 20 ethnologists have cooperated in administering the booklets to some 1800 persons. In 1960, Marshall Segall, the psychologist who actually designed the booklet, spent a year in Africa and there administered the tests to some 350 persons. An anthropology graduate student administered the tests in a door-to-door survey of 200 persons in Evanston, Illinois (U.S.A.), to provide our main European culture sample. Figures 1 and 2 show results for adults on the two illusions providing the largest differences. . . .

The Müller-Lyer data of Figure 1, the differences found by Allport and Pettigrew,[5] and the parallel results from the Sander parallelogram illusion in the present study lend themselves to an explanation in terms of the visual environment which we call the "carpentered-world" hypothesis. What we mean by this is perhaps most easily shown by the Sander parallelogram (Figure 3). In this illusion, the bias is to judge the left diagonal as longer. In the dominant theory of the optical illusion tradition,[6] this bias is understandable as a tendency to perceive the nonorthogonal parallelogram as a rectangular surface extended in space. In the carpentered Western culture such an inference habit has great ecological validity.[7] For we live in a culture in which straight lines abound, and in which per-

[5] Allport, Gordon W., and Thomas F. Pettigrew, "Cultural influence on the perception of movement: The trapezoidal illusion among the Zulus," *Journal of Abnormal Psychology*, vol. 55, 1957, pp. 104–113.

[6] Sanford, E. C., *A Course in Experimental Psychology, Part I: Sensation and Perception* (Boston: Heath, 1908).

[7] Brunswik, Egon, *Perception and the Representative Design of Psychological Experiments* (2nd ed.). (Berkeley: University of California, 1956).

FIGURE 1. Müller-Lyer Illusion

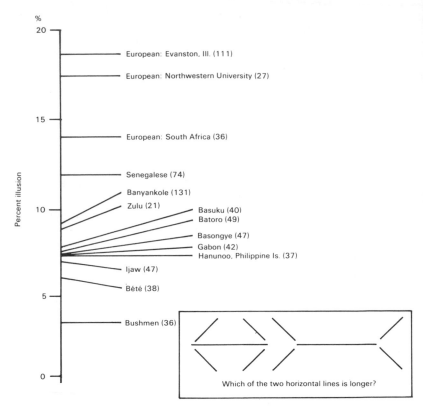

Note: The percent illusion is the percentage by which the arrowhead horizontal (left in the illustration) exceeds the tailed horizontal (right) when they are judged equal. The number of cases upon which the mean is based is indicated in the parentheses (adult data only). Most of the larger gaps are statistically significant; e.g., both the South African Europeans and the Senegalese differ significantly from all other groups, as do the Bushmen. The Banyankole differ significantly from the Ijaw.

haps 90 per cent of the acute and obtuse angles formed on our retina by the straight lines of our visual field are realistically interpretable as right angles extended in space. For those living where man-made structures are a small portion of the visual environment, and where such structures are constructed without benefit of saw, plane, straight edge, tape measure, carpenter's square, spirit level, chalk line, surveyor's sight, and plumb bob, both straight lines and "real" right angles are a rarity. As a result, the inference habit of interpreting all acute and obtuse angles as "really"

FIGURE 2. The Horizontal-Vertical Illusion.

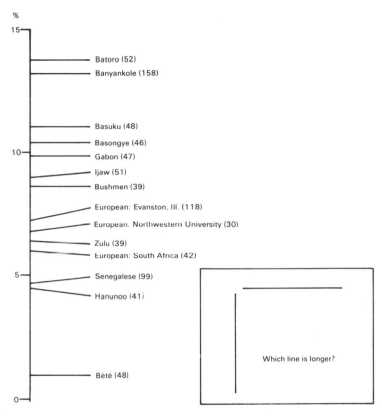

Note: The percent illusion is the extent to which the horizontal exceeds the vertical when the two are judged as equal. With regard to group differences, the Banyankole are significantly different from all lower groups, the Basuku from the Ijaw, the Evanstonians from the Ijaw and the Senegalese, the Bété from all other groups, and so on.

right angles extended in space would not be learned (or, if innate, would be extinguished). . . .

The interpretation of the illusion as a learned habit of inference is complicated by the frequently confirmed age trends for the illusion within the European culture.[8] Data from a separate sample of Evanston children,

[8] Pintner, Rudolf, and Margaret M. Anderson, "The Müller-Lyer illusion with children and adults," *Journal of Experimental Psychology*, vol. 1, 1916, pp. 200–

FIGURE 3. Sander Parallelogram: Which of the Two
Diagonals, *a* or *b*, Is Longer?

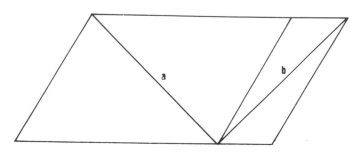

but using our same booklets,[9] show the following progression in mean per cent of illusion for age groups from 4 years to 9 years: 27%, 23%, 22%, 20%, 19%, and 17%. This age trend is confirmed for almost all cultures, although culture-to-culture differences are in general larger for children than for adults. The simplest application of our theory would have expected European adults, having had the longest influence on the culture, to have had more illusion than European children. The outcome is thus puzzling and complicating.

. . . The stimulus value of puzzling cross-cultural data is fully as great as that of well-understood data, and I should perhaps attempt no further explanation. However, my favored resolution at the moment is this: European children have fully mastered visual-locomotory coordination by the age of two or three. The inference habits useful in reaching for objects and locomoting around them are well established by that age. Soon thereafter they have also mastered the European inference conventions of *reading* two-dimensional drawings in terms of three-dimensional solids and displays. At this stage they are naive realists, unaware of the sensory data from which their real-object inferences have been constructed. Further maturation makes them more analytic, with greater access to the sensorial given, more able to hold the inferential processes in abeyance so as to report on the specific stimulus components. Supporting this development of analytic skills is learning the transmitter's role in the communication of three-dimensional content in two-dimensional drawing.

. . . Thus from a learned peak of acute-obtuse-inference illusion, our European children gradually and in part unlearn it or learn to hold it

210; Wohlwill, Joachin F., "Developmental studies of perception," *Psychological Bulletin*, vol. 57, 1960, pp. 249–288.

[9] Campbell, Donald T., and Solveig Cedarloo Wenar, *Perceptual and Cognitive Bias in Children* (in preparation).

partially in abeyance for certain tasks. The habitant of an uncarpentered world has never learned the inference-habit to so strong a degree. The notion that cultural differences in perception are to a considerable part tied up with our European conventions and great experience with regard to the two-dimensional representation of three-dimensional messages is supported by Hudson's [10] study of the dramatic misunderstandings which persons from uncarpentered worlds can make of European perspective drawings, and of the influence of both education and cultural isolation upon such inferences for both Africans and Europeans living in South Africa. . . .

Figure 2 shows the results of a quite different illusion in which the error is to exaggerate the length of the vertical line. It provides a quite different ordering of peoples, and new puzzles of interpretation. In our Evanston children's data for the horizontal-vertical no age trends at all are present. For the noncarpentered peoples, insofar as there are trends, children tend to have more of the illusion. I probably do not have as good an interpretation of these data as for the Müller-Lyer. Again, . . . we can profit from interesting differences even though they remain unexplained. However, here also the students of optical illusions in explaining the normal (European) case provided a basis for predicting cultural differences. Woodworth [11] states the theory concisely: "A short vertical line in a drawing may represent a relatively long horizontal line extending away from the observer. The horizontal-vertical illusion can be explained by supposing the vertical to represent such a foreshortened horizontal line." Sanford [12] cites Hering [13] and Lipps [14] as hypothesizing "an unconscious allowance for foreshortening, acquired through preponderating experience with squares lying in planes inclined with regard to the plane of vision."

Consider a man who stands on a flat plain, into which criss-crossed furrows have been plowed. Compare the retinal extensions of furrows which cross his line of sight from left to right with those which extend away from him. Relatively, those that extend away from him are much more foreshortened. They have a much shorter retinal extension per

[10] Hudson, W., "Pictorial depth perception in sub-cultural groups in Africa," *Journal of Social Psychology*, vol. 52, 1960, pp. 183–208.

[11] Woodworth, Robert S., *Experimental Psychology* (New York: Holt, Rinehart and Winston, 1938), p. 645.

[12] Sanford, E. C., *A Course in Experimental Psychology*, *op. cit.*, note 6, p. 238.

[13] Hering, Ewald, *Beiträge zur Physiologie* (Leipzig: Englemann, 1861–1864), p. 355.

[14] Lipps, Teodore, "Aesthetische Faktoren der Raumanschauung" in *Beiträge zur Psychologie und Physiologie der Sinnesorgane* (Hamburg and Leipzig: Voss, 1891), pp. 219–307.

ground-measured yard. Further, the furrows extending away from him along his line of regard are represented on the retina as vertical lines. For such a person, there might be great ecological validity in the inference habit of interpreting vertical linear extensions as greatly foreshortened lines in the horizontal plane extending away along the line of regard. Such an inference habit would have less validity for a person living in a rain forest in which the largest real surfaces in the visual regard were in fact vertical and in which tree trunks and hanging vines were the commonest source of vertical lines. Here the foreshortening of what comes to be represented as the visual vertical would be absent, the inference habits different, and the susceptibility to the horizontal-vertical illusion less. Canyon dwellers should be similar.

On such a continuum of environments, it might be reasonable to assume that the European indoors-dwellers, for whom vertical walls are as frequent as floors, would be intermediate. As an interpretation of Figure 2, it is comforting to note that the Bété, at the bottom, have a jungle environment, and that the Batoro and Banyankole live in high open country. But in detail, the data do not fit well. The Bushmen of the flat deserts should be at the top; the Zulu should be much higher, the Gabon, Ijaw, and Basongye much lower, and so on. If this ecology is a factor, as I do believe it is, it is obviously only one of many factors. . . .

PRACTICAL EFFORTS TO ASSURE TASK COMPREHENSION

The control details which I am going to discuss are products of common-sense considerations. They are routine mediational details which are usually compressed into fine print or left out of research reports altogether. Yet in such operational specifics lie the frontiers of epistemology. On what grounds does an experimenter decide whether an unexpected recording is a new phenomenon or an instrumentation error? What model of the philosophy of science will account for the substantial portion of the "data" which every experimenter disregards and fails to report?

Consider an extreme form of our cross-cultural task: Suppose that we parachuted an anthropologist and a test booklet into a totally isolated New Guinea tribe and that the anthropologist had first to learn the language without the help of an interpreter. The process of language learning would then become a part of the operations which we would have to detail. It would become obvious that no person ever learns another's language perfectly; that the existence of "interpreters" should not be taken for granted; that here is a problematic situation in which the cues and presumptions of communication need to be specified. It turns out that the anthropologist's main cue for achieved communication is similarity between the response of the other to a stimulus and the response which he himself would make. Disagreement turns out to be a sign of communication failure. How then can disagreement on an optical illusion test item be taken instead as a difference in perceiving the world? This is the focal problem justifying the somewhat tedious presentation of the administrative details in what follows.

Comprehension Checks

The instructions to the anthropologists read in part:

> It is essential that the data be collected under as standardized conditions as possible, and that all deviations from these procedures be recorded. The location and dimensions of the working area should permit display of the figures at a distance of four feet from the respondent, at his eye-level, and in a plane perpendicular to his line of vision. Lighting conditions should permit comfortable viewing of the drawings.
>
> Once rapport has been established, the experimenter should, insofar as cultural and semantic factors permit, conform to the following procedure:
>
> Have respondent sit in appropriate position. Instruct him as follows:
>
> "I am going to show you some drawings and ask you questions about them." Show page 1 (Figure 4). "What is the color of this line?" Point to red line. "What is the color of this line?" Point to

FIGURE 4. Test Item 1 from the Booklet (Comprehension Check)

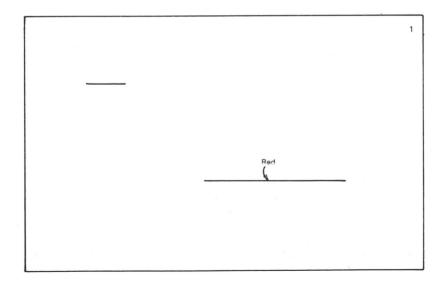

black line. "Which line is longer, the red or the black one?" *Note*: in all of the comparisons, the respondent, if possible, is to be forced to choose one line as longer, equal judgments not being allowed, unless rapport is seriously threatened. If equal judgments have to be accepted, modify the record sheets accordingly. Show page 2 (Figure 5). "Which of these two red lines is longer?" Record. Repeat page 2 procedure with pages 3 and 4 [Figures 6 and 7]. (Pages 1 through 4 are intended as comprehension checks. If the responses to these drawings are not correct, further efforts with that respondent may be considered a waste. If he demonstrates comprehension, the session should be continued.)

FIGURE 5. Second Inspection Page (Comprehension Check)

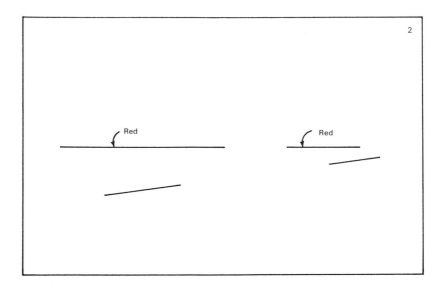

Thus on these first four items, if the respondent did not respond as the anthropologist would have, it was assumed that translation or comprehension or cooperation had failed. Yet on the subsequent items, we are prepared to accept such discrepancies in response as signs of differences in perception. What canons of applied epistemology are implicitly being invoked? The fourth check item is particularly relevant, for it is in the form of a Müller-Lyer drawing. How do we know the illusion is not causing the wrong response? It would take a 500 per cent illusion to produce it, while the strongest of the test items designed for scoring is 50 per cent. We find it incredible that cultures or persons exist for whom the

FIGURE 6. Third Task Page (Comprehension Check)

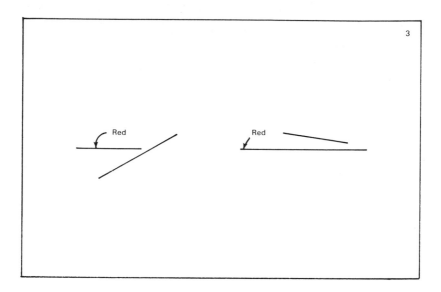

FIGURE 7. Fourth Task Page (Comprehension Check)

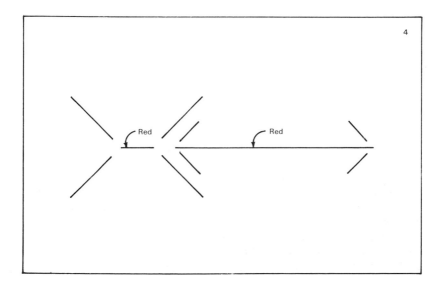

illusion is that strong. We prefer to say that they did not understand the task or were unwilling to cooperate or were blind and guessing. Are the grounds for this incredulity epistemologically legitimate? Or are they merely evidence of the ethnocentric bigotry of a Westerner?

Optimizing the Communicability of the Drawings

In the traditional form of the illusion, the parts of the drawing are all connected, and one asks, "Which horizontal line is the longer?" Such an assignment involves a number of European linguistic conventions which are unlikely to be widely shared. The term *line* itself may have no counterpart in many languages. Or, if it does it seems doubtful that the counterpart would imply only straight line, with an implicit end boundary where bends occur. To make sure that the comparison was not one of total figures including the distracting arrowheads and feathers, to make more certainly "thinglike" the things being compared, we separated the parts, producing a discontinuous line. We further printed the lines to be compared in red and the distractors in black. We could now ask, "Which of the two red lines is longer?" no longer needing to designate horizontal. We knew that these changes weakened the illusion substantially, but we felt that the increased certainty of communication was more important. . . .

Multiple Items in Mixed Order

When a respondent does not understand an assignment or does not wish to comply, he frequently prefers pseudocompliance to outright refusal or admission of ignorance. Responses under these conditions are typically not random, but instead are characterized by irrelevant regularities. Thus a noncomprehender might always pick the one on the right or the line with the arrowheads or might alternate left and right, possibly changing his rule of response halfway through, and so on. We wanted such irrelevant sources of order not to be confounded with the regularities of interest. For this reason, we represented each illusion by a number of separate drawings. The two types of figures were alternated randomly from left to right. The order of items was mixed in terms of degree of difference between the comparison lines. The ten Müller-Lyer pages had the following order-characteristics, in terms of the location of the tailed figure on the right or the left, and the percentage by which the arrowheaded line exceeded the tailed line in length: L, 30%; L, 0%; R, 20%; L, 25%; L, 5%; L, 40%; R, 45%; R, 10%; L, 50%; R, 15%; R, 35%; R, −5%. Because the orders were set down at random, the raw data sheets were nearly impossible to interpret. For analysis, we transformed the data into an orderly arrangement, using a 1 to indicate an illusion-supported response (i.e., choosing the tailed line as longer). Typical response patterns would look like this:

Item Illusion %	−5,	0,	5,	10,	15,	20,	25,	30,	35,	40,	45,	50
Presentation order	12	2	5	8	10	3	4	1	11	6	7	9
Illusion-supported												
response	R	L	L	R	R	R	L	L	R	L	R	L
Typical Evan-												
stonian	1	1	1	1	1	1	0	0	0	0	0	0
Typical Bushman	1	1	0	0	0	0	0	0	0	0	0	0

Where the data turn out to have consistent patterns of this sort, the patterned orderliness of both sets convinces us that the task is comprehended and that the two persons differ in their perceptions. But had the two rows been of this form:

Evanstonian	1	1	1	1	1	1	1	1	1	1	1	1
Bushman	0	0	0	0	0	0	0	0	0	0	0	0

our interpretation would have been less decisive. A most plausible hypothesis would have been that both misunderstood the task but in different ways. Had we still felt that visual perception was the explanation, we would have wanted to add many more test items at both ends until we had the two patterns agreeing at both extremes.

We had no such cases as these last two. But we did have cases that could not be interpreted, for which no statement of threshold seemed possible. Here are some Evanston cases:

1	1	0	0	0	1	0	1	1	1	1	1
1	0	0	0	0	1	1	1	0	1	1	0
1	0	0	1	1	0	1	0	0	0	0	0

For such nonscale types, our preferred interpretation was failure of communication or instability so extreme that perceptual performance could not be summarized. In the data reported in Figures 1 and 2, such cases have been eliminated. In borderline instances, the decision becomes arbitrary. For the analyses presented, a very strict rule has been used—only perfect cases and cases with a single reversal, i.e., cases like these:

Perfect	1	1	1	0	0	0	0	0	0	0	0	0
	1	1	1	1	1	0	0	0	0	0	0	0
	1	1	0	0	0	0	0	0	0	0	0	0

One reversal	1	1	1	0	1	0	0	0	0	0	0	0
	1	1	0	1	0	0	0	0	0	0	0	0
	1	1	1	0	1	1	1	0	0	0	0	0

By these strict standards, 10 per cent of the Evanston cases were lost, 22 per cent of the Bushmen, 18 per cent of the European South African, 9 per cent of the Basongye, 65 per cent of the Zulu, and so on.

Discarding cases is dirty business, rightfully suspect.[15] Leaving in obvious error, in varying amounts from culture to culture, is also bad. I do believe we take the path most common to science (although not to social science) by eliminating the nonscale, communication breakdown cases. Note a special problem of test design: *random* responding (or responding to irrelevancies) can often produce a *systematic* bias. It will, for example, make a person appear more stupid on an intelligence test. Because of the location of our items relative to the general illusion threshold, random responding would lead to an increase in the number of illusion responses, particularly for a low-illusion group. As it turned out, none of the good cases produced 1s on the three extreme items (40, 45, and 50 per cent). These three items thus come to serve as additions to the four comprehension checks. Similarly all cases gave a 1 to the −5 per cent item, where, indeed, this was the correct response, the illusion effect being combined with a true difference in the same direction.

Fortunately, the decision to discard cases is not a crucial one in the present instance. The percentage of lost cases shows no correlation with the magnitude of the illusion ($r = -.04$, N of 16 cultures). Further, within all groups, when all cases are pooled, there is a steady decrease in the percentage of 1s as one moves from the −5 per cent item toward the 50 per cent item. This recurrence of a common pattern assures us that in general there has been a communication of the task, plus an over-all similarity in function. And when we use all cases, scoring even the most errorful by the number of 1 responses, the cultural differences persist in essentially the same form and level of statistical significance.

EPISTEMOLOGICAL CONSIDERATIONS

We must not underestimate the fundamental nature of these practical problems and research decisions. *In essence, we could only observe differences in perception because these differences were small. Had any of our groups perceived in a radically different way from ourselves, we could not have determined that fact.* We could not have distinguished between

---

[15] See Kruskal, William H., "Some remarks on wild observations," *Technometrics*, vol. 2, 1960, pp. 1–3, for an introduction to the technical literature on the problem.

total failure of communication and total difference in perception. In the end, it is because in great bulk we perceive alike (respond alike) that we can note small differences in perception. The total context of agreement provides the firm platform from which we can note a particular, localized discrepancy. This supporting context of agreement includes that extensive basis of similar perceptions, similar classifications of substance into re-identifiable discrete objects, which has made the learning of the other's language possible. Lacking this, communication fails. Analogously, the blind person and the color-blind person never fully learn English. But they share enough common contours and hypothesized entities to learn that they perceive differently from the rest of us.

To repeat, were a culture to perceive in a radically different way, we could not confirm communication and hence could not ascertain perceptual differences. In emphasizing this we have endorsed the tenability of a cultural and linguistic solipsism. Arthur Child, one of the very few technically trained philosophers to have examined problems raised in the sociology of knowledge,[16] in an important though obscurely published paper has demonstrated with Malinowski's data the extreme difficulty of ascertaining that the members of another culture perceive things differently.[17] But like the present writer, he does not believe these difficulties are in all instances insurmountable. . . .

Within the area of applied epistemology, our methods illustrate one important general principle: Discrepancy can be noted and interpreted only against the background of an overwhelming proportion of nondiscrepant fit, agreement, or pattern repetition. This principle is found in operation in knowledge processes as varied as binocular vision and astronomy. Again and again in science, the equivocal interpretations are available: separate entity vs. same entity changed, moved, or perceived from a different perspective. And in all such instances where the second interpretation occurs, it is made possible by the overwhelming bulk of stable nonchanging background. Consider the reidentification of a single planet on successive nights, plus the inference that the planet migrates in an eccentric backtracking manner. Had Jupiter been the only star in the sky, this might never have been documented, certainly not by a nomadic people. Had all the stars been planets, it would also have gone unascertained. Had the oscillations in the locations of the fixed stars been so great as to subtend several degrees of visual angle, the backtracking would

[16] Child, Arthur, "The theoretical possibility of the sociology of knowledge," *Ethics*, vol. 51, 1941, pp. 392–418; "On the theory of the categories," *Philosophy and Phenomenological Research*, vol. 7, 1946–1947, pp. 316–335; "The problem of truth in the sociology of knowledge," *Ethics*, vol. 58, 1947, pp. 18–34.

[17] Child, Arthur, "The sociology of perception," *Journal of Genetic Psychology*, vol. 77, 1950, pp. 293–303.

not have been observed. It was the recurrent "fixedness" of 99.9 per cent of the stars which made the wanderings of the few planets interpretable as such. Similarly for binocular resolution, as illustrated in the stereoscope. If the great bulk of the detail in the two stereoscope pictures is similar, then minor discrepancies provide a gain in three-dimensional inference; the hypothesis becomes tenable that each eye is seeing the "same" thing from different angles. If all details differ, binocular resolution does not take place, and specific discrepancies are unused and unnoted. The more general point has been well made by Lorenz,[18] and I have expressed it in greater detail elsewhere.[19]

ANALOGOUS PROBLEMS IN DIAGNOSING ASPECTS OF CULTURE

A naive realistic approach to anthropology would assume that cultural differences were objectively directly available for any and all observers to "see." There would be no awareness of methodological problems, no recognition of the problematic character of knowing about another culture. Such an innocent epistemology could survive neither the experience of extensive fieldwork nor the comparison of interpretations between students of "the same" culture. As in other fields, the rejection of naive realism is made first by a move to complete subjectivity, to a radical empirical epistemology. At this stage, there is recognition of the fact that knowing involves the knower, is shaped by his characteristics. This recognition goes to the extreme of rejecting any other component, i.e., of denying all objectivity to knowledge. The stage of logical realism (or critical realism, or hypothetical realism, or corrigible realism) shares with radical empiricism an emphasis on the subjective relativity of all knowing. It shares with naive realism the aspiration to objective knowledge, invariant over points of observation or instruments. But it recognizes that such constructions will be fallibly known, through a process of hypothetical models only indirectly confirmed. The conditions of confirmation will never provide certainty and will often be totally lacking. From this point of view, scientific knowledge is not immediately available for the asking, but requires very special settings. . . .

[18] Lorenz, Konrad, "Gestaltwahrnehmung als Quelle wissenschaftlicher Erkenntnis," *Zeitschrift für Experimentelle und angewandte Psychologie*, vol. 6, 1959, pp. 118–165. Translated in *General Systems*, Yearbook of the Society for General Systems Research, vol. 7, 1962, pp. 37–56.

[19] Campbell, Donald T., "Methodological suggestions from a comparative psychology of knowledge processes," *Inquiry*, vol. 2, 1959, pp. 152–182; "Pattern matching as an essential in distal knowing," in K. R. Hammond (ed.), *The Psychology of Egon Brunswik* (New York: Holt, Rinehart and Winston, 1966).

The Necessity of a Base of Similarity in
Specifying Differences

The major conclusion from the optical illusion study was sort of a "postulate of impotence," that only under the very special condition of great perceptual similarity could one diagnose the particular nature of a perceptual difference; that had the differences been much greater they could not have been distinguished from total failure of communication. It is my thesis that this is not only unavoidably so for the optical illusions task, but is also so for all instances in which it has been learned that one culture differs in a specified manner from another. My methodological recommendation is that this anchoring base of similarities, usually left unconscious, be made explicit at least in methodological examples. This must remain an empty challenge without detailed analyses by anthropologists of instances in which they have successfully diagnosed specific cultural differences. . . . Informal and unreported discussions . . . provided beginning examples, however. Professor Ehrenfels pointed out * that the Tibetans stick out their tongues to symbolize friendly greeting, whereas for Europeans, the gesture symbolizes contempt. It is argued here that this diagnosis would have been impossible without a similarity in the meaning of the context of behaviors, such as the fighting or friendly sharing that followed. Ehrenfels also described the initial conditions in which he observed that the Bulgarians indicate assent by a horizontal wagging of the head, not a vertical one. As a traveler asking if indeed this road leads to such a city, his respondents indicated that he was correct both verbally and by head gesture. Had they used only the head gesture he would not have had the context of similarity in which to anchor the striking conclusion that the head gesture was being used in reverse.

Professor León-Portilla in conversation described the great difficulty in determining the meaning of the Aztec words for body parts because of the different conceptual segmenting involved. He agrees that the successful translation achieved (the successful instances of learning *how* they classified *differently*) was only made possible by the fact that many of the body-parts-segments were conceived similarly, including classifying human protoplasm into person-segments and within these the distinctions among arm, leg, head, and body. He reports that a similar situation exists in the study of Aztec religious concepts. The great array of similar religious concepts . . . makes possible the comprehension of certain religious concepts quite foreign to our way of thinking. . . .

* [Ed. note: This reference may be found in the original text by Northrop and Livingston.]

Identifying "The Same" Trait in Different Cultures

A recurrent problem in the comparative study of culture is that of identifying corresponding cultural items in two societies.[20] Analysis of this problem shows that it again requires the anchoring of the specific by a context. And concomitantly a limitation is placed upon its successful achievement. As Professor Northrop has repeatedly made explicit, our thinking on such matters may be biased by the carry-over of the atomistic radical empiricism of British associationism. In this instance it leads us to the anticipation that culture-elements are more certainly identifiable than culture complexes. The reverse is in fact the case.

An analogy may help. Consider the task of identifying corresponding dots of black on which two copies of a newspaper photograph are built. The task is impossible if the dots are taken singly, but becomes more possible the larger the area of the photographs available. Insofar as particular elements can be matched it is only because of the prior matching of the wholes. Similarly for matching elements between languages. A given word cannot usually be translated by a single word when it is in isolation, but can be when it is a part of a sentence or a speech. A paragraph is more accurately translated than a word. To the extent that the translation of a word is anchored, it is because the paragraph of which it is a part has been successfully translated.

In a similar way, it takes acquaintance with the larger cultural context to identify the appropriate parallel or classificatory assignment of any particular cultural item. This context dependence correspondingly removes the possibility of certainty and makes ever present the possibility of erroneously alleging cultural differences as a result of mismatching.

Triangulation Through the Own-Culture Bias of Observers

The achievement of useful hypothetically realistic constructs in a science requires multiple methods focused on the diagnosis of the same construct from independent points of observation, through a kind of triangulation.[21] This is required because the sense data or meter readings are now

---

[20] Sears, R. R., "Transcultural variables and conceptual equivalence," in B. Kaplan (ed.), *Studying Personality Cross-Culturally* (New York: Harper and Row, 1961), pp. 445–456; Norbeck, E., D. E. Walker, and M. Cohen, "The interpretation of data: Puberty rites," *American Anthropologist*, vol. 64, 1962, pp. 463–483.

[21] Campbell, Donald T., and Donald W. Fiske, "Convergent and discriminant validation by the multitrait-multimethod matrix," *Psychological Bulletin*, vol. 56, 1959, pp. 81–105; "Methodological suggestions from a comparative psychology of knowledge processes," *op. cit.*, note 19.

understood as the result of a transaction in which both the observer (or meter) and the object of investigation contribute to the form of the data. With a single observation at hand, it is impossible to separate the subjective and the objective component. When, however, observations through separate instruments and separate vantage points can be matched as reflecting "the same" objects, then it is possible to separate out the components in the data due to observer (instrument) and observed. It turns out that this disentangling process requires both multiple observers (methods) and multiple, dissimilar, objects of study.[22]

Applied to the study of the philosophy of a culture, this implies that our typical one-observer one-culture study is inherently ambiguous. For any given feature of the report it is equivocal whether or not it is a trait of the observer or a trait of the object observed. To correct this the ideal paradigm might be as shown in Figure 8 (a). In the most general model, two anthropologists from different cultures would each study a third and fourth culture. One of the four ethnographies resulting, the common attributes in ethnographies 1 and 3 not shared with 2 and 4 could be attributed to ethnographer A, the common attributes in 2 and 4 not elsewhere present to ethnographer B. Looking at row consistencies in the figure, the common attributes in ethnographies 1 and 2 not present in 3 and 4 could be attributed to culture C as "objectively" known. Attributes common to all four ethnographies are inherently ambiguous, interpretable as either shared biases on the part of the ethnographers or shared culture on the part of the societies studied. Note the desirability

FIGURE 8. Multiple- Ethnography Schedules to Extricate the Ethnographer-Contributed Content from the Culture- Studied Content

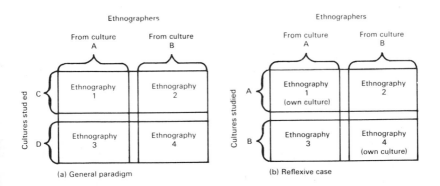

(a) General paradigm   (b) Reflexive case

[22] Campbell, Donald T., and Donald W. Fiske, "Convergent and discriminant validation by the multitrait-multimethod matrix," *op. cit.*, note 21.

in this regard of comparing ethnologists with as widely differing cultural backgrounds as possible. Insofar as the ethnologists come from the same culture, the replication of results becomes more a matter of reliability than validity, as these terms are used in discussions of psychological tests. Were such a study carried out by using four ethnographers, two from each ethnographer cultures A and B, studying separate villages of cultures C and D to avoid interference and collusion, then the attributes unique to any one of the ethnographies would be attributable to an equivocal pool of village specificities within its culture, to personality specifics of the ethnographer, and to interaction of specific ethnographer culture and studied culture. (If only one ethnologist were used from each culture, and if each of the two studied in turn the same village in the target cultures, then the features unique to any one of the four ethnographies would be equivocally due to ethnographer-culture interactions, time-order effects in which the ethnographer reacted differently to his second culture, time-order effects in which the society reacted differently to the second student of it, historical trends, and interactions among these.) The presence of these indeterminacies should neither be suppressed nor be allowed to overshadow the great gains in understanding which such multiple ethnographer studies would introduce.

While multiplicity of both ethnographer cultures and cultures studied is ideal, it would also be a great gain to achieve only the upper half of Figure 8 (a), i.e., two ethnographer cultures focused on the study of a single target culture. In all such triangulations, we again face the paradox of inability to use differences when these so dominate as to make it impossible to match the corresponding aspects of the reports being compared. The necessity of this common denominator provides one justification for Hockett's advocacy . . . of including material and behavioral cultural details even in ethnographies focused on the determination of the philosophy of the cultures.

Another version of the multiethnographer, multiple-target design is that in which two cultures study each other, as diagrammed in Figure 8 (b). Usually the focus is on ethnographies 2 and 3, A's report on B and B's report on A. Implicitly, however, A's description of A and B's description of B are contained as bases of reference. There is probably some scientific value to be gained from such reports, even at the level of mutual stereotype sets or of reputational consensus from neighboring peoples.[23] Once the evaluative component (each tribe viewing itself as

[23] Campbell, Donald T., and Robert A. LeVine, "A proposal for cooperative cross-cultural research on ethnocentrism," *Journal of Conflict Resolution*, vol. 5, 1961, pp. 86, 91.

best) is removed, such mutual stereotype sets show remarkable agreement in confirming the direction of group differences.

SUMMARY

Evidence has been presented demonstrating wide cultural differences in susceptibility to optical illusions. Inspection of the methodological details shows that the demonstration of these specific differences is dependent upon a great preponderance of similarity in perceptual processes. Had the cultures differed in all aspects, the differences in perception could not have been distinguished from failures of communication.

Analogously, it is asserted that a similar limitation exists in the description of cultural differences of other sorts. The recommendation is made that reports on cultural differences make more explicit the cultural communalities which provided the contextual anchoring for the interpretation of differences.

The general methodological theme of contextual matching as the basis for identifying particulars is also applied to the problems of identifying comparable culture traits in cross-cultural studies and removing the bias of the ethnographer's own culture in multiethnographer studies.

11   F. KENNETH BERRIEN

Familiarity, Mirror Imaging and Social Desirability in Stereotypes: Japanese versus Americans

In a previous study (Abate and Berrien, 1967) it was inferred that familiarity with an ethnic or national group tended to increase the validity of the stereotype. In that study Japanese students had more valid stereotypes

Reprinted from *International Journal of Psychology — Journal International de Psychologie*, 1969, Vol. 4, No. 3, pp. 207–215. By permission of IUPS and Dunod, Publisher, Paris, France.
This study was made possible through Contract Nonr-4806 between East-

of Americans than vice versa, and this finding was attributed to greater exposure of Americans to the Japanese (movies, TV, tourists, army of occupation) than vice versa (cf. Taft, 1966). The present report is a further test of the familiarity hypothesis, but raises additional questions concerning the mirror image hypothesis which has been proposed by Bronfenbrenner (1961), White (1961), and Osgood (1962). In effect these two hypotheses when considered side-by-side are contradictory, or more probably, counter-balancing mechanisms, the mirror-image tending to create unreal differences between the self-image and the stereotype of another, while familiarity tending to bring the stereotype more in line with some veridical standard.

A restatement of the two hypotheses may be in order. Both White and Bronfenbrenner, largely independently, were struck with the observation that in describing Russians, Americans attributed to them various uncomplimentary characteristics which they did not see in themselves. Upon questioning Russians the same process seemed to hold, except that the Americans in Russian eyes had many of the same uncomplimentary characteristics Americans attributed to the Russians. It seemed logical to suppose that such mirror images were in part generated by the hostilities which bathed relations between these two great powers. Bronfenbrenner saw mirror-imaging as an example of the strain toward consistency that has been a theme in the various cognitive theories of Heider (1958), Festinger (1957), and Osgood (1962).

The familiarity hypothesis is straightforward. The more one knows about people of a country the more accurate will be his stereotype as measured against some veridical standard. Familiarity may occur, of course, with various degrees of hostility. Familiarity may breed contempt or friendliness. Furthermore, unlike a Rorschach inkblot or the fictitious persons described by a series of adjectives used in the impression formation studies (Asch, 1946), national or ethnic groups possess certain veridical modal characteristics, by no means true of all individuals in the group, but nonetheless typical of the group as a whole (Allport, 1954). The cognition of these characteristics is enhanced by familiarity, other conditions being equal (Prothro and Melikian, 1955). The true features of another group may be in contrast with those of the perceiver's own group.

The social desirability of the characteristics employed to describe a target group may be a third dimension in stereotypes complicating the bal-

West Center, University of Hawaii and Group Psychology Branch, O.N.R. and was prepared while the author was Senior Specialist at East-West Center. He is grateful for the excellent collaboration of Drs. Abe Arkoff, University of Hawaii, and Shinkuro Iwahara, Tokyo University of Education.

ancing effects of familiarity versus mirroring. Thus target groups including one's own which are liked may be assigned characteristics considered socially desirable by the respondents and vice versa. It thus becomes a problem to separate the effects of affect toward the target from the social desirability of the descriptive characteristics. Moreover, if the social desirability of the particular descriptive terms colors the stereotypes, it would also obscure the effects of "mirroring" and familiarity.

METHOD AND SUBJECTS

The method and subjects were essentially the same as described in Abate and Berrien (1967). Respondents were presented with descriptions of 15 kinds of behavior drawn from the Edwards Personality Preference Schedule. The phrases in each of these descriptions were drawn from EPPS items. For example, deference and orderliness were defined as follows:

> To accept the leadership of others, get suggestions from others, find out what others think, follow instructions and do what is expected, praise others, tell others that they have done a good job, conform to custom and avoid the unconventional, let others make decisions.

> To keep things neat and orderly, have written work neat and organized, make plans before starting on a difficult task, have things organized, make advance plans when taking a trip, organize details of work, keep letters and files according to some system, have meals organized and a definite time for eating, have things arranged so that they run smoothly without change.

The subjects were instructed to judge how well these descriptions fitted Americans, Japanese in general. Each national group was considered individually. The subjects were requested to select from the descriptions those two which were *very* characteristic of the national group in question, three *rather* characteristic descriptions, five *neither* characteristic nor *un*characteristic descriptions, three *rather* uncharacteristic descriptions and two *very* uncharacteristic descriptions. Thus each behavior description was judged on a 5-point scale for each national group with a forced distribution of judgments. Forcing was used because, on the basis of a pilot study, it was found that subjects tended to use only the middle scale categories for all judgments unless compelled to do otherwise. Values of 1-5 were assigned to rating categories from very characteristic to very uncharacteristic. It should be noted that such a method is a departure from many stereotype studies which have used check lists of adjectives and permitted respondents to ascribe to a target population as many characteristics as seem appropriate. The analysis of such data presents certain difficulties which are avoided by the method adopted herein (Abate and Berrien, 1966).

Stereotype assessment forms were distributed to three sets of students: (a) undergraduate volunteers at the men's and women's colleges of Rutgers, The State University in New Jersey; (b) undergraduates in elementary psychology attending a number of universities in Tokyo; and (c) Japanese-American students at the University of Hawaii.

The samples consisted of 240 males and 240 females in both the Japanese and Hawaiian groups. The New Jersey samples consisted of 225 males and 118 females.

The social desirability (SD) of the behavior descriptions was determined by going back to Edwards' original and unpublished standardization data from American students. These data revealed the social desirability of the individual statements classified by categories. The sum of SD means for each of nine statements in each of the 15 categories made possible a ranking of the social desirability of these categories regardless of sex.[1] Comparable data were available for Japanese students developed by Iwahara and Sugimura (1965) and reported also by Berrien (1964). As in the American data, no significant sex differences were found. It must be borne in mind that this method of assessing the social desirability of the descriptive paragraphs is indirect. However a check on ratings thus obtained was made by presenting the paragraphs themselves to 59 men and 32 women (young adults in the Rutgers evening college) with instructions identical to those used in the stereotyping phrase: "Select the two characteristics most socially desirable in our culture; three rather socially desirable, etc." The correlation between the two methods was .90. Considering the fact that Edwards used high school students with some college experience, and the methods were different, this correlation provides considerable confidence that the rank orders are very similar.

RESULTS

The basic raw score stereotype data were reduced to ranks for purposes of analysis. The mean ratings of the 15 behavior descriptions were separately determined for each of the four respondent groups (male, female, Japanese, American) with respect to the stereotypes of Americans and Japanese. This means that the male and female sets of New Jersey respondents also gave self-stereotype ratings and ratings of Americans. The Japanese-Americans in Hawaii strictly speaking gave no self-stereotype but standing somewhat aloof, rated Americans and Japanese in general with both of which they had some familiarity.

The ranks assigned to each of the behavioral descriptions by "stimu-

[1] Edwards (1957) has shown that there are no significant differences between sexes in the social desirability ratings.

lus" and respondent sets are given in Table 1. . . . One way to determine the degree of similarity between any two profiles having a constant sum, or arrays of ranks such as those given in the tables, is to compute the rank-difference correlation.[2] Two correlation matrices separately by sex are presented in Table 2 . . . which are to be interpreted as indicating the degree to which the indicated profiles are similar or contrasting. Inspection of these two matrices shows no important sex differences. The coefficients are of the same order of magnitude in all corresponding cells, with only a few exceptions.

The partial correlations of the self versus the "other" stereotypes partialling out the social desirability of the descriptive paragraphs are given in Table 3. . . . Since it was not clear whether the Japanese-Americans were operating within the context of their Japanese or American culture, each SD ranking was employed to eliminate possible confounding.

Table 4 displays second order partial correlations in which the social desirability of *both* Japanese and New Jersey respondents have been partialled out for those zero order correlations that represent the agreement between different respondent samples about a given stimulus population. The Hawaiians, being in a somewhat anomalous situation, are compared with each of the self-stereotypes provided by the New Jersey and Japanese samples. These correlations are to be interpreted as indicators of the degree to which the different sets of respondents agree about a given stimulus population.

DISCUSSION

The zero and first order correlations given in Table 3 require some initial interpretation. They represent the degree to which respondents see themselves as similar or contrasting with "the other." It appears that for all sets of respondents except those from New Jersey the confounding contributed by the varying degrees of social desirability associated with the particular descriptions employed is not great. The chief exception occurs among the New Jersey females whose stereotype of the Japanese becomes more contrasting when the confounding is eliminated. With this correction the contrast between self and other is of the same order as for the Japanese respondents. Partialling out the effect of the American SD in the stereotype of the Japanese-Americans has a greater effect on the correlations than partialling out the Japanese SD. This suggests that the respondents in Hawaii, although of Japanese extraction, are more Ameri-

---

[2] It should be pointed out that because N in this case is the number of behavior descriptions derived from the scales in the EPPS and not number of observations, the significance of the correlations remains untested as are the differences between any two such correlations.

TABLE 1. RANK ORDERINGS OF STEREOTYPE RATINGS BY MALE AND FEMALE RESPONDENTS AND THE SOCIAL DESIRABILITY OF THE DESCRIPTIONS FOR BOTH SEXES[a]

	MALE RESPONDENTS						FEMALE RESPONDENTS						SD	
	Japanese		Jap.-American		American		Japanese		Jap.-American		American		Japanese American	
	(1)	(3)	(4)	(5)	(6)	(8)	(9)	(10)	(11)	(12)	(13)	(14)	(2)	(7)
Descriptions	Self	Amer.	Amer.	Jap.	Self	Jap.	Self	Amer.	Amer.	Jap.	Self	Jap.		
Achievement	12	9	15	14	15	13	11	8	14	10	15	13	13	13
Deference	14	2	2	10.5	4	12	14	2	3	13	2	12	8	7
Order	13	6	7	15	6	15	15	5	7	15	7	15	15	10
Exhibition	5	14	11	2	10	2	4	14.5	8	2	11	2	2	2
Autonomy	2	10	10	3	9	6	3	10	11	4	8.5	3.5	4	4
Affiliation	8	12	9	10.5	11	11	8	12	10	9	10	10	11	15
Introception	7	4	3	8	2	7	7	4	5	8	6	9	9	8
Succorance	9	5	5	6	5	3	9	6	4	7	4	7	10	6
Dominance	4	11	13	5	12	4.5	5	11	13	5	12	5	3	3
Abasement	15	1	1	9	1	4.5	13	1	1	11	1	8	6	5
Nurturance	11	8	8	12	8	10	10	9	9	14	8.5	11	12	14
Change	6	15	7	7	13	8	6	14.5	15	6	5	6	7	11
Endurance	10	3	6	13	7	14	12	3	6	12	13	14	15	12
Heterosexual	3	13	12	4	14	9	1	13	12	3	14	3.5	5	9
Aggression	1	7	4	1	3	1	2	7	2	1	3	1	1	1

[a]Low rank means least characteristic, least desirable.

TABLE 2. CORRELATIONS OF STEREOTYPE

MALE RESPONDENTS

	Japanese			Hawaiian		American		
	(1) Self	(2) SD	(3) Amer.	(4) American	(5) Japanese	(6) Self	(7) SD	(8) Jap.
(1)	—	.68	-.61	-.39	.83	-.3	.45	.56
(2)		—	-.32	-.08	.92	.1	.83	.82
(3)			—	.86	-.41	.82	.06	-.16
(4)				—	-.01	.96	.23	-.12
(5)					—	-.01	.78	.87
(6)						—	.35	.24
(7)							—	.80

FEMALE RESPONDENTS

	Japanese			Hawaiian		American		
	(9) Self	(2) SD	(10) Amer.	(11) American	(12) Japanese	(13) Self	(7) SD	(14) Jap.
(9)	—	.77	-.70	-.35	.93	-.42	.43	.64
(2)		—	-.38	.03	.82	-.03	.83	.93
(10)			—	.76	-.60	.81	.03	-.54
(11)				—	-.20	.95	.37	-.07
(12)					—	-.30	.63	.94
(13)						—	.32	-.14
(7)							—	.72

TABLE 3. PARTIAL CORRELATIONS (SOCIAL DESIRABILITY
CONTROLLED)

Respondents	Stimuli	Rhos	First order	Zero order
Japanese males	Self vs. Americans	(1)vs. 3.2	-.56	-.61
Japanese females	Self vs. Americans	(9)vs. 10.2	-.69	-.70
N. Jersey males	Self vs. Japanese	(6)vs. 8.7	-.07	.24
N. Jersey females	Self vs. Japanese	(14)vs. 13.7	-.56	-.14
Jap.-Amer. males	Amer. vs. Japanese	(4)vs. 5.7	-.30	-.01
Jap.-Amer. females	Amer. vs. Japanese	(11)vs. 12.7	-.46	-.20
Jap.-Amer. males	Amer. vs. Japanese	(4)vs. 5.2	.07	-.01
Jap.-Amer. females	Amer. vs. Japanese	(11)vs. 12.2	-.39	-.20

TABLE 4. COMPARISON OF PARTIAL 2ND ORDER CORRELATIONS
AND ZERO ORDER CORRELATIONS

		Correlations	
Respondents	Stimuli	Second order	Zero order
Males			
Japanese vs. New Jersey	Americans	.90	.82
Japanese vs. New Jersey	Japanese	.01	.56
Females			
Japanese vs. New Jersey	Americans	.79	.81
Japanese vs. New Jersey	Japanese	-.15	.64
Males			
Hawaii vs. Americans	Americans	.97	.96
Hawaii vs. Japanese	Japanese	.76	.83
Females			
Hawaii vs. Americans	Americans	.93	.85
Hawaii vs. Japanese	Japanese	.89	.93

can than Japanese, an interpretation which is in line with conclusions reached earlier from different data and reported by Berrien, Arkoff and Iwahara (1966).

Overall this table implies that even with SD partialled out the Japanese see the Americans as more contrasting with themselves than is the case for the New Jersey subjects when comparing themselves with the Japanese. The Hawaiian sample falls neatly between the other samples in this respect. Before speculating about the reasons for this let us look at other data.

Table 4 is an alternative way of considering how clearly the self-stereotype corresponds with the stereotype given by others, but with SD partialled out for *both* sets of respondents. That is to say, when Americans stereotype themselves and Japanese stereotype Americans, their respective evaluations of the descriptive phrases may confound the stereotypes. The second order correlations in Table 4 correct for both SD ratings. Thus .90 in the first row indicates the degree of agreement of the Japanese with the New Jersey males' self-stereotype, eliminating the evaluative effect in the descriptive terms. Two features of these data are salient. First, the correlations are positive (except one). This should not be interpreted as eliminating the mirror-image implications in Table 3. Table 4 indicates the agreement between different "observers" of a common target while Table 3 gives the similarity or contrast between two targets by single sets of observers. Second, the Japanese agree more closely with Americans about Americans than Americans agree with Japanese about Japanese. This is further confirmation of the hypothesis that knowledge about the stimulus group tends toward greater accuracy in the stereotype.

Moreover, by partialling out SD for both sets of respondents only minor changes occur in the Japanese views of Americans (.90 versus .82 and .79 versus .81), but a marked shift occurs in the agreement between respondents about the Japanese. From this and Table 2 the Americans appear to be more confounded by the social desirability of the particular descriptions than are the Japanese. This may in turn be a reflection of their greater knowledge of Americans such that even though they extend great friendliness toward Americans,[3] they do not allow the latter to over-shadow what they "know." Americans also have considerable friendliness toward the Japanese but less knowledge about them, and hence this affect tends to distort or reduce the correspondence of their stereotype with the self-image of the Japanese.

Table 3 has special implications with respect to the mirror image hypothesis because the first order correlations indicate a strong tendency, for the Japanese respondents especially, to see Americans as the reverse of themselves even when the good-bad dimension is statistically removed. Any of the cognitive balance theories would not predict such high negative correlations especially in the circumstance where the respondents profess considerable affect for the stimulus group.

One might speculate that the professed friendliness toward the Americans disguises a subtle hostility as a residue from the 1940–46 period. Such a hypothesis is difficult to accept, and further, is not supported by the second order correlations in Table 4, indicating a kind of reliability in the Japanese stereotypes of Americans. As Klineberg (1950) was perhaps the first to point out, stereotypes possess a "kernel of truth." From the data presented, it appears that the Japanese have a larger kernel of that truth respecting Americans than vice versa. It is of some interest also that the Japanese-Americans in Hawaii (Table 2) show high zero order correlations where their stereotypes are compared with the self-stereotypes of either the New Jersey or Japanese samples. Situated as they are between

---

[3] Data on this point are being analyzed and will be reported shortly. [Ed. note: See F. Kenneth Berrien, "Stereotype Similarities and Contrasts," *Journal of Social Psychology*, August 1969, 78:2, 173–183.]

East and West they are perhaps more knowledgeable about both national groups than either is about each other. The data fit this interpretation. Furthermore the existence of a mirror image (if it is close to the "truth") appears to be possible even when the descriptive terms are of equivalent social acceptance. In other words the present findings strongly suggest that contrasting images of self and others need not always be generated by disapproval of others. Cognitive contrasts are possible in the absence of affective differences.

When comparing the same sexes in Japan and New Jersey (Table 3, 1st order), one gets the impression that the Japanese appear to hold more contrasting views of self and other than is true of Americans. Given the fact that the strain-toward-consistency theories have been derived largely from occidental cultures, and especially American, one may wonder whether they are equally applicable to oriental respondents. The data suggest they are not. Further analyses of cognitive mechanisms in various cultures may lead to important revisions in these theories and also may have a bearing on international bargaining styles.

References

Abate, M. and F. K. Berrien. Validation of stereotypes: Japanese *vs.* American students. *Journal of Personality and Social Psychology*, December 1967, 7:4, 435–438.

Abate, M. and F. K. Berrien. *Explorations in the Process of Stereotyping National Groups.* Technical Report 3, University of Hawaii, Contract Nonr-4806, 1966.

Allport, G. W. *The Nature of Prejudice.* Cambridge: Addison-Wesley, 1954.

Asch, S. E. Forming impressions of personality. *Journal of Abnormal and Social Psychology*, 1946, *41*, 258–290.

Berrien, F. K., A. Arkoff, and S. Iwahara. *Japanese-Americans: Japanese? American? Japanese-American?* Paper read at Western Psychological Association, Long Beach, Calif., 1966.

Berrien, F. K. Japanese and American student personal values. Technical Report #13, Contract Nonr 404(10), New Brunswick, N.J.: Rutgers University, 1964.

Bronfenbrenner, U. The mirror image in Soviet-American relations. A social psychologist's report. *Journal of Social Issues*, 1961, *17*, 3, 45–56.

Edwards, A. L. *The Social Desirability Variable in Personality Assessment and Research.* New York: Dryden Press, 1957, 8–12.

Festinger, L. A. *A Theory of Cognitive Dissonance.* Evanston, Ill.: Row-Peterson, 1957.

Heider, F. *The Psychology of Interpersonal Relations.* New York: Wiley, 1958.

Iwahara, S. and T. Sugimura. Application of Edwards Personal Preference schedule to Japanese. *Japanese Journal of Educational Psychology*, 1965, *13*, 31–41.

Klineberg, O. *Tensions Affecting International Understanding.* Social Science Research Council, 1950.

Osgood, C. E. *An Alternative to War or Surrender.* Urbana: University of Illinois Press, 1962.

Prothro, E. T. and L. Melikian. Studies in stereotypes. V: Familiarity and the kernel of truth hypothesis. *Journal of Social Psychology*, 1955, 41:1, 3–10.

Taft, R. Accuracy of empathic judgments of acquaintances and strangers. *Journal of Personality and Social Psychology*, 1966, 3, 600–604.

White, R. K. *Misconceptions in Soviet and American Images.* Paper read at American Psychological Association, New York, 1961; also, Images in the context of international conflict. In H. C. Kelman (ed.), *International Behavior.* New York: Holt, Rinehart, Winston, 1965, Chap. 7.

12   A L F R E D L . B A L D W I N , C L A R A P .
B A L D W I N , V I C T O R C A S T I L L O -
V A L E S, a n d B O N N I S E E G M I L L E R

*Cross-Cultural Similarities in the
Development of the Concept of Kindness*

This study is part of a research program being carried on by the authors and their colleagues investigating some of the cognitive aspects of interpersonal relations (Baldwin, Baldwin, Hilton and Lambert, 1969; Baldwin and Baldwin, 1968). The basic assumption is that so-called *naive psychology* (Heider, 1958) forms the cognitive structure underlying judgments of other people's motivations, character traits, and personality characteristics.

By kindness people basically mean the strength of the desire to benefit

A report of this research was presented to Society of Inter-American Psychology — Mexico City, December 17, 1967.

Research reported in this paper was conducted at New York University and the Interuniversity Institute for Investigation in the Social Sciences in Yucatan and supported in part by the following Grant number MH 11039 from the National Institute of Mental Health.

The authors are grateful to Professor Fred Strodtbeck and Mr. Herman Konrad for their help in facilitating the data collection in Merida.

another person. A kind person is one who is motivated to help other people and who does not like to harm them. The problem of judging the kindness of another person from his actions is that an overt act that benefits another person may arise from a variety of circumstances besides the character trait of kindness. The benefit of another person may, for example, be the accidental consequence of an action that had a quite different intention. Or the benefit of another person may have been intentional but quite incidental to the motivation of the action, as when a firm subcontracts business to another firm because it is more profitable to do so. Or the benefit of another person may be an instrumental act intended to lead to some quite different result, as when a politician votes in favor of a colleague's bill in order to have a claim upon the colleague's vote on some future occasion.

Thus the context in which a benefit is brought about becomes essential in interpreting whether it is kind. In a previous study (Baldwin and Baldwin, 1968) ten pairs of stories explored some of the contextual factors involved in the judgment that an action is kind. They were described and named the *Kindness Picture-Story Measure*. In each pair of stories, the same benefit results — a boy gets a ball he wants, or a baby brother gets some toys to play with. The contexts of the benefit differ, however, within each pair. The subject is asked to judge in which of the two stories the action is kinder and to explain why he thinks so.

Situation 1 (intentionality) contrasts a benefit resulting from an intentional act in contrast to an unintentional one. [See Figures 1a and 1b.]

Situation 2 (choice) contrasts a situation where both of the person's alternative actions are beneficial to one where he has a choice between benefiting another person or not.

Situation 3 (obedience to mother) contrasts a benefit performed spontaneously with one performed after an authority has requested that it be done.

Situation 4 (self-sacrifice) contrasts a benefit that is performed at no cost to the actor with one that involves some sacrifice on his part.

Situation 5 (guest) contrasts a benefit to a person to whom there is a social obligation, as when he is a guest in one's home, with a benefit to the same person under circumstances where there is no social obligation.

Situation 6 (trade) contrasts a beneficial act performed as part of a trade of benefits with one that is performed with no expectation of a return.

Situation 7 (bribe) contrasts a favor done to another person when one has been offered a reward for doing it to one which does not involve any expectation of reward.

Situation 8 (returning a favor) contrasts benefiting another person when

FIGURE 1a. Kindness Picture Story Test, Situation 1

1a. Here's a boy playing outside. He wanted to play with a ball, but it was up on top of this box, and he couldn't reach it. Paul was playing on the other side of the box, and he didn't know that this boy wanted the ball. He put his boat on top of the box, and it knocked the ball down on the ground where the other boy could get it. He played with it and was very happy, but Paul didn't even know.

one is under the social obligation to benefit him in return for a previous favor or benefiting him when he has previously refused a favor.

Situation 9 (equalization of benefits) contrasts benefiting another person when one is undergoing suffering with benefiting another person when the actor is himself enjoying a benefit.

Situation 10 (amount of benefit) contrasts doing a favor for someone when it gets him out of a serious difficulty with doing the same favor for him when the benefit he receives from the favor is of little importance.

The original set of stories and pictures was written in English and involved toys and play situations that occur commonly in New York (Baldwin and Baldwin, 1968). For this study, a Spanish version involving

FIGURE 1b. Kindness Picture Story Test, Situation 1

1b. In this picture, the ball is up on the box again, and this boy wanted it. He called around the box and asked Paul if he would reach it for him. Paul said, "Sure," and reached up and pushed the ball to the ground where the other boy could get it. He played with it and had fun.

In which picture was Paul being the kinder—when he pushed the ball down accidentally and didn't even know the other boy wanted it, or when he knew that the other boy wanted it and got it down for him?

toys and play situations that are familiar to children in Merida, Yucatan, was developed.

The Mexican version of the Kindness Picture-Story Measure is not a translation of the measure used in the United States; instead it was devised by the authors, especially Professor Castillo-Vales, to represent the same contrasts as the English version, but each situation was adapted to the environment of children in Yucatan. It has already been shown that quite different alternative situations elicit very similar responses from subjects in New York. . . .

The first task of the research is to establish that adults in a society actually respond to the situations in a consistent, predictable way. If they do, then we can look upon the age differences in the judgments of children as a result of some socialization process bringing them into agreement with the adults in their own society. In a cultural comparison, of course, we want to know whether the adults in the two societies agree on their concepts of kindness.

The second task is to examine the development of the adult-like concept to determine at what age it emerges and how it develops.

This study reports two sets of data. One set of data is a sample of 646 people from New York distributed over various ages, social classes, and religious backgrounds. Table 1 shows the N's for each age group, and the percentages of subjects at various ages making the hypothesized judgment. The other set of data is a sample of 300 people from Merida, students in a private school, in preparatoria, and an adult sample composed of parents of the children in the study.

The responses of each subject are analyzed in two ways: first, in terms of whether his response agrees with the hypothesized adult response in the society; second, by a coding of the inquiry in which the subject tells why he thought the story he chose was the kinder. This coding reduces to four categories, labeled *A*, *B*, *C*, and *D*. *A* responses are those in which the subject's explanation does not point to any feature of the situation that discriminates between the two contrasting stories. In the third situation, for example, the response "he gave the baby some toys" is coded *A* because he gave the baby toys in both stories. The *A* category also includes such responses as "because he was kind," "because she wanted to be nicer to her friend," as well as "I don't know," completely irrelevant responses, and occasional thematic stories that the child tells under the instigation of the picture.

D responses are articulate explanations of the adult choice involving the factors that are hypothesized to underlie the adult answer. These can range from a mere repetition of the relevant aspect of the question to a sophisticated explanation of the concept.

B responses are articulate explanations of the reason for choosing the picture that is opposite to the predicted choice. In Situation 8, returning a favor, a *B* response is as follows: "Because if he lets him ride his bicycle, then he should lend him his skates. And in this one, I don't think it is right 'cause if he didn't let him ride his bicycle, how can he lend him his skates?"

Finally *C* responses, fortunately rare, are those where the child chooses the adult-like choice, but then explains it in some way that is logical but not in the manner that was intended. For example, in one situation, number 2, we intended the relevant feature to be the presence or absence of any choice. If the actor has no alternative but to benefit the recipient, it is less kind than if he has an opportunity to harm him but still chooses to benefit him. Some children read into this story that the big brother gives the little brother the nice toy to play with and then must be satisfied to play with the poor toy himself. We did not intend this self-sacrifice to be portrayed in the story, but some children read it in. Such an explanation is called a C response — it usually involves some understanding of naive psychology but not the particular understanding we were trying to test in that situation. Since C responses are rare, we will group them with A responses in our analysis. Like A's, they give us no information about the particular variable that a situation was intended to measure.

RESULTS

Table 1 shows the percentage of the people in each age group in each sample agreeing with the hypothesis. Significant differences between the New York and the Merida sample are indicated by x's in Table 1.

The first feature to be noted is that there are no significant differences between the college age samples from the two societies and that the age curves by that time are essentially level. In other words, there is no evidence that the adults in the two societies have different definitions of kindness.

Second, we can compare the development of the concept in the two societies. Two types of information are particularly relevant. One is the age curve showing the percentage of children who choose the same picture as the adults in the society. The other is the percentage of children at each age level in each sample who give B responses, i.e., who verbalize a reason for their choice that is opposite to the one given by adults. Table 2 shows the percentage of B responses in each age group in each sample and again the significant differences between the two cultural samples are indicated.

On many situations the development curves are extremely similar. Figure 2, for example, shows the percentage of the people in each age sample choosing the story showing intentionality in Situation 1. There is no significant difference at any age; by age 7 there is better than 90 per cent agreement on the choice, and this consensus holds for all subsequent ages. The coding of the inquiry shows that the percentage of D responses is very low at age 5 (17 per cent in the Merida sample and 23 per cent in the New York City sample); it climbs rapidly, like the percentage agreement curve.

In Situation 8, returning a favor, the two curves are also nearly identical, as shown in Figure 3. The two curves are never significantly different.

Even more interesting is the coding of the inquiry, because it illustrates a general finding in both societies. The developmental curve does not in-

TABLE 1. PERCENTAGE OF SUBJECTS AGREEING WITH KINDNESS HYPOTHESES AT DIFFERENT AGES IN NEW YORK CITY AND MERIDA, YUCATAN

| | | | Age | | | | | |
Situation	5	7	9	11	13	15	College	Adult
1 N.Y.	66	92	97	92	97	–	98	–
Merida	53	100	100	100	90	100	93	88
2 N.Y.	74	90	96	94	100	–	97	–
Merida	77	90	90	100	97	93	95	76
3 N.Y.	60	89 }	95 }	97 }	100	–	97	–
Merida	47	43^{xx} }	47^{xx} }	81^{x} }	100	97	96	91
4 N.Y.	47	68	81 }	84	97 }	–	96	–
Merida	50	53	63^{x} }	92	83^{x} }	97	93	94
5[a] N.Y.	39	56	80 }	85	–	–	83	–
Merida	47	57	40^{xx} }	69	83	70	83	73
6 N.Y.	66	92 }	90	88	95	–	90	–
Merida	53	73^{x} }	77	100	100	100	95	94
7 N.Y.	40	72 }	87 }	88	95	–	98	–
Merida	50	40^{x} }	63^{x} }	96	97	97	100	92
8 N.Y.	39	47	60	75	95	–	94	–
Merida	37	60	51	85	97	97	91	97
9 N.Y.	44	54	57	61	52		86	–
Merida	50	37	47	58	57	53	86	73
10[a] N.Y.	28	10 }	4	14	27	–	33	–
Merida	43	40^{xx} }	17	15	13	27	33	33
N N.Y.	62	142	181	163	38	–	110	–
Merida	30	30	30	26	30	30	59	33

[a]These are percentages based on sub-samples of the total group:

5	N		30	48	98	85			110	–
10	N		32	94	83	78	30	–	89	–

Levels of significance, difference between proportions: $x / p < .05$, $xx / p < .01$.

dicate merely a gradual acquisition of the adult understanding of the situation; *i.e.*, as soon as the child understands the problem, he acquires an adult-like solution of it. Instead, there is a substantial group of young children who give *B* responses, *i.e.*, who are articulate in saying that the child who benefits another in return for a favor is kinder than one who benefits another after the other had refused him a favor. For these children, the justification lies in the fact that the act is returning a favor. It is as if the moral obligation to return a favor makes the act kind rather than kindness being most clearly expressed in acts over and above the call of moral obligation. In this situation, these *B* responses occur in very similar frequency in both Merida and New York City. They occur in 10 to

TABLE 2. KINDNESS INQUIRY ANALYSIS: PERCENTAGE OF B
RESPONSES – NEW YORK AND MERIDA

Situation		5	7	Age 9	11	13	15	College	Adult
1	N.Y.	3	4	1	3	0	–	1	–
	Merida	3	0	0	2	7	0	5	0
2	N.Y.	0	1	1	1	0	–	0	–
	Merida	3	3	3	2	0	0	3	6
3	N.Y.	26	7	4	1	0	–	2	–
	Merida	13	50^{xx}	43^{xx}	12	0	3	3	9
4	N.Y.	15	13	9	7	3	–	1	–
	Merida	7	30^{x}	17	5	10	0	2	6
5	N.Y.	16	29	17	12	–	–	14	–
	Merida	7	10^{x}	37^{x}	22	7	10	6	21
6	N.Y.	11	5	9	11	5	–	5	–
	Merida	26^{x}	23^{x}	17	0	0	0	5	6
7	N.Y.	15	19	7	9	0	–	0	–
	Merida	10	50^{xx}	30^{x}	5	3	0	0	3
8	N.Y.	10	23	27	16	3	–	2	–
	Merida	20	27	20	10	3	3	5	0
9	N.Y.	15	29	28	25	27	–	7	–
	Merida	10	50^{xx}	46^{x}	36	30	13	9	21
10	N.Y.	25	77	87	82	73	–	66	–
	Merida	10^{x}	33^{xx}	50^{xx}	73	73	40	20^{xx}	30

Levels of significance, difference between proportions: x / $p < .05$, xx / $p < .01$.

20 per cent of the 5 years olds; they increase to 27 per cent at age 7 in Merida and 27 per cent at age 9 in New York City (see Figure 4). Then they decline with age.

It is very interesting that in these data these responses are opposite to the adult responses in each of the societies; thus, they are not simply explained in terms of the general commonality of two Western societies in the general Judeo-Christian tradition. These B responses show a very similar developmental curve among two groups of children who are widely separate. Even the wording of the argument for the B responses from Merida sounds like Spanish translations of the justifications given by New York City children. This suggests that there is something difficult about learning that kindness is doing more than what one is obliged to do and that at some point many children argue that kindness is merely fulfilling the obligation.

Not all the curves are similar, however. Situation 3 shows the greatest

FIGURE 2. Situation 1, Intentionality

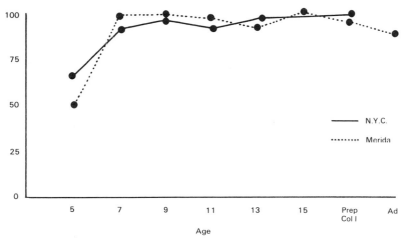

FIGURE 3. Situation 8, Returning a Favor

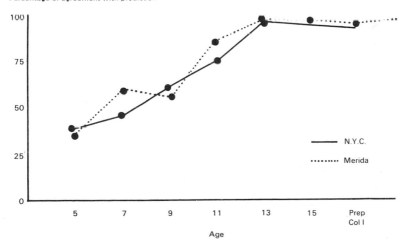

FIGURE 4: Situation 8. Coding of Inquiry

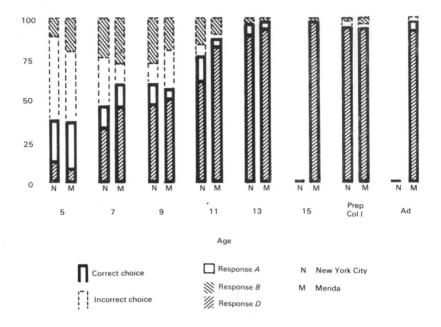

difference between the two cultures (see Figure 5). There is excellent agreement from age 13 on, but at ages 7 and 9, the New York City children agree with the adult response better than 85 per cent; in the Merida sample, the agreement with the adult response is around 50 per cent. Since the adult responses are alike in the two societies, this cannot be a case of two genuinely different cultural definitions of kindness.

One might argue that the Merida children are slower in picking up the adult concept, and if there were comparable differences in all the other situations, we might say that Merida children are socialized into adult values more slowly. On most situations, however, there is no evidence of any general difference in the rate of socialization.

The coding of the inquiry at these two age levels gives further information. In the New York City sample, there are very few B responses in Situation 3, and they are almost entirely at the 5 year level. In the Merida sample, however, nearly half of the 7 and 9 year olds argue that the boy is kinder when he obeys his mother than when he benefits his little brother without having to be asked to.

The stories are not identical, and thus might bear on the difference.

FIGURE 5. Situation 3, Coding of Inquiry

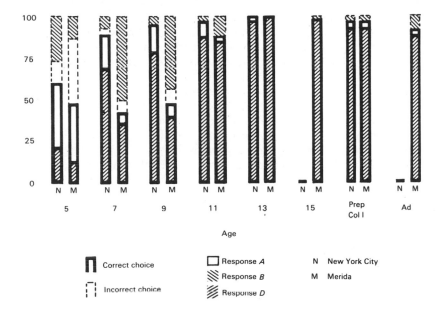

In one, the boy gives a little boy some toys; in the other, he visits with a little boy who had to stay in his hammock because he is sick. The difference is not obvious, but there may be one.

A more likely explanation is that obedience to parents is a stronger, more intensely socialized value in Merida than in New York City. Many observers have felt this is true. Therefore, children take longer to discover that benefiting other people over and above this obligation is even better than merely to obey.

There are other scattered significant differences revealed in Table 1, although none as marked as those in Situation 3. In Situations 4 (self-sacrifice), 6 (trade), and 7 (bribe), there are a total of five significant differences (at 5% level) among the eighteen differences tested. In each case, the New York sample agrees better with the adult response than the Merida sample. In Table 2 also there are scattered significant differences in Situations 4, 6, and 7, all indicating that B responses are more common in the Merida sample than in the New York sample. All three situations involve self-interest as an alternative motivation for the benefit. Thus, there appears some evidence that the Merida sample is slightly slower than the

New York sample in coming to the belief that a benefit is kinder when it does not also serve one's self-interest or if it involves self-sacrifice.

Finally, Situation 10 is interesting, not because the two cultures differ, but because it seems to pose the same dilemma for both cultures. In Situation 10, we have a child performing the same act (helping get a door open in New York City and lifting a big rock in Merida). In one case, this act gets the other boy out of serious trouble (gets him his new raincoat that he must wear home or helps him recover a peso that his mother had given him to buy sugar). In the other story, this act helps the boy get something that is trivial. When is the act kinder?

The youngest children apparently do not understand the problem; i.e., they don't really see any difference between the two stories (see Figure 6). They respond about 50 per cent one way or the other, and most of their reasons are classified A. From 5 to 9 there is a trend toward agreement that helping the boy out of serious trouble is kinder. By age 9 or so, there is almost a satisfactory consensus on this answer; the bulk of them are articulated by B-type justifications (Figure 7). From this age on there is a trend toward arguing that it is kinder to help the child when his need is not important. This response increases in frequency up to about 30 per cent among college age students and probably among adults in general. The clear B-type justifications decrease, but they are not entirely replaced by D-type justifications of the opposite position. There is an increase in A

FIGURE 6. Situation 10, Serious Trouble

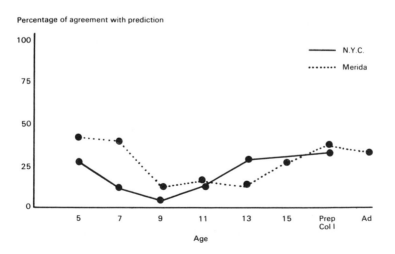

Percentage of agreement with prediction

FIGURE 7. Situation 10. Coding of Inquiry

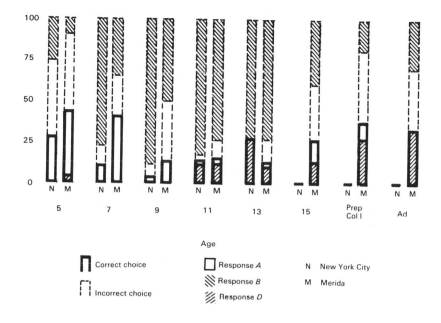

responses in Mexico reflecting genuine confusions. This situation seems to pose a real dilemma in which people tacitly recognize the force of both arguments. It is kinder to give another a big benefit rather than a small one. To give someone a dollar is kinder than a quarter. But there is a sort of obligation to help some boy out of serious trouble, especially if one can do so easily, and this is not particularly kind; it is just being decent. To help him out of a minor trouble is pure kindness. Curiously enough, the adults in the two societies resolve this dilemma in about the same proportions.

SUMMARY

This report has been based upon a study of kindness in two samples; one from New York City and one from Merida. There is what seems to me a remarkable agreement between the two samples on the meaning of kindness, the shape of the developmental curves, the difficulty in recognizing that kindness is benefiting other people over and above the call of obligation, and the resolution of the dilemma in Situation 10. There are differences in the growth curves, one of which perhaps reflects a difference in the emphasis the two societies put upon children's obedience to their parents.

References

Baldwin, A. L., C. P. Baldwin, I. M. Hilton, and N. W. Lambert. "The measurement of social expectations and their development in children." *Monographs of the Society for Research in Child Development*, 1969, 34:4, Serial No. 128.
Baldwin, C. P. and A. L. Baldwin. "Children's Judgments of Kindness." Unpublished manuscript, 1968.
Heider, F. *The Psychology of Interpersonal Relations*. New York: Wiley, 1958.

13   LEON A. JAKOBOVITS

Some Potential Uses of the Cross-Cultural
Atlas of Affective Meanings

The *Atlas of Affective Meanings* consists of affective ratings of 500 concepts given by groups of individuals in 15 language-culture communities around the world. In this paper we briefly discuss the nature of the data in the *Atlas* and present a few illustrations of how that information can be used in culturological investigations in comparative psycholinguistics. In the first section we give one possible characterization of the cross-

Paper presented at the XIth Interamerican Congress of Psychology, December 17th to 22nd, 1967, in Mexico City, to be published in *Proceedings of the XIth Interamerican Congress* (Mexico: Universidad Nacional Autonoma de Mexico).
[Ed. note: For a background description of the research, see the Introduction to this reader, and Charles E. Osgood, Semantic differential technique in the comparative study of cultures, *American Anthropologist*, June 1964, 66, 3, 171–200. (Reprinted in Leon A. Jakobovits and Murray S. Miron (eds.), *Readings in the Psychology of Language* (Englewood Cliffs, N.J.: Prentice-Hall, 1967).)
The *Atlas of Affective Meanings* by Charles Osgood and others will be published by the University of Illinois Press in 1972.]

culturally constant that may be viewed as substantive elements of a "world culture" and also examine some ways in which cultures impose a characteristically unique world-view upon the individual. In the second section we present (an) example of componential analysis involving . . . color. The third section illustrates a hypothesis-testing procedure of the *Atlas* data as applied to McClelland's theory of achievement motivation and economic development.

The *Atlas of Affective Meanings* is both a dictionary and a repository of information about cultural groups. For the comparative psycholinguist it may turn out to be what Murdock's *Human Relations Area Files* is for the anthropologist and social psychologist. Thus far in our work on what we refer to as "subjective culture" it has proved to be a useful tool for testing certain culturological hypotheses. In this paper, I would like to briefly outline some of the potential uses of the *Atlas* as a hypothesis-testing device and the nature of the information it contains about cultural groups.

SUBSTANTIVE CHARACTERIZATION OF THE CROSS-CULTURALLY COMMON AND THE CROSS-CULTURALLY UNIQUE

A striking fact that emerges in the comparative study of cultures is the contrast between the cross-culturally variable and the cross-culturally constant. Yet this is no less and no more than one should expect. For despite their varied nature (and frequent uniqueness), human societies everywhere share certain characteristics, a "world culture" that is imposed by the common sensory mold of the human species and the restrictions demanded by the requirements of cooperative interaction of social individuals.

What would a lexical inventory of world culture look like? Table 1 shows a few such concepts selected from the *Atlas*. Ten cultures are represented in this comparison: AE for American English, DH for Delhi Hindi [India], FF for Finnish, GK for Greek, HC for Hong Kong Cantonese, JP for Japanese, LA for Lebanese Arabic, ND for Netherlands Dutch, SW for Swedish, and YS for Yugoslav Serbo-Croat. The columns represent the nature of the shared affect: E+P+A+ refers to a portion of the semantic space (or "octant") encompassed by the three affective dimensions of Evaluation, Potency, and Activity and can conveniently be labeled as the "*good-strong-active* octant." Here we can find the concepts Airplane, Champion, and Space. Rabbit is *good-weak-active;* Saving is *good-strong* but neither *active* nor *passive;* Beard is *potent* but not particularly *good* or *active.* Notice a cluster of food objects in the *good* octant that is neutral with respect to Potency and Activity.

TABLE 1. SOME CONCEPTS WITH CROSS-CULTURAL AGREEMENT ON THEIR AFFECTIVE CODING[a]

$\begin{matrix}E+\\P+\\A+\end{matrix}$	$\begin{matrix}E+\\P_0\\A+\end{matrix}$	$\begin{matrix}E+\\P-\\A+\end{matrix}$	$\begin{matrix}E+\\P+\\A_0\end{matrix}$	$\begin{matrix}E+\\P_0\\A_0\end{matrix}$	$\begin{matrix}E_0\\P+\\A_0\end{matrix}$	$\begin{matrix}E-\\P_0\\A_0\end{matrix}$
Airplane Champion Space	Joke	Rabbit	Saving	Butter Cheese Dish Egg Map Vegetable	Beard	Smoke

[a]This analysis is based on the following 10 cultures: AE, DH, FF, GK, HC, JP, LA, ND, SW, and YS. The concepts shown exhibit agreement on seven of the ten cultures.
[Ed. Note: E+ = good; E- = bad
     P+ = strong; P- = weak
     A+ = active; A- = passive
     E_0 or P_0 or A_0 = neutral on the Evaluative, Potency or Activity rating dimension.
Ratings are made on a seven point scale with each rating dimension represented by a number of such scales. For example, on the Evaluative dimension, a subject might rate the word "Rabbit" on several scales such as the following:
 nice _: _ : _: _: _: _: _ awful
 sweet _: _ : _: _: _: _: _ sour
 good _: _ : _: _: _: _: _ bad]

Table 2 presents a more extended list involving 15 cultures — the previous 10 and 5 additional ones: FR for French, IT for Italian, MK for Mysore Kannada (Southern India), MS for Mexican Spanish, and TH for Thailand. The columns once again indicate the nature of the shared affect, and this time the differentiations are made along one dimension only. Certain obvious and expected communalities in this list are not surprising: indeed, they demonstrate a face validity of the *Atlas* data whose absence would have been cause for worry. There is cross-cultural unanimity in the designation of Cooperation, Friendship, Kindness, Pleasure, Success, Truth as *good* things. There is also perfect agreement as to the *badness* of Accident, Disease, Poison, Thief, and the *potency* of Elephant, Masculinity, Power, and Rock. Similarly, we find nearly perfect agreement on the *weakness* of Baby and Rabbit, the *high activity* of Airplane and Dancing, and the *passivity* of Old People and Pyramid.

On the other hand, certain cross-cultural communalities exhibited by this list would not have been easily predictable. Why should April, March, May, and August be *good* everywhere despite very different climatic environments? Although Suicide is intrinsically destructive of human life, one would have expected that because of its religious significance in some cultures (e.g., Japanese), some departure of its *badness* could have occurred. Not so. It is both instructive and, to this author at least, a source of profound satisfaction to notice the unanimous accept-

TABLE 2. ATLAS CONCEPTS EXHIBITING CROSS-CULTURAL AGREEMENT IN AFFECTIVE CODING[a]

E+		E-	P+	P-	A+	A-
Airplane	Lips	Accident	Airplane	Baby	Airplane	Old Age
Apple	Luck	Anger	Army	Rabbit	Boy	Old People
April	Machine	Cheating	Bridge		Cinema	Pyramid
Arm	Man	Death	Champion		Dancing	Rock
August	Map	Devil	City		Rabbit	
Automobile	March	Disease	Civilization		Singing	
Baby	Marriage	Fear	Elephant		Woman	
Bed	May	Greed	Hero			
Bird	Moon	Guilt	Hotel			
Blue	Mother	Hell	Justice			
Book	Music	Insane	Masculinity			
Boy	Name	Poison	Nationalism			
Bread	North	Suicide	Philosophy			
Bride	America	Thief	Power			
Bridegroom	Peace		Pyramid			
Brother	Picture		Railroads			
Butter	Pleasure		Revolution			
Chair	Progress		Rock			
Champion	Rabbit		School			
Child	Respect		Sea			
Cinema	Restaurant		University			
Civilization	Right Hand		World			
Cooperation	Salary					
Egg	Seed					
Eyes	Singing					
Father	Skin					
Friend	Space Travel					
Friendship	Story					
Game	Success					
Gramophone	Sunday					
Heaven	Sympathy					
Hero	Table					
House	Truth					
Kindness	University					
Knowledge	Vegetables					
Language	Water					
Laughter	Woman					

[a]Comparisons are made over 15 cultures (AE, DH, FF, FR, GK, HC, IT, JP, LA, MK, MS, ND, SW, TH, YS). For E+, E-, and P+, only those words exhibiting unanimous agreement were included. For P-, A+, and A-, the agreement across cultures is not perfect, but only words showing at least 80 per cent agreement are included here.

ancc of the *goodness* of Knowledge, Peace, and University, the *badness* of Cheating, Greed, and Anger, the *potency* of Justice, Philosophy, and School. At the same time, it may be sobering to reflect upon the unanimous acceptance of the *potency* of Army, Nationalism, and Revolution.

The cross-cultural similarities as well as the differences are reflected in the summary presentation of all the *Atlas* concepts in Table 3, which presents the distribution of concept allocations in the 27 octants of our semantic space for 10 cultures. The skewness of the distribution is a striking fact. The semantic world is not filled out equally in all regions.

Good things outnumber *bad* things by 5 to 1; *strong* things outnumber *weak* ones by 13 to 1; *active* things have a 2 to 1 edge over *passive* things. Here lies a profound psycholinguistic truth whose lesson is at the moment not entirely clear. Why should the concept universe give such a decided edge for the *good*, the *strong*, and the *active* over the *bad*, the *weak*, and the *passive?* The perception of these qualities is surely a sub-jectively imposed organization, and one cannot find an easy answer in the objective reality that surrounds us.

If we now switch our attention to cross-cultural differences to be found in Table 3, they turn out to be no less intriguing than the similarities. Take for example the question of what is the most salient octant for the various cultures. We find that for American English and Yugoslav Serbo-Croat it is *good* and *strong* but neutral on *activity;* for Greek and Hong Kong Cantonese it is *good, strong,* and *active;* for Delhi Hindi and Leba-nese Arabic it is *good, strong,* and *passive;* for Finnish it is *good* and *active* but neutral on *potency.* Note that for Japanese and Netherlands Dutch there is no strongly salient octant; apparently a more differentiated con-cept universe is preferred. Note also the almost complete absence of con-cepts in the *good, strong, active* octant for Delhi Hindi and Lebanese Arabic. How is one to interpret these differences? There cannot be any doubt from these results that cultural membership is indeed an associa-tion with weighty consequences: it imposes upon the individual a world-view that is as distinctively characteristic as it is far reaching and pro-found.

AN EXAMPLE OF COMPONENTIAL ANALYSIS

Up to now, we have dealt with certain aspects of the *Atlas* data in terms of simple raw scores on the three main affective dimensions. It is possible to make use of the *Atlas* data in the form of comparisons at a more ab-stract level involving a componential analysis based on intuitive classifica-tions of selected concepts within the *Atlas.* . . .

An example of a componential analysis done on a different set of *Atlas* concepts is given in Tables 4 and 5. Six concepts were selected as mem-bers of the concept class of color. In this case physical and psycho-physi-ological considerations suggest three convenient components: *Brightness, Saturation,* and *Hue.* The terms White ("+") and Gray ("−") represent an adequate contrast for *Brightness.* For *Saturation,* Red and Blue are contrasted with Yellow and Green respectively, on the rationale that at equal physical purity (*i.e.,* in terms of wave length) Red and Blue appear psychologically more saturated than Yellow and Green. The contrast for *Hue* is in terms of the longer wave length distribution (Red and Yellow)

TABLE 3. OCTANT DISTRIBUTION OF 500 ATLAS CONCEPTS IN TEN LANGUAGE/CULTURE COMMUNITIES[a]

	E+ P+ A+	E+ P+ A0	E+ P+ A-	E+ P0 A+	E+ P0 A0	E+ P0 A-	E+ P- A+	E+ P- A0	E+ P- A-	E0 P+ A+	E0 P+ A0	E0 P+ A-	E0 P0 A+	E0 P0 A0
American English (AE)	20	33	6	5	8	4	1	1	0	1	4	2	0	4
Delhi Hindi (DH)	0	23	32	1	20	0	0	0	0	0	3	2	0	10
Finnish (FF)	11	9	2	22	5	0	7	2	0	2	6	5	2	5
Greek (GK)	27	13	1	15	21	1	1	0	0	1	2	0	0	4
Hong Kong Cantonese (HC)	31	12	1	9	16	0	1	1	0	1	2	1	1	8
Japanese (JP)	8	13	2	10	14	2	2	0	0	3	9	3	2	11
Lebanese Arabic (LA)	1	23	32	3	18	1	1	0	0	0	3	1	0	5
Netherlands Dutch (ND)	14	5	2	12	13	3	4	4	2	6	6	1	3	6
Swedish (SW)	10	8	1	13	30	1	0	1	0	3	2	0	3	16
Yugoslav Serbo-Croat (YS)	3	27	20	2	10	3	2	1	0	1	4	3	1	8
Average	12	17	10	9	16	2	2	1	0	2	4	2	1	8

	E0 P0 A-	E0 P- A+	E0 P- A0	E0 P- A-	E- P+ A+	E- P+ A0	E- P+ A-	E- P0 A+	E- P0 A0	E- P0 A-	E- P- A+	E- P- A0	E- P- A-
American English (AE)	1	0	0	0	0	1	2	0	0	2	1	2	4
Delhi Hindi (DH)	0	0	1	0	0	0	0	0	1	0	0	6	1
Finnish (FF)	2	0	0	0	0	0	8	1	1	3	1	2	4
Greek (GK)	0	0	0	0	0	0	0	1	1	0	0	7	3
Hong Kong Cantonese (HC)	2	0	0	0	0	0	0	1	1	3	0	5	3
Japanese (JP)	3	0	0	0	0	0	1	1	1	3	2	5	1
Lebanese Arabic (LA)	0	0	1	0	0	2	2	1	0	0	0	7	3
Netherlands Dutch (ND)	4	0	0	0	0	0	2	0	1	2	0	2	0
Swedish (SW)	2	0	0	0	0	0	0	1	1	1	3	6	3
Yugoslav Serbo-Croat (YS)	1	0	0	0	0	2	1	1	1	1	1	5	2
Average	2	0	0	0	0	1	2	1	1	2	1	5	2

[a]Entries represent percentages to the nearest unit.

TABLE 4. A COMPONENTIAL ANALYSIS OF THE ATLAS COLOR TERMS

| | | Components | |
Color Term	Brightness	Saturation	Hue
White	+	0	0
Gray	–	0	0
Red	0	+	+
Yellow	0	–	+
Green	0	–	–
Blue	0	+	–

Component	Relevant contrast
Brightness	White vs. Gray
Saturation	Red vs. Yellow Blue vs. Green
Hue	Red vs. Blue Yellow vs. Green

TABLE 5. TESTS OF AFFECTIVE RELEVANCE OF THREE COMPONENTS OF COLOR

	AE	DH	FF	FR	GK	HC	IT	JP	LA	MK	MS	ND	SW	TH	YS	Summary
							Evaluation									Brightness
W/Gray	+	–	+	+	+	+	+	+	+	+	+	+	+	+	+	14/1
																Saturation
R/Y	+	–	–	+	+	+	–	+	–	–	–	–	–	–	+	17/13
B/G	+	+	+	+	–	+	–	+	+	–	+	+	–	+	+	
																Hue
R/B	+	–	+	–	–	–	–	–	–	+	–	–	–	+	–	8/22
Y/G	–	+	+	–	–	–	–	–	–	+	–	–	–	+	–	
							Potency									Brightness
W/Gray	+	–	–	–	–	+	+	–	+	+	+	–	–	–	+	7/8
																Saturation
R/Y	+	+	+	+	+	+	+	+	+	+	+	+	+	+	+	25/5
B/G	+	+	–	+	–	+	+	+	–	–	+	+	+	–	+	
																Hue
R/B	+	–	–	+	+	+	–	+	–	+	+	+	+	+	+	12/18
Y/G	–	–	–	–	–	–	–	–	–	–	–	+	–	–	–	
							Activity									Brightness
W/Gray	+	+	+	+	+	+	+	+	–	–	+	+	–	+	+	12/3
																Saturation
R/Y	+	–	–	+	+	+	–	+	–	+	+	+	+	–	–	21/9
B/G	+	+	+	–	+	+	–	–	+	+	+	+	+	+	+	
																Hue
R/B	+	–	+	+	–	–	+	+	+	+	+	–	+	–	+	19/11
Y/G	–	+	+	–	–	+	+	–	+	–	–	+	+	+	+	

contrasted with the shorter wave length distribution (Blue and Green). Table 5 presents the test for affective relevance of the 3 color components for 15 cultures. The summary ratios at the extreme right indicate the following relationships. *Brightness* reflects a clear relevance for Evaluation and Activity such that high brightness goes with *high positive evalu-*

ation and *high activity. Saturation* is clearly relevant for Potency, viz. higher saturation goes with *higher potency*, and less clearly with Activity, viz. higher saturation goes with *high activity*. Finally, for *Hue* the Blue-Green side of the spectrum is clearly *more positively evaluated* than the Red-Yellow side. It is interesting, and reassuring, to be able to report that recent data obtained with physical color patches varying in known physical values of brightness, saturation, and hue corroborate this componential analysis based on color words. Color patches having higher brightness values, as saturation and hue were kept constant, were rated significantly *better* in the 4 cultures tested. When brightness and hue were kept constant, more saturated color patches were rated significantly more *potent*, and finally, when brightness and saturation were kept constant, Blue was rated significantly *better* than Red or Yellow. In addition to this corroboration the color patch data were more powerful and showed additional contrasts not reflected by the color word ratings — a finding which is hardly surprising.

AN EXAMPLE OF A HYPOTHESIS-TESTING APPLICATION

This final section illustrates a different use of the *Atlas,* that of testing a specific hypothesis that, in the present instance, is based on Professor David McClelland's theory of need achievement in the economic sphere as expounded in his book, *The Achieving Society.* The aspect of Professor McClelland's theory that is under examination here is the notion that the economic achievement of a country is partially determined by the presence within a culture of individuals with a high achievement motivation whose entrepreneuring spirit can be recruited to managerial and business positions where they can actively promote their country's economic development. The high achieving person is depicted as possessing characteristics that make him effective in promoting economic development. These characteristics include a perception of the self as *active* and *potent* and operating on an environment that is *more passive* and relatively *weaker,* giving him possibilities of manipulation and promotion of change. The high achieving person also has a dim view of tradition and the past, looks out toward a bright future, values knowledge, and welcomes competition. This characterization of the high achieving person was generalized in the present instance to the cultural level: certain predictable differences in the affective meaning of concepts ought to occur between economically advantaged and disadvantaged cultures in our *Atlas* sample, since the prevalent achievement syndrome within a culture ought to be reflected in that culture's predominant evaluations of concepts relevant to achievement. With this view in mind, 22 concepts were selected from the *Atlas* that were thought on an intuitive basis to be relevant to the achievement motive. Predictions were then made with respect to the expected differences in Evaluation, Potency, and Activity for the ratings of these concepts between the culturally advantaged and disadvantaged cultures in our *Atlas* sample. The concepts and predictions are shown in Table 6. The predicted difference in each case is indicated by the numerals "1" and "2" reflecting the rank order of means to be expected. Thus, I, Myself was predicted to be higher on Potency and Evaluation ("1") for the economically advantaged cultures; Competition was predicted to be *better, stronger,* and *more active;* Tradition was predicted to be *less good, less potent,* and *less active,* and so on. In all, 50 predictions were made. Table 7 presents the mean ratings of the 22 concepts on each of the 3 factors for 6 economically advantaged cultures (American English, French, Italian, Japanese, Netherlands Dutch, Swedish) and 6 economically disadvantaged cultures (Delhi Hindi, Hong Kong Cantonese, Lebanese Arabic, Mysore Kannada, Mexican Spanish, Thailand). In this table, there are 66 possible comparisons (22 concepts × 3 factors), 50 of which were included in the predictions. The results of the comparisons

TABLE 6. PREDICTED DIFFERENCE BETWEEN ECONOMICALLY ADVANTAGED AND ECONOMICALLY DISADVANTAGED COMMUNITIES ON 22 SELECTED CONCEPTS[a]

Concepts	Evaluation (E) Adv.	Disadv.	Potency (P) Adv.	Disadv.	Activity (A) Adv.	Disadv.
World			2	1	1	2
Brain			1	2	1	2
Body			1	2	1	2
I (Myself)			1	2	1	2
People, Most			2	1	2	1
Borrow Money	2	1	2	1	2	1
Competition	1	2	1	2	1	2
Education	1	2	1	2		
Prayer	2	1	2	1	2	1
Luck			2	1	2	1
Knowledge	1	2	1	2		
Neutrality	2	1	2	1	2	1
Choice	1	2	1	2	2	1
Purpose	1	2			2	1
Future	1	2			1	2
Hope	2	1	2	1		
Tradition	2	1	2	1	2	1
Past	2	1	2	1	2	1
Present	1	2			1	2
Death			2	1	2	1
Sunday			2	1	2	1
Pleasure			2	1		

[a]The numerals "1" and "2" stand for higher and lower E-P-A scores, respectively.
(— — — — — —) = predictions confirmed by data.
(———————) = predictions confirmed by data and statistically significant
          (i.e. a difference of half-a-scale unit or larger).

in relation to the predictions are indicated in Table 6. The predicted comparisons that were confirmed by the data are underlined. A solid line indicates confirmation by a difference that can be considered significant (*i.e.*, a difference of half-a-scale unit or larger). A broken line indicates a difference in the predicted direction that does not reach statistical significance. A test of the adequacy of the predictions is given by the following observations: (1) 32 of the 50 predictions were in the proper direction, and 11 of these were significant; (2) none of the predictions made were ever significant in the opposite direction; (3) of the 18 predictions made with respect to the Activity factor, 16 were in the proper direction, and 9 of these were significant; (4) of the 66 possible comparisons in Table 7, 10 were statistically significant; of these, 9 were correctly predicted. They can be summarized as follows: *higher activity* on the part of the advantaged cultures for I, Myself, Body, Competition, and Future; *more passivity* for Neutrality, Tradition, Past, Death, and Sunday; *more potency* for Competition; the one significant difference that was not pre-

TABLE 7. AVERAGE E-P-A SCORES FOR SIX "ECONOMICALLY ADVANTAGED" AND SIX "ECONOMICALLY DISADVANTAGED" COMMUNITIES[a]

Concepts	Economically advantaged			Economically disadvantaged		
	E	P	A	E	P	A
World	-.12	1.27	.80	.28	1.62	-.71
Brain	.84	.75	1.28	.56	.40	1.12
Body	.84	.61	1.39	.66	.29	.35
I (Myself)	.59	.39	1.40	.40	.04	.40
People, Most	-.25	.22	.02	-.23	-.02	.09
Borrow Money	-1.15	-.38	-.42	-1.90	-.74	-.02
Competition	.59	1.22	1.09	.41	.63	.51
Education	.66	.88	.06	1.07	.91	-.13
Prayer	.43	.22	-.85	.94	.32	-.35
Luck	.95	.02	-.13	.50	.15	.32
Knowledge	1.01	1.01	-.01	.99	1.41	-.07
Neutrality	.11	-.35	-.87	.02	-.05	-.15
Choice	.23	.06	-.05	.30	.27	-.08
Purpose	.33	.39	.05	.39	.16	.38
Future	.65	.85	.64	.20	.67	-.23
Hope	.76	.56	.20	.47	.65	.10
Tradition	.28	.33	-.91	.06	.10	.50
Past	.27	.06	-.95	.19	.02	.01
Present	.17	.24	1.02	.09	.19	.75
Death	-1.92	.16	-1.74	-2.01	.24	-.72
Sunday	1.13	-.69	-.12	.35	-.19	.53
Pleasure	1.21	.40	1.40	.90	-.06	.97

[a]The communities in the "economically advantaged" and "economically disadvantaged" sets are, respectively:
(1) AE, FR, IT, JP, ND, SW,   (2) DH, HC, LA, MK, MS, TH

U.S.A.	Japan	India-Delhi	Mysore
France	Netherlands	Hong Kong	Mexico
Italy	Sweden	Lebanon	Thailand

dicted was *higher evaluation* for Sunday on the part of the advantaged cultures. It is clear then that the hypothesis can be considered adequately confirmed only in the case of the Activity factor. . . .

14   WALLACE E. LAMBERT,
            MOSHE ANISFELD, AND
            GRACE YENI-KOMSHIAN

Evaluational Reactions of Jewish and
Arab Adolescents to Dialect
and Language Variations

Several recent investigations have demonstrated that one's perception of another person is markedly modified when the latter changes his speech style from one dialect or language to another. Lambert, Hodgson, Gardner, and Fillenbaum (1960) showed that English-speaking Canadian college students judged the personalities of bilingual male speakers much more favorably when listening to taped recordings of them speaking English in contrast to the style of French typically used by French Canadians. This finding held for both monolingual English Canadians and those who were bilingual in French and thus able to understand the French as well as the English content of the recordings. On the other hand, college-age French-Canadian listeners perceived the same bilingual speakers more

    Wallace E. Lambert, Moshe Anisfeld, Grace Yeni-Komshian, "Evaluational Reactions of Jewish and Arabic Adolescents to Dialect and Language Variations," *Journal of Personality and Social Psychology*, Vol. 2, No. 1, July 1965, pp. 84–90. Copyright (1965) by the American Psychological Association, and reproduced by permission.
    This research was supported by a grant from the Carnegie Corporation of New York. We are grateful to Avraham Lavie of Bar-Ilan University, Israel, for translating questionnaires into Arabic and for conducting the experiment with Arab subjects. We are also indebted to Itshak Levin (Bar-Ilan University) for help in translating questionnaires into Hebrew. Roberta Preston helped us greatly in the statistical analysis of the data.

favorably when they spoke in English — a result that was interpreted as a minority group's adoption of the majority group's views. These negative views, however, were apparently restricted to Canadian-style French since neither the English nor French-Canadian listeners downgraded to any noticeable degree one speaker who used European-style French. A more recent study by Anisfeld and Lambert (1964) showed that younger French-Canadian subjects did not downgrade the French-Canadian guises of bilingual speakers. In fact, 10-year-old monolingual French-Canadian children had a much more favorable view of the French Canadian in contrast to the English guises of young bilingual speakers. On the other hand, French-Canadian children who had become bilingual in English, and who gave other indications of being comfortably identified with both cultural groups, made few invidious comparisons one way or the other between the French and English guises of bilingual speakers.

Anisfeld, Bogo, and Lambert (1962) examined listeners' reactions to speakers who changed from standard English to English as spoken by Jewish immigrants to North America. It was found that gentile listeners reacted less favorably to a speaker when his speech was accented than when it was in the standard English style. Jewish listeners showed ambivalence in their evaluations of persons with a Jewish accent, liking certain traits and disliking others.

The findings of these three studies indicate that speech variations play an important role in social perception and that the technique of matching guises of the same speaker may be a useful means of examining the stereotyped thinking of members of one cultural, ethnic, or social group when they consider typical representatives of other groups. The major purpose of the present study was to apply the technique in Israel, a setting where language and dialect variations are presumed to have particularly important social and political implications. For example, with regard to language differences, one can examine the stereotyped images Jews and Arabs have of one another by comparing the changes in listeners' perceptions of bilingual speakers whose Hebrew and Arabic guises are matched. Dialect differences are also of potentially great significance in Israel since people can be identified as Jews of European background by their Ashkenazic [1] style of Hebrew or as emigrants from Yemen by their distinctive dialect. In contrast to European Jews, the Yemenites in Israel are said to be regarded as less sophisticated and possibly less cultured. Both the Arabic-Hebrew and the Ashkenazic-Yemenite contrasts were examined in the present investigation.

---

[1] The Ashkenazic style of Hebrew speech refers in this paper to modern Hebrew as spoken in Israel by Jews of European descent.

METHOD

Subjects

Jewish Subjects. Forty high school students, 15–16 years of age, from a Tel-Aviv school noted for its high academic standards, volunteered to spend one morning of their 1961 summer vacation to participate in the study. There were 28 girls and 12 boys in all. Most were born in Israel of European parentage, except for 3 whose parents came from Syria and Iraq. All students were taking a course in Arabic as part of their curriculum. The educational and economic backgrounds of the parents place the sample in Israel's middle class.

Arab Subjects. The Arab students ranged in age from 13 to 18 years with a mean age of 14.5. They all belonged to a scout group in Jaffa. There were 29 in all, 23 boys and 6 girls. They were from Grades 6 to 8 in Christian schools where instruction is conducted mainly in Arabic, although they also study Hebrew, English, and French. All spoke Arabic in their homes and half reported that they used both Arabic and Hebrew with friends. Thus, the Arab subjects as a group were more bilingual in Arabic and Hebrew than were the Jewish subjects. More than half of their parents were born in what is now Israel and the rest in other parts of the Arab world. The social class, estimated from what the youngsters stated their fathers' occupations were, is generally lower than that of the Jewish subjects, making them, as a group, either lower-middle or upper-lower social class.

Procedure

Jewish Subjects. The experiment was conducted in an auditorium of the school normally attended by the subjects. All instructions and questionnaires were given in Hebrew by the second author, an Israeli. Tape recordings were made of speakers reading a 2.5-minute philosophical passage (the same used in the previous studies mentioned) in either Hebrew or Arabic. Speakers were selected who were sufficiently bilingual in Hebrew and Arabic or in the Ashkenazic and Yemenite dialects of Hebrew to satisfy several competent judges that they would sound genuine to most listeners. One, who habitually used the Ashkenazic version of Hebrew, was able to imitate a Yemenite manner of speaking Hebrew so that it sounded nativelike rather than caricatured. A second speaker was a professional actor whose native dialect was Yemenite but who could imitate the Ashkenazic form quite well. Although it was possible to detect traces of Yemenite style in his standard Hebrew, his guises were still used in order to have one natural and one acquired manner of speaking the two dialects.

Two speakers were chosen for the Hebrew-Arabic comparison. One was a senior high school student whose native language was Hebrew and who had learned Arabic in school and through usage. He was a native of Israel of European parentage. The other was a young Arab who spoke Hebrew with an accent similar to that of Jews of Arabic-speaking background. They were judged to speak both languages well enough to be taken as native speakers in each of their guises by most listeners.

The guises of any speaker were separated maximally on the tape. The first voice heard on the tape — that of another speaker — was used as a filler to acquaint the subjects with the rating procedure.

Arab Subjects. The study was carried out in Jaffa in the building where the Scouts met regularly on Friday afternoon, with the Scoutmaster present. All instructions were administered by a professor of Arabic. For the Arab subjects, one speaker was the same Arab bilingual used with the Jewish subjects and the second was a Jew from Syria who was perfectly bilingual in Hebrew and Arabic. The two guises of speakers were maximally separated on the tape, and were preceded and interspersed with other speakers. Competent bilingual judges agreed that the variations in guises of the speakers sounded authentic.

General. The instructional set given all subjects was to listen attentively to a series of speakers reading a standard passage and to imagine, much as one does when he hears a voice for the first time over a phone or on the air, what type of person each speaker was. Subjects were told that some would be speaking Hebrew and some Arabic, but they were to disregard the language differences, which purportedly were used to make the task more interesting, and to concentrate on the speaker in order to make accurate judgments of his personality. They were given a rating sheet to be used for each voice listing the 20 traits presented in Table 1, with 6-point rating scales, each labeled from "very little" to "very much." They were to start rating whenever they got a clear notion of a speaker's personality. About half of the subjects made their ratings of the traits in the order presented in Table 1, while the remainder had the traits listed in reversed order.

At the bottom of each sheet, they were asked to express their feelings about the speaker on four social-distance scales: I would befriend this person; I would accept this person as a relative by marriage; I would accept this person as a neighbor; and I would help this person if he were in need. They answered "yes" or "no" to each question.

It should be realized that the selection of speakers for both parts of the study was made with the help of Israeli teachers of Arabic and Hebrew. However, we did not have the advice and assistance of professional linguists in this matter. There is no problem in the case of the speakers used with the Jewish subjects because an important control was used.

After all voices had been rated, the tape was replayed for the Jewish subjects, and they indicated what linguistic-ethnic group they thought each speaker belonged to. If they stated that an Ashkenazic guise was that of an Ashkenazi or a Sabra (a native of Israel) and that the matched guise was that of a Yemenite, their ratings for the pair were used for analysis in the Ashkenazi-Yemenite comparisons. For the Hebrew-Arabic guise comparisons, the ratings of subjects were used if they identified one guise as Arabic and the other as either Ashkenazic or Sephardic (North African Jews). However, we were not permitted to take the extra time for this check with the Arab subjects and therefore are open to the criticism of linguists who might question the judgments of language teachers about the adequacy of the speakers used.

Standard Attitude Measures. This part of the study was carried out with the Jewish subjects only, since we were advised not to administer standard attitude questionnaires to the Arab subjects. When the Jewish subjects had completed the rating of personality traits, they were given a second booklet that included three different measures of attitudes.

1. The attitude rating scales made use of 18 bipolar scales (see Table 2) for measuring attitudes toward Ashkenazic Jews, Arabs, and Yemenite Jews. Subjects were given instructions in the use of the scales, for example, to indicate whether Arabs in general were "interesting" or "boring" on a 6-point rating scale. These scales are similar in form to those used for the evaluation of speakers.

2. An 18-item attitude questionnaire designed to measure attitudes toward Yemenites was then administered. Sample items were: Yemenite Jews contribute to the richness of the Israeli society; the intellectual capacities of the Yemenites are clearly lower than those of Ashkenazic Jews. Subjects were given six choices for agreeing or disagreeing with each item in this and in the following questionnaire. Eleven out of 18 were written with a negative theme.

3. Finally, a 7-item attitude questionnaire about Arabs was administered. A sample item is: Arabs must be considered a bad influence on Jewish culture and civilization. In this case, the Israeli advisors suggested that all the items have a negative theme.

RESULTS AND DISCUSSION

The algebraic difference (D score) between the ratings given to the two guises of each speaker was obtained for each subject on each of the 20 traits. For the Jewish subjects, only the ratings based on correct identification of both guises of a speaker were employed in the analysis. Thus, there were two D scores on each trait for those subjects who correctly identified the two guises of both speakers, but only one D score for subjects who correctly identified the two guises of one of the two speakers. An average D score was taken for those subjects who had two D scores in order to obtain one entry for each subject on each trait. For all Arab subjects, average D scores were used in the analysis since no data on guise identification was available.

For each trait, the sum of the D scores for all subjects was tested for the statistical significance of its departure from zero. The results of this analysis, using t tests for correlated samples, are presented in Table 1. Positive and negative signs were added to the t values to indicate which guise was more favorably evaluated.

Jewish Subjects

Ashkenazic and Yemenite Jewish Guise Comparisons. The results are presented in the first column of Table 1. The pattern of findings suggests that Yemenite in comparison to Ashkenazic Jews were considered by Ashkenazic Jews as less intelligent, ambitious, and wealthy, as less socially acceptable (cleanliness, prestige, potential neighbor), and as less honest and reliable. However, the Yemenite Jews were viewed as having a greater sense of humor.

Hebrew and Arabic Guise Comparisons. The results are presented in the second column of Table 1. The pattern suggests that the Jewish subjects held stereotyped views of Arabs, considering them less humorous, less friendly, less honest, and less desirable as friends or potential marriage partners.

It is not clear why the Arabs were viewed as more wealthy. This would not fit the social facts of Arab life in Israel, but it might reflect a wider view on the part of the subjects: they may have interpreted wealth in this case in terms of land possessions and seen their own country as small in comparison to the enormity of the Arab world.

Arab Subjects

Hebrew and Arabic Guise Comparisons. The pattern of findings (third column of Table 1) suggests that Arab subjects considered members of the Jewish group less capable (intelligence and confidence), less dependable (good-hearted, friendly, honest), and less desirable for marriage than their own people. They also tend to be more willing to help members of their own group than Jews in time of need.

It is of particular interest that the Jewish and Arab subjects responded to representatives of one another's group in mutually antagonistic manners in the sense that both samples of subjects saw their own group as more honest, friendly, good-hearted, and more desirable as relatives

TABLE 1. COMPARATIVE EVALUATIONAL REACTIONS OF JEWISH
AND ARAB SUBJECTS TO BILINGUAL GUISES OF SPEAKERS

| | Reactions to Ashkenazic and Yemenite Jewish guises | Reactions to Hebrew and Arabic guises | |
	Jewish subjects t^a	Jewish subjects t^b	Arabic subjects t^b
Trait			
Height	.40	.61	.59
Good looks	1.18	1.58	.43
Leadership	-1.36	.35	-.20
Sense of humor	-2.73**	2.25*	.06
Intelligence	3.50***	1.08	-2.07*
Honesty	3.35***	3.06***	-1.83
Self-confidence	-1.44	-.58	-2.22*
Friendliness	-.14	1.96	-1.85
Generosity	.77	1.49	-.14
Entertainingness	-1.53	1.82	-.82
Nervousness	.49	-.13	-.82
Good-heartedness	.64	1.86	-2.64**
Reliability	3.41***	1.48	.10
Ambition	2.30*	.71	-1.17
Stability	-.79	-.56	-.32
Good character	-.30	.54	-.58
Likability	1.01	.92	-1.45
Wealth	2.60**	-2.39*	.07
Cleanliness	4.74***	.47	-1.05
Prestige	2.31*	.14	-.95
Social distance responses			
1. Would befriend	.82	2.16*	-.25
2. Would accept as relative by marriage	.44	3.02***	-2.30*
3. Would accept as neighbor	3.75***	1.25	-.53
4. Would help if in need	1.00	.65	-2.04

Note. Entries are two-tailed tests of significance based on a total N of 32 for the Jewish subjects and on N of 29 for the Arab subjects.

[a]A positive sign indicates that the Ashkenazic guises were evaluated more positively than the Yemenite guises of the same speakers. Negative entries indicate the opposite.

[b]Positive entries indicate that the Hebrew guise was judged more favorably and negative entries mean that the Arabic guise was judged more favorably.

*$p < .05$.
**$p < .02$.
***$p < .01$.

through marriage. Mutual distrust of this sort would certainly restrict social interaction, since members of neither group would initiate a friendly overture if they anticipated the others to react in a relatively dishonest, unfriendly, and selfish manner.

Standard Attitude Measures and Evaluational Reactions to Matched Guises

In Table 2 the comparative attitude ratings of Ashkenazic and Yemenite Jews, and of Ashkenazic Jews and Arabs, are presented in detail for the Jewish subjects. It will be noted that a quite different pattern of results emerged when attitudes were measured by rating scales. In this case, the

TABLE 2. COMPARISONS OF JEWISH SUBJECTS' ATTITUDE RATINGS OF ASHKENAZIC
JEWS VERSUS YEMENITE JEWS AND OF ASHKENAZIC JEWS VERSUS ARABS

Trait	Comparisons of Ashkenazic and Yemenite Jews t	Comparisons of Ashkenazic Jews and Arabs t
Interesting	-5.01***	-.55
Unprejudiced	.80	1.64
Courageous	-1.17	2.33*
Good looking	1.13	2.75***
Friendly	-2.50*	1.03
Honest	-4.25***	1.03
Intelligent	1.19	5.07***
Good-hearted	-3.15***	4.55***
Pleasant	-1.68	4.77***
Good-mannered	2.53**	5.19***
Truthful	-1.60	2.58**
Successful	10.50***	9.27***
Self-confident	6.77***	4.49***
Permissive	-1.19	3.67***
Reliable	1.15	7.68***
Leadership	10.25***	6.67***
Cheerful	-1.82	2.52**
Hard working	-1.60	4.39***

Note. The total N is 40. A positive entry signifies that Ashkenazic Jew is rated more favorably than the Yemenite Jew or the Arab. A negative entry signifies the opposite.

Only the favorable adjective of any pair is presented here. The complete list of adjectives and traits used in this study, in both languages, may be obtained from the first author.

*$p < .05$.
**$p < .02$.
***$p < .01$.

Jewish subjects considered Yemenite Jews significantly *more* interesting, friendly, honest, and good-natured than Ashkenazic Jews, but less good-mannered, successful, self-confident, and leader-like. In the second column, it is apparent that Arabs were rated lower on nearly all traits, significantly so on courage, good looks, intelligence, good-naturedness, pleasantness, manners, truthfulness, successfulness, self-confidence, permissiveness, reliability, leadership, cheerfulness, and capacity for hard work.

Seven identical traits were used for rating both guises and attitudes toward the different cultural groups. These are listed in Table 3, where the reactions evoked by the two procedures are compared. There are remarkably sharp contrasts in these data. In terms of attitude ratings, Yemenite Jews were considered by Jewish subjects as *more* friendly and honest, equally intelligent, reliable, and good-looking, and less self-confident and leaderlike than Ashkenazic Jews. However, as revealed by the comparison of reactions to matched guises, Yemenite Jews were viewed as *less* honest, intelligent, and reliable, similar in friendliness and good looks, and somewhat more self-confident and leaderlike than Ashkenazic Jews. In every case but one (good looks) where there is a reliable difference

TABLE 3. COMPARABLE TRAITS FOR GUISE EVALUATIONS AND
ATTITUDE RATINGS

| | Ashkenazic-Yemenite Jew comparisons | | Hebrew-Arab comparisons | |
| | Ashkenazic-Yemenite Jewish guises | Ratings of Ashkenazim and Yemenite Jews | Hebrew-Arabic guises | Ratings of Ashkenazim and Arabs |
Trait	t	t	t	t
Good looks	1.18	1.13	1.58	2.75***
Friendliness	-.14	-2.50*	1.96	1.03
Honesty	3.35***	-4.25***	3.06***	1.03
Intelligence	3.50***	1.19	1.08	5.07***
Self-confidence	-1.44	6.77***	-.58	4.49***
Reliability	3.41***	1.15	1.48	7.68***
Leadership	-1.36	10.25***	.35	6.67***

Note. Positive entries signify that the guise and attitude ratings for Ashkenazim or Hebrews were more favorable than for Yemenite Jews or Arabs, and negative entries indicate the opposite.
*p < .05.
***p < .01.

on one form of rating, it is not different or reversed on the other form. The same type of contrasts are apparent in the reactions of Jewish subjects to Arabs. From the attitude ratings, Arabs were considered relatively less good-looking, intelligent, self-confident, reliable, and leaderlike people, whereas the view revealed in the guise ratings was that Arabs were less honest and friendly, but not reliably different as far as appearance, intelligence, self-confidence, reliability, or leadership is concerned.

These contrasts may be due in part to procedural differences. The matched-guise technique directs attention to individuals whose language style makes them representative of a particular linguistic and ethnic group, whereas the rating scale, like most standard measures, directs attention to an ethnic group in general, giving it a stereotyped label such as "Yemenite Jews." Furthermore, in the case of the Hebrew-Arabic contrasts, the style of Arabic used by the individual speakers was classical, similar to the Arabic the subjects studied in school, whereas "Arabs" in general use the colloquial form of the language.

Table 4 presents the intercorrelations of three measures: the evaluational reactions to matched guises, the attitude questionnaires, and the attitude rating scales. For the matched guises (Items 1 and 4 in Table 4), a mean D score was calculated for each subject by considering his reactions to a particular pair of guises on all traits except height, nervousness, and wealth since they were not clearly evaluative in nature. The higher a subject's score, the more favorable was his reaction to Ashkenazic in contrast to Yemenite guises (Item 1) or to Hebrew in contrast to Arabic guises (Item 4).

For the attitude questionnaires (Items 2 and 5 in Table 4) a total score was determined for each subject by considering his reactions to all questions, the higher the score, the more favorable the attitude toward Yem-

TABLE 4. CORRELATIONS OF EVALUATIONAL REACTIONS AND
ATTITUDE MEASURES: JEWISH SUBJECTS

Item	1	2	3
1. Ashkenazic-Yemenite Jewish guise comparisons	—	−.42*	−.39*
2. Attitude questionnaire toward Yemenite Jews		—	.47***
3. Rating scales of attitudes toward Yemenite Jews			—
	4	**5**	**6**
4. Hebrew-Arabic guise comparisons	—	−.36*	.00
5. Attitude questionnaire toward Arabs		—	.40*
6. Rating scales of attitudes toward Arabs			—

Note. Comparisons of guises were determined by considering all traits except height, nervousness, and wealth. The higher the score, the more favorable is the evaluation on all 17 traits of the Ashkenazic or Hebrew guises over the Yemenite Jewish or the Arabic guises. For the two attitude measures, the higher the score, the more favorable is the reaction to the group.
*$p < .05$, $N = 32$.
***$p < .01$.

enite Jews (Item 2) and toward Arabs (Item 5). Similarly, total scores for the attitude rating scale (Items 3 and 6 in Table 4) were determined by considering ratings on all 18 scales, and again, the higher the score the more favorable the attitude toward Yemenite Jews (Item 3) and toward Arabs (Item 6).

The correlations in Table 4 are low if one considers that all three procedures measure the same components of attitude. The fact that the rating scales and attitude questionnaires correlate only in the 40s is difficult to explain; it may be due in part to differences of form and wording. The matched-guise and rating-scale techniques used the same rating form but, as already noted, there are major procedural differences that could account for the low and inconsistent correlations. The two measures correlate to a significant but low degree in the case of the Hebrew-Yemenite comparison ($r = −.39$), but not at all in the case of the Hebrew-Arabic comparison ($r = .00$).

The correlations in Table 4 are similar in magnitude to those found in earlier studies using the matched guise technique (Anisfeld et al., 1962; Lambert et al., 1960) in that D scores based on ratings of matched guises showed low or insignificant correlations with standard measures of attitudes. These low correlations suggested that in expressing evaluational reactions to the matched guises of speakers, subjects drew on stereotypes about the groups in question in their attempts to make accurate judgments about the speakers' personalities and that community-wide stereotyped reactions may have played a more important role in the personality judgments than did personal attitudes towards the groups represented by the speakers.

The results of the present study, particularly the contrasts presented in Table 3, suggest a supplementary explanation for the low and inconsistent correlations noted in Table 4. First, standard attitude items usually direct the respondent's attention to ethnic or national groups as a whole (e.g., The trouble with Jews is . . . or The more I get to know Negroes . . .) while the matched-guise procedure directs the subject's attention to individuals whose distinguishable speech characteristics identify them as members of the groups in question. Furthermore, standard measures of attitudes are often transparent in the sense that subjects can comprehend what is being measured and can easily distort their actual attitudes by responding in what they feel is a socially appropriate manner. The instructional set accompanying the matched-guise technique, however, makes it unlikely that subjects will realize the true purpose of the procedure. In view of the marked contrasts between the two procedures revealed in the present study, the hypothesis suggests itself that the matched-guise technique, in contrast to standard measures of attitudes, evokes more private emotional and conceptual reactions. This is, of course, only a hypothesis, for until further research directed specifically at this question is conducted there are as yet no empirical grounds for actually deciding which is the better procedure for evoking "private" or "uncensored" attitudes.

References

Anisfeld, Elizabeth and W. E. Lambert. Evaluational reactions of bilingual and monolingual children to spoken languages. *Journal of Abnormal and Social Psychology*, 1964, 69, 89–97.

Anisfeld, M., N. Bogo, and W. E. Lambert. Evaluational reactions to accented English speech. *Journal of Abnormal and Social Psychology*, 1962, 65, 223–231.

Lambert, W. E., R. C. Hodgson, R. C. Gardner, and S. Fillenbaum. Evaluational reactions to spoken languages. *Journal of Abnormal and Social Psychology*, 1960, 60, 44–51.

V

Comparative Studies
of Social Roles
and Interaction

15   HARRY C. TRIANDIS, VASSO VASSILIOU
AND MARIA NASSIAKOU

Role Perception, Behavioral Intentions,
and Perceived Social Behaviors:
Three Cross-Cultural Studies
of Subjective Culture

AN INTRODUCTION TO THE
MEASUREMENT OF SUBJECTIVE CULTURE

In a review of the literature on the influence of culture on cognition, Triandis (1964a) employed a number of constructs which appear useful

Abridged from Harry C. Triandis, Vasso Vassiliou, Maria Nassiakou, "Three Cross-Cultural Studies of Subjective Culture," *Journal of Personality and Social*

in the analysis of the way persons perceive their social environment, that is, in the analysis of "subjective culture." The review focused on the concept of *categorization*, the *relationships among categories*, the *evaluation of the categories*, the subjects' *behavioral intentions towards the categories*, the subjects' *behavioral norms towards the categories*, and the subjects' *values*.

The evidence showed substantial differences among subjects from different cultures in the way they categorize experience. *Categorization* is inferred from the observation that similar stimuli elicit the same response from groups of subjects. Thus, persons of dark skin often elicit similar behaviors from certain American subjects (e.g., the response "I would exclude from the neighborhood"). Inclusion of a person in a given category, for example, the category *Negro*, depends on the characteristics of the stimulus persons. Certain criterial attributes (e.g., skin color) are far more important than others in categorization. Persons in one culture may use criterial attributes in different ways from persons in another culture. The content of categories is largely culturally determined and is closely related to the language system employed by members of a particular culture.

The *relationships among the categories* employed by the subjects are also in part determined by culture. Thus, some subjects see strong relationships among two categories — for example, the category *Negro* is strongly related to the category *musical* — while other subjects do not. Stereotyping is the result of categorization and is used by subjects as a means of simplifying their social environment. It provides a certain amount of predictability to the events of the social environment.

A particularly important connection among categories is the relationship between a category and sets of categories implying *evaluation*. Osgood's (1965) cross-cultural work with the semantic differential suggests that there are three important relationships between concepts: their evaluation, as well as the perception of their potency and their activity.

Psychology Monograph Supplement, Vol. 8, No. 4, Part 2, April 1968, pp. 1–41. Copyright (1968) by the American Psychological Association, and reproduced by permission.

    [The] Monograph is an abbreviated version of "Some Cross-Cultural Studies of Subjective Culture" and "Some Cultural Differences in the Perception of Social Behaviors," by the same authors, which are Technical Reports Numbers 45 and 49 of the contract to study communication, cooperation, and negotiation in culturally heterogeneous groups between the University of Illinois and the Advanced Research Projects Agency and the Office of Naval research, Contract NR 177–472, Nonr 1834(36); Fred E. Fiedler, Lawrence M. Stolurow, and Harry C. Triandis, principal investigators. . . .

For example, Negroes may be seen as "good," "powerful," and "active" by one group of subjects and as "bad," "powerful," and "active" by another group. Evaluation is typically the most important of these connections, since it accounts for most of the variance in all of the studies reported by Osgood and his colleagues.

People also have *behavioral intentions* towards categories. Thus, subjects give highly reliable responses to the Behavioral Differential (Triandis, 1964b) items such as:

Negro, female, physician

would   :__:__:__:__:__:__:__:__:__: would not

admire the ideas of this person

A behavioral intention is simply a statement that the subject intends to do something to a person or object represented by a particular category or a set of categories. When the subject is asked to indicate what behaviors he considers *appropriate* toward the category, we obtain a measure of his *behavioral norms*.

When we analyze the responses of subjects to large sets of categories, we observe certain regularities. Such regularities may be indications of the *values* that underlie such responses. Thus, we might observe highly positive responses to semantic or behavioral differentials when the categories are "educational concepts." We can then infer a positive value for education.

Roles constitute a particularly important type of category to which subjects respond. A *role* is a patterned sequence of learned behaviors performed by a person in an interaction situation (Sarbin, 1954). This pattern of behaviors is normative in the sense that it is particularly appropriate for persons holding specified positions in a social system. From the early use of the role concept (Linton, 1936), it has been recognized that it refers to the dynamic or action component of the *status* of an individual in a social system. Status was defined by Linton as a collection of rights and duties; he distinguished between ascribed and achieved status, pointing out that the most frequent bases of status are ascribed. Linton considered the following bases of status differentiation as universal: sex, age, family relationships, social class, and/or caste. Most societies also differentiate roles according to the skills of different individuals, their titles, and conscious formations of social units, such as clubs, etc.

In order to study the perception of roles, we have adapted and extended the work within the methodological framework utilized in previous investigations of behavioral intentions (Triandis, 1964a, 1964b). In these earlier studies, subjects responded to a behavioral differential in which a stimulus person is judged on a series of bipolar scales.

A female Negro physician

would :__:__:__:__:__:__:__:__: would not
                    admire the ideas of

would not :__:__:__:__:__:__:__:__: would
                    let go first through door

would :__:__:__:__:__:__:__:__: would not
                         hit

Three domains are sampled when using this instrument: the stimulus persons, the social behaviors, and the subjects making the responses. In a typical study, the responses of a homogeneous sample of subjects are summed. A matrix of 100 (stimuli) × 50 (behaviors) may be the basic input to a factor analysis of the correlations among the behaviors. The purpose is to find basic "clusters of behaviors" and thus describe in the most simple way how a particular sample of subjects intends to behave toward each stimulus person. Triandis (1964b) found five independent factors from such an analysis: *Respect* (e.g., admire the ideas, obey), *Marital Acceptance* (marry, love), *Friendship Acceptance* (gossip, accept as intimate friend), *Social Distance* (exclude from the neighborhood, not accept as kin by marriage), *Subordination* (be commanded by, not treat as a subordinate). In that study, two samples of behaviors were employed with the same stimulus persons and subjects; it was shown that the independent factor analyses of the two samples gave essentially the same factors. Triandis, Tanaka, and Shanmugam (1966) showed that when the stimulus persons and the social behaviors remain the same, while the subjects change (Illinois, U.S.A.; Mysore, India; Tokyo, Japan), the factor structures of the behaviors are again the same. It remains to be shown whether a similar instrument will likewise prove useful in understanding the structure of roles and role behavior.[1]

In the work mentioned above, the sample of social behaviors was obtained from content analyses of American novels. In the present study the sample of behaviors was obtained from standardized procedures involving direct elicitation from subjects. Thus, while all the other work employed samples of "American behaviors," in the present study each of the cul-

---

[1] On the other hand, when the stimulus persons are changed (Triandis, Fishbein, & Hall, 1964) the factor structures of the behaviors do change. For example, the social distance factor is particularly relevant when American white subjects judge stimulus persons who include Negroes and whites. When race is not included in the study, the social distance factor merges with other factors. This has been encountered with both semantic and behavioral differential work, and has been referred to by Osgood (1962) as the concept/scale interaction phenomenon.

tures was allowed to yield its own sample of behaviors. Furthermore, in previous work the instructions asked the subjects to indicate how they would or would not behave toward the stimulus persons, in the sense that it is "likely" that they would or would not behave in particular ways. However, in the present study we asked the subjects to tell us what is "appropriate" behavior in their culture, and the stimulus persons were replaced by roles (e.g., father-son; prostitute-client), so that the judgments were made on whether it is appropriate in a particular culture for a father to behave in particular ways toward his son or for a prostitute to behave in certain ways toward her client.

STUDY I: A CROSS-CULTURAL STUDY OF ROLE PERCEPTIONS

The Role Differential Method

The American instructions appear below. The Greek instructions were careful translations of the same text.

> In every society there are certain ideas about what kinds of behaviors are appropriate for a person to undertake in relation to another person. For instance, in our society, at least in certain circles, a man lets a woman go first through a door. Some of these behaviors are very clearly specified and well understood, but other behaviors are not so clearly specified. Also, some behaviors are very clearly specified in one country, but not so clearly specified in another.
>
> In the present study we are trying to obtain your opinions about what are the appropriate behaviors in your culture. We are doing this in many countries, and with people from many cultures. By culture we mean the man-made part of the human environment. This includes not only cars and electric appliances, etc., but also the ideas about what is right or wrong, etc. When we say *your* culture, we mean the circle of people who are most like yourself—in race, religion, social class, neighborhood, nationality, region of the country, etc. So, when we ask you to tell us whether in your culture a particular behavior is appropriate, we are asking you to tell us how your friends, neighbors, relatives, and other people like yourself feel about the appropriateness of the behavior.
>
> Note that we are not asking you to make a moral judgment. It is not a question of whether a person ought to do something, but whether, in general, he does do it. In other words, if you and your friends feel that cheating on your income tax is not morally correct, but you go ahead and do it anyway because everybody else that you know does it, then we want you to tell us that you would cheat when filling out your income tax. Give us the actual, not the ideal.

Inside this questionnaire you will find a role-pair on the top of
each page and a set of behavior scales under the pair. For instance:

Male-Female

X
would :_:_:_:_:_:_:_:_:_: would not
let go first through door

You are asked to check by placing an X at the degree of certainty
that a particular behavior is considered appropriate in your culture-
group. Notice that there is a convention about the order of the people that appear in the role-pair. The first member of the pair is the
actor. The second is the person acted upon. Thus, the item Female-
Male refers to the question whether a female would let a male go
first through the door. Here your answer might be:

Female-Male

X
would :_:_:_:_:_:_:_:_:_: would not
let go first through door

Such an answer would indicate that this is unlikely, but not too
rare.

The information that you are going to give us is going to be completely confidential. We will use it only in statistical form for cross-
cultural comparisons. Thus, please express yourself freely in responding
to this questionnaire.

For each culture there were two sets of social behaviors (A and B); as
noted earlier, each set consisted of 52 behaviors. In addition, 8 behaviors
were added from the Triandis (1964b) study, so as to have a round number of 60 behaviors in each analysis, and also to have "marker variables"
that permit comparison with the previous study.

Because the complete role differential involved a very large number of
judgments (100 roles judged on 120 scales = 12,000 in the United
States), it was randomly divided into 17 groups of items. Each subject
responded to 1/17 of the total, thus permitting subject completion of
the questionnaire in approximately 1 hour. In addition, each subject responded to 50 common items, to allow for a check of the reliability of the
groups of subjects. Thus, there were 17 types of questionnaires. Each type
of questionnaire was responded to by at least 15 subjects in each culture.
Approximately 275 Americans and 300 Greeks participated in this phase
of the study. [See Table 1.]

Analyses

The responses of the subjects to each questionnaire type (N of 15 or
more) were combined. Thus, matrices of 100 roles by 60 behaviors and

TABLE 1. ROLE PROFILES OF A FEW ROLES IN TWO CULTURES

Role	America	Greece
Mother-son	Stand up for	Help
	Reward	Cooperate with
	Love	Study with
	Admire	Reward
	Show concern for	Advise
	Protect	Teach
	Buy gift for	Admire
	Praise	Be interested in
	Go to movie with	Feel sympathetic toward
	Cry for	Love
	Wish good luck to	Enjoy
	Share responsibility with	Not be enemy of
	Not discuss with	Not feign
	Command	Not grow impatient with
	Idolize	Not be indifferent to
	Kiss	Not feel inferior to
	. . .	Not hate
		Not anger
		Not despise
		Cry for
		Feel sorry for
		Not compete with
		Not have fun with
		Not exploit
		Not be jealous of
Foreman-laborer	Argue with	Reprimand
	Disagree with	Scold
	Command	Appoint
	Not confess sins to	Exploit
	Be annoyed by	Advise
	Treat as a subordinate	Teach
	Teach	Not ask for advice
	Correct	Not thank for goods
	Advise	Not ask for help
	Reprimand	Not apologize
	Look down upon	Not express gratitude to
	. . .	Not fear
Man-God	Confess sins to	Be enemy of
	Not teach	Feign
	Not correct	Grow impatient with
	Not advise	Be indifferent to
	Not reprimand	Be indignant with
	Not look down upon	Compete with
	Not treat as a subordinate	Be enemy with
	Not argue with	Be rival of
	Not disagree with	Show abhorrence of
	Not be annoyed by	Not cry with
	Not compliment	Not fear
	Not accept	Not caress
	Not go to a movie with	Not cheat
	Not cuddle	Cooperate with
	Not marry	Advise
	Not accept as intimate friend	Teach
	Not kiss	Ask for advice

TABLE 1. *Continued*

Role	America	Greece
Man-God (*continued*)	Work well for	Thank
	Learn with help of	Show love for
	Depend upon	Express understanding of
	Be afraid of	Cry for
	Idolize	Be interested in
	Ask for help	Not compete with
	Complain to	Not have fun with
	Envy	Not exploit
	Not blame for failure	Not feign
	Not throw rocks at	Not be rival of
	Not be enemy of	Not be jealous of
		Not annoy
		Not quarrel with
		Not reprimand
		Not scold
		Not complain to
		. . .

92 roles by 60 behaviors were obtained in the United States and in Greece, respectively. Four independent factor analyses were performed on the matrices of intercorrelation (60×60) of the behaviors (Set A and Set B from Illinois and Set A and Set B from Greece).

Sets A and B of the American role differential each yielded 10 interpretable factors; the Greek role differential Set A yielded only 5, and Set B, only 7 interpretable factors. The computer program rotates successively a decreasing number of factors obtained in each factor analysis. This permits the use of both the "relative drop" in the eigenvalues and the interpretability of the factors in the various solutions as criteria for the determination of the most satisfactory number of factors to be rotated. In general these two criteria give identical results, but when this was not so, we erred in the direction of showing fewer rather than more factors. The latter decision is based on our experience in factor analysis, which suggests that the last factors, accounting for little variance, are often not replicable. This decision may have eliminated some of the culture-specific factors from each of the analyses. Tables 2 and 3 show the results of these factor solutions. The correspondence between Sets A and B, *within* both cultures, is rather high, showing high reliability for the procedures employed. However, the correspondence of the factors *across* cultures is lower, though not very low. In both cultures, the first factor includes Associative versus Dissociative behaviors, though the content of the factors is quite culture-specific. The second factor involves Hostility, though the American factor suggests Contempt, rather than hostility. The third factor in both cultures is Superordination-Subordination. Factor IV (American) and Factor V (Greek) suggest Intimacy. While the above-

TABLE 2. HIGHEST LOADING OF ROLE DIFFERENTIAL BEHAVIOR
FACTORS AFTER VARIMAX ROTATION — AMERICAN

Set A		Set B	
Acceptance vs. prejudice			
Factor I (30% of variance)		Factor I (28% of variance)	
Be prejudiced against	-.94	Fear	-.94
Compliment	.92	Exclude from	
Be afraid of	-.94	neighborhood	-.94
Stand up for	.84	Be eager to see	.90
Be interested in	.93	Laugh at jokes of	.86
Exclude from		Let join own club	.83
neighborhood	-.92	Respect	.86
Reward	.84	Be prejudiced	
Not admire	-.80	against	-.89
Blame for failure	-.86	Not admire	-.77
Argue with	.81	Swear at	-.74
Contempt			
Factor II (14% of variance)		Factor II (15% of variance)	
Lie to	.75	Cheat	.82
Go to meeting with	-.75	Sympathize with	-.85
Enjoy meeting	-.80	Enjoy company of	-.85
Laugh at	.82	Laugh at	.79
Learn with help of	-.76	Go shopping with	-.77
Superordination			
Factor III (6% of variance)		Factor III (6% of variance)	
Command	.77	Inspect work of	.71
Advise	.65	Feel superior to	.69
Treat as a subordinate	.62	Order to do something	.66
Be annoyed by	.58	Counsel	.56
Look down upon	.50	Punish	.36
Intimacy			
Factor IV (4% of variance)		Factor IV (4% of variance)	
Kiss	.84	Kiss	.78
Cuddle	.83	Cuddle	.83
Love	.43	Punish	.38
Marry	.35	Be captivated by charm	.35
Tutoring			
Factor V (7% of variance)		Factor V (5% of variance)	
Teach	.81	Tutor	.69
Buy gift for	.82	Accept views of	.73
Admire character of	.69	Approve of	.51
Not work well for	.50	Ask for advice	-.47
Kinship			
Factor VI (5% of variance)		Factor VI (5% of variance)	
Accept as close kin	.61	Accept as close kin by marriage	.76
Ask for help of	.58	Follow instructions of	.50
Depend upon	.50	Introduce to own friends	.48
Be annoyed by	.57	Like	.42
Complain to	.62	Ask for advice of	.38

TABLE 2. Continued

Set A		Set B	
		High intensity	
Factor VII (6% of variance)		Factor VII (10% of variance)	
Cry for	-.72	Mourn for	-.80
Help	-.69	Understand	-.76
Protect	-.59	Be proud of	-.72
Be enemy of	.59	Be loyal to	-.69
Throw rocks at	.31	Not eat with	.53
		Envy	
Factor VIII (4% of variance)		Factor VIII (5% of variance)	
Envy	.84	Envy	.88
Be friend of	.48	Admire ideas of	.64
		Intense hostility	
Factor IX (3% of variance)		Factor IX (3% of variance)	
Throw rocks at	.77	Fight with	.61
Accept as kin by marriage	-.31	Avoid	.45
		Work acceptance	
Factor X (3% of variance)		Factor X (2% of variance)	
Work well for	.66	Work with	.47
Work for	.66	Wish good luck to	-.34

Note. Total variance accounted: Set A, 82%; Set B, 83%.

mentioned four factors appear to be common across cultures, the remaining factors are definitely culture-specific. It is possible that accidents of sampling of the social behaviors resulted in factors in the Greek Set B which do not appear in the Greek Set A. Thus, there is a factor of Suspicion and a factor of Overt Agression only in Set B. Ingroup Concern for Consensus is a Greek factor. Tutoring, Kinship, and four other minor factors are entirely American.

STUDY II: A CROSS-CULTURAL STUDY OF BEHAVIORAL INTENTIONS

Method and Results

It was hypothesized that the factor structure of the behavior norms, as measured by the role differential, would be the same as the factor structure of behavioral intentions, as measured by the behavioral differential. To test this hypothesis, an American and a Greek Behavioral Differential was constructed which used the 60 behaviors, obtained in the role differential study. [See Tables 4 and 5.]

Ninety-six stimuli were constructed from all possible combinations of *age* (young, middle-aged, old, very old), *race* (white, Negro), *sex* (male, female), *occupation* (physician, sales clerk, unskilled laborer), and *En-*

TABLE 3. HIGHEST LOADING OF ROLE DIFFERENTIAL BEHAVIOR
FACTORS AFTER VARIMAX ROTATION — GREEK

	Set A		Set B	
Factor I	Associative vs. dissociative (38.7%)		Associative vs. dissociative (54.0%)	
	Help	.72	Be Friend of	.88
	Reward	.82	Invite	.86
	Advise	.83	Discuss	.87
	Hate	-.90	Argue with	-.80
	Mutually hate	-.91	Infuriate	-.85
	Feel antipathy	-.88	Be indignant with	-.87
	Grow impatient with	-.80	Be proud of success of	.79
	Be indignant with	-.82	Hate	-.84
			Respect	.71
Factor II	Hostility (17.0%)		Hostility (7.3%)	
	Quarrel with	.87	Quarrel with	.78
	Exploit	.76	Annoy	.78
	Cheat	.73	Accuse	.70
	Be jealous toward	.81	Avoid	.64
	Lie to	.69		
Factor III	Superordination (11.7%)-Subordination		Subordination (7.1%)	
	Thank for presents	.84	Is dependent on	.78
	Apologize	.80	Accept commands of	.73
	Asks for help	.84	Fear	.67
Factor IV	Ingroup concern for consensus (5%)		Ingroup concern for consensus (5%)	
	Adore the same God with	.52	Adore the same God with	.60
	Is saddened by attitude of	.73	Admire	.65
	Desire good attitude of	.76		
Factor V	Intimacy (3.2%)		Intimacy (2.5%)	
	Pet	.60	Sex-Love	.89
	Cry for	.67	Love	.25
Factor VI			Suspicion (2.6%)	
			Be cautious	.70
			De discriminating	.60
Factor VII			Overt aggression (2.5%)	
			Throw rocks at	.67
			Hit	.55
	Total accounted by 5 factors: 75.6%		Total accounted by 7 factors: 81.3%	

glish fluency (speaks fluent English, speaks poor English). In Greece the *race* element was changed to a *religion* (Greek, Orthodox, Jewish) element to include stimuli that elicit a maximum of social distance (see Triandis & Triandis, 1962) and *English fluency* was changed to *Greek fluency*. These stimulus persons were presented to subjects with instructions used in previous studies involving the behavioral differential. Thus, the subject was not instructed to indicate an "appropriate behavior" for people like him in his culture (as was the case in the role differential), but to indicate his actual *behavioral intentions* towards the stimulus person.

Discussion of the Culture-Common Factors of Studies I and II

In a previous study, Triandis (1964b) examined the behavioral component of social attitudes. Using the behavioral differential, he established

TABLE 4. FACTORS OF AMERICAN BEHAVIORAL DIFFERENTIAL

Factor		Loading
I: Respect (21.0% of total variance)		
	Go to meeting with	.73
	Learn with help of	.75
	Stand up for	.73
	Reward	.73
	Depend upon	.77
	Enjoy working for	.72
	Enjoy meeting	.79
	Admire character of	.76
	Praise	.79
	Admire	.74
II: Hostility (13.5%)		
	Argue with	.75
	Correct	.83
	Blame for failure	.76
	Dislike	.72
	Disagree with	.74
III: Marital acceptance (10.6%)		
	Love	.77
	Accept as close kin by marriage	.71
	Marry	.76
IV: Friendship (11.3%)		
	Help	.87
	Protect	.77
	Wish good luck to	.76
V: Superordination (8.4%)		
	Treat as subordinate	.74
	Command	.73
VI: Deep emotional involvement (6.4%)		
	Confess sins to	.67
	Idolize	.56
	Cry for	.51

Note. Total cumulated variance accounted for = 71.2%.

the existence of five factors. The first factor was extremely similar to the Respect factor of Table 4 (it had high loadings on *admire character, admire ideas, cooperate in political campaign,* etc.). The second was similar to the Marital factor of Table 4. The third was somewhat similar to the Friendship factor of Table 4, being defined by high loadings on *would gossip with, would be partners in athletic games with,* and *would eat with.* The fourth was a Social Distance factor (*exclude from the neighborhood, prohibit from voting*) which appears similar to the Hostility factor of Table 4. The fifth factor was Subordination-Superordination and is very similar to one of the factors of Table 4. Thus, the factors of the previous study were replicated in the present study.

In the present series of studies the Associative-Dissociative and Superordination-Subordination factors appeared repeatedly. Hence, the present results lend support to the notion that solidarity and dominance are the

TABLE 5. FACTORS OF GREEK BEHAVIORAL DIFFERENTIAL

Factor		Loading
I: Associative vs. dissociative (40.0% of the variance)		
	Be enemy of	.76
	Be rival of	.71
	Show love to	-.80
	Express understanding of	-.79
	Be interested in	-.81
	Be grateful for interest of	-.80
	Be friend of	-.80
	Enjoy	-.80
	Feel sympathetic towards	-.77
	Love	-.85
	Thank for goods	-.86
	Exploit	.77
	Cheat	.88
	Help	-.88
	Reward	-.85
II: Friendship (9.6% of variance)		
	Annoy	.60
	Ask for advice	.59
	Have fun with	.59
	Cooperate with	.66
	Promise	.62
	Apologize to	.66
	Study with	.69
III: Hostility (5.5% of the variance)		
	Hate	.60
	Fear	.60
	Feel inferior to	.57
IV: Superordination (4.8% of variance)		
	Reprimand	.69
	Scold	.51
	Have difficulty understanding	-.49
V: Active avoidance (5.9% of the variance)		
	Have difficulty understanding	.63
	Show abhorrence of	.60
	Detest	.52
VI: Attempts at acceptance by high-status persons (4.8% of variance)		
	Complain to	.68
	Boast to	.59
	Boast of success to	.51

Note. Total variance accounted by 6 factors: 70.6%.

two basic dimensions of social interaction, a result that is in agreement with similar studies (Foa, 1964), with studies of animal social psychology (e.g., Mason, 1964), and analysis of verbal usage (Brown, 1965). Straus (1964) has reviewed a large number of studies which suggest that these two dimensions are central in family relations and in socialization.

In our unrotated factors we repeatedly found the dimensions of affect (evaluation), dominance (potency) (Foa, 1964), and intensity (activity). Thus, these three dimensions appear to be the most important in the perception of social behavior. The correspondence of these results with the Schutz (1958) theory of interpersonal relations is quite striking. Our three dimensions correspond to Schutz's *affection, dominance,* and *inclusion*. Their correspondence with the basic dimensions of connotative meaning (Osgood et al., 1957) is interesting and needs discussion. We note that Triandis and Lambert (1958) have already suggested that there is a similarity between the dimensions of the perception of emotional expressions and those of meaning. They noted that Schlosberg's (1954) dimensions of *pleasantness-unpleasantness, attention-rejection,* and *tension-sleep* correspond to *evaluation, potency,* and *activity*. More recently, Osgood (1966) reanalyzed several studies of emotional expression and concluded that the basic dimensions are *evaluation, control,* and *activity*, and they correspond very closely to the dimensions of connotative meaning.

Another correspondence can be noted with analyses of personality. La-Forge and Suczek (1955) have presented a theory of interpersonal personality which postulates the factors love-hate, dominance-submission, and intensity. More recently, Lorr and McNair (1965) presented a theory in which dominance-submission and affection-hostility appear as approximately orthogonal components.

All of these studies involved subjects responding to verbal stimuli or attitudinal items, or giving verbal responses to a judgmental task. Perhaps the correspondence between the factor analytic studies performed in these diverse domains is the result of a methodological artifact: all studies do nothing more than reflect the structure of the meaning of words (evaluation, potency, activity). This pessimistic conclusion appears incorrect when we note the results that Longabaugh (1966) reported on observations of social behavior of children in six cultures. The data were obtained by the Whiting and Lambert six-culture project from 67 girls and 67 boys living in rural communities in Mexico, Africa, India, Philippines, Okinawa, and New England.

Five-minute samples of child behavior were collected by observers. About 20,000 acts were coded. The behaviors were categorized into 12 categories: gives help, suggests responsibility (e.g., taking adult role), reprimands, attempts to dominate, calls attention to self, acts sociable (e.g., greets), gives support or approval, contacts physically, succorance (e.g., asks for help), sociable physical assault, nonsociable physical assault, symbolic aggression. One measure was obtained when the frequency with which each child enacted each behavior was divided by the total amount of time he was observed. Another measure was obtained by dividing the frequency with which a child enacted a particular category by the total frequency of enacting of any behavior. These two measures were highly correlated. Correlations among the categories of behavior were obtained, using all 134 children. Several factor analyses were performed and three-, four-, and five-factor solutions were rotated. In summarizing all these analyses it is fair to say that the first measure resulted in five factors (nurturance, aggression, dependence, egocentrism-altrocentrism, and impulsivity), and the second measure resulted in four factors (amount of participation, dominance, exploitation, and association). The author employed somewhat different names, but labels given in factor analyses are idiosyncratic. It is most likely that Longabaugh would agree with our interpretation of his factors, particularly since he himself stated that the two major axes that emerge from his factor analyses are *interpersonal power and positive/negative interpersonal disposition* (pp. 93–94). Comparison of his results with ours suggests adequate correspondence. Thus, *total participation* suggests our *activity* factor; *nurturance* and *association* suggest our *association-dissociation* factor; *aggression* and *exploitation* suggest our *hostility* factor; *dependence* and *dominance* suggest our *subordination-superordination* factor. We conclude that our major factors, with the exception of *intimacy-formality*, were obtained in Longabaugh's study. The absence of the intimacy-formality factor seems hardly surprising, since very few of the behaviors emitted by children are likely to be characterized as formal.

Implications for Studies of National Character

The approach used in the present study may be used in analyses of certain aspects of national character. Triandis and Vassiliou (1967) have present some evidence which suggests that the two most central distinguishing features of Greek national character are extreme competitiveness and an unusual response to authority figures. Specifically, there is warm acceptance of ingroup authority figures and cold rejection of outgroup authority figures.

Extreme competitiveness is found through examination of the differential behaviors towards members of the ingroup as opposed to members of the outgroup. The ingroup is defined to include members of a person's immediate family, friends, the friends of these friends, and people who show concern. Within the ingroup the appropriate behaviors are not only cooperative but also self-sacrificing (the principle of the "philotimo"). However, between ingroup and outgroup members *extreme* competition is appropriate. Behavior towards members of the ingroup is characterized by cooperativeness, extreme nurturance, as well as anxiety and concern about their welfare. By contrast, behavior towards members of the outgroup is characterized by suspicion and hostility, as well as extreme competitiveness. The competitiveness theme is also found in sociological analyses of ancient Greek culture (Gouldner, 1965) and anthropological analyses of a modern Greek village (Friedl, 1962). Friedl used the term "contact unit" to describe the ingroup.

Some Greek behaviors appear "antiauthoritarian." But antiauthoritarian does not refer to the opposite of authoritarianism, as defined in the classic study by Adorno et al. Greek antiauthoritarianism is a by-product of the distinction between ingroup and outgroup. Our data show that the Greeks submit to authority only in the ingroup. For example, in most cultures a person with special skills or knowledge would be considered an authority figure. In Greece, unless he is an ingroup member, that is, appears concerned, he is quite likely to be ignored. Thus, Greek antiauthoritarianism is characterized by acts of ignoring authority figures rather than by acting out against them.

A benevolent government which is perceived as concerned with the citizen's welfare is likely to receive acceptance similar to the acceptance experienced by ingroup authority figures. On the other hand, a government which is seen as unconcerned will be ignored or rejected.

Most Greek outgroup authority figures are likely to perceive themselves as defied when they are ignored, and as a result they take extreme measures to enforce compliance.

The severity of punishment employed by such authority figures is exemplified by the use of a death penalty, by the military, for mere insubordination (a 1966 case of a conscientious objector who was found insubordinate because he refused to bear arms).

The Greek responses to the man-God role (small respect and friendship, but little rejection), the university student-administrator role (same pattern), and to other authority roles such as officer, club member-president of club suggest the tendencies described above. Furthermore, the Greek subjects show more acceptance of ingroup authority figures than do the American subjects.

Another characteristic of Greek national character mentioned by both Gouldner and Friedl is the extreme use of division of labor and specialization of function. A farmer might not repair a wall in his farm until the proper "master" comes to do the job for him (Friedl, 1962, pp. 34–37). This can also be thought of as a by-product of extreme competitiveness towards outgroup members, since this limits the competition to only one activity, the one the individual is quite good at, so that he can think of himself as the best. However, this emphasis on being the best does not necessarily lead to excellent workmanship. Extreme competitiveness often results in defensive devaluation of the work activity itself, as though the individual places himself above the contest by spending little time, doing a poor job, and often not bothering with the completion of the job. As demonstrated by Triandis and Vassiliou (1967), the above-mentioned characteristics produce extremely negative reactions by Americans working with Greeks. The results of the present study converge in some important respects with those of Triandis and Vassiliou. We noted that the role differential results suggest that when there is a status gap there is greater exchange of respect between members of a role pair in America than there is in Greece. This finding would suggest a lower competitiveness in such roles in America than in Greece. In Greece, not only do high-status persons give little respect to low-status persons, but also low-status persons give little respect to high-status persons.

There is little friendship, in Greece, between role-pair members who are in contest settings, such as Protestants and Catholics, and also in situations where a client receives help from a professional (lawyer, psychologist, etc.), but there is a great deal of friendship towards tourists, who are treated as members of the ingroup because of an age-long hospitality norm which is an important aspect of the culture. Similarly, there is less respect, friendship, rejection, superordination and subordination in both the God-man and the man-God roles in Greece than there is in America. This further suggests a non-involvement with the high-status person by the Greeks. It should be emphasized that the described type of antiauthoritarianism avoids involvement with outgroup authority figures, but when the Greek is forced to interact with powerful figures he may display outward signs of subservience. This is understandable when it is remembered that behavior is not only determined by role perceptions and interpersonal attitudes, but also by the perceived probabilities of negative and positive reinforcement and the values of such reinforcements. Since authority figures control such reinforcements, it is understandable that when responding to them subjects will not only be guided by their attitudes but also by their expectations of reinforcement.

STUDY III: SOME CROSS-CULTURAL DIFFERENCES IN THE PERCEPTION OF SOCIAL BEHAVIORS

It is a frequent observation among persons who have engaged in social interactions with persons from other cultures that their behaviors are

sometimes "misinterpreted" and their intentions "misunderstood." For
example, a person from one culture may provide what he considers to
be "friendly criticism" to a person from another culture only to discover that the other person interprets it as "hatred." Or, a person from
Culture A behaves in a manner which he considers extremely "positive"
toward a person from Culture B. However, the individual from Culture
B perceives the behavior as "neutral," and in turn, the individual from
Culture A feels that he is "given the cold shoulder." His negative reaction is then perceived as negative and a vicious circle of mutual negative reinforcement takes place. One possible explanation of such mis-
interpretations is that the meaning of the social behavior is not the same
across cultures.

Method

Selection of a Sample of Social Behaviors. In Study I we asked
samples of American and Greek students to supply sentence completions
to a set of 100 roles. The instructions required the subjects to supply
a social behavior which they considered appropriate and likely to occur
within each of these roles (e.g., father hits son). Samples of about 10,000
behaviors were obtained from each culture, and these were subjected to
facet and factor analyses. A variety of factor analytic approaches (including two-mode factor analysis) yielded four culture-common factors.
The four major culture-common factors were (a) Giving versus Denying
Affect (defined by high loadings on the behaviors such as *to love, to
admire, to help* versus *to hate, to despise, to be prejudiced against*); (b)
Giving versus Denying Status (defined by high loadings on behaviors
such as *obey, be commanded by, accept criticism of* versus *treat as a
subordinate, command, give advice to*); (c) Intimacy versus Formality
(e.g., *to have sexual intercourse with, to marry, to pet* versus *to appoint
to important position, to send letter inviting to dinner, let join own
club*); and (d) Hostility (e.g., *throw rocks at, insult, exclude from the
neighborhood*). Sixty American and 60 Greek behaviors having high
loadings on one or another of these four culture-common factors were
selected for the present study.

Procedure. The 120 behaviors mentioned were translated into
the other language, so that a list of 120 behaviors was available in each
culture. The list was then presented to psychology student subjects
with Thurstone equal-appearing interval scale instructions (Edwards,
1957). The Ballin and Farnsworth (1941) graphic-rating method was
used. The four continua utilized by the subjects in making their judgments were defined as follows:

> *Giving Versus Denying Affect.* Giving affect means to feel positively

about the other person. *To love* is an example of a social behavior which is high on "giving affect." *To hate* is an example of denying affect. Read all behaviors listed in this sheet. Select the one behavior which you consider to be most extreme in giving affect and place it in Category 11. Then select the one behavior which you consider to be the most extreme in denying affect and place it in Category 1. Then, judge the other behaviors in this list and place each of them in one of the 11 categories provided to you.

Giving Versus Denying Status. Giving status means to make the other person feel strong, powerful, great. Denying status means to make the other person feel weak, powerless, small. *To beg* is an example of giving status, *to command* is an example of denying status. Read all behaviors . . .

Formal Versus Intimate Behaviors. Extremely formal behaviors are the type that a head of state would undertake when interacting with another head of state. *To send written invitation to a formal dinner* is a formal behavior. Intimate behaviors are behaviors that are likely to occur within the family. *To have sexual intercourse with* is a very intimate behavior. Of course, this does not mean that all family behaviors are intimate or all behaviors between heads of state are formal. In between the two extremes there are behaviors which might be called informal. Read all behaviors . . .

Hostile Behaviors. Hostile behaviors involve doing something which hurts another person. This dimension looks superficially like the denying of affect dimension, but there is actually a difference. For example, a mother may love her child and yet beat him. *To beat* under these conditions would be high in hostility and also high in *giving* affect. Read all behaviors . . .

The subjects were provided with 11-point scales on which they entered the serial number associated with each behavior. The end-points of the scales were labeled as follows: Gives affect–Denies affect; Gives status–Denies status; Formal-Informal-Intimate; No trace of hostility–Maximum hostility.

Subjects. Three samples of psychology undergraduates were employed: American males, American females, Greek females (there are no males studying psychology in Greece). Since 120 behaviors had to be judged on four dimensions and it was felt that the 480 judgments would lead to fatigue and unreliability, the judgments were randomly divided into four equal sets. Each subject completed 120 judgments. Since each of the subjects responded to a different combination of behavior-scale judgments, and since they were also instructed not to make a judgment if they felt that the dimension was irrelevant, the number of judgments obtained had unequal Ns. The Ns for the Greeks ranged from 5 to 45, with a median of 25. The Ns for the Americans ranged from 7 to 30, with a median of 20.

Analysis. The medians of the distributions of the judgments as well as the interquartile range of these distributions were recorded. The medians of the judgments on the four dimensions were intercorrelated. Table 6 shows the correlations ($N = 120$) between the samples.

The medians and interquartile ranges obtained for each behavior were employed to determine whether cultural differences existed in the judgments of the behaviors. Only differences significant beyond the .01 level were considered. Thus, we preferred to focus on only the most extreme cultural differences.

Results

Cross-Cultural Similarities. It is clear that the meaning of the four dimensions employed in the two cultures is very similar; otherwise we would not have obtained the high correlations of Table 6. In fact, the meanings across cultures is about as similar as it is across sex groups. Furthermore, Table 7 shows that the subjects did not make the discriminations that we expected them to make. Giving affect apparently implies giving status (e.g., *to marry* involves giving high affect and

TABLE 6. CORRELATIONS BETWEEN THE MEDIANS OF THE BEHAVIORS ON THE FOUR DIMENSIONS[a]

| | Correlations between Mdns of: | | |
Dimension	American males and females	American females and Greek females	American males and Greek females[b]
Affect	.94	.89	.90
Status	.83	.89	.86
Intimacy	.43	.58	.62
Hostility	.91	.90	.90

Note. All correlations are significant beyond the .001 level.
[a]$N = 120$.
[b]There are no males studying psychology in Greece.

TABLE 7. CORRELATIONS AMONG THE FOUR DIMENSIONS FOR AMERICAN AND GREEK FEMALES[a]

Dimensions	Americans	Greeks
Affect and status	.82**	.84**
Affect and intimacy	-.12	.24*
Affect and hostility	-.89**	-.93**
Status and intimacy	-.11	.03
Status and hostility	-.76**	-.84**
Intimacy and hostility	.13	-.18*

[a]$N = 120$.
*$p < .05$.
**$p < .001$.

status) and low hostility despite our attempts to make the subjects discriminate between these dimensions.

As Table 8 indicates, there are numerous differences in the perception of social behaviors. Many of these differences appear meaningful to those of us who have been exposed to the two cultures under study. Further research is needed to establish the importance of such differences in the determination of the outcomes of social behavior.

It is notable that on 23 behaviors the Greeks see more intimacy than do the Americans and on only 8 is there the reverse pattern. This result is consistent with the findings of Studies I and II, where we found more intimacy within roles in Greece than in America.

The implication of such differences is that an American interacting with a Greek might behave inappropriately for the level of intimacy that is appropriate at a particular time, because he may not realize that more intimacy is required before the particular behavior is permissible. Thus, for example, he may try to *kiss,* to *quarrel with,* to *ask for advice of,* to *advise,* to *laugh at jokes of,* to *correct,* etc., before the Greek sees that the relationship is ripe for such intimacies. On the other hand, he may wait too long before he *invites to dinner, congratulates, mourns for,* etc., than would be appropriate from the Greek's point of view, since, for instance, a dinner invitation does not require as much intimacy in Greece as it requires in the United States.

Another kind of "cross-cultural interaction mistake" would be not to realize the significance of certain behaviors in terms of their implications for denying affect. Thus, *to be indifferent to, to punish,* etc., are seen as denying affect to a much greater extent in Greece than in America. The Greek on his side can make the cultural mistake of assuming that he is reinforcing the American more than he really is when he *helps him, advises him, praises, appreciates him,* etc.

We might speculate that the degree to which a behavior is seen as involving the giving of affect is related to the extent to which it is reinforcing (using Thibaut & Kelley's [1959] language — the extent to which it provides rewards). Those behaviors that are seen as denying affect provide negative reinforcement, that is, are costly to the person receiving the behavior. Similarly, giving status and not showing hostility might be conceived as rewarding, while denying status and showing hostility may be thought to be costs.

Any social situation can be characterized by the exchange of reinforcements that are received or given, the level of intimacy (related to the time during which the social relationships exist), and the relative status of the two participants. The cross-cultural differences in the perception of the meaning of these behaviors suggest that it is possible for members

TABLE 8. CULTURAL DIFFERENCES IN THE PERCEPTION OF SOCIAL BEHAVIORS

Dimension: Status		Dimension: Intimacy		Dimension: Hostility	
Greeks see more giving status than do Americans for: Compete with Reward Flatter Discuss with Inform Learn with help of Compliment Look up to Greeks see more denying status than do Americans for: Be impatient with Be indifferent to Be embarrassed by To accuse To envy To inspect work of To protect	Greeks see less giving status than do Americans for: Accept as close kin by marriage Have sexual intercourse with	Greeks see more intimacy than do Americans for: To annoy To quarrel with To ask for advice of To scold To study with To advise To complain to To be grateful to To hit To be friend of To learn with help of To laugh at jokes of To enjoy company of To correct To like To kiss To go to movies with To protect To wish good luck to To share responsibility with To work with To be loyal to To date	Greeks see less intimacy than do Americans for: To despise Compete Ask for forgiveness Invite to dinner Congratulate Depend upon Mourn for Follow instructions Be commanded by	Greeks see more hostility than do Americans for: To quarrel To compete To exploit To cheat To be indifferent to Feel inferior to Punish To be sarcastic to Accept orders from Laugh at Cheat Blame for failure Dislike Envy	Greeks see less hostility than do Americans for: Grow impatient with Anger Be prejudiced against Greeks see no hostility while Americans see some for: Feel sorry for Teach Talk to Be friend of Compliment Argue with Approve of Confess sins to Go to movies with Work for Be proud of Understand

of two cultures to perceive the same situation in very different terms, and for the exchange of reinforcements to be very different for the two individuals.

Interaction mistakes can occur because of differences in the perception of social behavior, not only on the main dimensions of affect and intimacy, but also on correlated dimensions, such as status or hostility. For example, it is reasonable to speculate that when there is a status gap, the high-status person may be allowed to deny status and the low-status person would be required to give status. Misunderstandings may occur if a low-status American misperceives the amount of status he is giving by *accepting as a close kin by marriage*, or a low-status Greek may misperceive the amount of status he is giving by *competing with, flattering, discussing with, informing, complimenting,* and *looking up to.* In other words, the latter set of behaviors may seem very status-giving to the Greek, while the American sees them as only moderately status-giving. Thus, a Greek may expect appropriate behavior by the American in exchange for the extra status the Greek has conferred on him. If the American fails to perceive the Greek's behavior as giving status, the Greek is likely to perceive him as ungrateful.

Finally, Americans may see less hostility in *quarreling with, competing with,* etc. and thus behaviors which the Americans see as involving very little implication of hostility may arouse considerable hostility among Greeks. On the other hand, the Greeks may see little implication about hostility for *growing impatient with* while Americans see it as rather hostile.

Thus, the present study suggests that a variety of "misunderstandings" may occur between members of two cultures due to differences in the perception of social behaviors.

Clearly, these are suggestions that need to be tested in further research, but they indicate considerable fruitfulness of the present approach in the determination of which behaviors are appropriate in a cross-cultural setting.

Toward a Theory of Behavioral Intentions and Social Norms

Our task, as social psychologists, is to predict and understand social behavior. To accomplish this task we propose to define in this section a number of concepts, to show how the behavioral and the role differentials can provide operational measures of these concepts, and to state a set of testable theoretical sentences which relate these concepts with observable behavior.

We begin with the definitions. A person has *general intentions* (e.g., to be helpful), and *behavioral intentions* (e.g., to clean the dishes), and these behavioral intentions are expressed in *behavior* recognizable as "dish-cleaning." It appears clear that the determinations of both behavior and behavioral intentions is largely situational. For example, if there are no dishes to be cleaned it is unlikely that we will observe this behavior, or that the person will have the behavioral intention to clean dishes. The behavior also depends on the person's *knowledge* (does he know how to wash dishes), his previous *habits* (does he usually wash dishes), and the possible *intrinsic satisfaction* with the behavior (does he enjoy washing dishes). In addition, there are *behavioral norms* concerning this behavior, which may be defined by the person's roles (male-female, husband-wife, guest-host, etc.).

On the other hand, the *general intention* is less situationally determined, does not depend on such a large number of factors, and may therefore be a more appropriate focus for a theory of social behavior.

The general intentions may be considered as underlying the behavioral intentions. This interpretation suggests that the factors we obtained in our factor analyses of the behavioral differential are *general intentions*. Thus, to show Respect, Friendship, Superordination, etc., appear to be the appropriate variables for a theory of social behavior. What is measured by a *particular* behavioral differential scale may be too specific, and may be too often distorted by situational factors, to be a useful variable, but what is measured by a behavioral differential factor should be of theoretical concern.

The correspondence between the factors of the role differential and the factors of the behavioral differential suggests that the *general behavioral norms* (the factors of the role differential) correspond to the *general intentions*. The results of Study III above suggest that as a first approximation (ignoring the nonindependent and culture-specific factors) we may employ only three dimensions: (*a*) giving versus denying affect, (*b*) giving versus denying status, and (*c*) intimacy versus formality. Thus, as a first approximation, we have three "basic" dimensions which may be used in theory building. Each role occupies a point in a three-dimensional space defined by these dimensions. Similarly, each behavioral intention may be located in the same space.

A person, P, who finds himself in a particular social situation occupies any of several roles (a *role set*) in relation to the other person, O. A role set consists of the roles which are salient in a given P-O relationship. For example, the roles male-male, roommate-roommate, white-Negro, Jewish-Christian may be salient. However, the work with the behavioral differential suggests that unequal weights are given to the various roles in the determination of the particular behavioral intentions that are appropriate for the total role set of P and O. Thus, the white-Negro role will be more salient in the case of the behavioral intention "to accept as kin by marriage" than in the case of the intention "to admire the ideas of." On the other hand, the roles male-male and roommate-roommate will be more salient in the determination of the behavioral intentions "to accept as athletic partner" than the roles white-Negro or Jewish-Christian (see Triandis, 1964b, for the data collected from Illinois students). In other words, while each role defines *a behavioral set* (i.e., a set of behaviors that have high probability of occurrence between persons in that role) the role set determines a *mean behavioral set* — that is, a set of behaviors that have probabilities that are weighted averages of the probabilities of the corresponding behavior sets.

We will now suggest the correspondence between our theoretical terms and our role and behavioral differential measures. Each behavioral differential scale measures one *behavioral intention*. A behavioral differential factor measures a general intention. Each role differential scale measures a *behavioral norm*. A role differential factor measures a *general behavioral norm*. The role differential scales corresponding to a particular role which have been marked by subjects with high intersubject agreement (i.e., small variance in the subjects' judgments) constitute a *behavioral set*. The several behavioral sets that correspond to the roles that are salient in a given social situation are weighted differentially to determine the *mean behavioral set*. The weights are obtained from analyses of variance, as described in Triandis (1964b).

Figure 1 provides a graphic representation of a behavioral set that corresponds to a role set. To simplify the discussion we ignore the status

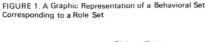

FIGURE 1. A Graphic Representation of a Behavioral Set
Corresponding to a Role Set

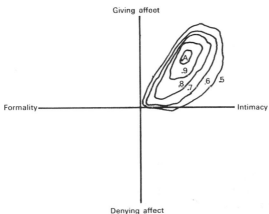

dimension. Thus, each behavioral intention may be represented by a point in a two-dimensional space determined by two dimensions of general intention: intimacy and giving affect. The particular role set calls for behaviors that are intimate and involve giving of positive affect. Some of these behaviors have high probability, while others have somewhat lower probability. The equiprobability contours of Figure 1 have a "center of gravity" which corresponds to the location of the most salient roles of the corresponding role set in the two-dimensional space. Figure 1 is an oversimplification, since it employs only two general intentions. A more complete theory would employ certainly three and possibly five or more dimensions.

It is obvious that this theory of social behavior is oversimplified. Clearly, roles are not the only determinants of social behavior. Other variables, for example, the length of the acquaintance between P and O, their cognitive similarity, the history of reinforcements that each has given to the other, the interpersonal reinforcement probabilities, the power of one to reinforce the other, etc., will also determine the location of the behavior set. We propose that the effect of the length of acquaintance will be to shift the center of gravity of the equiprobability contours towards the intimacy pole of the intimacy dimension; the effect of cognitive similarity will be to provide positive reinforcements and hence a shift of the center of gravity toward the giving of affect pole of the affect dimensions. It is likely that if P expects O to reinforce him if he emits a certain kind of behavior, this will raise the probability of the behavior; that is, this will cause one of the high equiprobability contours to cross the location of that particular behavior on the map of Figure 1. If O has much power, it is likely that the center of gravity will again move toward the giving of affect pole.

Thus, the theory we propose is still very sketchy. Nevertheless, it indicates how role and behavioral differential data may be used in the determination of the equiprobability curves. Once we learn how the center of gravity shifts as a function of the length of acquaintance, cognitive similarity, etc., we will be able to obtain a graphic representation of the mean behavior set that corresponds to a particular social situation. Such graphs provide a quantitative statement concerning the probability of each behavioral intention. The theoretical probabilities of each behavioral intention can then be correlated with the observed frequencies of the corresponding behaviors.

The application of this approach to interpersonal adjustment in situations where P and O belong to different cultures is likely to be fruitful. Consider, for example, the roles foreman-laborer and laborer-foreman. . . . Thus, in Figure 2, the role differential responses of Americans and Greeks are used to determine the centers of gravity of the behavior sets that correspond to the two roles. Behavioral intentions located near these centers of gravity are assumed to have a high probability of occurrence. The way a particular foreman behaves is his *enacted role*. The way a laborer expects the foreman to behave is the laborer's *expectation concerning the* foreman's *role*.

FIGURE 2. "Centers of Gravity" for Two Roles: Laborer-Foreman and Foreman-Laborer

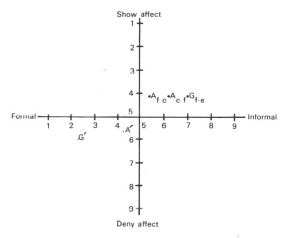

For the situation in which an American foreman is interacting with a Greek laborer we note a difference between the foreman's probable enacted role (A_{f-1}) and the laborer's expectation of how the foreman should behave (G_{f-1}) on the intimacy dimension. The Greek will expect the American foreman to show much more personal interest and even pry into his personal affairs, while the American's behavior will fall seriously short of this expectation. Thus, the American will appear cold and aloof. The Triandis and Vassiliou (1967) data of stereotypes of Americans working with Greeks and Greeks working with Americans are entirely consistent with this analysis. Furthermore, the Greek's probable enacted role (G_{1-f}) will differ from the American's expectations of what a laborer should do (A_{1-f}) on both the affect and intimacy dimensions. The Greek will behave in ways which are more hostile and more formal than what the American expects of him. This will disturb the American, who is likely to react by behaving in an even more cold and formal manner, and the Greek is likely to shift his behavior even further toward formality and hostility, so that the final role-pair interaction may be centered around A' and G'.

Much more research is needed to test these speculations, but this approach has the advantage that it makes possible quantitative predictions about the probabiliies of certain kinds of behaviors. It appears worthy of further investigation.

References

Ballin, M. and P. R. Farnsworth. A graphic rating method for determining the scale values of statements in measuring social attitudes. *Journal of Social Psychology*, 1941, *13*, 323–327.

Brown, R. *Social Psychology*. New York: Free Press, 1965.

Edwards, A. L. *Techniques of Attitude Scale Construction*. New York: Appleton-Century-Crofts, 1957.

Foa, U. G. Cross-cultural similarity and difference in interpersonal behavior. *Journal of Abnormal and Social Psychology*, 1964, *68*, 517–522.

Friedl, E. *Vasilika: A Village in Modern Greece*. New York: Holt, Rinehart & Winston, 1962.

Gouldner, A. W. *Enter Plato: Classical Greece and the Origins of Social Theory*. New York: Basic Books, 1965.

LaForge, R. and R. Suczek. The interpersonal dimension of personality: III. An interpersonal checklist. *Journal of Personality*, 1955, *24*, 94–112.

Linton, R. *The Study of Man*. New York: Appleton-Century, 1936.

Longabaugh, R. The structure of interpersonal behavior. *Sociometry*, 1966, *29*, 441–460.

Lorr, M. and D. McNair. Expansion of the interpersonal behavior circle. *Journal of Personality and Social Psychology*, 1965, *2*, 823–830.

Mason, W. A. Sociability and social organization in monkeys and apes. In L. Berkowitz (ed.). *Advances in Experimental Social Psychology*, Vol. *I*. New York: Academic Press, 1964.

Osgood, C. E. Studies of the generality of affective meaning systems. *American Psychologist*, 1962, *17*, 10–28.

Osgood, C. E. Cross-cultural comparability in attitude measurement via multilingual semantic differentials. In I. D. Steiner and M. Fishbein (eds.). *Current Studies in Social Psychology*. New York: Holt, Rinehart & Winston, 1965.

Osgood, C. E. *Speculation on the Structure of Interpersonal Intentions*. Technical Report No. 39, 1966, Group Effectiveness Research Laboratory, University of Illinois, Office of Naval Research.

Osgood, C. E., G. J. Suci, and P. H. Tannenbaum. *The Measurement of Meaning*. Urbana: University of Illinois Press, 1957.

Sarbin, T. R. Role theory. In G. Lindzey (ed.). *Handbook of Social Psychology*. Cambridge: Addison-Wesley, 1954.

Schlosberg, H. Three dimensions of emotion. *Psychological Review*, 1954, *61*, 81–88.

Schutz, W. C. *FIRO: A Three-Dimensional Theory of Interpersonal Behavior*. New York: Holt, Rinehart & Winston, 1958.

Straus, M. A. Power and support structure of the family in relation to socialization. *Journal of Marriage and the Family*, 1964, 26, 318–326.

Thibaut, J. W. and H. Kelley. *The Social Psychology of Groups.* New York: Wiley, 1959.

Triandis, H. C. Cultural influences upon cognitive processes. In L. Berkowitz (ed.). *Advances in Experimental Social Psychology.* New York: Academic Press, 1964. (a)

Triandis, H. C. Exploratory factor analyses of the behavioral component of social attitudes. *Journal of Abnormal and Social Psychology*, 1964, 68, 420–430. (b)

Triandis, H. C., M. Fishbein, and E. R. Hall. *Person Perception among American and Indian Students.* Technical Report No. 15, 1964, Group Effectiveness Research Laboratory, University of Illinois, Office of Naval Research.

Triandis, H. C., and W. E. Lambert. A restatement and test of Schlosberg's theory of emotion with two kinds of subjects from Greece. *Journal of Abnormal and Social Psychology*, 1958, 57, 187–196.

Triandis, H. C., Y. Tanaka, and A. V. Shanmugam. Interpersonal attitudes among American, Indian, and Japanese students. *International Journal of Psychology*, 1966, 1, 177–206.

Triandis, H. C. and L. M. Triandis. A cross-cultural study of social distance. *Psychological Monographs*, 1962, 76 (21, Whole No. 540).

Triandis, H. and V. Vassiliou. Frequency of contact and stereotyping. *Journal of Personality and Social Psychology*, 1967, 7, 316–328.

16 URIE BRONFENBRENNER

Response to Pressure from Peers versus Adults among Soviet and American School Children

PROBLEM

The experiment to be reported here is part of a more extensive research project investigating the differential impact of adults and peers on the

Reprinted from the *International Journal of Psychology — Journal International de Psychologie*, 1967, Vol. 2, No. 3, pp. 199–207. By permission of IUPS and Dunod, Publisher, Paris.

This paper was first presented, in slightly condensed form, at the Symposium

behavior and personality development of children in different cultural contexts. Our earlier studies had pointed to important differences from culture to culture in the part taken by peers vis-a-vis adults in the socialization process. For example, in Germany the family appears to play a more central and exclusive role in upbringing than it does in the United States, where children spend a substantially greater proportion of their time outside the family in peer group settings (Devereux, Bronfenbrenner and Suci, 1962). The influence of peers emerged as even stronger, however, among English children, who were far more ready than their American age-mates to follow the lead of their companions in socially disapproved activities rather than adhere to values and behaviors approved by parents and other adults (Devereux, Bronfenbrenner and Rodgers, 1969). In other words, the evidence suggested that in both these Western countries, especially in England, peers often stood in opposition to adults in influencing the child to engage in anti-social behavior.

In contrast, field observations in the Soviet Union (Bronfenbrenner, 1963) indicated a rather different pattern. In that country, in keeping with the educational principles and methods developed by Makarenko (1952) and others, an explicit effort is made to utilize the peer group as an agent for socializing the child and bringing about an identification with the values of the adult society (Bronfenbrenner, 1962). Accordingly we were led to the hypothesis that in the Soviet Union, in contrast to America or England, children are less likely to experience peer pressure as conflicting with adult values and hence can identify more strongly with adult standards for behavior.

RESEARCH DESIGN AND PROCEDURES

An opportunity to investigate this hypothesis was provided during the author's visits as an exchange scientist at the Institute of Psychology in Moscow in 1963 and 1964. With the cooperation of Soviet colleagues, it was possible to carry out a comparative study of reaction to pressure from peers vs adults in six American ($N = 158$) and six Soviet ($N = 188$) classrooms at comparable age and grade levels (average age of 12 years in both countries, 6th graders in US, 5th graders in USSR, where school entrance occurs one year later).

To measure the child's responsiveness to pressure from adult vs peers

on Factors in Personality Development at the XIXth International Congress of Psychology, Moscow, USSR, August 1966. It was presented in the United States by Edward C. Devereux, Jr. at the Meeting of the American Sociological Association, August 29-September 1, 1966, Miami, Florida. The research was supported by a grant from the National Science Foundation of the US.

we employed the following experimental procedure.[1] Children were asked to respond to a series of conflict situations under three different conditions: 1) a *base* or *neutral* condition, in which they were told that no one would see their responses except the investigators conducting the research; 2) an *adult* condition in which they were informed that the responses of everyone in the class would be posted on a chart and shown to parents and teachers at a special meeting scheduled for the following week; and 3) a *peer* condition, in which the children were notified that the chart would be prepared and shown a week later to the class itself. The conflict situations consisted of 30 hypothetical dilemmas such as the following:

The Lost Test

You and your friends accidentally find a sheet of paper which the teacher must have lost. On this sheet are the questions and answers for a quiz that you are going to have tomorrow. Some of the kids suggest that you not say anything to the teacher about it, so that all of you can get better marks. What would you *really* do? Suppose your friends decide to go ahead. Would you go along with them or refuse?

GO ALONG WITH MY FRIENDS			REFUSE TO GO ALONG WITH MY FRIENDS		
absolutely certain	fairly certain	I guess so	I guess so	fairly certain	absolutely certain

Other items dealt with such situations as going to a movie recommended by friends but disapproved by parents, neglecting homework to join friends, standing guard while friends put a rubber snake in the teacher's desk, leaving a sick friend to go to a movie with the gang, joining friends in pilfering fruit from an orchard with a "no trespassing" sign, wearing styles approved by peers but not by parents, running away after breaking a window accidentally while playing ball, etc.

A Russian-language version of the same thirty items was prepared, with minor variations to adapt to the Soviet cultural context. Each response was scored on a scale from -2.5 to $+2.5$, a negative value being assigned to the behavior urged by age-mates. To control for a positional response set, scale direction was reversed in half of the items. The

---

[1] This procedure was developed by the author in collaboration with the other principal investigators for the project as a whole: E. C. Devereux, Jr., G. J. Suci, and R. R. Rodgers, who also carried out the American phase of the experiment.

situations were divided into three alternate forms of 10 items each, with a different form being used for each experimental condition. Thus under any one condition a child could obtain a score ranging from — 25 to + 25 with zero representing equal division between behavior urged by peers and adults. Split-half reliabilities for the ten-item forms ranged from .75 to .86 under different experimental conditions; the reliability of the total score (*i.e.*, sum across all three conditions) was .94. All reliability coefficients are corrected for length of test by the Spearman-Brown formula.

The basic research design involved a double Latin square with experimental treatments, constituting the three rows, classrooms appearing in the columns, and forms distributed randomly, with the restriction that each form appear only once in each column and twice in each row. This basic pattern was repeated twice in each culture, once for boys and once for girls, for a total of four sets of double Latin squares (three conditions by six classrooms in four sex-culture combinations). In order to equate for varying numbers of boys and girls in each classroom, the individual cell entries used for the primary analysis of variance were the mean scores obtained by all boys or girls in a given classroom under a particular experimental condition. In this model, classrooms and forms were treated as random variables, and culture, experimental treatment, and sex of child as fixed effects. It is, of course, the latter three which constitute the primary focus of interest in the experiment.

RESULTS

Mean values obtained by boys and girls in each culture under the three experimental conditions are shown in Table 1, relevant mean differences and corresponding significance levels in Table 2. Several findings emerge from this analysis. First of all, there is clear evidence that Soviet

TABLE 1. MEAN SCORES OBTAINED BY BOYS AND GIRLS IN THE
US AND THE USSR UNDER THREE EXPERIMENTAL CONDITIONS

Subjects	*I* Base	*II* Adult	*III* Peer	*IV. M across* Conditions
Boys				
Soviet	12.54	14.21	13.18	13.30
American	1.02	1.57	.16	.92
Difference	11.52	12.64	13.02	12.38
Girls				
Soviet	15.13	17.02	16.90	16.33
American	3.83	4.35	2.38	3.52
Difference	11.30	12.67	14.52	12.82
Both sexes				
Soviet	13.84	15.62	15.04	14.82
American	2.43	2.96	1.27	2.22

TABLE 2. DIFFERENCES IN TOTAL SCORE AND EXPERIMENTAL EFFECTS BY CULTURE AND SEX

	I *Soviet*	*II* *American*	*III. Effect* *across both* *cultures (Sov.* *+ Amer.)*	*IV. Cultural* *Difference* *(Soviet* *– Amer.)*
Total scores				
1. Both sexes (Girls + Boys)	14.82	2.22	–	12.60**
2. Sex differ. (Girls – Boys)	3.03	2.60	5.63**	.43 ns
Shift scores (Girls + Boys) [1]				
3. Ad[2]-peer conflict (Ad – Peer)	.58	1.69	2.27**	-1.11 ns
4. Ad shift (Ad – Base)	1.78	.53	2.31	1.25
5. Peer shift (Base – Peer)	-1.20	1.16	-.04	-2.36
6. Ad shift – Peer shift	2.90	-.63	2.35 ns	3.61*

*significant at .05
**significant at .01
[1]None of the shift effects showed a significant interaction by sex;
[2]Ad = Adult.

children are far less willing than their American age-mates to say that they will engage in socially disapproved behavior. The mean scores for Russian boys and girls (Table 1, col. IV) average about 13 and 16 respectively, values that are clearly on the adult side of the continuum. The corresponding American averages of approximately 1 and 3.5 are barely over the dividing line, indicating that the children are almost as ready to follow the prompting of peers to deviant behavior as to adhere to adult-approved standards of conduct. The above cultural difference is highly significant across both sexes (Table 2, Line 1).

Second, the data indicate that both in the USSR and in the United States, boys are more inclined to engage in socially undesirable activity than girls. The absence of a reliable sex by culture interaction (Table 2, Col. IV) indicates that the sex difference was no larger in one country than in the other. It is noteworthy that despite the differing conceptions of the role of women in the two societies, females in the Soviet Union as in the United States lay greater claim to virtuous behavior, at least up to the age of twelve!

Third, turning to the experimental effects, we learn (Table 2, Line 3) that in both countries children gave more socially approved responses when told that their answers would be seen by adults than when faced with the prospect of having their statements shown to classmates. Although American youngsters exhibited a greater shift than their Soviet counterparts, a fact which suggests stronger conflict between peer and adult influences in the United States, this cultural difference is not statistically significant (Table 2, Line 3, Col. IV). A reliable difference does appear, however, for the remaining independent degree of freedom which measures whether the two shifts from base condition differed from each other; that is, whether there was any difference in direction or degree between the shift from base to adult condition and that from base to peer condition. As indicated in Table 2 (Line 6), Soviet children shifted more when subjected to pressure from grown-ups, whereas Americans were slightly more responsive to pressure from peers. The components entering into this difference are shown in Lines 4 and 5 of the same table. Although the cultural differences cannot be subjected to an independent statistical test, since they are incorporated in the single degree of freedom tested in Line 6, they do provide a more detailed picture of the differing reactions of children in the two countries to pressure from grown-ups vs. age-mates. Thus we see from Line 4 that although both Russian and American youngsters gave more socially acceptable responses in moving from the neutral to the adult condition, this shift was more pronounced for the Soviet children. Moreover, under pressure from peers (Line 5), there was a difference in direction as well as degree. When told that classmates would see their answers, American pupils indicated greater readiness to engage in socially-disapproved behavior, whereas Soviet children exhibited increased adherence to adult standards. In other words, in the USSR, as against the United States, the influence of peers operated in the same direction as that of adults.

DISCUSSION

Our original hypothesis has been sustained in a number of respects. First, in contrast both to American and English children, Russian youngsters showed less inclination to engage in anti-social activity. Second, although pressure from adults induced greater commitment to socially approved behavior in both cultures, Soviet children were more responsive to the influence of grown-ups than of peers, whereas their American age-mates showed a trend in the opposite direction. Putting it another way, pressure from peers operated differently in the two countries. In the USSR, it strengthened commitment to adult-approved behavior; in the United States it increased deviance from adult standards of conduct.

If, as our data strongly suggest, the social context is a powerful determinant of behavior, then we should expect differences in responses to be associated not only with molar social structures like cultures but also smaller units such as classroom groups. This expectation can be tested from our data by determining whether, in each culture, there were significant classroom effects; the error term used for this comparison was the mean square for individual differences within classrooms. Table 3

TABLE 3. VARIANCES AMONG CLASSROOM MEANS UNDER THREE
EXPERIMENTAL CONDITIONS

	American	Soviet
Base	36.01**	43.40**
Adult	13.43	9.25
Peer	45.77**	17.01

**F significant at .01.

shows the variance of classroom means in each country under each of
the three experimental conditions. The accompanying significance levels
reveal that there are reliable classroom differences in both countries, but
only under base or peer conditions, never in the adult condition. It
would appear that the tendency to conform to peer group norms operates only in the absence of monitoring by parents and teachers, and threat
of exposure to adults has the effect of dissolving pressure to conform to
peer standards. Although the pattern of classroom variances under the
three experimental conditions differs in the two countries — the highest
mean square occurs under peer condition in the United States and base
condition in the USSR — this cultural variation was not significant. Nor
were there any reliable classroom differences associated with the sex of
the child.

What about individual differences within classrooms? Is there a
greater tendency for children to conform to classroom norms in one
country than in the other? The data of Table 4 reveal that there is
such a cultural difference, but for one sex only. Although American
boys show slightly higher individual variation than either Soviet boys
or American girls, these differences are not significant. Soviet girls, however, show a surprisingly strong tendency to respond as a classroom

TABLE 4. AVERAGE VARIANCE OF INDIVIDUALS WITHIN
CLASSROOMS

	American	Soviet	Ratio US/USSR
Boys	df = 75	df = 103	
Base	5.70	5.03	1.13
Adult	6.10	5.23	1.17
Peer	6.05	5.71	1.06
Total	14.07	11.55	1.22
Girls	df = 71	df = 73	
Base	4.28	2.08	2.06**
Adult	4.98	1.73	2.88**
Peer	5.36	2.03	2.64**
Total	11.31	3.02	3.74**

**F significant at .01

group, with little individual deviance. The variances are about half the size of those for any other group, and significantly smaller. Finally, individual differences for the Russian girls were smallest when exposed to pressure from adults. It will be recalled that the Soviet girls were the most adult-oriented of the four groups of subjects. Under all those conditions, including peer pressure, their mean scores were above 15, closer to the maximum possible 25 than to the borderline of anti-social behavior represented by zero on the scale. Given this combination of especially high means with extremely low variances, we may conclude that it is Soviet girls in particular who support adult standards of behavior and, both as individuals and as a classroom collective, experience and exert social pressure to conform to these standards.

The finding that in both societies adult pressure dissolved group solidarity suggests some opposition between adult values and peer interests in the Soviet Union as well as in the United States. The fact remains, however, that at least in our data, readiness to resist promptings to anti-social behavior, and responsiveness to adult influence, were greater among Russian than among American children. In addition, the results showed that in the USSR peer groups exerted some influence in support of adult standards, whereas in America they encouraged deviance from adult norms.

Although these results are in accord with our original hypothesis, and indeed perhaps for this very reason, it is important to stress the limitations of the study. To begin with, our samples were rather small, only six classrooms, comprising less than 200 cases, in each culture. Second, both samples were essentially accidental, the American classrooms being drawn from two schools in a small city in upstate New York, the Russian from three *internats* or boarding schools, in Moscow. The latter fact is especially important since one of the reasons for the widespread introduction of boarding schools in connection with the educational reform carried out in the Soviet Union during the past decade was to make possible more effective character education in the school environment. It is therefore possible that pupils in the internats are more strongly identified with adult values than those attending day schools. For this reason, the experiment here described is currently being carried out, through the collaboration of the Institute of Psychology, in six other Moscow classrooms in schools of the more conventional type where the students live at home. At the same time, the experiment is also being repeated in a series of classrooms in a large American city more comparable to Moscow.

Even if these further and more relevant replications confirm the trends revealed by the present data, two additional questions remain.

First there is the matter of the generalizability of the results outside the experimental setting. Although carried out in school classrooms, the research remains in effect a laboratory study dealing with hypothetical situations rather than behavior in real life. What evidence is there that in fact American children are more likely than their Soviet age-mates to engage in anti-social behavior? None in the present study. The present investigator has reported elsewhere, however, some field observations of Soviet children which described a pattern quite in accord with the findings of the present research. For example, "In their external actions they are well-mannered, attentive, and industrious. In informal conversations, they reveal strong motivation to learn, a readiness to serve their society . . . Instances of aggressiveness, violation of rules, or other anti-social behavior appear to be genuinely rare' '(Bronfenbrenner, 1963).

Finally, we must bear in mind that both the earlier observations and present experimental study were carried out with children at a particular age level, namely late childhood and early adolescence. We are therefore left with the all-important question, unanswered by our data, as to how these same youngsters will behave as adults. Do children who at the age of 12 or 13 yield to peer pressures toward anti-social behavior continue to show such reactions in later years? Does early commitment to the values of the adult society endure? Does the presence of such a commitment in adulthood require that the norms of behavior among children be fully compatible with those of grown ups, or does some conflict of interest further the development of capacities for independent thought and responsible social action? Our results shed little light on these important questions.

Despite the acknowledged limitations of the study, it permits several inferences, both theoretical and practical. With respect to the former, the experiment demonstrates that social pressure has appreciable effects in such differing social systems as those of the Soviet Union and the United States. At the same time, the research indicates that these effects can vary significantly as a function of the larger social context. Where the peer group is to a large extent autonomous, as it often is in the United States, it can exert influence in opposition to values held by the adult society. In other types of social systems, such as the USSR, the peer group, and its power to affect the attitudes and actions of its members, can be harnessed by the adult society for the furtherance of its own values and objectives. This fact carries with it important educational and social implications. Thus it is clear that in the Soviet Union the role of the peer group is in large part the result of explicit policy and practice. This is hardly the case in the United States. In the light of the increasing evidence for the influence of the peer group on the behavior and psychological development of children and adolescents, it is questionable whether any society, whatever its social system, can afford to leave largely to chance the direction of this influence, and realization of its high potential for fostering constructive development both for the child and this society.

References

Bronfenbrenner, U. Soviet methods of character education. *American Psychologist*, 1962, 17, 550–564.
Bronfenbrenner, U. *Upbringing in Collective Settings in Switzerland and the USSR.* Paper presented at the XVIIth International Congress of Psychology, Washington, D.C., 1963.
Devereux, E. C., U. Bronfenbrenner, and G. J. Suci. Patterns of parent behavior in the United States of America and the Federal Republic of Germany: A cross-national comparison. *International Social Science Journal* (UNESCO), 1962, 14:3, 488–506.
Devereux, E. C., U. Bronfenbrenner, and R. R. Rodgers. Child-rearing in England and the United States: A cross-national comparison. *Journal of Marriage and the Family*, 1969, 31:2, 257–270.
Makarenko, A. S. *O Kommunisticheskom Vospitanii* (On Communist Upbringing). Moscow: Gosudarstvennoe Uchebno-pedagogicheskoye Izdatel'stvo, 1952.

17   R O B E R T   D .   M E A D E

An Experimental Study of Leadership in India

INTRODUCTION

The experimental studies of Lippitt (1940) and Lippitt and White (1943) demonstrated that democratic leadership generally produces higher mo-

Reprinted from *The Journal of Social Psychology*, 1967, Vol. 72, pp. 35–43. Copyright (1967) by The Journal Press, 2 Commercial Street, Provincetown, Mass.

This research was conducted while the author was visiting Fulbright Professor at Balwant Rajput College, Agra, U.P., India.

rale, less aggression, and greater productivity than does authoritarian leadership. Shaw (1955) found that authoritarian leaders produce a better performance but a lower morale than do democratic leaders in a sample of college men. His observations, however, were over a much shorter period of time than were those of Lippitt and White. Greer (1953) found that people in a neighborhood who are nominated as leaders by their peers tend to be more equalitarian or democratic than are those not nominated, and Hollander (1954) reports a negative correlation between authoritarianism and leadership nomination in a military situation.

It should be noted that all of the studies cited here have used Ss [Subjects] or respondents who have grown up in the American culture, which has had a long history of democratic traditions. Being reared in such a culture might very well be expected to produce Ss who react more favorably to democratic leadership than to one that is more dictatorial. People who are basically more authoritarian might react differently from people who are more democratic, and a study by Haythorne *et al.* (1956) gives some evidence that this is the case. They found a tendency for increased morale, more effective communication, and increased cooperation when both leaders and followers score high on a test of authoritarianism. An extensive study by Sanford (1950), using questionnaire and interview data, also suggests different reactions from people who are high in authoritarianism. He reports that adults who score high on scales designed to measure authoritarianism prefer ". . . status ladened leadership, to accept strongly-directive leadership and to talk in terms of 'power' words when categorizing 'good' leaders" (Sanford, p. 170). He found such concern with power and strong direction from leaders to be considerably less among people who score low on the same scale.

The trends reported by these studies suggest that, in a culture which is more strongly authoritarian than that in America, authoritarian leadership would produce better morale and productivity than would democratic leadership, results essentially opposite from those of Lippitt and White. That such a culture exists in the Republic of India is evidenced by data reported by Meade and Whittaker (1967), who found that a sample of college students in that country scored significantly higher on the California F. Scale than did five other national groups. Related to this, a study by Ghei (1966) reported that both male and female college students score higher on the deference scale of the Edwards Personal Preference Schedule than do American students. Sociological and anthropological accounts of family, religious, and school organizations have also given adequate documentation for this conclusion [see Lewis (1962)].

Studies of leadership in India have been confined to those employing questionnaires [e.g., Govindarajan (1964) and Krishnan (1965)] or general survey methods [e.g., Kothurkar and Pendse (1962) and Inamdar and Pendse (1962)]. The present study was undertaken to determine the effect of authoritarian and democratic leadership on productivity and morale in the atmosphere of a boys' club in India.

METHOD

1. Subjects

Twenty-four grade-school boys between the ages of 10 and 11 living in a city in northern India acted as Ss. They were recruited from their school as volunteers to join a club for the purpose of making a number of useful and artistic articles. All Ss were Hindus and the four major caste groupings were represented.

2. Apparatus

Materials and tools necessary for the construction of kites, maps, and crayon drawings were used throughout the progress of this investigation.

3. Independent and Dependent Variables

The two conditions of the independent variable were the type of leadership, authoritarian or democratic, which was exercised by the leaders in a club-like atmosphere. The dependent variables, measures of morale, were the total number of absences during the progress of the study, the number of Ss indicating a desire to continue with the club activities at the conclusion of each part of the study, and expressions of preference for the authoritarian or democratic leader. Productivity was assessed through ranking the quality of work done when the projects had been completed. As the study progressed and most groups did not complete all of the work in the allotted time, it was possible to add three additional dependent variables: number of projects completed in the allotted time, number of additional club meetings necessary to complete the projects, and the total number of man-hours required to complete the projects. These latter measures, while not entirely independent of each other, provided additional assessments of productivity effectiveness.

4. Procedure

For three weeks prior to the beginning of the experiment proper, the two leaders, third-year college men hired for the project, were coached on the techniques of both authoritarian and democratic leadership described by Lippitt and White (1943, p. 487). Two observer-assistants were trained at the same time and later were assigned to one of the leaders to observe his behavior as well as that of the participating group members. The chief function of these observers was to watch the leaders and determine that they were exercising the role appropriately and especially to assure that the democratic atmosphere did not take on characteristics of *laissez-faire* leadership also described by Lippitt and White but not tested here.

During the training period the leaders also worked with another boys' club in a neighboring school to practice each type of leadership under E's direction.

Before the experiment proper began, four groups of boys with six members in each were formed. Each group was made up of boys who had nominated each other as those with whom they would like to work. Assignment of the groups to the different experimental conditions was done randomly. Two groups, one with authoritarian leadership atmosphere and one with democratic leadership atmosphere, met on Mondays and Wednesdays, while the other two groups with a similar leadership arrangement met on Tuesdays and Thursdays. Leader "A" exercised authoritarian leadership with the Monday-Wednesday group and democratic leadership with the Tuesday-Thursday group. Leader "B" exercised democratic leadership with the Monday-Wednesday group and authoritarian leadership with the Tuesday-Thursday group.

It was originally intended that all groups work on three projects, the completion of which was estimated to require six weeks although no time limit was suggested to the boys. In actual practice, three of the four groups required additional meetings to complete their projects. Recess, for a week, was observed before the club meetings resumed again. On resumption, all groups changed leadership in such a way that each one was now operating under a different leader as well as a different leadership atmosphere. As an example, boys who had experienced democratic leadership from Leader "A" worked the second six-week period under Leader "B" who exercised authoritarian leadership. They also worked on a different but similar set of projects.

Each boy worked with a teammate of his own choosing on three projects during each six-week period and on three similar projects during the second six-week period, and mutual assistance between members of different teams was neither encouraged nor discouraged. In the democratic groups, the leader suggested 10 different projects on which the boys could work and encouraged them to suggest other tasks that might be done. From the materials available, however, only three of them appeared to be feasible at that time and these were soon selected. These same projects were arbitrarily assigned to the authoritarian groups. The projects were as follows: make a crayon copy of a picture of Taj Mahal, construct a flat kite, make a map of the world, make a crayon copy of a picture of Red Fort, construct a box kite, and make a map of India. Each set of teammates worked on and completed all six projects. The complete schedule of leaders, leadership atmosphere, and projects was counterbalanced. All four groups experienced both leaders, both atmospheres, and construction of all projects.

Two different clubs met simultaneously for one-hour sessions in the late afternoon in two different rooms of the same school. The clubs terminated when all sets of teammates had completed all six projects. On termination, each S was asked by the observer to state under whose direction, Leader "A" or Leader "B," he would like to continue were the activities to resume.

Finally, five teachers from the school where the clubs met, who prior to this time had not witnessed the activities of the clubs, were asked to rank each set of six projects in terms of quality. A rank of 1 was to be assigned to the sample whose workmanship was considered best and a rank of 12 to the one considered poorest. Work was to be judged in terms of neatness, precision, and freedom from errors. The average ranking for each of the six projects was determined and was used as a qualitative measure of output under authoritarian and democratic leadership.

RESULTS

Data for all groups working in an authoritarian leadership atmosphere were pooled, as were the data for all groups working in a democratic atmosphere. The total number of absences, number wishing to continue, number of projects completed on time, extra days required, and total man-hours required for each condition of leadership are presented in Table 1. The number of boys expressing a preference for the authoritarian and democratic leaders is also presented in this table. Finally, the number of projects whose average rank placed them qualitatively in the top half of all projects in its class is presented in the last line of Table 1 in the category, "quality of work."

The statistic χ^2, corrected for continuity, has been applied to these data and is also reported in Table 1. The expected frequencies were determined by assuming that their division was equally probable for each type of leadership.

At the .01 level of confidence, there was a greater rate of absenteeism in the democratic than in the authoritarian groups, the boys preferred their authoritarian leader over the democratic one, and fewer days were re-

TABLE 1. MEASURES OF MORALE AND PRODUCTIVITY IN
DEMOCRATIC AND AUTHORITARIAN LEADERSHIP IN INDIA

Leadership effectiveness measure	Leadership atmosphere		χ^2
	Democratic	Authoritarian	
Total absences	44	15	13.28**
Number wishing to continue	12	23	2.86
Projects completed on time	19	31	2.42
Extra days required	16	6	9.44**
Total man-hours required	340	287	4.48*
Preferred leader	3	21	12.04**
Quality of work	11	25	5.69*

*$p < .05$.
**$p < .01$.

quired to complete the work under the authoritarian leader. At the .05 level of confidence, a greater number of man-hours were required to complete the projects in the democratic groups and the work was judged to be of better quality in the authoritarian groups.

While there was a tendency for a greater number of Ss working with the authoritarian leadership atmosphere to wish to continue the club activities, the difference was not significant. There was also a tendency for the democratic groups to finish fewer projects in the allotted time but this, too, was not statistically significant.

The data for all conditions were also pooled for each leader as an individual without respect to the type of leadership atmosphere he was exhibiting. Leader "A" was slightly superior to Leader "B" by having more projects completed in the allotted time (26 opposed to 24), having more Ss prefer his leadership (13 opposed to 11), and quality of work done under his leadership (20 in top half as opposed to 16). Leader "B" was slightly superior to Leader "A" with respect to number of Ss wishing to continue with the club activities (18 vs. 17), fewer absences (26 vs. 33), fewer extra days required to complete the projects (8 vs. 10), and total number of man-hours utilized (312 vs. 315). When these data were compared with the same statistic, χ^2 corrected for continuity, none approached a level of confidence sufficient for rejection of the null hypothesis.

The Lippitt and White study made elaborate report of instances of cooperation, rivalry, hostility, and aggression exhibited by Ss. No such assessment was undertaken in the present investigation. However, when each leader and assistant was asked at the end of the study to attempt a general retrospective statement relevant to the tendencies toward aggression in each type of atmosphere, all four agreed that there was more aggression in the democratically led groups than under authoritarian leadership.

DISCUSSION

Except for the type of projects on which Ss worked and a slight increase in group size (six instead of five), the conditions of the present experiment were similar to those used by Lippitt and White. However, more reliance was placed on quantitative data and no transcripts of conversations among Ss were made. Thus, no formal quantitative assessment of tendencies toward harmony or discord in either kind of leadership atmosphere could be made. Both the leaders and assistants expressed the belief that fewer acts of aggression occurred in conditions of authoritarian leadership than under democratic leadership.

When one considers the quantitative measures, a number of conclusions can be made. The number of projects completed in the allotted time, the extra time required, and the total number of man-hours utilized indicate that Ss whose leadership was authoritarian were the more productive. The rankings of the excellence of work done by Ss demonstrated that work done under authoritarian leadership was of a higher quality than that done under democratic leadership. That the morale of Ss working under authoritarian leaders was higher than that in democratic leadership was indicated by lower rate of absenteeism, the greater number wishing to continue in the authoritarian conditions, and the number of Ss expressing a preference for the authoritarian leader. These results obtained with Ss in India are, then, opposite from those of Lippitt and White who used American Ss.

Lippit and White explain their results by assuming that leadership effectiveness is conditioned to a great extent by the degree to which the followers' individual and group needs are met. They assumed that fewer needs were frustrated where the leader allowed a free expression of these needs and their modes of satisfaction. Such expression was possible and follow-through more efficient where the leader was democratic. Less satisfaction was attained where the leader acted in an authoritarian manner and thus minimized the expression or satisfaction of the needs of the group and its members.

While the data of the present study support the opposite conclusions, there need be no alteration in their theoretical explanation. The critical factor here appears to be that leadership effectiveness is related to satisfaction of followers' needs and the efficiency with which the leader promotes them. The authoritarian social and family structure typical of India is such that children grow up being told what to do and to have decisions made for them. Later, this same kind of atmosphere is carried forward into the schools. They have, therefore, had little opportunity to learn to rely on their own initiative or that of others their own age which made up the group membership of the present study. As a result, when leadership is democratic, few Ss were capable of or willing to participate by making suggestions or in decision making. Such a state of affairs led to a lowering of both the quantitative as well as the qualitative aspects of productivity. Failures such as these would be expected to contribute as well to a higher level of frustration and a lowering of morale.

The authoritarian leadership, being similar to that to which Ss were better accustomed, led to a more comfortable situation for them. Needs were satisfied more adequately and fewer frustrating situations occurred. Being conditioned to authoritarian leadership, individuals as well as the group functioned more effectively, and both the quantity and quality of work remained high. Such an atmosphere of accomplishment would be expected to produce the higher level of morale which was observed in the authoritarian, as compared to the democratic, conditions.

These results, along with those of Haythorne *et al.* (1956), demonstrate that cultural and personality differences are important considerations determining the effectiveness of the type of leadership atmosphere. Authoritarian dependency, where it exists, is more likely to be fulfilled where the leader acts in an authoritarian way. In individuals and cultures which are less authoritarian, such leadership is less effective.

The present results were obtained from a rather specialized type of situation and age group for the purpose of comparability with the Lippitt and White study. Generalizations concerning the effectiveness of leadership in other situations within the same culture or to the other subcultures, religions, and castes of India involve considerable risk, and further study would be required to ascertain the relevance of the results of this study for larger group situations, such as that found in government. In spite of the authoritarian structure of life in India, the long history of authoritarian rule by foreign nations and local monarchs is generally regarded as instrumental in their choosing a democratic form of government on achieving independence in 1948. The results presented here suggest that a more autocratic form of government might have been more satisfactory. However, democratic procedures are now being taught and emphasized in the schools, and there is also considerable enthusiasm for participation in national and local governments and elections (Wiser and Wiser, 1963). The joint family system with its tendency to strong authoritarian leadership is also beginning to break down [see Lewis (1962)]. If tendencies such as these continue, follow-up studies in future years may very well reveal results that are more congruent with those of Lippitt and White.

SUMMARY

In a boys' club setting, groups of six 10-year-old Hindu boys living in northern India worked with both an authoritarian and a democratic leader. Subjects worked for six weeks under each kind of leadership and completed a total of six projects. Measures of absenteeism, the wish to continue club activities, and expressed preference to continue under one particular leader indicated that morale was higher under the authoritarian leadership atmosphere than under the democratic leadership atmosphere. Number of projects completed on time, extra days required, and total man-hours expended indicated that productivity was higher under the authoritarian leader than under the democratic leader. The quality of work done under the authoritarian leader was judged to be superior. These findings, opposite from those made on American Ss by Lippitt and White, are explained by assuming that, in a culture with a relatively high level of authoritarianism, needs are more adequately met in an authoritarian leadership atmosphere than in a democratic leadership atmosphere.

References

Ghei, S. A cross-cultural study of need profiles. *J. Personal. & Soc. Psychol.*, 1966, 3, 580–585.

Govindarajan, T. Vocational interests of leaders and non-leaders among adolescent school boys. *J. Psychol. Res. (Madras)*, 1964, 8, 124–130.

Greer, F. Neighborhood leaders. In D. Courtney, F. Greer, J. Masling, and H. Orlans. *Naval, Neighborhood and National Leaders*. Philadelphia, Pa.: Inst. Res. Hum. Relat., 1953.

Haythorne, W., A. Couch, D. Haefner, P. Langham, and L. Carter. The effects of varying combinations of authoritarian and equalitarian leaders and followers. *J. Abn. & Soc. Psychol.*, 1956, 53, 210–219.

Hollander, E. Authoritarianism and leadership choice in a military situation. *J. Abn. & Soc. Psychol.*, 1954, 49, 365–370.

Inamdar, N. and V. Pendse. Panchayat leadership: A case study. *J. Univ. Poona*, 1962, 15, 188–193.

Kothurkar, V. and V. Pendse. A study of social prejudice in three India villages: The problem of Nav-Buddhas. *J. Univ. Poona*, 1962, 15, 123–129.

Krishnan, B. The leadership qualities among college students as measured by "L" Scale of Mysore Personality Inventory. *Psychol. Studies (Mysore)*, 1965, 10, 23–36.

Lewis, O. *Village Life in Northern India*. New York: Vintage, 1962.

Lippitt, R. An experimental study of the effect of democratic and authoritarian group atmospheres. *Univ. of Iowa Studies in Child Welfare*, 1940, 16, 43–195.

Lippitt, R. and R. White. The "social climate" of children's groups. In R. Barker *et al.* (eds.). *Child Behavior and Development*. New York: McGraw-Hill, 1943.

Meade, R. and J. Whittaker. A cross-cultural study of authoritarianism. *J. Soc. Psychol.*, 1967, 72, 3–7.

Sanford, F. *Authoritarianism and Leadership*. Philadelphia, Pa.: Inst. Res. Hum. Relat., 1950.

Shaw, M. A comparison of two types of leadership in various communications nets. *J. Abn. & Soc. Psychol.*, 1955, 50, 127–134.

Wiser, W. and C. Wiser. *Behind Mud Walls*. Berkeley, Calif.: Univ. Calif. Press, 1963.

Honesty toward Compatriot and Foreigner: Field Experiments in Paris, Athens, and Boston

Previous experiments by Feldman (1967) examined the cooperative behavior of Parisians, Athenians, and Bostonians toward compatriots and foreigners in casual encounters. When foreign and compatriot experimenters (Es) asked random samples in each city to "do a favor" for them, the Parisians and Bostonians treated compatriots better than foreigners, but the Athenians treated foreigners better than compatriots. In these experiments subjects (Ss) could grant the request or refuse it, but there was no opportunity to materially profit from the encounter. The three experiments reported here investigate relative honesty toward compatriot and foreigner in Paris, Athens, and Boston. In addition, two of the experiments utilize occupational encounter rather than casual encounter.

Most previous attempts to investigate comparative behavior in different socio-cultural environments have focused upon the nation to define the population under investigation (Milgram, 1960; Schachter, et al., 1954). We depart from this practice of studying "national characteristics," because of the heterogeneous nature of the sub-populations which often make up nation states. *The basic paradigm consists of controlled standardized observations of behavioral episodes that have been initiated via the intervention of a member of the experimental team.*

Roy Feldman, "Honesty toward compatriot and foreigner: Field experiments in Paris, Athens and Boston," *Proceedings, 76th Annual Convention, APA,* 1968, pp. 375–376. Copyright (1968) by the American Psychological Association, and reproduced by permission.

This research was supported, in part, by a grant from the Comparative International Studies Program of the Harvard Department of Social Relations and by a grant from the Milton Fund of Harvard University. The investigator acknowledges research assistance from the following: Jean Plas, John Williamson, P. B. Doeringer, Demetrius Bubas, and Cornelius Passani. Special thanks for advice and criticism are due to Stanley Milgram, Jean-Pierre Gruère, and Victor Ernoult. Of course none of these are responsible for errors or faults in this investigation.

METHOD

Experiment 1: Falsely Claiming Money

In a casual encounter on the street, Ss had the opportunity to materially profit by falsely claiming money from a stranger. The E approached S and asked if S had just dropped a 5-franc note (or appropriate Greek or United States currency). Actually, S had not dropped the money.

Experimenters. Two male Es were used in each city, a compatriot and a foreigner. In Paris and Athens the foreigner was a citizen of the U.S. In Boston the foreigner was French. The compatriot and foreigner both addressed Ss in the native language of the city involved. Interviews with Ss after the termination of the experiment indicated that Ss identified the foreign E as foreign.

Selection of Subjects. Each time the experiment was begun for each S, E selected the fourth man to pass him. This insured that E did not bias the sample by selecting Ss on the basis of personal criteria. The fourth man coming toward E and passing him was the automatic and compulsory choice of E as the next S. When E completed the experimental procedure with an S, he recorded the outcome and began the same procedure to select a new S.

Location. The site of the experimental procedure was: Washington Street, in front of Jordan Marsh and Filene's in Boston; Boulevard Haussmann, in front of Galeries LaFayette in Paris; Venizelou Street in Athens, from the university until just before Omonia Square.

Procedure. A dress classification previously shown to correlate with S's behavior was used for each S (Feldman, 1967). Each S was classified into one of three categories according to the clothes he wore at the time of the experiment. A compatriot and a foreign E operated at each location at matched times of the day. After an S selection, E approached from behind S and said, "Excuse me, sir. Did you just drop this dollar bill?" The S's positive or negative response and dress classification were then recorded. For half of the Ss in each city (total $N = 160$ in each city) the approximate equivalent of $1.00 U.S. currency was offered. For the other half of the Ss, the note of the next highest denomination was offered. A set of typical S interviews was obtained following the experiment. No Ss knew they were involved in an experiment, and none of the interviewed Ss knew they were interviewed. The interviewer walked along the crowded street and positioned himself to be walking beside S just as the experimental episode terminated. When an S took money from E and walked on, the interviewer turned to S and said, "Hey, is that guy giving money away?" Almost all Ss approached in this manner proceeded to give their version of the experimental episode.

Experiment 2: Cashier Experiment

In making a variety of small purchases, a few "pennies" over the actual cost were added to the payment by E, who then slowly left the store. The overpayment actually amounted to from one-fourth to one-third of the total purchase. The behavior of the cashier in keeping or returning the overpayment of E was recorded. In the previous experiment, S had to overtly take the money which did not belong to him. Here S only had to tacitly accept the overpayment. The encounter, however, was with one occupational group and more structured than in the first experiment.

Experimenters. Two male experimenters were used in each city. Nationalities were the same as in Experiment 1.

Selection of Shops. One necessity in this experiment was to make a relatively large number of purchases on a relatively small budget. Pastry shops were selected because of their large number in each city and because relatively good guides were available in all three cities to compile lists of all the pastry shops in each city from which a random sample was drawn. In Paris, e.g., all 20 arrondissements appeared in the random sample.

Procedure. The E entered the shops selected and requested an item or items which cost approximately 20¢ U.S. currency. After being told the cost of his purchase, E paid that sum plus about 25% above the total cost, gave the cashier a chance to count the money and slowly began to walk out of the shop. The main measure was whether or not the cashier returned the overpayment.

Experiment 3: Taxi Cab Charges

This study investigated whether or not compatriots and foreigners were charged the same fare over identical routes.

Experimenters. A compatriot and a foreign E conducted the experiment in each city. Nationalities matched Experiment 1.

Subjects. Cabs were "hailed" in different parts of the city. The same cab driver was sometimes the S for both compatriot and foreign E.

Locations. Most taxi rides were taken between public places. Locations were matched in each city by using similar types of destinations such as railroad stations, the stock exchange, a postoffice, an observatory, and a hospital.

Procedure. The compatriot and foreign E did this experiment at the same time of day and within minutes of each other. The compatriot addressed the driver in his native language. The foreigner did not directly ask for his destination, but handed the driver a slip of paper with his destination written on it in script by a compatriot and read the destination location from the slip of paper. The dependent variable was the cost of the ride to the compatriot as compared to the cost to the foreigner.

RESULTS

Experiment 1: Falsely Claiming Money

No significant differences were found between the treatment of compatriot and foreigner within cities. Significant differences were found between cities ($p < .05$). Six per cent of the Parisians, 13% of the Athenians, and 17% of the Bostonians falsely claimed money from a strange compatriot or foreigner. Five per cent of the Parisians took 5 francs from the American foreigner. Fifteen per cent of the Athenians took 20 drachmas from the American foreigner. Twenty-seven per cent of the Bostonians took 1 dollar from the French foreigner. The American stereotype of the Parisian was not confirmed in comparison with how the Bostonian treats a fellow citizen under the same circumstances: the Bostonians falsely took money 14% of the time from their compatriots, but the Parisians only claimed money falsely 2.5% of the time from the American foreigner.

A trend was observed for the proportion of takers to decrease as the amount of money increased, but the absolute number of takers was too small to be very confident of the trend. The lower the socioeconomic classification the higher was the proportion of takers from both foreigners and compatriots.

Experiment 2: Cashier Study

No difference was found between the treatment of compatriot and foreigner in Paris, Athens, or Boston. Fifty-four per cent of the shops kept the overpayment in Paris (39% of universe sampled); 51% in Athens (31% of universe sampled); and 33% in Boston (18% of universe sampled).

Experiment 3: Taxi Charges

Foreigners and compatriots were charged equivalent amounts in Boston and Athens, and no compatriot believed that he was deliberately taken by any other than the most direct route known to the driver. In Paris, however, the American foreigner was charged a higher fare significantly more often than the French compatriot ($p < .05$) in an ingenious variety of ways.

DISCUSSION

Although initially it was thought that there might be some unidimensional area called "cooperation," it now appears that "doing a favor for a stranger" and "honesty toward a stranger" may well be quite separate factors which have been incompletely paired in a fourfold table with casual encounter and occupational encounter. The three experiments presented here all involved "honesty." The two experiments described by Feldman (1967) concerned asking Ss to "do a favor" for a stranger.

Whereas Ss asked to "do a favor" for a stranger usually discriminated between compatriot and foreigner (Feldman, 1967), this was not usually true in the studies of "honesty" described here. Findings in Athens and Boston are in accord with this interpretation. The case of the Parisian taxi drivers, however, who were dishonest to the American foreigners but not to compatriots, was an exception. Confidence in the generality of our interpretation can be improved if occupational encounter is experimentally paired with "doing a favor" for a stranger. Discrimination of compatriot and foreigner by cashiers and taxi drivers asked to do a favor for the stranger would add considerable power to this interpretation. It would also weaken the rival hypothesis that discrimination of compatriots and foreigners is correlated with casual versus occupational encounter.

References

Feldman, R. E. "The Response to Compatriot and Foreigner Who Seek Assistance: Field Experiments in Paris, Athens, and Boston." Unpublished doctoral dissertation, Harvard University, 1967.

Milgram, S. "Conformity in Norway and France: An Experimental Study of National Characteristics." Unpublished doctoral dissertation, Harvard University, 1960.

Schacter, S., J. Nuttin, C. deMonchau, P. H. Maucorps, D. Osmon, H. Duijker, R. Rommetveit, and J. Israel. Cross-cultural experiments on threat and rejection. *Human Relations*, 1954, 7, 405–439.

Communication, Creativity, and Problem-Solving Ability of Middle- and Working-Class Families in Three Societies

One of the most crucial phenomena for the analyst of social class is variation in family organization. Such data can help us to go beyond mere categorization of class differences to an understanding of at least one set of factors which establish and maintain the boundaries between social strata. This paper tests the assumption that one of these factors underlying many other social class differences is the ability of the family groups to deal with the kind of novel and problematic situations characteristic of a rapidly changing urban-industrial society.

A second assumption is that the social organization of working-class families represents a partly dysfunctional response to certain structural pressures, such as unemployment and overcrowding. The patterns of organization developed in response to these pressures are reasonable adaptations to the immediate pressures, but these same organizational patterns are also assumed to be responsible for some of the difficulties experienced by working-class families in adapting to social change.

The larger study from which this analysis is drawn was designed to test the latter assumption with a number of different family organization variables. This paper presents data on only one of these family organization variables — communication. The paper is primarily focused on an empirical test of the first assumption: that there are large social class differences in the ability of family groups to deal with novel problem situations. Consequently, the first hypothesis tested is that working-class families have a lower ability to solve a laboratory problem than middle-class families. It should be noted, however, that confirmation of this

Reprinted from *The American Journal of Sociology*, Vol. 73, No. 4, January 1968. Copyright 1968 by The University of Chicago.

Revision of a paper read at the 1966 meeting of the American Sociological Association. Financial support for this research was provided by the National Science Foundation, the University of Minnesota Graduate School, and the United States Educational Foundation in India. . . .

hypothesis provides evidence in favor of the assumptions on which it was based only to the extent that ability to cope with the laboratory problem reflects the ability of the family to deal with at least certain classes of natural setting problems.[1]

Assuming that the hypothesized differences in group problem-solving ability do in fact exist, what accounts for these differences? The issue is extremely complex, and undoubtedly many factors are at work, including individual differences in intellectual capacity. Without denying the existence of other factors, the present investigation was designed to test the hypothesis that one of the factors accounting for social class differences in family problem-solving ability is to be found in patterns of communication. This hypothesis is based on the assumption that group problem solving is impeded if members of the group lack the communicative skills to share items of information needed for the solution, or if the organization of the group inhibits such communication.[2]

[1] For a discussion of the validity of the measurements obtained by means of performance in this task see Murray A. Straus, "Methodology of a laboratory experimental study of families in three societies," *Yearbook of the International Sociological Associations* (in press); Murray A. Straus and Irving Tallman, "SIMFAM: A Technique for Observational Measurement and Experimental Study of Families" (mimeographed paper available on request); Murray A. Straus, "The influence of sex of child and social class on instrumental and expressive family roles in a laboratory setting," *Sociology and Social Research*, LII (October, 1967), 7–21. Two 16 mm. sound films are also available. The first is a verbatim film record of a family going through the experiment. The "Family Crisis Periods" is a film of a television broadcast explaining the research and including excerpts from the first film.

[2] Robert O. Blood and Donald M. Wolfe, *Husbands and Wives* (New York: Free Press, 1960); Ray L. Birdwhistell, "An approach to communication," *Family Process*, I (September, 1962), 194–201; D. Cartwright and A. Zander (eds.), *Group Dynamics: Research and Theory* (Evanston, Ill.: Row, Peterson, 1960); Barry E. Collins and Harold Guetzkow, *A Social Psychology of Group Processes for Decision-making* (New York: John Wiley & Sons, 1964); Nathan B. Epstein and William A. Westley, "Patterns of intra-familial communication," *Psychiatric Research Reports*, Vol. XI (December, 1959); Bernard Farber and William C. Jenne, "Family organization and parent-child communication: Parents and siblings of a retarded child," *Monographs of the Society for Research in Child Development*, Vol. XXVIII, Serial No. 91 (1963); A. Paul Hare, Edgar F. Borgatta, and Robert F. Bales, *Small Groups: Studies in Social Interaction* (New York: Alfred A. Knopf, Inc., 1955); Reuben Hill, J. Mayone Stycos, and Kurt Back, *The Family and Population Control* (Chapel Hill: University of North Carolina Press, 1959); G. Karlsson, *Adaptability and Communication in Marriage: A Swedish Prediction Study of Marital Satisfaction* (Uppsala: Almqvist and Wiksells, 1951); Basil Bernstein, "Language and social class," *British Journal of Sociology*, II (1960), 271–76; Basil Bernstein, "Social class and linguistic development: A theory of social learning," in A. H. Halsey (ed.), *Education, Economy and Society* (New York: Free Press, 1961); E. P. Hollander, *Leaders, Groups and Influence* (New York: Oxford University Press, 1964); Mirra Komarovsky, *Blue-Collar Marriage*

After examining the communicative patterns needed for effective group action, the paper next considers the content to be communicated. Specifically, it is assumed that the solution of novel problems demands a flow of ideas to be tried as possible solutions — a variable which will be termed "creativity" in this paper. Furthermore, because of their poorer education and less varied life experiences, it is assumed that working-class persons have had less opportunity to develop the mental flexibility needed for this type of creativity. Consequently, a third hypothesis tested in this research predicted lower creativity scores for the working-class sample.

A final major assumption to be examined in this paper is Inkeles' "Industrial Man" theory which holds that, irrespective of culture, urban-industrial societies pose a similar set of adaptive problems for their members and provide a similar set of resources for meeting these problems. Consequently, despite differences due to the unique features of each culture, the structural pressures impinging on the working class (such as lack of privacy, and insufficient resources to make planning a meaningful act) result in a similar set of social class differences in all urban-industrial societies.[3] To test this hypothesis, the research was replicated in Bombay, India; Minneapolis, Minnesota; and San Juan, Puerto Rico. These three societies were chozen in part on the basis of prior familiarity and convenience but primarily because the extreme cultural contrasts which they present make possible a stringent test of this hypothesis.

SAMPLE AND METHOD

Sample

To be included in the working-class, a child had to have a father engaged in manual work.[4] In Minneapolis, 64 per cent of the eligible families

---

(New York: Random House, 1964); Lee Rainwater, *Family Design: Marital Sexuality, Family Size, and Contraception* (Chicago: Aldine Publishing Co., 1965); Leonard Schatzman and Anselm Strauss, "Social class and modes of communication," *American Journal of Sociology*, LX (January, 1955), 329–38; E. H. Schein, "Interpersonal communication, group solidarity, and social influence," *Sociometry*, XXIII (1960), 148–61; R. C. Ziller, "Communication restraints, group flexibility, and group confidence," *Journal of Applied Psychology*, XLII (1958), 346–52.

3 See Alex Inkeles, "Industrial man: The relation of status to experience, perception and value," *American Journal of Sociology*, LXVI (July, 1960), 1–31. [Ed. note: A portion of Inkeles' paper is reprinted in this reader.]

4 The number of other children in the family was not used as a selection criterion, nor was the legal status of the union. It should be noted that the requirement of a natural child of at least twelve years of age undoubtedly produced an atypical working-class sample. This is because of the instability characteristic of

who were asked to participate did so. In San Juan 88 per cent co-operation was secured, and in Bombay the figure was 93 per cent.[5] The sample sizes are Bombay 64, Minneapolis 64, and San Juan 45.

The study was conducted in a university small-groups laboratory in Minneapolis, and in a room of the Puerto Rico Vocational Rehabilitation Center in San Juan. In Bombay rooms in a neighborhood school and in a municipal recreation center were used. Except for the light operator, all staff with whom the family interacted in San Juan and Bombay spoke the native language.

Task

The problem presented to the family was a puzzle in the form of a game played with pushers and balls. This task is a greatly simplified version of procedures first developed by Swanson and later modified by Hamblin.[6] The choice of this task was in part based on the assumption that the

---

slum families everywhere. See Straus, *op. cit.*, for further details on the sampling procedures.

[5] The unusually high rate of participation in the Bombay experiment is probably due to a number of factors. First, the research was conducted at a more leisurely and careful pace, since it was my main responsibility for an entire academic year. Second, the head research assistant on the project, who had the responsibility of contacting all the families, was a person of unusual ability in establishing rapport with families of all social levels. Third, I was aided by the tradition of hospitality which is so marked in many Eastern cultures. The people of India, even more than those of European cultures, want to make a good impression on foreigners and to assist them in the task which brought them to their country.

Even the Minneapolis co-operation rate, although lower than hoped for, represents a substantial success because of the difficulty which is assumed to be present in getting a family group to come to a laboratory for research. The payment of $10 or Rs. 10 undoubtedly contributed to this success, especially for the working-class families. Perhaps also important was the use of the child as the unit for sample selection, since many parents will take part in activities which they would otherwise avoid if the activity is concerned with, or for, the welfare of their children. Finally, the personal calls for appointments probably played a part. The importance of personal calls is further suggested by the fact that the lowest rate of participation occurred in the city where telephone calls rather than personal visits were used to make the initial appointment, and the families were left to come to the laboratory on their own. In San Juan and Bombay, on the other hand, an assistant called for and brought each family to the laboratory.

[6] Robert L. Hamblin, "Group integration during a crisis," *Human Relations*, XI (1958), 57–76; Robert L. Hamblin, "Leadership and crisis," *Sociometry*, XXI (December, 1958), 322–35; and Guy E. Swanson, "A preliminary laboratory study of the acting crowd," *American Sociological Review*, XVIII (October, 1953), 522–33.

lower-class persons "do not verbalize well in response to words alone," [7] or, as Miller and Swanson put it, the lower-class person tends to think and learn in a physical or motoric fashion. "Such people can think through a problem only if they can work on it with their hands. Unless they can manipulate objects physically they cannot perform adequately." [8] It was hoped that a task which involved physical manipulation of objects would allow for such motoric thinking.

It is difficult to describe adequately this task and the associated observational and scoring procedures within the space limitations of this article. Consequently, a methodological paper has been prepared for those needing such information.[9] However, it is hoped that the partial description which follows will be sufficient for purposes of understanding the findings.

The game was played on a court about 9 × 12 feet marked on the floor, with two target boards at the front, as shown in Figure 1. Also at the front of the room were three pairs of red and green lights. There was one pair of lights for each member of the family, and a blackboard to post scores after each period of play. Each family was told that the problem was to figure out how to play the game. The instructions given were ambiguous and designed to emphasize speed in performance and the need to play as a team. There were eight three-minute play periods. The family's task was to infer the rules of the game with the aid of green lights flashed for correct, and red lights for incorrect, moves and to use this information to exceed the average of "other families who have played this game."

Reaction to the Task

The middle-class families in Minneapolis and San Juan almost immediately become engrossed in the game and appeared to enjoy the experience from the start. There seemed to be a considerable feeling of accomplishment in solving the experimental problem (figuring out the rules of the game from the light signals). In fact, a number of families wanted to continue after the experiment was over, and others suggested that the game be marketed commercially.

However, the first working-class family tested seemed initially to be

[7] See Frank Riessman, *The Culturally Deprived Child* (New York: Harper & Row, 1962), especially p. 77.

[8] Daniel R. Miller and Guy E. Swanson, *Inner Conflict and Defense* (New York: Holt, Rinehart & Winston, 1960). See also J. McV. Hunt, *Intelligence and Experience* (New York: Ronald Press, 1961); and papers on preschool enrichment programs in the *Merrill Palmer Quarterly*, Vol. X, No. 3 (July, 1964), all of which deal with this issue.

[9] Straus and Tallman, *op. cit.*

FIGURE 1.

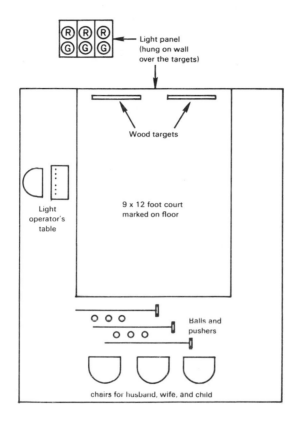

anxious and frightened by the laboratory setting, although once the game started they too became absorbed in it. To reduce this initial anxiety, the following steps were subsequently taken: the staff wore sports clothes, the subjects were met at the building entrance, coffee or soft drinks were served prior to the experiment, the instructions were simplified, and what can be called the "bumbling experimenter role" was played. This involved getting slightly tangled in the tape used to mark off the playing court and asking the subjects to help put down the tape. These maneuvers appeared successful in reducing the social distance between experimenter and families and in making them feel more at ease. Once the game started, almost all families in all groups appeared to enjoy the game and at the same time to have become involved in the objective of learning the rules and maximizing their scores.

In Bombay, however, difficulties of another and more serious nature occurred. The task as just described proved too strange and difficult for the families in the pretest. To have kept to the original rules would have meant that the problem was insoluble for almost all families. It was therefore necessary to simplify the problem by eliminating certain rules. The simplified task was within the capabilities of the middle-class families. On the other hand, even these simplifications were not sufficient, and additional simplification was necessary to put the problem within the grasp of the Bombay working-class families.

It should be clear then that in Bombay there were such vast differences between social classes in their ability to solve this task that no comparison of mean scores is needed to support the problem-solving ability hypothesis within that society. Nevertheless, we will present the problem-solving ability scores for Bombay because, as subsequent sections will try to show, these scores are useful for within-class analysis.

PROBLEM-SOLVING ABILITY SCORES

The problem-solving ability score is based on the lights used to indicate correct and incorrect actions to the subjects. Green lights were used to indicate a correct action, and red lights indicated violation of some rule of the game. Electric counters wired to each signal light, therefore, recorded the number of successes and errors. The data reported here on the problem-solving ratio (Figure 2) are the proportion that the green lights are of all lights flashed during each trial.

Figure 2 presents the problem-solving ratio for each of the four trials. As previously noted, the class differences in Bombay were so large they could not be encompassed within the same measurement instrument. Nevertheless, scores for Bombay are presented here to show that the strategy of abandoning "phenomenal identity" in the task, in order to maintain "conceptual equivalence," appears to have been successful, at least to the extent that roughly similar learning curves are shown for both social class groups in all three societies.[10]

The importance of subjecting the families to a task which was at a roughly equivalent level of difficulty *relative to their ability* arises because the problem-solving ability score is only one of a large number of variables measured in this study. Among these other variables are the communication and creativity scores (presented later in this paper) as well as measures of intrafamily power and supportive interaction described in other papers. All of these scores would have been rendered non-compar-

[10] See the discussion in Henry W. Riecken *et al.*, "Narrowing the gap between field studies and laboratory experiment in social psychology: A statement of the summer seminar," *Social Science Research Council Items*, VIII (December, 1954), 37–42.

FIGURE 2. Mean Problem-Solving Ratios

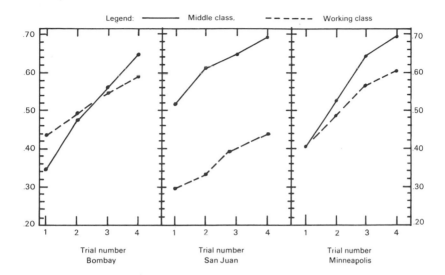

Legend: ———— Middle class, – – – – – Working class

Trial number
Bombay

Trial number
San Juan

Trial number
Minneapolis

able if one sample had been presented with the frustration of a task which was completely beyond their ability, or another sample with a task which was ridiculously easy. In short, by maintaining a roughly constant level of difficulty, relative to their ability, it is believed that a *psychologically equivalent* task, even though not a *phenomenally identical* task, was presented and that this made possible comparison of the social class groups in respect to the family interaction variables which form the larger framework of this study.

Turning now to the problem-solving scores of the San Juan families, it is clear from the wide band separating the middle-class and the working-class family curves in Figure 2 that there are extremely large differences between social classes in family problem-solving ability in that society. Although a statistical test is hardly necessary to establish confidence in differences this large and this consistent, the mean problem-solving ratio scores for all four trials are a convenient summary statistic for purposes of comparison. The middle-class families in San Juan had a mean of 63.0 compared to 36.8 for the working-class families $(F = 20.2, p < .01)$.[11]

[11] The F-ratios for Bombay and Minneapolis reported in this paper are all based on 1 and 16 degrees of freedom, and for San Juan on 1 and 32 degrees of freedom. In the case of San Juan, the error term used was the within-cells variance of a $2 \times 2 \times 2$ design. In the case of Bombay and Minneapolis, the error term was the variance obtained by pooling the six four-factor interactions and the five-

For the Minneapolis sample, however, the parallel comparison produced a mean of 57.2 for the middle-class families and 50.5 for the working-class families. This difference is consistent with the hypothesis, but it is not statistically significant ($F = 3.36$, $p < .10$). This is because this measure includes the first two trials, where class differences in Minneapolis were non-existent or small. A test of the hypothesis based on the fourth trial does reveal a statistically significant difference ($F = 4.61$, $p < .05$). Thus, the Minneapolis working-class families were equally able to deal with the basic features of the problem *in the first two trials,* but they were less able than the middle-class families to discover the last details and secure a nearly perfect score. In fact, among the sixteen working-class control group families who continued with the task as described in this paper for an additional four trials, there were two who, even after eight trials, obtained scores of under 50, indicating more errors than successes, and an additional two who had scores of under 70 per cent. By contrast, none of the sixteen middle-class control group families had a score under 70 during the eighth trial.

Although social class differences found for the Minneapolis families are not as dramatic as those in Bombay or San Juan, it is believed that the hypothesis of relatively low family group problem-solving ability was confirmed for this sample also. This conclusion is based in part on the statistical data and in part on the judgment that the task was not sufficiently difficult to reveal the class differences which actually exist in the Minneapolis sample. In retrospect, therefore, it would have been preferable to have used a more difficult task for the Minneapolis sample than for the San Juan sample, rather than the identical task. However, at that stage of the research, it was still believed that an identical task could be

---

factor interaction in a $2 \times 2 \times 2 \times 2 \times 4$ design. The choice of the pooled variance as the error term was based on the following considerations: (1) the alternative of using the five-factor interaction was tried and found to be unstable in the sense that certain differences between groups which were quite small occasionally turned out to be significant, whereas in other instances large and theoretically meaningful differences were found by these criteria to be not significant. The pooled variance, however, consistently produced significant F's where the differences were large, and non-significant F's where the differences were small. (2) Several of the analyses were recomputed by collapsing the fifth factor. This yielded a $2 \times 2 \times 2 \times 2$ design with four observations per cell. The F-ratios obtained by using the within-cells variance in this design were almost exactly comparable to those obtained by means of the pooled variance error terms, but frequently differed from those obtained using the five-factor interaction as the error term. (3) No theoretical predictions were made for the four-factor and five-factor interactions. (4) In view of the above, and the computational efficiency of the five-factor analysis of variance, it was decided to use the pooled variance as the error term throughout this study.

used in all three societies. Had the necessity of making the modifications which were subsequently made for Bombay been realized at the time, we would not have adhered so rigidly to the principle of phenomenal identity for the San Juan and Minneapolis phases of the study.

So far we have established a between-class difference in problem solving for all three societies. The balance of this paper investigates certain within-class factors which could underlie the inferior problem-solving ability of the working-class families. Among the many possible explanations, only the following will be examined: (1) lack of motivation on the part of the working-class families resulting in their not striving to solve the problem; (2) greater anxiety over having to perform in public and the resulting constriction of performance; (3) inability to maintain lines of communication needed for a rapid solution to the problem; and (4) ideational poverty.

DIFFERENTIAL MOTIVATION AND ANXIETY

The first two of the above listed explanations, if true, would preclude further analysis of the data, since they essentially challenge the validity of the data. Consequently, it is important to examine them before proceeding. Fortunately, in respect to the "differential motivation to participate" explanation, two types of data are available. The first comes from over-all observation of the families as they attempted to solve the experimental task. Although individual families varied in respect to the intensity of their participation and striving, at no point was it possible to gather the impression that involvement in the task was any more or less prevalent among the working-class families. In fact, it was often painful to watch the efforts of the working-class families, since their involvement was so great and the effort expended usually disproportionate to the success achieved.

Of course, such impressions are subject to unconscious bias in favor of the methodological soundness of the experiment. Consequently, as one means of providing more objective data, an "activity level" score was obtained for each family. This score, which is the number of times a ball was pushed during each trial, provided at least one objective measure of task involvement. The results show a high level of activity for both the middle- and the working-class families, with no significant difference between them.[12]

[12] The mean activity scores were: Bombay, middle class 168, working class 145 ($F = 1.56$, n.s.); Minneapolis, middle class 155, working class 193 ($F = 5.02$, $p < .05$, but note that this is in the opposite direction from that predicted on the basis of the differential motivation theory); and San Juan middle class 222, working class 194 ($F = 0.51$, n.s.).

A second methodological artifact which could account for the class differences is more difficult to deal with, since objective evidence comparable to the activity score is not available. This is the argument that the experimental situation was more strange and anxiety-producing for the working-class families than it was for the middle-class families, since the latter are accustomed to interacting with professional persons, whereas the former tend to fear them because of a generalization from their dealings with the police and other government officials.[13] It has already been noted that such a difference in situation anxiety was present before the game started. However, it has also been pointed out that, because of the engrossing nature of the task, once the family began to try to solve the puzzle, class differences in at least the external manifestations were not discernible. Moreover, the anxiety argument also runs the other way, since the middle-class families might have been more concerned over the adequacy of their performance in an academic situation. Unfortunately, there is no really objective evidence which could be used to support or refute either argument. Consequently, the possibility that differential anxiety either enhanced or reduced the "true" class difference must be kept in mind.

COMMUNICATION AND GROUP PROBLEM SOLVING

An alternative to the "differential motivation" and the "differential anxiety" explanations of the social class differences in problem-solving ability is what may be called the "communication block" explanation or hypothesis. This hypothesis arose from observing that one of the most striking class differences was a markedly lower amount of communication among members of working-class families. Informal observation of the working-class families' attempts to solve the problem further suggested that these differences in amount of communication were a major factor accounting for the poor performance of the working-class families. The solution of the experimental problem is relatively simple, but it also depends on fitting several elements together and perhaps also on breaking perceptual sets concerning the correct mode of play. For example, one member of the family may discover that the ball must hit one of the boards rather than, as most people initially guess, roll between them. An-

---

[13] It should be noted, however, that even if we do ascribe the poor performance of the working-class families to anxiety in a "middle-class biased" situation, this can be considered a finding rather than entirely a methodological artifact. This is because a modern industrial society presents many such situations, and adequate performance in situations of this type is needed by working-class families if they are to adapt to the modern industrial order.

other member of the family may discover that the color of the ball must match that of the pusher. In the middle-class families, such discoveries tended to be immediately announced. Each member of the family then had the central elements of the solution available to him. But in the working-class families, such communications were rare. Instead there was frequently either an almost complete autonomy or a tendency to rely on inefficient non-verbal communication, that is, watching the others and attemping to imitate them.

An extreme case was San Juan family number 34. The wife had figured out all the rules by the end of the second trial; but she told no one. The husband observed that his wife was getting almost entirely green lights (indicative of successful play) and tried to imitate her, but unsuccessfully. This family played all eight three-minute trials without, *as a group*, achieving the solution which takes most middle-class families only one trial. Even more extreme instances occurred in Bombay. For example, in one family, the son had determined the rules of the game but the parents had not. During all of one trial and half of another trial, the son obtained almost all green lights and the parents almost all red lights, and the father from time to time mentioned various incorrect modes of play. The son said nothing during this time and finally started playing the game incorrectly despite the red lights he received from then on. Similar blocks in communication were observed between working-class husbands and wives. In short, the working-class families appeared not to have shared enough information to achieve a rapid solution to the problem.

A *post hoc* interpretation of this type needs to be tested empirically. A conclusive test requires a fresh experiment in which communication is experimentally controlled.[14] In the absence of such an experiment, the cross-sectional data of the present study can provide at least a partial test of this interpretation. For this purpose, a rough measure of the amount of communication between family members was obtained by totaling all the verbal and nonverbal interactions between family members.[15]

It is evident from the data in Table 1 that in all three societies the working-class families had a markedly lower volume of intrafamily communication. In fact, in San Juan, the working-class sample averaged less than half the number of communications which characterized the middle-class sample. Moreover, since the measure used in this study includes non-verbal communication, it greatly understates the actual difference in verbal communication.

[14] An experimental test of this theory is now being undertaken by Irving Tallman. It is briefly described in Straus and Tallman, *op. cit.*, pp. 23–25.

[15] These interactions were recorded to obtain measures of intrafamily power and support, as described in Straus and Tallman, *op. cit.*

TABLE 1. SOCIAL CLASS DIFFERENCES IN FAMILY
COMMUNICATION

Sample	Social class	Mean communication score	F	$p \leq$
Bombay	Middle	129 ⎫	5.81	.05
	Working	98 ⎭		
Minneapolis	Middle	131 ⎫	23.38	.01
	Working	67 ⎭		
San Juan	Middle	173 ⎫	11.92	.01
	Working	134 ⎭		

Although these social class differences in communication indirectly support the communication block hypothesis, more direct support for the hypothesis would be provided if the communication scores were found to be positively correlated with problem-solving ability. The coefficients are .36 for San Juan, .15 for Minneapolis, and .27 and .43 for Bombay.[16] Thus, despite the plausibility of the communication block theory, these results suggest that only in Bombay and San Juan can much of the variation in problem-solving ability be attributed to lack of intra-family communication.

As a final check on the communication block theory, the partial correlation between social class and problem-solving ability with communication held constant was computed for Minneapolis and San Juan. If differences in communication underlie the class difference in problem-solving ability, then we would expect that controlling for communication would lower the correlation between social class and group problem-solving ability. The partial correlation analysis did reveal some reduction in the association between social class and the problem-solving score. For Minneapolis, holding constant communication reduced the correlation of social class with problem solving from .24 to .20 — a reduction of 17 per cent in the size of the correlation. For San Juan, the partial correlation of social class with problem solving, holding constant communication, is .44 compared to .55 for the two-factor correlation — a reduction of 20 per cent. Thus, the present data provide at least modest evidence in favor of the communication block theory. However, as previously noted, even though the theory is confirmed, communication as measured in this study accounts for only a small part of the social class difference in family group problem solving.

[16] The first of these correlations is for the working-class part of the sample and the second for the middle-class part. Two correlations were necessary because, as previously explained, it was necessary to use an easier problem for the working-class group in Bombay.

Restricted Communication as Environmental Adaptation

Although the data and interpretations just presented suggest that the restricted intrafamily communication patterns of the working-class families are dysfunctional for solving the type of problem presented in this research, it does not follow that such a minimal communication pattern is generally dysfunctional for families occupying positions at the low end of the socioeconomic hierarchy. In fact, the minimal communication pattern might well represent an appropriate adaptation to their actual life circumstances. For many of these families, the objective fact is that there are so few alternatives actually available to them that no amount of communication or joint problem-solving effort is likely to effect a significant improvement in their lives. Moreover, the volume of communication found among the middle-class families could well prove intolerable for families crowded six or more people to a room, such as the Bombay working-class families. In such circumstances, the low frequency and restricted channels of communication may constitute part of a "norm of civil inattention," which enables at least a modicum of individuality and separate identity to be maintained.[17]

CREATIVITY

Having accounted for only a relatively small part of the social class difference in problem-solving ability in terms of class differences in communication, I shall now try my luck with a cognitive theory. Among the many theoretically relevant variables which need investigation in this context are originality of thought and the ability to break perceptual sets, that is, the cluster of behaviors generally described under the heading of creativity.

Measurement of Creativity

The data for scoring creativity in this study were from a verbatim listing of the suggestions for ways of playing the game offered by each family member, irrespective of either the practicality of the idea or whether it was actually tried out.[18] Some families were almost com-

---

[17] See in this connection, Frank Riessman, "Low income culture: The strengths of the poor," *Journal of Marriage and the Family,* XXVI (November, 1964), 417–21. On the norm of civil inattention, see Erving Goffman, *Behavior in Public Places* (New York: Free Press, 1963), pp. 83–88; and Edward Gross and Gregory P. Stone, "Embarrassment and the analysis of role requirements," *American Journal of Sociology,* LXX (July, 1964), 1–15.

[18] A verbal statement of the innovation was *not* necessary for it to be scored for creativity. A more complete description together with a manual for this technique of creativity scoring is given in Straus and Tallman, *op. cit.* I would like to express my appreciation to Fraine E. Whitney for development of the original version of the creativity scoring manual.

pletely perseverative in their actions. During the goal-blocking trials, they never varied from the modes of play developed in the first four trials. The social interaction aspect of creativity was clearly observed in a few families in which one member suggested an innovation in mode of play and was immediately brought back into line by comments such as, "That's not the way this sort of game is played." At the other extreme were the almost completely uninhibited families who tried everything they thought of, for example, pushing the ball from between the legs while facing away from the target and using various alternations of colors and players.

The validity of using innovations in game-playing as a measure of creativity is, of course, not known. However, (1) the behaviors scored by this technique are congruent with the main conceptualizations of creativity.[19] (2) The measure has proved fruitful in the analysis of a different set of issues.[20] (3) The behaviors used to index creativity in this study have the advantage of being based on a motor performance rather than a purely verbal performance and should, therefore, be more suited to tapping the creativity of working-class persons.[21]

Creativity Scores

In all three societies, the data in Table 2 indicate that the middle-class families exhibited greater creativity (i.e., a larger number and range of ideas for solving the problem) than did the working-class families.[22]

---

[19] See the papers in H. H. Anderson, *Creativity and Its Cultivation* (New York: Harper & Row, 1959).

[20] See Jacqueline H. Straus and Murray A. Straus, "Family Roles and Sex Differences in Creativity of Children in Bombay and Minneapolis," *Journal of Marriage and the Family*, Vol. XXX (February, 1968).

[21] Even if one assumes that the test is nonetheless biased in favor of the middle class, this assumption merely changes the interpretation of the findings rather than invalidating them. This is because most accounts of working-class life leave the reader impressed with the extent to which upward social mobility is a goal of the slum dweller. In relation to Latin America, see Carolina Maria de Jesus, *Child of the Dark* (New York: E. P. Dutton & Co., 1963); Oscar Lewis, *Five Families* (New York: Basic Books, 1959); and Oscar Lewis, *The Children of Sanchez* (New York: Basic Books, 1961). The slum dweller may not perceive the correct channels or efficient means for such mobility, but there is little doubt that most wish to leave their present status. This fact makes the "class-biased" test argument take on a different meaning, for it is precisely these middle-class tasks which the working-class person must master to achieve his aspirations. Therefore, the measure of creativity used in this experiment, if it is valid for the middle class, is also an important pattern of behavior for the mobility goals of the majority of the working-class families. See also n. 14 above.

[22] It must again be emphasized that one cannot compare the Bombay, Minneapolis, and San Juan grand means and conclude from data of this type that families in San Juan are less creative in dealing with the experimental problem than are families in Bombay or Minneapolis. This is because, as was previously noted, the

TABLE 2. SOCIAL CLASS DIFFERENCES IN FAMILY CREATIVITY

Sample	Social class	Mean creativity score	F	$p \leq$
Bombay	Middle	24.4 ⎱	5.13	.05
	Working	20.5 ⎰		
Minneapolis	Middle	16.3 ⎱	6.18	.05
	Working	11.5 ⎰		
San Juan	Middle	24.4 ⎱	7.73	.01
	Working	21.3 ⎰		

Since the data just presented show important social class differences in creativity, it is appropriate to investigate the extent to which these differences could underlie the social class differences in problem-solving ability. The correlation between creativity and problem-solving ability was therefore computed for each sample. The resulting coefficients are .30 for the San Juan sample, .24 for Minneapolis, and .67 and .25 for the Bombay working-class and middle-class samples.[23]

Partial correlation analysis was used to determine the extent to which social class differences in problem-solving ability can be accounted for by differences in creativity. Holding constant creativity produced a small reduction in the size of the correlation between social class and problem solving (from .24 to .20 for Minneapolis and from .55 to .49 for San Juan). Thus, the variable measured under the heading "creativity" does seem to be one of the factors which underlie social class differences in the problem-solving ability of families in both Minneapolis and San Juan.

SUMMARY AND CONCLUSIONS

Families in Bombay, India; Minneapolis, Minnesota; and San Juan, Puerto Rico, were studied to investigate social class differences in family

---

task was modified to suit local conditions in each society. Moreover, even if the task had remained identical, descriptive comparisons such as this are still likely to be invalid because different observers were used in each society, and they recorded and scored the suggestions made in the local language. Consequently, although there was a high degree of agreement between observers *within* each society, the *numerical* comparability of the scores between societies is unknown. Nevertheless, as has been argued in the methodological paper on this research, such data can have internal validity within a society and therefore can legitimately be used to test the comparability of relationships among variables cross-culturally. It is the latter use which is the objective of the present study. See the discussion of "Measurement and Measurement of Association in Cross-National Research," in Straus, *op. cit.* (n. 2 above).

[23] See n. 17 above.

group problem-solving ability. A gamelike task was used, rather than a verbal problem, because such a task enables working-class persons to make use of "motoric" thinking. Despite the use of a task which should minimize the educational advantage of the middle class, the working-class families in each of the three societies revealed a markedly poorer ability to solve the problem than was the case with the middle-class families. In fact, in Bombay the differences were so great that the problem-solving ability of the working class could not be measured with the same task as was used for the middle class, since the task was completely beyond the ability of the working-class families.

Three theories concerning the causes of the social class differences in group problem-solving ability were tested. The first of these, a "differential motivation" theory, was tested by means of an activity-level score which is believed to reflect the intensity of involvement in the experimental task. This test revealed no important class difference in involvement and hence was rejected.

Second, a "communication block" theory was tested. In all three societies, the working-class families had substantially less communication with each other than was the case with the middle-class families. It is believed that this lack of communication interfered with the pooling of information and hence accounts for part of the working-class families' difficulty in solving the problem. This interpretation was further supported by the results of a correlation analysis which showed that communication is correlated with problem-solving ability and that the social class difference in problem solving is reduced when communication is held constant.[24]

[24] It may be true, as Riessman and others claim, that non-verbal forms of communication are more highly developed among the working class than among the middle class. But the evidence of this study, which is based on a motor situation in which both verbal and non-verbal communication could be used by the families, suggests that non-verbal communication, even if more highly developed, is not a match for verbal symbols in attempting to solve even such relatively simple tasks as determining the rules of this game. At the same time it must be recognized that in this paper the low volume of verbal communication of the working-class families has been viewed in essentially negative terms because the focus of the analysis is on a process which apparently requires a pattern of communication not generally practiced by working-class families. However, in so doing, it is by no means meant to deny the possibility—indeed the likelihood—that the pattern of communication characteristic of the working class constitutes an adaptation to and a method of coping with the difficult environment which they face. Research taking this latter perspective is of great importance for understanding the social world of the slum, but is beyond the scope of this paper (see Frank Riessman, "Low-Income Culture: The Strengths of the Poor," op. cit.), and the discussion of "Restricted Communication as Environmental Adaptation" earlier in this paper.

Third, a cognitive theory was tested using a measure of ideational fluency and flexibility believed to reflect creativity. This also revealed large differences in favor of the middle class in all three societies. However, less of the variation in problem-solving ability could be attributed to variation in creativity than to variation in communication. Since the problem used for this research is a group task, the greater importance of communication is not surprising.

In conclusion, to the extent that performance on this laboratory problem is indicative of performance in solving novel problems in the natural setting, the findings suggest that deficiencies in communication and also, but to a lesser extent, creativity are among the factors which underlie the lower problem-solving ability of working-class families. However, many other factors must also be operative, since neither communication nor creativity accounted for a very large proportion of the variation in problem-solving ability.

One of most important conclusions to emerge from the present study concerns the cross-cultural comparability of urban social class differences. Despite the tremendous variation in the culture of the three societies from which the samples were drawn, a considerable concordance was found in the way middle-class families are differentiated from working-class families. Specifically, in all three societies the middle-class families were more effective problem-solving groups, and in all three societies the middle class demonstrated a greater ideational fluency and flexibility. Most important of all from the viewpoint of sociology is the much higher volume of communication among members of middle-class families, suggesting that in all three societies the social structure of middle-class nuclear families is more closely interwoven than is the case in the working class.

Finally, let us return to the "industrial man" theory which holds that "to the degree a nation's social structure approximates the model of a full-scale primary industrial society, to that degree will it more clearly show the social class differentiated structure of responses we have delineated, and do so over a wider range of topics, problems, or areas of experience." [25] The findings of the present study do indeed show differences in communication, creativity, and problem-solving ability of families which are consistent with the social class differences delineated in Inkeles' analysis. However, contrary to the "industrial man" theory, the findings also show that the more urbanized and industrialized the society, the *smaller* the social class differences in these behaviors. Thus, to the extent that these three societies represent the continuum of societies along the urban-industrial axis, it would appear that the effect of more closely ap-

[25] Inkeles, *op. cit.*, p. 29.

proximating the urban-industrial society end of the continuum attenuates rather than creates the type of social class differences which form the focus of Inkeles' analysis.[26]

[26] Indeed, certain of the data presented by Inkeles himself can be interpreted as supporting the attenuation rather than the causal hypothesis, for example, the data on job satisfaction.

VI

Comparative Studies of
Man and Modern Society

20 CHARLES MORRIS
   AND LYLE V. JONES

Ways to Live: Value Scales and Dimensions

The purpose of this paper is to illustrate some methodological approaches
to the study of human values, and to cite results obtained when these
approaches are applied in a cross-cultural investigation of ways in which
college students from the United States, India, Japan, China, and Nor-

Charles Morris and Lyle V. Jones, "Value Scales and Dimensions," *The Journal
of Abnormal and Social Psychology*, Vol. 51, No. 3, 1955, pp. 523–535. Copyright (1956) by the American Psychological Association and reproduced by permission.

This study is part of a larger project made possible by grants from The Rocke-
feller Foundation, Division of Humanities.

255

way say they would like to live. Emphasis is directed toward (a) the development of a scale for the measurement of value, (b) the isolation and definition of variables to serve as primary value dimensions, and (c) the utilization of both the measurement scale and the value dimensions to characterize differentially the value systems of the five culturally defined samples.

The material to be analyzed consists of ratings of 13 possible ways to live by male college students from each of the five cultures. The "Ways to Live" document on which the ratings were obtained appears as Table 1. The various ways to live represent, for the most part, conceptions of a desirable life as embodied in the main religious and ethical traditions. They may be regarded as fragments of value-orientations as that term is used by Kluckhohn and his collaborators (1951).

For administration in Japan, China, and Norway, the document was translated into the native language; it was administered in English to students in India and the United States.

The material was collected in the countries in question, from the United States during 1945–52, from India during 1949–1950, from Japan in 1949, from China in 1948, and from Norway in 1952. The number of cases in these samples is respectively 252, 724, 192, 523, and 149. The Japanese data were collected at the Universities of Kyoto and Tokyo; the Norway data are from the University of Oslo. The material from the United States came from three Eastern universities, while the data from China and India came from a number of schools and universities throughout these countries. In all cases efforts were made to find persons from various fields of study. At a later time the make-up of these samples will be analyzed in greater detail, with acknowledgments of the help given by many people in the gathering of the data.

In what follows, when reference is made to "India," and the like, it must be remembered that this is but a short way of referring to "the male college students sampled from India." No claim is made that the samples adequately portray these cultures as a whole. They function in this study primarily as controls in the investigation of two problems: Are the ratings in the various cultures scalable, and if so, are they scalable in such a way as to permit cross-cultural measurements and comparisons? Is it possible to isolate a number of dimensions common to the 13 ways to live under investigation, and if so, does the resulting structure hold across cultures?

It is frankly recognized that the present study fails, in several specific ways, to utilize the most exact and theoretically desirable of available methodological procedures. First, a graphical method of curve fitting is used in our scale analysis rather than one of the more precise analytic techniques; second, for the factor analysis, correlations are derived not

TABLE 1. WAYS TO LIVE

Instructions: Below are described thirteen ways to live which various persons at various times have advocated and followed.

Indicate by numbers which you are to write in the margin how much *you yourself like or dislike each of them. Do them in order. Do not read ahead.*

Remember that it is not a question of what kind of life you now lead, or the kind of life you think it prudent to live in our society, or the kind of life you think good for other persons, *but simply the kind of life you personally would like to live.*

Use the following scale of numbers, placing one of them in the margin alongside each of the ways to live:

7 I like it *very much*
6 I like it *quite a lot*
5 I like it *slightly*
4 I am *indifferent* to it
3 I dislike it *slightly*
2 I dislike it *quite a lot*
1 I dislike it *very much*

Way 1. In this "design for living" the individual actively participates in the social life of his community, not to change it primarily, but to understand, appreciate, and preserve the best that man has attained. Excessive desires should be avoided and moderation sought. One wants the good things of life but in an orderly way. Life is to have clarity, balance, refinement, control. Vulgarity, great enthusiasm, irrational behavior, impatience, indulgence are to be avoided. Friendship is to be esteemed but not easy intimacy with many people. Life is to have discipline, intelligibility, good manners, predictability. Social changes are to be made slowly and carefully, so that what has been achieved in human culture is not lost. The individual should be active physically and socially, but not in a hectic or radical way. Restraint and intelligence should give order to an active life.

Way 2. The individual should for the most part "go it alone," assuring himself of privacy in living quarters, having much time to himself, attempting to control his own life. One should stress self-sufficiency, reflection and meditation, knowledge of himself. The direction of interest should be away from intimate associations with social groups, and away from the physical manipulation of objects or attempts at control of the physical environment. One should aim to simplify one's external life, to moderate those desires whose satisfaction is dependent upon physical and social forces outside of oneself, and to concentrate attention upon the refinement, clarification, and self-direction of one's self. Not much can be done or is to be gained by "living outwardly." One must avoid dependence upon persons or things; the center of life should be found within oneself.

Way 3. This way of life makes central the sympathetic concern for other persons. Affection should be the main thing in life, affection that is free from all traces of the imposition of oneself upon others or of using others for one's own purposes. Greed in possessions, emphasis on sexual passion, the search for power over persons and things, excessive emphasis upon intellect, and undue concern for oneself are to be avoided. For these things hinder the sympathetic love among persons which alone gives significance to life. If we are aggressive we block our receptivity to the personal forces upon which we are dependent for genuine personal growth. One should accordingly purify oneself, restrain one's self-assertiveness, and become receptive, appreciative, and helpful with respect to other persons.

Way 4. Life is something to be enjoyed — sensuously enjoyed, enjoyed with relish and abandonment. The aim in life should not be to control the course of the world or society or the lives of others, but to be open and receptive to things and persons, and to delight in them. Life is more a festival than a workshop or a school for moral discipline. To let oneself go, to let things and persons affect oneself, is more important than to do — or to do good. Such enjoyment, however, requires that one be self-centered enough to be keenly aware of what is happening and free for new happenings. So one should avoid entanglements, should not be too dependent on particular people or things, should not be self-sacrificing; one should be alone a lot, should have time for meditation and awareness of oneself. Solitude and sociality together are both necessary in the good life.

Way 5. A person should not hold on to himself, withdraw from people, keep aloof and self-centered. Rather merge oneself with a social group, enjoy cooperation and companionship, join with others in resolute activity for the realization of common goals. Persons are social and persons are active; life should merge energetic group activity and cooperative group enjoyment. Meditation, restraint, concern for one's self-sufficiency, abstract intellectuality, solitude, stress on one's possessions all cut the roots which bind persons together. One should live outwardly with gusto, enjoying the good things of life, working with others to secure the things which make possible a pleasant and energetic social life. Those who oppose this ideal are not to be dealt with too tenderly. Life can't be too fastidious.

Way 6. Life continually tends to stagnate, to become "comfortable," to become "sicklied o'er with the pale cast of thought." Against these tendencies, a person must stress the need of constant activity — physical action, adventure, the realistic solution of specific problems as they appear, the improvement of techniques for controlling the world and society. Man's future depends primarily on what he does, not on what he feels or on his speculations. New problems constantly arise and always will arise. Improvements must always be made if man is to progress. We can't just follow the past or dream of what the future might be. We have to work resolutely and continually if control is to be gained over the forces which threaten us. Man should rely on technical advances made possible by scientific know-

TABLE 1. *Continued*

ledge. He should find his goal in the solution of his problems. The good is the enemy of the better.

Way 7. We should at various times and in various ways accept something from all other paths of life, but give no one our exclusive allegiance. At one moment one of them is the more appropriate; at another moment another is the most appropriate. Life should contain enjoyment and action and contemplation in about equal amounts. When either is carried to extremes we lose something important for our life. So we must cultivate flexibility, admit diversity in ourselves, accept the tension which this diversity produces, find a place for detachment in the midst of enjoyment and activity. The goal of life is found in the dynamic integration of enjoyment, action, and contemplation, and so in the dynamic interaction of the various paths of life. One should use all of them in building a life, and no one alone.

Way 8. Enjoyment should be the keynote of life. Not the hectic search for intense and exciting pleasures, but the enjoyment of the simple and easily obtainable pleasures: the pleasures of just existing, of savory food, of comfortable surroundings, of talking with friends, of rest and relaxation. A home that is warm and comfortable, chairs and a bed that are soft, a kitchen well-stocked with food, a door open to the entrance of friends — this is the place to live. Body at ease, relaxed, calm in its movements, not hurried, breath slow, willing to nod and to rest, grateful to the world that is its food — so should the body be. Driving ambition and the fanaticism of ascetic ideals are the signs of discontented people who have lost the capacity to float in the stream of simple, carefree, wholesome enjoyment.

Way 9. Receptivity should be the keynote of life. The good things of life come of their own accord, and come unsought. They cannot be found by resolute action. They cannot be found in the indulgence of the sensuous desires of the body. They cannot be gathered by participation in the turmoil of social life. They cannot be given to others by attempts to be helpful. They cannot be garnered by hard thinking. Rather do they come unsought when the bars of the self are down. When the self has ceased to make demands and waits in quiet receptivity, it becomes open to the powers which nourish it and work through it; and sustained by these powers it knows joy and peace. To sit alone under the trees and the sky, open to nature's voices, calm and receptive, then can the wisdom from without come within.

Way 10. Self-control should be the keynote of life. Not the easy self-control which retreats from the world, but the vigilant, stern, manly control of a self which lives in the world, and knows the strength of the world and the limits of human power. The good life is rationally directed and holds firm to high ideals. It is not bent by the seductive voices of comfort and desire. It does not expect social utopias. It is distrustful of final victories. Too much cannot be expected. Yet one can with vigilance hold firm the reins to his self, control his unruly impulses, understand his place in the world, guide his actions by reason, maintain his self-reliant independence. And in this way, though he finally perish, man can keep his human dignity and respect, and die with cosmic good manners.

Way 11. The contemplative life is the good life. The external world is no fit habitat for man. It is too big, too cold, too pressing. Rather it is the life turned inward that is rewarding. The rich internal world of ideals, of sensitive feelings, of reverie, of self-knowledge is man's true home. By the cultivation of the self within, man alone becomes human. Only then does there arise deep sympathy with all that lives, an understanding of the suffering inherent in life, a realization of the futility of aggressive action, the attainment of contemplative joy. Conceit then falls away and austerity is dissolved. In giving up the world one finds the larger and finer sea of the inner self.

Way 12. The use of the body's energy is the secret of a rewarding life. The hands need material to make into something: lumber and stone for building, food to harvest, clay to mold. The muscles are alive to joy only in action, in climbing, running, skiing, and the like. Life finds its zest in overcoming, dominating, conquering some obstacle. It is the active deed which is satisfying, the deed adequate to the present, the daring and adventuresome deed. Not in cautious foresight, not in relaxed ease does life attain completion. Outward energetic action, the excitement of power in the tangible present — this is the way to live.

Way 13. A person should let himself be used. Used by other persons in their growth, used by the great objective purposes in the universe which silently and irresistibly achieve their goal. For persons and the world's purposes are dependable at heart, and can be trusted. One should be humble, constant, faithful, uninsistent. Grateful for the affection and protection which one needs, but undemanding. Close to persons and to nature, and secure because close. Nourishing the good by devotion and sustained by the good because of devotion. One should be a serene, confident, quiet vessel and instrument of the great dependable powers which move to their fulfillment.

from the scale values of responses (on an equal interval scale) but from arbitrary integers assigned to response categories (on an ordinal scale); finally, an alternative to the complete regression solution (Thurstone, pp. 511–515) is used to estimate factor scores for each sample. In each case, however, application of the labor-saving approximations appears sufficiently precise for the fallible data under analysis. The high degree of internal consistency found in the scaling analysis justifies the use of the graphical approach. For the factor analysis, it is demonstrated that the relation between scale values of response categories and arbitrary integer values of categories not only is monotonic, but is very nearly linear. (The product-moment r between scale values of upper category limits on our common scale and arbitrary equidistant interval limits is computed to be .995). Thus, the use of arbitrary integer values in the correlational work is demonstrated to involve a legitimate near-linear transformation. Certainly, no part of the major findings can be attributed to the use of such satisfactorily approximate techniques.

DEVELOPMENT OF A SCALE

In the form in which they were collected, the ratings obtained on the value schedule lend themselves to analysis by a successive-intervals scaling method. The value of scaling the data can be recognized readily. It would be erroneous to assume that the seven response categories are equidistant. This is an empirical question, and can only be solved by a test of the linearity of the relationship between a set of arbitrary integers assigned to response categories and corresponding values of response categories derived from the use of an equal-interval metric. Application of a successive-intervals scaling method provides such a metric, and thus allows the legitimate use of more powerful analytic procedures.

Alternative scaling operations, all within the same theoretical context, are presented by Guilford (1954, pp. 223–262). In determining scale values of the six category limits of our seven-interval scale, there was utilized the first of the methods described by Guilford (1954, pp. 226–229). In all cases, normal deviates associated with cumulative proportions of response between .03 and .97 were included. It is assumed that the distribution of judgments of each stimulus on an interval scale is normal. (More precisely, the necessary assumption is weaker than this, and can be demonstrated to hold whether or not the distributions are normal [Rozeboom & Jones].)

Scales are first derived separately for the value data from each of the five samples.[1] The resulting five sets of upper category limits are pre-

---

[1] The raw data, in the form of cumulative proportions of response in the seven categories, for each of the five samples, are filed with the American Documenta-

sented in the first five rows of Table 2.[2] Since a major purpose of our scaling procedure is cross-cultural comparison, it is desirable to have a common scale, which, as presented in Table 2, is a simple average over the five cultures. For all scales, a zero scale value is assigned the presumed point of indifference, which corresponds to the center of the fourth (middle) response category.

TABLE 2. SUCCESSIVE INTERVALS SCALE VALUES OF UPPER CATEGORY LIMITS

Scale	N	Category					
		1	2	3	4	5	6
U.S.	252	-1.417	-.709	-.216	.216	.872	1.701
India	724	-1.151	-.606	-.213	.213	.818	1.562
Japan	192	-1.284	-.752	-.266	.266	.803	1.574
China	523	-1.356	-.687	-.233	.233	.854	1.628
Norway	149	-1.477	-.732	-.220	.220	.718	1.730
Common Scale		-1.337	-.697	-.230	.230	.813	1.639

For each way to live, estimates of scale values and dispersions are determined on the common scale for each culture. These estimates are graphical, determined from plots, on normal probability paper, of cumulative proportion of response against scale values of upper-category limits. On the assumption of normality of distributions, these plots should be linear; straight lines are drawn by visual inspection so as to minimize the average discrepancy, in vertical (proportion) units, of the points from their corresponding line. Scale values are read from the graphs for the point at which each straight line passes the median. Standard deviations also are read from each graph, as the scale distance between the median and the 84th (or 16th) percentile. This latter procedure is simply a shortcut method for finding the reciprocal of the slope for each line, a value easily demonstrated to be an estimate of the standard deviation of each distribution. For the purpose of illustrating this approach, there has been chosen the way to live on which the most extreme cultural differences were found, Way 13. The graphs on Way 13 for the five cultures are presented in Figure 1.

Scale values of each way of life for the five cultures are reported in Table 3, and corresponding standard deviation estimates appear in Table 4. Following the procedure presented by Edwards and Thurstone (1952), theoretical cumulative proportions of response in the successive response

tion Institute. They may be obtained as Document No. 4650 from ADI Auxiliary Publications Project, Photoduplication Service, Library of Congress, Washington 25, D.C., by remitting in advance $1.25 for microfilm or $1.25 for photocopies.

[2] Mr. Karl-Erik Waerneryd gave substantial help in the determination of the scales and the scale values of the ways.

FIGURE 1. Cumulative Proportions of Response Plotted
Against Scale Values of Upper Category Limits, Way 13

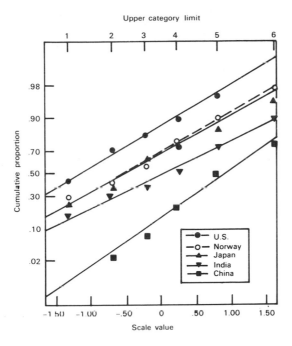

TABLE 3. SCALE VALUES OF THE WAYS TO LIVE

Way	U.S.	India	Japan	China	Norway	Sum	Average
1	.80	1.36	.70	.59	.83	4.28	.86
2	-.78	.08	.09	-.67	-.25	-1.53	-.31
3	.18	.91	.87	.72	.96	3.64	.73
4	-.26	-.21	-.18	-.49	-.55	-1.69	-.34
5	.20	.54	.44	.75	-.07	1.86	.37
6	.47	.93	.65	.85	.62	3.52	.70
7	1.24	.46	.21	.51	.66	3.08	.61
8	.26	.19	-.22	.03	-.02	.24	.05
9	-.60	-.33	.03	-.87	-.25	-2.02	-.40
10	-.09	.98	.46	.22	.24	1.37	.27
11	-.71	-.15	-.10	-.91	-.70	-2.57	-.51
12	.33	.39	.04	.35	.22	1.33	.27
13	-1.17	.06	-.52	.92	-.56	-1.27	-.25
Sum	-.13	5.21	2.47	1.56	1.13	10.24	
Average	-.01	.40	.19	.12	.09		.158

categories, computed from the scale value and standard deviation of each
distribution, are compared with actual observed proportions. Discrepancies for each culture, averaged over the 13 ways to live, appear in the

TABLE 4. STANDARD DEVIATIONS OF THE WAYS TO LIVE

Way	U.S.	India	Japan	China	Norway	Sum	Average
1	.74	.90	.93	.96	.90	4.43	.89
2	.83	1.06	.87	1.04	1.07	4.87	.97
3	.91	.91	1.01	.88	1.13	4.84	.97
4	1.00	1.18	.96	1.09	1.11	5.34	1.07
5	.91	1.04	.93	.95	.90	4.73	.95
6	.88	1.02	.83	.84	.82	4.39	.88
7	1.11	1.02	1.21	1.06	1.25	5.65	1.13
8	1.03	1.21	1.13	1.20	1.16	5.73	1.15
9	.83	.98	.93	.96	.90	4.60	.92
10	.99	1.12	1.05	1.15	1.15	5.46	1.09
11	.89	.98	.97	1.09	.92	4.85	.97
12	.88	.99	.94	.86	.89	4.56	.91
13	1.05	1.27	1.11	.88	1.09	5.40	1.08
Sum	12.05	13.68	12.87	12.96	13.29	64.85	
Average	.93	1.05	.99	1.00	1.02		.998

TABLE 5. AVERAGE DISCREPANCIES OF PREDICTED FROM
OBSERVED CUMULATIVE PROPORTIONS OF RESPONSE UNDER TWO
CONDITIONS OF SCALING

| | | Average absolute discrepancy | |
Sample	Sample size	Common scale	Separate scales
U.S.	252	.014	.013
India	724	.011	.010
Japan	192	.015	.015
China	523	.012	.011
Norway	149	.022	.017
Sum		.074	.066
Average		.015	.013

"Common Scale" column of Table 5. It is to be emphasized that these discrepancies result from use of the common scale. The resulting grand average discrepancy of .015 attests to the unusually good fit of the scaling model to the data. In the final column of Table 5 appear discrepancies obtained when, instead of a common scale for all cultures, estimates are obtained for each culture with the use of its own, distinct scale (see Table 2). As is expected, discrepancies under these conditions are reduced even further. It is interesting to note from Table 5 that size of average discrepancy varies inversely with sample size. This finding offers indirect support for the assumption of normality in the populations from which the samples are drawn; discrepancy values indicate the degree of departure of observed distributions from the normal distribution, and, if population distributions were normal, sample discrepancies would be expected to vary with N.

Discussion of these results, noting similarities and differences among the five samples, is presented in a later section.

THE FACTOR ANALYSES

Two experimentally independent factor analyses were performed, one based upon responses of 250 United States male college students, the other based upon an India sample of 250 male students (selected from the 252 United States and the 724 India students upon whom scaling was based).* . . .

FACTOR INTERPRETATIONS

For the interpretation of factors, particular attention is directed toward factor loadings which differ from zero by at least .25. The choice of this value is essentially arbitrary. Ways for which factor loadings exceed .25 are presented below, together with brief summaries of their content and their actual factor loadings. Factor names are supplied to facilitate discussions and are viewed as less than perfect representations of factor content.

UNITED STATES ANALYSIS

Factor A: *Social Restraint and Self-Control*

Way 10. Dignity, self-control, without retreat from the world .56
1. Refinement, moderation, restraint; participation in social life to understand and preserve the best attainments of man .... .39
3. Sympathy, concern for others, restraint of self .... .25
4. Abandonment; sensuous enjoyment of life; delight in people and things; solitude and sociality are both necessary .... —.30

The stress is upon conservation, rather than upon the initiation of change. Restraint and self-control are not for the sake of withdrawal into self, but for conscientious, responsible, intelligent participation in the world, holding firm to high ideals. The antithesis of the trait is unrestrained and irresponsible enjoyment. (Factor A accounts for 5.3% of the total variance, 16% of the common factor variance.)

On this factor India ranks the highest, with China and the United States exhibiting relatively low scores. All five factor scores are positive.

Factor B: *Enjoyment in Action*

Way 5. Live outwardly, energetically, cooperatively, for group achievement and enjoyment .... .55
12. Outward, energetic action .... .42
8. Carefree, relaxed, secure enjoyment .... .39

* [Ed. note: See the original article for the full presentation.]

10. Dignity, self-control, without retreat from the world — .32
2. Go it alone; avoid outward activity; know self; be
self-sufficient .... —.41
11. Give up the world and develop the inner self .... —.50

The stress is upon action, vitality, enjoyment. There is no tolerance for self-discipline, but there is maintained at least loose control of the physical and social environment. The antithesis of the trait is the highly controlled development of the inner self. (Factor B accounts for 9.2% of the total variance, 27% of the common factor variance.)

On this factor China and the United States have, in order, the highest scores, while Japan exhibits the lowest score. The spread between the highest and the lowest scores is exceeded only by the spread of scores on Factor D (receptivity and sympathetic concern). All five scores are positive.

Factor C: Withdrawal and Self-Sufficiency

Way 9. Quiet receptivity to nature yields a rich self ...... .61
2. Go it alone; avoid outward action; know self; be
self-sufficient .... .47
11. Give up the world and develop the inner self .... .35
6. Constant activity, striving for improved techniques
to control nature and society .... —.27

The stress is upon inwardness, self-sufficiency, closeness to nature. Control over other persons and things is avoided, but not control over one's self. The antithesis of the trait is outward activity for the sake of progress in the control of the world. (Factor C accounts for 7.2% of the total variance, 21% of the common variance.)

On this factor the relative positions which were obtained on Factor B are essentially reversed: the United States and China are here the low scorers while Japan and India score relatively high. All five scores, however, are negative.

Factor D: Receptivity and Sympathetic Concern

Way 13. Let oneself be used; remain close to persons and to
nature .... .60
3. Sympathy, concern for others, restraint of self .... .48
10. Dignity, self-control, without retreat from the world .29
5. Live outwardly, energetically, cooperatively, for group
achievement and enjoyment .... .28
2. Go it alone; avoid outward activity; know self; be
self-sufficient .... —.25
4. Abandonment; sensuous enjoyment of life; delight in
people and things; solitude and sociality are both
necessary .... —.27

The stress is upon the fulfillment of the needs of others through receptivity and devotion. This requires restraint of greed, passion, and self-concern. Both an emphasis on self-knowledge (while avoiding society) and on self-centered enjoyment are antithetic to the trait. (Factor D accounts for 7.4% of the total variance, 22% of the common variance.)

This factor shows the greatest range of scores of any factor, with China and India high and the United States low and standing apart from the other groups, it alone having a negative score.

Factor E: Self-Indulgence

Way 4. Abandonment; sensuous enjoyment of life; delight in people and things; solitude and sociality are both necessary .... .50
12. Outward energetic action .... .40
3. Sympathy, concern for others, restraint of self .... —.27

The stress is upon adventurous activity for the sake of pleasure and self-enjoyment. Self-control is lacking, nor is there an attempt to control others, but rather to enjoy others without becoming dependent upon them. The antithesis of the trait is self-sacrifice, affection, concern for others. (Factor E accounts for 4.9% of the total variance, 14% of the common variance.)

This factor has a much smaller range of scores than any other factor, and all the scores are negative. The scores for Norway and China are more negative than those of the other cultural groups.

INDIA ANALYSIS

Factor A': Social Restraint and Self-Control

Way 10. Dignity, self-control, without retreat from the world .42
1. Refinement, moderation, restraint. Participation in social life to understand and preserve the best attainments of man .... .40
2. Go it alone; avoid outward action; know self; be self-sufficient .... .28
8. Carefree, relaxed, secure enjoyment .... —.25
4. Abandonment; sensuous enjoyment of life; delight in people and things; solitude and sociality are both necessary .... —.32

Factor A' is essentially the same as United States Factor A. (Factor A' accounts for 5.3% of the total variance, 18% of the common factor variance.)

The order of scores on this factor is the same as on United States Factor A except for the reversal of Japan and Norway.

Factor B': Enjoyment and Progress in Action

Way 5. Live outwardly, energetically, cooperatively, for group
achievement and enjoyment .... .52
     12. Outward, energetic action .... .52
      6. Constant activity, striving for improved techniques
to control nature and society .... .46
      2. Go it alone; avoid outward action; know self; be
self-sufficient .... —.28
     11. Give up the world and develop the inner self ..... —.29

Factor B' is very similar to United States Factor B. Way 8, however, has a near-zero loading here, and is supplanted by Way 6 which emphasizes technical progress through action. Way 10 does not exhibit the negative loading which it had on the United States factor; the loading here is near zero. (Factor B' accounts for 7.7% of the total variance, 27% of the common variance.)

The relative score of India is here somewhat higher than on Factor B, and is now higher than Norway. Otherwise the order of scores by cultures is the same.

Factor C': Withdrawal and Self-Sufficiency

Way 11. Give up the world and develop the inner self ..... .54
     9. Quiet receptivity to nature yields a rich self ...... .49
     2. Go it alone; avoid outward action; know self; be
self-sufficient .... .43

Factor C' is very similar to United States Factor C. Notable is the lack of appearance of Way 6, which exhibits a negative loading of the United States factor. (Factor C' accounts for 7.1% of the total variance, 24% of the common variance.)

There are minor reversals in the positions of India and Japan, and of China and the United States, when compared to Factor C. The scores of India and Japan are now positive.

Factor D': Receptivity and Sympathetic Concern

Way 13. Let oneself be used; remain close to persons and to
nature .... .52
     3. Sympathy, concern for others, restraint of self .... .25
    10. Dignity, self-control, without retreat from the world .24
     5. Live outwardly, energetically, cooperatively, for group
achievement and enjoyment .... .23

Factor D' is very similar to United States Factor D, although Ways 2 and 4 here exhibit loadings close to zero instead of negative loadings.

(Factor D' accounts for 4.3% of the total variance, 15% of the common variance.)

The order of scores is the same as in Factor D, except that India here has a slightly higher score than China. The score for Norway has become slightly negative.

Factor E': Self-Indulgence

Way 4. Abandonment; sensuous enjoyment of life; delight in people and things; solitude and sociality are both necessary .... .53

      8. Carefree, relaxed, secure enjoyment .... .28

      3. Sympathy, concern for others, restraint of self .... —.26

Factor E' is quite similar to United States Factor E. The major difference is the replacement of Way 12 by Way 8. Hence E' implies less activistic and adventurous traits than E, and relatively more emphasis on sensuous enjoyment. (Factor E' accounts for 4.6% of the total variance, 16% of the common variance.)

The range of factor scores remains very small, as on Factor E. The United States, however, now has a higher score than India.

CHARACTERIZATION OF THE FIVE GROUPS IN TERMS OF SCALE VALUES AND FACTOR SCORES

The aim of this section is to characterize and compare the five national groups in terms of the analytic results presented in the two preceding sections. For the most part no attempt will be made to "explain" differences and similarities which are noted.[3] And since the India and United States factor analyses are so similar, only the factor scores based upon the United States factors will be used in the comparisons. Those who are interested in such differences as would be introduced by the India factors may compare Figure 3 with Figure 2.

While statements concerning the United States students are based on the sample of 252 men, it should be noted that a very similar scale was obtained from a larger sample of 1,546 male students drawn from all sections of the country. Also the median ratings of the two groups, for each of the 13 ways, are very similar. Hence the statements made on the

---

[3] It is planned to interpret as far as possible these and other findings in a book, *Varieties of Human Value*, to be published in 1956 by the University of Chicago Press. This will include a comparison of the factors obtained from the 13 ways with the three dimensions of value which were postulated in earlier books, *Paths of Life* and *The Open Self*. (C.M.) [Charles Morris' *Varieties of Human Value* was published by the Univ. of Chicago Press in 1956. The Eds.]

FIGURE 2. Factor Scores of the Five Samples: United States Analysis

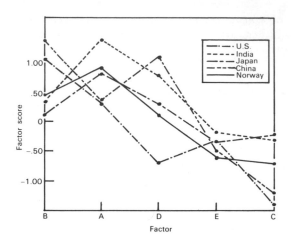

FIGURE 3. Factor Scores of the Five Samples: India Analysis

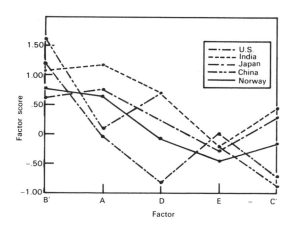

basis of the smaller sample may be considered applicable to the larger sample, which is considered more representative of the population of male college students in the United States.

The United States

Factor B (enjoyment in action) has a score higher than in any other group except China. Factor A (social restraint and self-control) is also positive, but lower than found elsewhere. The three other factor scores are negative, two of them (D, receptivity and sympathetic concern; C, withdrawal and self-sufficiency) being lower than in any other group. While Factor E (self-indulgence) has in general a low score, the United States is second highest on this score.

The over-all picture would seem to be that of a highly activated and extroverted orientation, less subject to social restraints and less open to receptivity and inwardness than any of the other four groups of college men. This interpretation on the basis of factor scores needs to be qualified, however, by the very high rating of Way 7, a rating much higher than in any other group. Way 7 stresses flexibility and many-sidedness, and explicitly provides a place for contemplation and enjoyment as well as for action. Since it accepts some values represented by each factor, but none of them to an extreme or exclusive degree, it has no high positive or negative loadings on any of them, United States or Indian. Way 7 is the only way for which this is true. Hence the importance of Way 7 for American students is not reflected in any interpretation or comparison based on factor scores alone.

It is noteworthy that Way 3, which stresses sympathetic concern for others, has a much lower scale value in the American sample than elsewhere, and Way 6, which represents the pioneering spirit, while relatively high in the American group, has the lowest scale value assigned to this alternative. The extreme rejection of Way 13 is also striking.

Whatever may be the explanation, for the United States students, the highest scale values are associated with those ways exhibiting lowest communalities (product-moment $r = -.79$). This relation does not hold to any such degree in the other samples.

India

The factor scores of India differ considerably from the United States scores. Instead of the order B, A, E, D, C, there appears the order A, D, B, E, C. Thus "social restraint and self-control" and "receptivity and sympathetic concern" are higher than the "enjoyment in action" factor which dominated so strongly the United States profile. Factor A (social restraint and self-control) is in fact much higher in India than elsewhere. And Factor C (withdrawal and self-sufficiency), while the lowest of India's factor scores, is noticeably higher than in the United States.

Way 7 is rated lower in India than in the United States; it is sixth in rank instead of first. Ways 1 and 10 have much the highest scale values assigned to these alternatives, and Ways 3 and 6 are markedly higher than in the United States. The fact that Ways 1 and 6 are both highly favored (though Way 1 more than Way 6) suggests considerable tension in the Indian students between preservation of the cultural heritage and reconstruction of the existing society. Way 13 has the highest standard deviation, and this may reflect the same situation. Perhaps the strong acceptance of Way 10, stoical in its emphasis, serves to mitigate or buffer this tension.

Japan

The pattern of preferences is very similar to that of India, although the actual factor scores tend to be lower. Japan is lower than any of the other groups in the acceptance of Factor B (enjoyment in action), and exhibits the greatest acceptance of Factor C (withdrawal and self-sufficiency). The scale values of the ways are also in general considerably lower than those of India. The only ways rated higher by Japan than by others are Ways 2, 4, 9, 11, each of which reflects the value of solitude; the differences between Japan and India on these ways are, however, slight.

The Japanese sample exhibits the lowest scale value given to Way 7, and yet this alternative has the largest standard deviation, suggesting heterogeneity of attitude toward Way 7. The high favor shown for Ways 3 and 10, the differentially high position of Ways, 2, 4, 9, and 11, and the relatively low ratings of Ways 5 and 13 show that the Japanese student of 1949 differed markedly in his values from those of the dominant Japanese leaders of World War II.

China

The factor pattern for China is more similar to that of the United States than it is to the pattern found in Japan and India. The order of factor scores is B, D, A, E, C. The score for Factor B (enjoyment in action) is the highest score given to that factor. The single striking difference between the Chinese and the American factor scores is on Factor D (receptivity and sympathetic concern). This is due in part to the fact that Way 13 was rated higher in China than any other alternative, while it was rated lowest in the United States. It must be remembered that the Chinese data were secured in the last stage of the conflict between the Communists and the Nationalists; receptivity to, and concern for, one side or the other was almost inevitable. The same fact is equally relevant in interpreting the very high rating of Way 5, a rating much higher than in the other cultural samples. All of this is not to say that the high Chinese score on Factor D is solely situational. Way 13 in particular embodies many values of the traditional Chinese heritage, both in its neo-Confucianist and Taoist forms.

There is a marked difference between the Chinese value pattern and the Japanese and Indian patterns. This is revealed in the factor scores, but even more clearly in the scale values: Ways 5 and 13 are rated very much higher in China, and Ways 2, 4, 9, and 11 are definitely rated lower. The similarity of the Chinese pattern to that of the United States (except for Factor D) and its dissimilarity to that of India or Japan (again, except for Factor D) shows how obsolescent is the bare and unqualified opposition of East and West.

Norway

Way 3 receives the highest rating, a rating higher than is given elsewhere. The second place goes to Way 1. Next in order is Way 7, which has a scale value second to that of the United States, although considerably lower. The ratings for Way 7 show the highest standard deviation, as was the case in Japan and the United States. Ways 4 and 5 receive the lowest ratings given to those alternatives. One notes with some surprise that Way 12 is rated lower than in China, India, or the United States, and its standard deviation is low.

The order of factor scores is A, B, D, E, C. The line on Fig. 2 which connects these scores tends to fall about midway between the highest and lowest scores of the other groups, suggesting a "middle way" attitude. Factor B (enjoyment in action) is not as high as in China or the United States and not as low as in India or Japan; Factor C (withdrawal and self-sufficiency) is not as high as in Japan or India, nor as low as in China or the United States. However, on Factor E (self-indulgence) Norway has the lowest of the five scores.

The factor profile of Norway is seen on Figure 2 to be very similar to that of Japan. This does not negate the view that Norway occupies a somewhat intermediate position between, say, Japan and the United States. For profile similarity is not, alone, an adequate measure of cultural similarity. In the present instance the factor scores are considerably lower for Norway than for Japan. And with respect to the scale values Norway is higher than Japan on five of the alternatives and higher than the United States on another five. The sum of the absolute differences of the scale values of Norway and Japan is only slightly more than half of the sum of the differences of the scale values of Japan and the United States. The sum of the absolute differences of the scale values of Norway and the United States is less than any similar sum in which the United States is paired with one of the three Asiatic groups. Norway is akin to the United States in the acceptance of Way 7, but it does not reject the ways stressing receptivity and inwardness as violently as do the American students.

GENERAL COMMENTS

The total variance accounted for by the five United States factors is 34%. Based upon product-moment correlations from test-retest ratings by 21

United States students, with an interval of three weeks, an estimate of the mean reliability of the ways is .67. Hence, the five factors account for about 50% of the total nonerror variance. This means that there is much which is unique in the individual ways over and above what is reflected in the five common factors. This explains the importance in comparing the five groups of taking account of the scale values of the individual ways, and not merely of the factor scores. But even when this is done it should be emphasized that the methods and materials employed in this study do not in themselves provide a sufficient basis for a comprehensive comparison of cultures or groups within cultures. The "Ways to Live" document was here used to study how persons say they would like to live, and not how they do live. The present study deals with values in only one sense of the term, that is, with what Kluckhohn calls "conceptions of the desirable." The relation between how persons would like to live and how they in fact do live has not been the problem of this study.

The mean factor scores on the United States factors are as follows: India, .42; China, .24; Japan, .15; Norway, .05; United States, −.19. On the India factors the order is the same, except that Japan precedes China. In terms of average scale values for the 13 ways to live the order is again, India, Japan, China, Norway, United States. These orders indicate in a rough way the degree of acceptance of different ways to live within a culture. In these terms the two Western groups show less cultural diversity than do the Asiatic groups.[4] On the other hand, as the ratings for Way 7 indicate, students of the United States and Norway seem to favor diversity within the single person more than the Eastern students do.

In the five groups certain of the ways tend to be favored more highly than others. Thus the average of the five scale values is high for Ways 1, 3, and 6, and low for Ways 2, 4, 9, and 11. It may be noted that the first set of ways embodies values important for the continuing operation of a society (stressing as they do the conservation of what has been achieved, sympathetic concern for others, and reconstruction in the face of new problems), while the latter set is essentially individualistic in orientation and contains no stress on social responsibility.

SUMMARY

To the problem of measuring human values have been applied both psychometric scaling analysis and factor analysis. With respect to the "Ways to Live" document, which aims to embody basic human values, the main results of the analysis are as follows:

---

[4] Of course, one cannot rule out the possibility that these orders may be the results of differing interpretations and/or uses of the rating categories.

1. The ratings of the 13 ways are scalable; the scales obtained for the five groups are similar enough to justify the formation of a common scale, and on this scale quantitative comparisons can be made within and across the cultures. The scales obtained are interval scales and permit the use of statistics appropriate to such scales. The question of whether a nonarbitrary zero point can be determined (i.e., whether a ratio scale can be found) has not been examined here. But if one assumes a zero point (such as the mid-point of the fourth interval of the original seven response categories), then ratio comparisons can be made relative to that assumed zero point.

2. Some evidence for the existence of a value structure holding across cultures is given in the similarity of the results of the Indian and United States orthogonal factor solutions. The actual ratings of the ways differed considerably in these two cultures, but the factors (dimensions) proved to be very much the same. Whether the result obtained in these two cultures holds also for other cultures could be determined only by further factor analyses. But to the extent that it does hold, it is possible to compare quantitatively the value patterns of different cultures in terms of common value dimensions.*

3. How this can be done was suggested by a comparison of the ratings of various ways to live by American, Norwegian, Chinese, Japanese, and Indian students. It is believed that the results obtained by the combined use of factor scores and scale values show that this method has penetration and power, and does not merely reproduce the obvious.

References

Edwards, A. L., and L. L. Thurstone. An internal consistency check for scale values determined by the method of successive intervals. *Psychometrika*, 1952, 17:169–180.

Guilford, J. P. *Psychometric Methods.* (2nd Ed.) New York: McGraw-Hill, 1954.

Kluckhohn, C. Values and value-orientations in the theory of action. In T. Parsons and E. A. Shils (eds.). *Toward a General Theory of Action.* Cambridge, Mass.: Harvard University Press, 1951.

Rozeboom, W. W. and L. V. Jones. The validity of the successive intervals method of psychometric scaling. *Psychometrika*, 1956, 21, 165–183.

Thurstone, L. L. *Multiple-factor Analysis.* Chicago: University of Chicago Press, 1947.

* [Ed. note: See discussion on this point in the Introduction to this reader, and especially in Charles Morris, *Varieties of Human Value* (Chicago: University of Chicago, 1956).]

21   DAVID C. McCLELLAND

The Achievement Motive in Economic Growth

From the beginning of recorded history, men have been fascinated by the fact that civilizations rise and fall. Culture growth, as Kroeber has demonstrated, is episodic, and sometimes occurs in quite different fields.[1] For example, the people living in the Italian peninsula at the time of ancient Rome produced a great civilization of law, politics, and military conquest; and at another time, during the Renaissance, the inhabitants of Italy produced a great civilization of art, music, letters, and science. What can account for such cultural flowerings? In our time we have theorists like Huntington, who stresses the importance of climate, or Toynbee, who also feels the right amount of challenge from the environment is crucial, though he conceives of the environment as including its psychic effects. Others, like Kroeber, have difficulty imagining any general explanation; they perforce must accept the notion that a particular culture happens to hit on a particularly happy mode of self-expression, which it then pursues until it becomes overspecialized and sterile.

My concern is not with all culture growth, but with economic growth. Some wealth or leisure may be essential to development in other fields — the arts, politics, science, or war — but we need not insist on it. However, the question of why some countries develop rapidly in the economic sphere at certain times and not at others is in itself of great interest, whatever its relation to other types of culture growth. Usually, rapid economic growth has been explained in terms of "external" factors — favorable opportunities for trade, unusual natural resources, or conquests that have opened up new markets or produced internal political stability. But I am interested in the *internal* factors — in the values and motives men have that lead them to exploit opportunities, to take advantage of favorable trade conditions; in short, to shape their own destiny.

Reprinted from Bert F. Hoselitz and W. E. Moore (eds.), *Industrialization and Society*. The Hague: Mouton, 1963. Copyright, UNESCO. This paper is a summary of the author's book, *The Achieving Society*, published by Van Nostrand Co. in Princeton, N.J., in 1961.

[1] A. L. Kroeber, *Configurations of Culture Growth*. Berkeley, California: University of California Press, 1944.

This interest is not surprising; I am a psychologist — and, furthermore, a psychologist whose primary research interest is in human motivation, in the *reasons* that people behave as they do. Of course, all people have always, to a certain extent, been interested in human motivation. The difference between their interest and the twentieth-century psychologist's interest is that the latter tries to define his subject matter very precisely and, like all scientists, to measure it. How can human motives be identified, or even measured? Psychologists' favorite techniques for conducting research in this area have always been the interview and the questionnaire. If you want to know what a man's motives are, ask him. Of course, you need not ask him directly; but perhaps, if you talk to him long enough in an interview, or ask him enough in a questionnaire, you can infer what his motives are — more or less — the same way that, from a number of clues, a detective would infer who had committed a crime.

Whatever else one thinks of Freud and the other psychoanalysts, they performed one extremely important service for psychology: once and for all, they persuaded us, rightly or wrongly, that what people said about their motives was not a reliable basis for determining what those motives really were. In his analyses of the psychopathology of everyday life and of dreams and neurotic symptoms, Freud demonstrated repeatedly that the "obvious" motives — the motives that the people themselves thought they had or that a reasonable observer would attribute to them — were not, in fact, the real motives for their often strange behavior. By the same token, Freud also showed the way to a better method of learning what people's motives were. He analyzed dreams and free associations: in short, fantasy or imaginative behavior. Stripped of its air of mystery and the occult, psychoanalysis has taught us that one can learn a great deal about people's motives through observing the things about which they are spontaneously concerned in their dreams and waking fantasies. About ten or twelve years ago, the research group in America with which I was connected decided to take this insight quite seriously and to see what we could learn about human motivation by coding objectively what people spontaneously thought about in their waking fantasies.[2] Our method was to collect such free fantasy, in the form of brief stories written about pictures, and to count the frequency with which certain themes appeared — rather as a medical technician counts the frequency with which red or white corpuscles appear in a blood sample. We were able to demonstrate that the frequency with which certain "inner concerns" appeared in these fantasies varied sys-

[2] John W. Atkinson (ed.), *Motives in Fantasy, Action, and Society.* Princeton, N.J.: D. Van Nostrand, 1958.

tematically as a function of specific experimental conditions by which we aroused or induced motivational states in the subjects. Eventually, we were able to isolate several of these inner concerns, or motives, which, if present in great frequency in the fantasies of a particular person, enabled us to know something about how he would behave in many other areas of life.

Chief among these motives was what we termed "the need for Achievement" (n Achievement) — a desire to do well, not so much for the sake of social recognition or prestige, but to attain an inner feeling of personal accomplishment. This motive is my particular concern in this paper. Our early laboratory studies showed that people "high" in n Achievement tend to work harder at certain tasks; to learn faster; to do their best work when it counts for the record, and not when special incentives, like money prizes, are introduced; to choose experts over friends as working partners; etc. Obviously, we cannot here review the many, many studies in this area. About five years ago, we became especially interested in the problem of what would happen in a society if a large number of people with a high need for achievement should happen to be present in it at a particular time. In other words, we became interested in a social-psychological question: What effect would a concentration of people with high n Achievement have on a society?

It might be relevant to describe how we began wondering about this. I had always been greatly impressed by the very perceptive analysis of the connection between Protestantism and the spirit of capitalism made by the great German sociologist, Max Weber.[3] He argues that the distinguishing characteristic of Protestant business entrepreneurs and of workers, particularly from the pietistic sects, was not that they had in any sense invented the institutions of capitalism or good craftmanship, but that they went about their jobs with a new perfectionist spirit. The Calvinistic doctrine of predestination had forced them to rationalize every aspect of their lives and to strive hard for perfection in the positions in this world to which they had been assigned by God. As I read Weber's description of the behavior of these people, I concluded that they must certainly have had a high level of n Achievement. Perhaps the new spirit of capitalism Weber describes was none other than a high need for achievement — if so, then n Achievement has been responsible, in part, for the extraordinary economic development of the West. Another factor served to confirm this hypothesis. A careful study by Winterbottom had shown that boys with high n Achievement usually came from families in

---

[3] Max Weber, *The Protestant Ethic and the Spirit of Capitalism*, trans. Talcott Parsons. New York: Charles Scribners and Sons, 1930.

which the mothers stressed early self-reliance and mastery.[4] The boys whose mothers did *not* encourage their early self-reliance, or did not set such high standards of excellence, tended to develop lower need for achievement. Obviously, one of the key characteristics of the Protestant Reformation was its emphasis on self-reliance. Luther stressed the "priesthood of all believers" and translated the Bible so that every man could have direct access to God and religious thought. Calvin accentuated a rationalized perfection in this life for everyone. Certainly, the character of the Reformation seems to have set the stage, historically, for parents to encourage their children to attain earlier self-reliance and achievement. If the parents did in fact do so, they very possibly unintentionally produced the higher level of *n* Achievement in their children that was, in turn, responsible for the new spirit of capitalism.

This was the hypothesis that initiated our research. It was, of course, only a promising idea; much work was necessary to determine its validity. Very early in our studies, we decided that the events Weber discusses were probably only a special case of a much more general phenomenon — that it was *n* Achievement as such that was connected with economic development, and that the Protestant Reformation was connected only indirectly in the extent to which it had influenced the average *n* Achievement level of its adherents. If this assumption is correct, then a high average level of *n* Achievement should be equally associated with economic development in ancient Greece, in modern Japan, or in a preliterate tribe being studied by anthropologists in the South Pacific. In other words, in its most general form, the hypothesis attempts to isolate one of the key factors in the economic development, at least, of all civilizations. What evidence do we have that this extremely broad generalization will obtain? By now, a great deal has been collected — far more than I can summarize here; but I shall try to give a few key examples of the different types of evidence.

First, we have made historical studies. To do so, we had to find a way to obtain a measure of *n* Achievement level during time periods other than our own, whose individuals can no longer be tested. We have done this — instead of coding the brief stories written by an individual for a test, we code imaginative literary documents: poetry, drama, funeral orations, letters written by sea captains, epics, etc. Ancient Greece, which we studied first, supplies a good illustration. We are able to find literary documents written during three different historical periods and dealing with similar themes: the period of economic growth, 900 B.C.–475 B.C.

---

[4] M. R. Winterbottom, "The relation of need for achievement to learning and experiences in independence and mastery," in Atkinson, *op. cit.*, pp. 453–478.

(largely Homer and Hesiod); the period of climax, 475 B.C.–362 B.C.; and the period of decline, 362 B.C.–100 B.C. Thus, Hesiod wrote on farm and estate management in the early period; Xenophon, in the middle period; and Aristotle, in the late period. We have defined the period of "climax" in economic, rather than in cultural, terms, because it would be presumptuous to claim, for example, that Aristotle in any sense represented a "decline" from Plato or Thales. The measure of economic growth was computed from information supplied by Heichelheim in his *Wirtschaftsgeschichte des Altertums.*[5] Heichelheim records in detail the locations throughout Europe where the remains of Greek vases from different centuries have been found. Of course, these vases were the principal instrument of Greek foreign trade, since they were the containers for olive oil and wine, which were the most important Greek exports. Knowing where the vase fragments have been found, we could compute the trade area of Athenian Greece for different time periods. We purposely omitted any consideration of the later expansion of Hellenistic Greece, because this represents another civilization; our concern was Athenian Greece.

When all the documents had been coded, they demonstrated — as predicted — that the level of *n* Achievement was highest during the period of growth prior to the climax of economic development in Athenian Greece. (See Table 1.) In other words, the maximum *n* Achievement level preceded the maximum economic level by at least a century. Furthermore, that high level had fallen off by the time of maximum prosperity, thus foreshadowing subsequent economic decline. A similar methodology was applied, with the same results, to the economic development of Spain in the sixteenth century [6] and to two waves of economic development in the history of England (one in the late sixteenth century and the other at the beginning of the industrial revolution, around 1800).[7] The *n* Achievement level in English history (as determined on the basis of dramas, sea captains' letters, and street ballads) rose, between 1400–1800, *twice*, a generation or two before waves of accelerated economic growth (incidentally, at times of Protestant revival). This point is significant because it shows that there is no "necessary" steady

[5] F. Heichelheim, *Wirtschaftsgeschichte des Altertums.* Leiden: A. W. Sijthoff, 1938.

[6] J. B. Cortes, "The achievement motive in the Spanish economy between the thirteenth and the eighteenth centuries," *Economic Development and Cultural Change*, 1960, IX, 144–163.

[7] N. M. Bradburn and D. E. Berlew, "Need for achievement and English economic growth," *Economic Development and Cultural Change*, October 1961, X:1, 8–20.

TABLE 1. AVERAGE *n* ACHIEVEMENT LEVEL PLOTTED AT MIDPOINTS
OF PERIODS OF GROWTH, CLIMAX, AND DECLINE OF ATHENIAN
CIVILIZATION AS REFLECTED IN THE EXTENT OF HER TRADE AREA
(MEASURED FOR THE SIXTH, FIFTH, AND FOURTH CENTURIES B.C. ONLY)

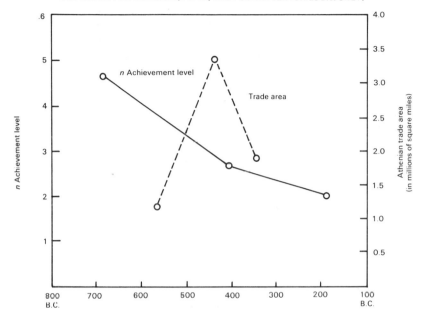

Time in centuries before Christ

decline in a civilization's entrepreneurial energy from its earlier to its
later periods. In the Spanish and English cases, as in the Greek, high
levels of *n* Achievement preceded economic decline. Unfortunately, space
limitations preclude more detailed discussion of these studies here.

We also tested the hypothesis by applying it to preliterate cultures of
the sort that anthropologists investigate. At Yale University, an organized
effort has been made to collect everything that is known about all the
primitive tribes that have been studied and to classify the information
systematically for comparative purposes. We utilized this cross-cultural
file to obtain the two measures that we needed to test our general hypothesis. For over fifty of these cultures, collections of folk tales existed
that Child and others had coded,[8] just as we coded literary documents

[8] I. L. Child, T. Storm, and J. Veroff, "Achievement themes in folk tales related to socialization practices," in Atkinson, *op. cit.*, pp. 479–492.

and individual imaginative stories, for *n* Achievement and other motives. These folk tales have the character of fantasy that we believe to be so essential for getting at "inner concerns." In the meantime, we were searching for a method of classifying the economic development of these cultures, so that we could determine whether those evincing high *n* Achievement in their folk tales had developed further than those showing lower *n* Achievement. The respective modes of gaining a livelihood were naturally very different in these cultures, since they came from every continent in the world and every type of physical habitat; yet we had to find a measure for comparing them. We finally thought of trying to estimate the number of full-time "business entrepreneurs" there were among the adults in each culture. We defined "entrepreneur" as "anyone who exercises control over the means of production and produces more than he can consume in order to sell it for individual or household income." Thus an entrepreneur was anyone who derived at least seventy-five per cent of his income from such exchange or market practices. The entrepreneurs were mostly traders, independent artisans, or operators of small firms like stores, inns, etc. Nineteen cultures were classified as high in *n* Achievement on the basis of their folk tales; seventy-four per cent of them contained some entrepreneurs. On the other hand, only thirty-five per cent of the twenty cultures that were classified as low in *n* Achievement contained any entrepreneurs (as we defined it) at all. The difference is highly significant statistically (Chi-square $= 5.97$, $p < .02$). Hence data about primitive tribes seem to confirm the hypothesis that high *n* Achievement leads to a more advanced type of economic activity.

But what about modern nations? Can we estimate their level of *n* Achievement and relate it to their economic development? The question is obviously one of the greatest importance, but the technical problems of getting measures of our two variables proved to be really formidable. What type of literary document could we use that would be equally representative of the motivational levels of people in India, Japan, Portugal, Germany, the United States, and Italy? We had discovered in our historical studies that certain types of literature usually contain much more achievement imagery than others. This is not too serious as long as we are dealing with time changes within a given culture; but it is very serious if we want to compare two cultures, each of which may express its achievement motivation in a different literary form. At last, we decided to use children's stories, for several reasons. They exist in standard form in every modern nation, since all modern nations are involved in teaching their children to read and use brief stories for this purpose. Furthermore, the stories are imaginative; and, if selected from those used in the earliest grades, they are not often influenced by temporary political events. (We were most impressed by this when reading the stories that every Russian child reads. In general, they cannot be distinguished, in style and content, from the stories read in all the countries of the West.)

We collected children's readers for the second, third, and fourth grades from every country where they could be found for two time periods, which were roughly centered around 1925 and around 1950. We got some thirteen hundred stories, which were all translated into English. In all, we had twenty-one stories from each of twenty-three countries about 1925, and the same number from each of thirty-nine countries about 1950. Code was used on proper names, so that our scorers would not know the national origin of the stories. The tales were then mixed together, and coded for *n* Achievement (and certain other motives and values that I shall mention only briefly).

The next task was to find a measure of economic development. Again, the problem was to insure comparability. Some countries have much greater natural resources; some have developed industrially sooner than others; some concentrate in one area of production and some in another. Economists consider national income figures in per capita terms to be the best measure available; but they are difficult to obtain for all countries, and it is hard to translate them into equal purchasing power. Ultimately, we came to rely chiefly on the measure of electricity produced: the units of measurement are the same all over the world; the figures are available from the 1920's on; and electricity is the *form* of energy (regardless of how it is produced) that is essential to modern economic development. In fact, electricity produced per capita correlates with estimates of income per capita in the 1950's around .90 anyway. To equate for differences in natural resources, such as the amount of water power available, etc., we studied *gains* in kilowatt hours produced per capita between 1925 and 1950. The level of electrical production in 1925 is, as one would expect, highly correlated with the size of the gain between then and 1950. So it was necessary to resort to a regression analysis; that is, to calculate, from the average regression of gain on level for all countries, how much gain a particular country should have shown between 1925 and 1950. The actual gain could then be compared with the expected gain, and the country could be classified as gaining more or less rapidly than would have been expected on the basis of its 1925 performance. The procedure is directly comparable to what we do when we predict, on the basis of some measure of I.Q., what grades a child can be expected to get in school, and then classify him as an "under-" or "over-achiever."

The correlation between the *n* Achievement level in the children's readers in 1925 and the growth in electrical output between 1925 and

1950, as compared with expectation, is a quite substantial .53, which is highly significant statistically. It could hardly have arisen by chance. Furthermore, the correlation is also substantial with a measure of gain over the expected in per capita income, equated for purchasing power by Colin Clark. To check this result more definitively with the sample of forty countries for which we had reader estimates of n Achievement levels in 1950, we computed the equation for gains in electrical output in 1952–1958 as a function of level in 1952. In turned out to be remarkably linear when translated into logarithmic units, as is so often the case with simple growth functions. Table 2 presents the performance of each of the countries, as compared with predictions from initial level in 1952, in standard score units and classified by high and low n Achievement in 1950. Once again we found that n Achievement levels predicted significantly ($r = .43$) the countries which would perform more or less rapidly than expected in terms of the average for all countries. The finding is more striking than the earlier one, because many Communist and underdeveloped countries are included in the sample. Apparently, n Achievement is a precursor of economic growth, not only in the Western style of capitalism based on the small entrepreneur, but also in economies controlled and fostered largely by the state.

For those who believe in economic determinism, it is especially interesting that n Achievement level in 1950 is *not* correlated either with *previous* economic growth between 1925 and 1950, or with the level of prosperity in 1950. This strongly suggests that n Achievement is a *causative* factor — a change in the minds of men which produces economic growth rather than being produced by it. In a century dominated by economic determinism, in both Communist and Western thought, it is startling to find concrete evidence for psychological determinism, for psychological developments as preceding and presumably causing economic changes.

The many interesting results which our study of children's stories yielded have succeeded in convincing me that we chose the right material to analyze. Apparently, adults unconsciously flavor their stories for young children with the attitudes, the aspirations, the values, and the motives that they hold to be most important.

I want to mention briefly two other findings, one concerned with economic development, the other with totalitarianism. When the more and less rapidly developing economies are compared on all the other variables for which we scored the children's stories, one fact stands out. In stories from those countries which had developed more rapidly in both the earlier and later periods, there was a discernible tendency to emphasize, in 1925 and in 1950, what David Riesman has called "other-directedness" namely, reliance on the opinion of particular others, rather

TABLE 2. RATE OF GROWTH IN ELECTRICAL OUTPUT (1952-1958)
AND NATIONAL N ACHIEVEMENT LEVELS IN 1950; DEVIATION
FROM EXPECTED GROWTH RATE[a] IN STANDARD SCORE UNITS

National n achievement levels (1950)[b]		Above expectation		Below expectation
High n Achievement				
3.62	Turkey	+1.38		
2.71	India[c]	+1.12		
2.38	Australia	+ .42		
2.32	Israel	+1.18		
2.33	Spain	+ .01		
2.29	Pakistan[d]	+2.75		
2.29	Greece	+1.18	3.38 Argentina	- .56
2.29	Canada	+ .08	2.71 Lebanon	- .67
2.24	Bulgaria	+1.37	2.38 France	- .24
2.24	U.S.A.	+ .47	2.33 U. So. Africa	- .06
2.14	West Germany	+ .53	2.29 Ireland	- .41
2.10	U.S.S.R.	+1.61	2.14 Tunisia	-1.87
2.10	Portugal	+ .76	2.10 Syria	- .25
Low n Achievement				
1.95	Iraq	+ .29	2.05 New Zealand	- .29
1.86	Austria	+ .38	1.86 Uruguay	- .75
1.67	U.K.	+ .17	1.81 Hungary	- .62
1.57	Mexico	+ .12	1.71 Norway	- .77
.86	Poland	+1.26	1.62 Sweden	- .64
			1.52 Finland	- .08
			1.48 Netherlands	- .15
			1.33 Italy	- .57
			1.29 Japan	- .04
			1.20 Switzerland[e]	-1.92
			1.19 Chile	-1.81
Correlation of n Achievement			1.05 Denmark	- .89
level (1950) x deviations from			.57 Algeria	- .83
expected growth rate = .43, p < .01.			.43 Belgium	-1.65

[a]The estimates are computed from the monthly average electrical production figures, in millions of Kwh, for 1952 and 1958, from United Nations, *Monthly Bulletin of Statistics* (January, 1960), and *World Energy Supplies,* 1951-1954 and 1955-1958, (Statistical Papers, Series J).

The correlation between log level 1952 and log gain 1952-58 is .976

The regression equation based on these thirty-nine countries, plus four others from the same climatic zone on which data are available (China-Taiwan, Czechoslovakia, Rumania, Yugoslavia), is: log gain (1952-58) = .9229 log level (1952) + .0480.

Standard scores are deviations from mean gain predicted by the regression formula (M = -.01831) divided by the standard deviation of the deviations from mean predicted gain (SD = .159).

[b]Based on twenty-one children's stories from second-, third-, and fourth-grade readers in each country.

[c]Based on six Hindi, seven Telegu, and eight Tamil stories.

[d]Based on twelve Urdu and eleven Bengali stories.

[e]Based on twenty-one German Swiss stories, mean = .91; twenty-one French Swiss stories, mean = 1.71; over-all mean obtained by weighting German mean double to give approximately proportionate representation to the two main ethnic population groups.

than on tradition, for guidance in social behavior.[9] *Public opinion* had, in these countries, become a major source of guidance for the individual. Those countries which had developed the mass media further and faster

[9] David Riesman, with the assistance of Nathan Glazer and Reuel Denney, *The Lonely Crowd.* New Haven, Conn.: Yale University Press, 1950.

— the press, the radio, the public-address system — were also the ones who were developing more rapidly economically. I think that "other-directedness" helped these countries to develop more rapidly because public opinion is basically more flexible than institutionalized moral or social traditions. Authorities can utilize it to inform people widely about the need for new ways of doing things. However, traditional institutionalized values may insist that people go on behaving in ways that are no longer adaptive to a changed social and economic order.

The other finding is not directly relevant to economic development, but it perhaps involves the means of achieving it. Quite unexpectedly, we discovered that every major dictatorial regime which came to power between the 1920's and 1950's (with the possible exception of Portugal's) was foreshadowed by a particular motive pattern in its stories for children: namely, a low need for affiliation (little interest in friendly relationships with people) and a high need for power (a great concern over controlling and influencing other people).

The German readers showed this pattern before Hitler; the Japanese readers, before Tojo; the Argentine readers, before Peron; the Spanish readers, before Franco; the South African readers, before the present authoritarian government in South Africa; etc. On the other hand, very few countries which did not have dictatorships manifested this particular motive combination. The difference was highly significant statistically, since there was only one exception in the first instance and very few in the second. Apparently, we stumbled on a psychological index of ruthlessness — i.e., the need to influence other people (n Power), unchecked by sufficient concern for their welfare (n Affiliation). It is interesting, and a little disturbing, to discover that the German readers of today still evince this particular combination of motives, just as they did in 1925. Let us hope that this is one case where a social science generalization will not be confirmed by the appearance of a totalitarian regime in Germany in the next ten years.

To return to our main theme — let us discuss the precise ways that higher n Achievement leads to more rapid economic development, and why it should lead to economic development rather than, for example, to military or artistic development. We must consider in more detail the mechanism by which the concentration of a particular type of human motive in a population leads to a complex social phenomenon like economic growth. The link between the two social phenomena is, obviously, the business entrepreneur. I am not using the term "entrepreneur" in the sense of "capitalist": in fact, I should like to divorce "entrepreneur" entirely from any connotations of ownership. An entrepreneur is someone who exercises control over production that is not just for his personal consumption. According to my definition, for example, an executive in a steel production unit in Russia is an entrepreneur.

It was Joseph Schumpeter who drew the attention of economists to the importance that the activity of these entrepreneurs had in creating industrialization in the West. Their vigorous endeavors put together firms and created productive units where there had been none before. In the beginning, at least, the entrepreneurs often collected material resources, organized a production unit to combine the resources into a new product, and sold the product. Until recently, nearly all economists — including not only Marx, but also Western classical economists — assumed that these men were moved primarily by the "profit motive." We are all familiar with the Marxian argument that they were so driven by their desire for profits that they exploited the workingman and ultimately forced him to revolt. Recently, economic historians have been studying the actual lives of such entrepreneurs and finding — certainly to the surprise of some of the investigators — that many of them seemingly were not interested in making money as such. In psychological terms, at least, Marx's picture is slightly out of focus. Had these entrepreneurs been above all interested in money, many more of them would have quit working as soon as they had made all the money that they could possibly use. They would not have continued to risk their money in further entrepreneurial ventures. Many of them, in fact, came from pietistic sects, like the Quakers in England, that prohibited the enjoyment of wealth in any of the ways cultivated so successfully by some members of the European nobility. However, the entrepreneurs often seemed consciously to be greatly concerned with expanding their businesses, with getting a greater share of the market, with "conquering brute nature," or even with altruistic schemes for bettering the lot of mankind or bringing about the kingdom of God on earth more rapidly. Such desires have frequently enough been labeled as hypocritical. However, if we assume that these men were really motivated by a desire for achievement rather than by a desire for money as such, the label no longer fits. This assumption also simplifies further matters considerably. It provides an explanation for the fact that these entrepreneurs were interested in money without wanting it for its own sake, namely, that money served as a ready quantitative index of how well they were doing — e.g., of how much they had achieved by their efforts over the past year. The need to achieve can never be satisfied by money; but estimates of profitability in money terms can supply direct knowledge of how well one is doing one's job.

The brief consideration of the lives of business entrepreneurs of the past suggested that their chief motive may well have been a high n Achievement. What evidence have we found in support of this? We made two approaches to the problem. First, we attempted to determine whether individuals with high n Achievement behave like entrepreneurs; and second, we investigated to learn whether actual entrepreneurs, particularly the more successful ones, in a number of countries, have higher n Achievement than do other people of roughly the same status. Of course, we had to establish what we meant by "behave like entrepreneurs" — what precisely distinguishes the way an entrepreneur behaves from the way other people behave?

The adequate answers to these questions would entail a long discussion of the sociology of occupations, involving the distinction originally made by Max Weber between capitalists and bureaucrats. Since this cannot be done here, a very brief report on our extensive investigations in this area will have to suffice. First, one of the defining characteristics of an entrepreneur is *taking risks* and/or innovating. A person who adds up a column of figures is not an entrepreneur — however carefully, efficiently, or correctly he adds them. He is simply following established rules. However, a man who decides to add a new line to his business *is* an entrepreneur, in that he cannot know in advance whether his decision will be correct. Nevertheless, he does not feel that he is in the position of a gambler who places some money on the turn of a card. Knowledge, judgment, and skill enter into his decision-making; and, if his choice is justified by future developments, he can certainly feel a sense of personal achievement from having made a successful move.

Therefore, if people with high n Achievement are to behave in an entrepreneurial way, they must seek out and perform in situations in which there is some moderate risk of failure — a risk which can, presumably, be reduced by increased effort or skill. They should not work harder than other people at routine tasks, or perform functions which they are certain to do well simply by doing what everyone accepts as the correct traditional thing to do. On the other hand, they should avoid gambling situations, because, even if they win, they can receive no sense of personal achievement, since it was not skill but luck that produced the results. (And, of course, most of the time they would lose, which would be highly unpleasant to them.) The data on this point are very clear-cut. We have repeatedly found, for example, that boys with high n Achievement choose to play games of skill that incorporate a moderate risk of failure. Table 3 represents one study. The game was adapted from one used by the psychologist Kurt Lewin. Each child was given a rope ring and told that he could stand at any distance that he preferred from the peg, to try to throw the ring over the peg. The children with high n Achievement usually stood at middle distances along the peg, where the chances of success or failure were moderate. However, the

TABLE 3. PERCENTAGE OF THROWS MADE BY 5-YEAR-OLDS WITH HIGH
AND LOW DOODLE *n* ACHIEVEMENT AT DIFFERENT DISTANCES FROM
THE PEG AND SMOOTHED CURVE OF PROBABILITY OF SUCCESS AT
THOSE DISTANCES

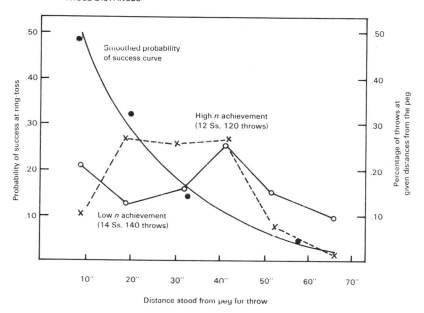

26 Ss, 10 throws each. Plotted at midpoints of intervals of 11 inches beginning with closest distance stood
(4"–14", 5"–15", etc.)

children with low *n* Achievement evinced no particular preference for
any position. They more frequently stood at extremes of distance —
either very close to the peg, where they were sure to throw the ring over
it, or very far away, where they were almost certain not to. They thus
manifested behavior like that of many people in underdeveloped countries who, while they act very traditionally economically, at the same
time love to indulge in lotteries — risking a little to make a great deal on
a very long shot. In neither of the two last examples do the actors concentrate on the realistic *calculated* risk, as do the subjects with high *n*
Achievement.

We have recently concluded a somewhat analogous study, which indicated that boys with high *n* Achievement tend to perform better and to
work harder under conditions of moderate risk — boys not only in the
United States, but also in Japan, Brazil, and India. In each of these

countries, the boys with high n Achievement did not invariably perform a laboratory task better than the boys with low n Achievement. They did better only under conditions involving some degree of competition, some risk of doing worse than others or of not getting a sense of personal achievement. There was still another group of boys in the sample from each country. These boys were identified by their optimistic attitude toward life in general, as manifested in their answers to a questionnaire. The members of these groups always had more success than the others, no matter what the competitive or risk situation was. I like to think of these boys as the conscientious ones, who will do their work cheerfully and efficiently under any kind of incentive conditions. They may form the backbone of the civil service, because they can tolerate routine; but they will not be the business entrepreneurs, because the latter constantly seek situations in which they can obtain a sense of personal achievement from having overcome risks or difficulties.

Another quality that the entrepreneur seeks in his work is that his job be a kind that ordinarily provides him with accurate knowledge of the results of his decisions. As a rule, growth in sales, in output, or in profit margins tells him very precisely whether he has made the correct choice under uncertainty or not. Thus, the concern for profit enters in — profit is a measure of success. We have repeatedly found that boys with a high n Achievement work more efficiently when they know how well they are doing. Also, they will not work harder for money rewards; but if they are asked, they state that greater money rewards should be awarded for accomplishing more difficult things in games of skill. In the ring-toss game, subjects were asked how much money they thought should be awarded for successful throws from different distances. Subjects with high n Achievement and those with low n Achievement agreed substantially about the amounts for throws made close to the peg. However, as the distance from the peg increased, the amounts awarded for successful throws by the subjects with high n Achievement rose more rapidly than did the rewards by those with low n Achievement. Here, as elsewhere, individuals with high n Achievement behaved as they must if they are to be the successful entrepreneurs in society. They believed that greater achievement should be recognized by quantitatively larger reward.

We are now investigating to learn whether business executives do, in fact, have higher n Achievement. Our analysis of this question is not yet finished; but Table 4 indicates what, on the whole, we shall probably find. Four conclusions can be drawn from it. (1) Entrepreneurs ("junior executives") have higher n Achievement than do a comparable group of non-entrepreneurs ("adjusters"), whose chief job was quasi-judicial (tax

TABLE 4. PERCENTAGES OF DIFFERENT TYPES OF EXECUTIVES HIGH
IN *n* ACHIEVEMENT IN THE U.S.A. AND TURKEY (AFTER DATA
SUPPLIED BY N. M. BRADBURN)

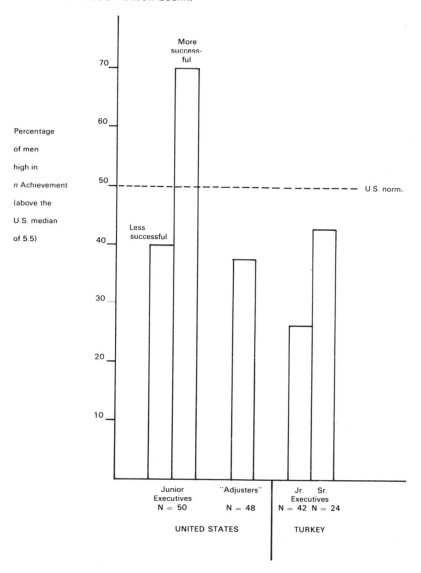

Percentage
of men
high in
n Achievement
(above the
U.S. median
of 5.5)

claim and insurance adjusters). A very careful study in the General Electric Company has confirmed this finding: on the average, production managers have higher n Achievement than do staff specialists of comparable education and pay. (2) The more successful junior executives have higher n Achievement than the less successful ones. (3) Turkish executives have a lower *average* level of n Achievement than American executives. This finding supports the general impression that the "entrepreneurial spirit" is in short supply in such countries. (4) Nevertheless, the more successful Turkish executives have a ligher level of n Achievement than do the less successful ones. This confirms our predictions that n Achievement equips people peculiarly for the business executive role — even in a country like Turkey, where business traditions are quite different from those of the West.

There are two successful, and one unsuccessful, methods by which the business community recruits people with the "entrepreneurial spirit" — with high n Achievement. The unsuccessful way is easiest to describe and is still characteristic of many underdeveloped countries. In a study of the occupational likes and dislikes of boys in Japan, Brazil, Germany, India, and the United States, we found that (as Atkinson had predicted on theoretical grounds) the boys with high n Achievement usually aspire toward the occupation of highest prestige *which they have a reasonable chance to enter and to succeed.*[10] For example, their ambitions will be centered on the professions, which are the highest prestige occupations in most countries — *if* the boys themselves are from the upper class and thus have the opportunity and backing to enter the professions. In other words, when the business leadership of a country is largely recruited from the elite (as it is in many countries, because only the elite has access to capital and to government), it will *not* tend to attract those with high n Achievement who are not from the upper class.

Developments in many of the Western democracies were quite different. In the most rapidly advancing countries, business leadership was drawn, at least in the early stages, largely from the middle elasses. A business career was the highest prestige occupation to which a middle-class boy with high n Achievement could aspire — especially if he were a member of a disliked minority group, like the Protestants in France or the Jews in many countries, to whom other channels of upward mobility were closed. Thus a constant "natural" flow of entrepreneurial talent from the middle classes provided economic leadership of a high quality.

[10] J. W. Atkinson, "Motivational determinants of risk-taking behavior," *Psychological Review*, 1957, LXIV, 359–372.

The other successful method of recruiting entrepreneurial talent is the one that has been adopted, for example, in the U.S.S.R. There, the central government took a severe, achievement-oriented, "pass-or-fail" attitude toward its plant managers, so that only the "fittest" survived. We believe that those "fittest" were the ones with the highest *n* Achievement, although we have no supporting evidence as yet. In the free enterprise system, the recruiting method may be compared to a garden in which all plants are allowed to grow until some crowd the others out. In the Soviet system, it is comparable to a garden in which plants that have not reached a specified height by a certain time are weeded out. In many underdeveloped countries, it is comparable to a garden where only certain plants are permitted to live in the first place, so that the gardener has to take them whatever size they attain. Of course, no country represents a pure type; but perhaps the analogy, oversimplified though it is, helps to illustrate my point.

What produces high *n* Achievement? Why do some societies produce a large number of people with this motive, while other societies produce so many fewer? We conducted long series of researches into this question. I can present only a few here.

One very important finding is essentially a negative one: *n* Achievement cannot be hereditary. Popular psychology has long maintained that some races are more energetic than others. Our data clearly contradict this in connection with *n* Achievement. The changes in *n* Achievement level within a given population are too rapid to be attributed to heredity. For example, the correlation between respective *n* Achievement levels in the 1925 and 1950 samples of leaders is substantially zero. Many of the countries that were high in *n* Achievement at one or both times may be low or moderate in *n* Achievement now, and vice versa. Germany was low in 1925 and is high now; and certainly the hereditary makeup of the German nation has not changed in a generation.

However, there is substantiating evidence that *n* Achevement is a motive which a child can acquire quite early in life, say, by the age of eight or ten, as a result of the way his parents have brought him up. Winterbottom's study of the importance of early self-reliance and achievement training has been supplemented by a much more detailed inquiry by Rosen and D'Andrade.[11] They actually entered the homes of boys with high and low *n* Achievement and observed how the boys were treated by their parents while they were engaged in various kinds of work, e.g., stacking blocks blindfolded. The principal results are

[11] B. C. Rosen and R. G. D'Andrade, "The psychosocial origins of achievement motivation," *Sociometry*, 1959, *XXII*, 185–218.

summarized in Table 5, which indicates the differences between the parents of the "high *n* Achievement boys" and the parents of boys with low *n* Achievement. In general, the mothers and the fathers of the first group set higher levels of aspiration in a number of tasks for their sons. They were also much warmer, showing positive emotion in reacting to their sons' performances. In the area of authority or dominance, the data are quite interesting. The mothers of the "highs" were more domineering than the mothers of the "lows," but the *fathers* of the "highs" were significantly *less* domineering than the fathers of the "lows." In other words, the fathers of the "highs" set high standards and are warmly interested in their sons' performances, but they do not directly interfere. This gives the boys the chance to develop initiative and self-reliance.

What factors cause parents to behave in this way? Their behavior certainly is involved with their values and, possibly, ultimately with their religion or their general world view. At present, we cannot be sure that

TABLE 5. MEAN DIFFERENCES IN THE BEHAVIOR OF PARENTS OF SONS WITH LOW AND HIGH *n* ACHIEVEMENT WORKING IN TASK SITUATIONS[a]

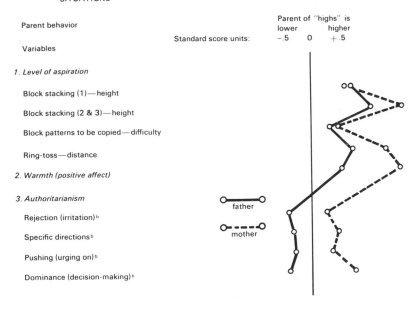

[a]After Rosen and D'Andrade.
[b]Parents of "highs" predicted to be lower, permitting more independence.

Protestant parents are more likely to behave this way than Catholic parents — there are too many subgroup variations within each religious portion of the community: the Lutheran father is probably as likely to be authoritarian as the Catholic father. However, there does seem to be one crucial variable discernible: the extent to which the religion of the family emphasizes individual, as contrasted with ritual, contact with God. The preliterate tribes that we studied in which the religion was the kind that stressed the individual contact had higher *n* Achievement; and in general, mystical sects in which this kind of religious self-reliance dominates have had higher *n* Achievement.

The extent to which the authoritarian father is away from the home while the boy is growing up may prove to be another crucial variable. If so, then one incidental consequence of prolonged wars may be an increase in *n* Achievement, because the fathers are away too much to interfere with their sons' development of it. And in Turkey, Bradburn found that those boys tended to have higher *n* Achievement who had left home early or whose fathers had died before they were eighteen.[12] Slavery was another factor which played an important role in the past. It probably lowered *n* Achievement — in the slaves, for whom obedience and responsibility, but not achievement, were obvious virtues; and in the slave-owners, because household slaves were often disposed to spoil the owner's children as a means for improving their own positions. This is both a plausible and a probable reason for the drop in *n* Achievement level in ancient Greece that occurred at about the time the middle-class entrepreneur was first able to afford, and obtain by conquest, as many as two slaves for each child. The idea also clarifies the slow economic development of the South in the United States by attributing its dilatoriness to a lack of *n* Achievement in its elite; and it also indicates why lower-class American Negroes, who are closest to the slave tradition, possess very low *n* Achievement.[13]

. . . In the present state of our knowledge, we can conceive of trying to raise *n* Achievement levels only in the next generation — although new research findings may soon indicate *n* Achievement in adults can be increased. Most economic planners, while accepting the long-range desirability of raising *n* Achievement in future generations, want to know what can be done during the next five or ten years. This immediacy inevitably focuses attention on the process or processes by which executives or entrepreneurs are selected. Foreigners with proved entrepre-

[12] N. M. Bradburn, "The Managerial Role in Turkey" (unpublished doctoral dissertation, Harvard University, 1960).

[13] B. C. Rosen, "Race, ethnicity, and achievement syndrome," *American Sociological Review*, 1959, XXIV, 47–60.

neurial drive can be hired, but at best this is a temporary and unsatisfactory solution. In most underdeveloped countries where government is playing a leading role in promoting economic development, it is clearly necessary for the government to adopt rigid achievement-oriented standards of performance like those in the U.S.S.R.[14] A government manager or, for that matter, a private entrepreneur, should have to produce "or else." Production targets must be set, as they are in most economic plans; and individuals must be held responsible for achieving them, even at the plant level. The philosophy should be one of "no excuses accepted." It is common for government officials or economic theorists in underdeveloped countries to be weighed down by all the difficulties which face the economy and render its rapid development difficult or impossible. They note that there is too rapid population growth, too little capital, too few technically competent people, etc. Such obstacles to growth are prevalent, and in many cases they are immensely hard to overcome; but talking about them can provide merely a comfortable rationalization for mediocre performance. It is difficult to fire an administrator, no matter how poor his performance, if so many objective reasons exist for his doing badly. Even worse, such rationalization permits, in the private sector, the continued employment of incompetent family members as executives. If these private firms were afraid of being penalized for poor performance, they might be impelled to find more able professional managers a little more quickly. I am not an expert in this field, and the mechanisms I am suggesting may be far from appropriate. Still, they may serve to illustrate my main point: if a country short in entrepreneurial talent wants to advance rapidly, it must find ways and means of insuring that only the most competent retain positions of responsibility. One of the obvious methods of doing so is to judge people in terms of their *performance* — and not according to their family or political connections, their skill in explaining why their unit failed to produce as expected, or their conscientiousness in following the rules. I would suggest the use of psychological tests as a means of selecting people with high *n* Achievement; but, to be perfectly frank, I think this approach is at present somewhat impractical on a large enough scale in most underdeveloped countries.

Finally, there is another approach which I think is promising for recruiting and developing more competent business leadership. It is the one called, in some circles, the "professionalization of management." Harbison and Myers have recently completed a world-wide survey of the

[14] David Granick, *The Red Executive*. Garden City: Doubleday and Co., 1960.

efforts made to develop professional schools of high-level management. They have concluded that, in most countries, progress in this direction is slow.[15] Professional management is important for three reasons. (1) It may endow a business career with higher prestige (as a kind of profession), so that business will attract more of the young men with high *n* Achievement from the élite groups in backward countries. (2) It stresses *performance* criteria of excellence in the management area — i.e., what a man can do and not what he is. (3) Advanced management schools can themselves be so achievement-oriented in their instruction that they are able to raise the *n* Achievement of those who attend them.

Applied toward explaining historical events, the results of our researches clearly shift attention away from external factors and to man — in particular, to his motives and values. That about which he thinks and dreams determines what will happen. The emphasis is quite different from the Darwinian or Marxist view of man as a creature who *adapts* to his environment. It is even different from the Freudian view of civilization as the sublimation of man's primitive urges. Civilization, at least in its economic aspects, is neither adaptation nor sublimation; it is a positive creation by a people made dynamic by a high level of *n* Achievement. Nor can we agree with Toynbee, who recognizes the importance of psychological factors as "the very forces which actually decide the issue when an encounter takes place," when he states that these factors "inherently are impossible to weigh and measure, and therefore to estimate scientifically in advance." [16] It is a measure of the pace at which the behavorial sciences are developing that even within Toynbee's lifetime we can demonstrate that he was mistaken. The psychological factor responsible for a civilization's rising to a challenge is so far from being "inherently impossible to weigh and measure" that it has been weighed and measured and scientifically estimated in advance; and, so far as we can now tell, this factor is the achievement motive.

[15] Frederick Harbison and Charles A. Myers, *Management in the Industrial World.* New York: McGraw-Hill, 1959.

[16] Arnold J. Toynbee, *A Study of History* (abridgment by D. C. Somervell; Vols. I–VI). New York: Oxford University Press, 1947.

On Happiness in Industrial Man

Ever larger segments of the world's population are living and will come to live in what is now commonly called "industrial society." The standard complex of institutions — most notably the factory — associated with this system daily becomes more widely diffused into a variety of traditional and even "primitive" cultural contexts. These institutions rather rigorously prescribe a set of norms, with regard to such matters as dress, time, order, and authority, which must be conformed to, at least during the time that individuals are engaged in their industrial and related occupations. This aspect of the diffusion of the industrial order is easily recognized.

It is less evident that the distinctive roles of the industrial system also foster typical patterns of perception, opinions, beliefs, and values which are not institutionally prescribed but arise spontaneously as new subcultures in response to the institutional conditions provided by the typically differentiated role-structure of modern industrial society. This paper reports an exploratory comparative study of the influence of these standard environments on attitudes, which yielded considerable evidence that the process is effective and pervasive.

In this investigation I take the institutional pattern or setting as given and the responses to it, particularly those not explicitly required by the institutional forms, as the dependent variable. The individual and groups

Abridged from Alex Inkeles, "Industrial Man: The Relation of Status to Experience, Perception, and Value." Reprinted from *The American Journal of Sociology*, Vol. 66, July 1960. Copyright 1960 by the University of Chicago.

This is a revised and somewhat abridged version of a report prepared for the Conference on Political Modernization which met in June, 1959, under the auspices of the Committee on Comparative Politics of the Social Science Research Council. I am particularly indebted to the Committee's chairman, Professor Gabriel Almond, for support and encouragement. The data were assembled with the aid of a grant from the Ford Foundation, supplemented by the Russian Research Center at Harvard. Dr. Elmo C. Wilson generously made available special tabulations from studies undertaken by International Research Associates, Inc. Jay Greenfield rendered creative research assistance.

of individuals, not institutions, are the central concern, and we study variation not in formal institutional arrangements but in individual and collective social perception and action. Only one institutional complex is considered here, namely, that which characterizes the modern large-scale bureaucratic industrial system. What is not given, namely the response to it, will be sought in a number of different realms but in each case will be measured through reported experiences and expressed attitudes and values.

The underlying theory is very simple. It is assumed that people have experiences, develop attitudes, and form values in response to the forces or pressures which their environment creates. By "environment" we mean, particularly, networks of interpersonal relations and the patterns of reward and punishment one normally experiences in them. They include not only access to facilities and items of consumption, necessary and conspicuous, but also such intangibles as prestige, the comforts of security, respectful treatment, calculability in the actions of significant others, and so on. The theory holds that, within broad limits, the same situational pressures, the same framework for living, will be experienced as similar and will generate the same or similar response by people from different countries. This is, of course, not a denial of individual variation, of personality as a determinant of perception, cognition, or affect. Neither is it meant to deny the effect of traditional cultural ways on behavior. These will mute the independent effect of the industrial institutional environment, but it is assumed that they cannot eliminate it. Rather, its force is sufficiently great to assert itself clearly despite the countervailing influence of personal idiosyncracy and traditional cultural ways of thinking and feeling. Insofar as industrialization, urbanization, and the development of large-scale bureaucratic structures and their usual accompaniments create a standard environment with standard institutional pressures for particular groups, to that degree should they produce relatively standard patterns of experience, attitude, and value — standard, not uniform, pressures. The situation of worker and manager may be relatively standard in the factory, wherever it is located, but relative to each other these positions are by no means uniform.

The test of the assumption is very simple. It is made by comparing the perceptions, attitudes, and values of those in comparable positions in the typical hierarchies of modern society, in particular the occupational, educational, and socioeconomic. If the "foreign" (read: "industrial"), externally introduced institutional environment plays no role, there should be no pattern or similarity in the response of incumbents of a given type of position from country to country. If there is a pattern — if, for example, workers are everywhere less "happy" or "optimistic," or more insistent on obedience in children, than are engineers — this can come only from the similarity of their situation in the hierarchical setting of occupation, income, or education, since on the basis of their nationality or culture alone they should obviously differ.

To discern this influence of the industrial environment is, of course, not the same as determining either its extent or its intensity. The pressure generated by the institutional setting of industrialism may affect only a narrow range of experience and attitude — possibly only that relating to work experience. It may exert only a moderate influence, producing only a small part of the variance, the main part being accounted for by other factors, such as traditional cultural orientations. These are important problems for further elucidation. For now, we restrict ourselves to a statement of the main proposition — *that men's environment, as expressed in the institutional patterns they adopt or have produced to them, shapes their experience, and through this their perceptions, attitudes and values, in standardized ways which are manifest from country to country, despite the countervailing randomizing influence of traditional cultural patterns.* I trust it will be understood without great elaboration that this proposition is stated so unequivocally only to facilitate clear exposition. The hypothesis is tentative, a guide to the exploration which this paper reports and not a dictum or an empirically established fact. We are equally interested in proof and disproof and must expect to find both supporting, negating, and ambiguous evidence.

I can hardly claim novelty for the proposition. The idea that the institutions in which men live shape their character and their views is old indeed. So is the more refined notion that a man's distinctive standing and role within the social structure will influence not only his perspective on the world but his wishes, beliefs, and values as well. Probably very few will argue that any people can indefinitely, or even for very long, utilize the material and institutional forms of industrial society without also absorbing some of its culture. At the same time, very few will argue that the industrial system is indeed so standardized or its influence so compelling as to permit no variation in the culture of those who share it. The obvious task of serious investigation, therefore, is to determine with some degree of precision where and how far the institutions of industrial society impose or foster the development of new subcultures wherever they are introduced and in what realms of life and to what degree traditional patterns maintain a relative independence of or immunity to the influence of the industrial institutional system.

There are two main avenues open to us. The first would be to designate certain attitudes or values as indices of the industrial "subculture" and then to test the degree of association between these indices and the level of industrialization in various countries. This is essentially the path taken by Davis and Lipset in their comparative studies. Both used the percentage of males engaged in non-agricultural pursuits, and the per capita consumption of energy, as indices of industrialization. For his dependent variable, Davis studied the degree of urbanization; Lipset, the extent and stability of democratic political processes.[1] If we were to follow this path, our dependent variable would be the proportion of the population in each country holding a certain belief or sharing a particular value presumed to be fostered by the industrial milieu — for example, the belief that most human problems can ultimately be solved by technological advances.

There are several reasons for not adopting this procedure. Indices of industrialization tend to generalize to the population, as a whole, characteristics which may in fact be intensely developed in only one segment. An outstanding example would be the Soviet Union, which is highly and intensely industrialized, but in which about half the population is engaged in agriculture. In such cases a nationwide index of the industrial subculture might be low, not because the industrialized segment of the population failed to show the expected characteristic, but because so large a part of the population was not integrated into the industrial structure. Our theory applies only to those segments of the population whose life conditions are standardized through industrial or other large-scale bureaucratic organizations.

Another reason for not adopting this method is that the average level of response for a nation may so heavily reflect traditional cultural orientations, or recent events, as to mask the independent influence of the industrial environment. To control this would require matching countries sharing the same traditional culture but varying in degree of industrialization. On the face of it, many would deny the possibility of meaningfully accomplishing this, even if the pool of countries available for matching were much larger than it is.

The most compelling reason for not relying on a single national average as an index of the industrial subculture, however, lies in the nature of the theory being tested. The idea that the industrial institutional order carries with it a distinctive industrial culture does not necessarily mean that the culture is the same for all who live in industrial society. This commonly made assumption can be quite misleading. We should,

---

[1] Kingsley Davis and Hilda H. Golden, "Urbanization and the Development of Pre-Industrial Areas," in Paul K. Hatt and Albert J. Reiss, Jr. (eds.), *Cities and Society* (rev. ed.; Glencoe, Ill.: Free Press, 1957), pp. 120–40; Seymour M. Lipset, "Some social requisites of democracy: Economic development and political legitimacy," *American Political Science Review*, LIII (March, 1959), 69–105.

rather, expect that, in accord with the differences among positions in
the modern occupational hierarchy, the different occupational groups
will have differentiated attitudes and values. What is likely to be common to industrial societies, therefore, is not a single idea or a set of
commonly held ideas but a particular *structure* of experience, attitude,
and value which takes its form from the occupational structure.

Our expectation, that the distinctive feature of the industrial culture is a structure of response characteristic of the occupational hierarchy
as a whole, also accounts for our not adopting the simple alternative of
studying just one distinctive group, such as factory workers. From
country to country the proportion of factory workers giving a particular
answer might be quite different, yet in each country the workers might
stand in a fixed relation to the other strata. This regularity would not be
evident at all if we studied only one typical occupational group in different societies. We therefore take as our unit of analysis not a national
average or a score for a particular group but the structure of response
in some status hierarchy representing the entire nation or, at least, its
industrialized segment.

We will speak of the existence of a structure of response when the
proportion in each stratum (occupation, prestige, income, or educational
group) reporting certain experiences or holding particular views rises
or falls more or less regularly as we ascend or descend the hierarchy. We
will speak of a cross-national *pattern*, with which we are most concerned,
when the structure of response is more or less the same as we move from
country to country — that is, when the direction and, to some degree,
the magnitude of the changes in proportion are similar in different national populations.

We assume that the industrial order fixes the situation of different
groups relative to each other in a more or less invariant fashion. We also
assume that occupational groups, as units, respond distinctively to
their occupational environment and the world outside it according to
their situation and the characteristic pressures it generates. Insofar as
these assumptions are correct, we should expect to find a cross-national
pattern of response on many issues directly and indirectly related to the
typical pattern of experience in the roles common in industrial society.
The similarity in the structure of response as we move from country to
country may exist, even though the average response varies widely from
one nation to another. The typical response of any population may be
strongly shaped by its traditional culture, and that of any particular
group in some country may be influenced by a unique local situation.
But, by focusing on the occupational hierarchy as a whole, country by
country, we at once control both the effect of traditional culture at the

national level and the special circumstances affecting one or another occupational group at the "local" level.

To test these assumptions, we should, ideally, have data gathered for this specific purpose. Our samples should come from a variety of countries selected to represent diverse cultural traditions, and the sample from each country should be restricted to those holding strictly comparable positions in each respective society's industrial sector. The questionnaires would be carefully translated to insure comparability of meaning. But what is actually available is very far from meeting the optimum requirements. I have had to rely on already completed studies drawn from a file of the reports of various national survey agencies,[2] the one major international compilation edited by Hadley Cantril,[3] the few, more systematic, comparative studies such as those undertaken by UNESCO[4] and International Research Associates, Inc. (INRA),[5] and sundry other scattered sources. None of these studies was designed for the purpose for which we wish to use them. The selection of countries is highly variable. The sample subgroups are frequently not equivalent from country to country, and it has been necessary to use other criteria of stratification than occupational status, which is most relevant to our theory. The questions used in different countries are often only very approximate equivalents. Under the circumstances, failure to find the expected patterns would be somewhat inconclusive as a test of our hypothesis. On the other hand, the presence of so many potentially randomizing influences in the data means that the emergence of the expected pattern, even if weakly manifested, may be taken as highly suggestive of the probable predictive power of the theory. . . .*

[2] Particularly useful were the Italian agency *Doxa Bolletino published in Milan* (hereinafter cited as "*Doxa*"), the releases of the Netherlands Institute of Public Opinion in Amsterdam (hereinafter cited as "NIPO"), and the bulletins of the Australian Gallup Polls of Melbourne (hereinafter cited as "AGP").

[3] Hadley W. Cantril (ed.), *Public Opinion, 1935–1946* (Princeton, N.J.: Princeton University Press, 1951).

[4] William Buchanan and Hadley Cantril, *How Nations See Each Other* (Urbana: University of Illinois Press, 1953).

[5] During 1958 they undertook a substantial number of comparative surveys, released through the *New York Herald Tribune*. Additional tabulations were made available through the courtesy and cooperation of Dr. Elmo Wilson. Although the Gallup affiliates in various countries often ask the same question at more or less the same time, detailed consolidated results suitable for comparative study are generally not available. Some reconstruction is possible from the bulletins released by the individual affiliates.

* [Ed. note: A section of Professor Inkeles' paper on "The Realm of Work" has been deleted in this reprinting because of space limitations. See the original paper for the full presentation.]

ON HAPPINESS

Granted that happiness is a very elusive thing, we may yet make so bold as to study it and to do so through so crude a device as a public-opinion poll. Of course we should not naïvely accept what a man says when we ask him, "Are you happy?" But neither is it reasonable to assume that whatever he says means the opposite. That would be all too regular and a sure key to the truth. Some men will be truly cheerful but suspect our purpose; fear of the "evil eye," or a trait of personality, may lead them to deny publicly their true feeling. If everyone answered the question in a random and, in that sense, meaningless way, we would expect by chance that 50 per cent in any population would say "Yes," 50 per cent "No," and that no control variable such as age, sex, or income would reveal anything but this 50/50 division.

Common sense tells us that some groups produce more people who feel they are happy than do others, and with reason. Those about to commit suicide tell their friends, doctors, or diaries that they are miserable; those who are about to get divorced are likely to report their marriage is unhappy. Admittedly, where there are pressures which make people disguise their true feelings, their more or less public report of how they feel will certainly reduce the clarity of the relationship between the objective situation and their true inner feeling. If, despite this built-in and essentially uncontrollable distortion, we still find strong and meaningful connections between a man's situation and what he says about his happiness, then we must assume that the "real" connection is, if anything, not weaker but stronger than the one which emerges in our data.

Both direct and indirect questions have been used in an effort to assess individual happiness. An identical direct question was put to people in the U.S., England, France, and Canada during 1946. By contrast to the Anglo-Saxon trio, the French emerge as dour indeed: in the other countries a third or more were "very happy," but in France only 8 per cent. Forty per cent of the French said they were "not very happy," as against a maximum of 10 per cent elsewhere.[6] Much the same question was asked in 1949 by at least six of the Gallup affiliates, with similar results. Only 11 per cent of the French were "very happy," as against a range of from 26 per cent in Norway to 52 per cent in Australia.[7] Unfortunately, we do not have cross-tabulations by stratification variables for

---

[6] Cantril (ed.), *op. cit.*, p. 281.

[7] AGP, Nos. 569–78 (February-March, 1949). The other countries were Holland (43 per cent), the United States (43 per cent), and the United Kingdom (39 per cent).

either of these two studies, by comparable data from Italy and Britain leave little doubt that, when these are made, we will find in each society that such happiness as anyone cares to admit will be found oftenest among those in the more advantaged strata of society.

In the British study men were asked: "In the last twenty-four hours, have you had a hearty laugh?" Women were asked whether they had had a "good cry," an effort being made to disarm them by prefacing the question with the statement: "Many doctors say it is good to give vent to your feelings by crying once in a while." Although the questions do not deal directly with happiness, they very probably measure much the same thing. The proportion who had laughed in the last twenty-four hours decreased, and the proportion who had cried increased, as one descended the socio-economic scale (Table 1). The differentiation was sharp, however, only in the case of the very poor, who had laughed only half as often and had cried twice as often as did those in the middle and upper economic classes.

TABLE 1. LAUGHING AND CRYING IN ENGLAND BY CLASS AND SEX[a]

Economic class	Percentage who laughed in last 24 hours (men only)	Percentage who cried in last 24 hours (women only)
Well-to-do	47	12
Average	50	11
Below average	41	16
Poor	26	27

[a]Reported in *Doxa Bolletino*, Vol. V, No. 6 (April, 1956).

I have asked many people, including several large audiences, to predict the outcome of this poll. The great majority invariably expected the working class to laugh more often. They express surprise at the findings and generally question me closely as to the time and country involved.[8] On learning the study was done in England, they invariably offer an *ad hoc* explanation, based on assumptions about the character of English society, and regularly volunteer the opinion that certainly in Italy the results would be different. Unfortunately the same question seems not to have been asked in sunny Italy. But its smiling workers and singing

[8] These audiences were generally composed of faculty and students, supplemented by people in the college or university community who attend lectures "open to the public" — safely characterized as solidly middle class. Despite their high average level of education, they seemed to harbor a stereotype of the working class which in important respects is strikingly analogous to that held by southern whites about the poor, irresponsible, but "happy" Negro.

peasants have been asked two other questions which should serve our purpose. The first was simple and straightforward: "Just now do you feel happy or unhappy?" The second was more complex: "Could you summarize in a few words the state (or balance) of your life today?" The respondents were then offered a choice of six sentences suggesting various combinations and degrees of pain and joy ranging from "Life has given me only joys and satisfactions," to "Life has given me only pain and disillusionment."

The results are fairly unambiguous but, as is so often true of such data, by no means completely so. For example, on the first "test" the lowest proportion of happy people is found among one of the more favored groups — the managers (*dirigente*), a category which seems to include free professionals. On the other hand, this group is quite "normal" on the second test, reporting life to be full of pain and disillusionment less often than any other group. Leaving aside such complications, however, we may conclude that on the whole, in Italy no less than in Britain, happiness is much more commonly reported by the advantaged strata of society, while sadness and despair are more standard in the manual and depressed classes. Of course, the well-to-do have no monopoly on happiness, nor does a majority of the working class report itself miserable. In all classes the central tendency is toward some mixture of happiness and pain. But at the extremes the general pattern we have found elsewhere is manifested here as well. As we ascend the occupational ladder, the proportion who are "very" or "fairly" happy rises from 29 per cent among farm laborers and ordinary workers to 47 per cent among employers.[9] Similarly, at the other extreme, workers report themselves as unhappy two-and-a-half times as often as do the employers and managers. Among the manual classes the ratio of the happy to the unhappy is as low as 1:1, whereas in the more advantaged groups it is almost 5:1.

Much the same pattern is shown in the second test. The life of much pain and little joy is claimed by about 50 per cent of workers and farm laborers, by as few as 23 per cent of the managers and professionals, and by about one-third of employers and farm owners (Table 2).

To assess happiness in a number of countries simultaneously we must, unfortunately, use a question which can at best be taken as only a rough approximation of those dealing directly with happiness, namely, one inquiring about "satisfaction." What happiness is may be somewhat ambiguous, but we are generally clear that it deals with an *emotional*

---

[9] There is, however, not much to choose between the lowest categories who are clustered around the 30 per cent level (cf. *Doxa*, No. 12 [April, 1948]).

TABLE 2. BALANCE OF JOY AND PAIN IN LIFE IN ITALY, IN PERCENTAGES BY OCCUPATION[a]

Occupation	More pain than joy[b]	More joy than pain[c]	A balance of joy and pain[d]	No answer
Employer	32	20	45	3
Manager	23	23	56	–
Farm owner and operator	33	20	46	1
White collar	28	15	55	2
Artisan	36	12	51	1
Worker	48	11	41	–
Farm laborer	51	11	38	1

[a]*Doxa Bolletino,* No. 12 (April, 1948).
[b]Includes the response: "Life has given *only* pains and disillusion."
[c]Includes: "Life has given me *only* joys and satisfactions."
[d]Includes: "Many pains but also many joys" and "Few pains and few joys." Among workers and farm laborers and employees the choice of "few joys" predominated markedly; among managers, the reverse; and by the remainder the two alternatives were equally chosen.

state. "Satisfaction" is a much more ambiguous term, and, when not further specified, it can mean satisfaction with one's financial situation, social or political advancement, family life, or any one of a number of things. Furthermore, "happiness" may be translated fairly well from one language to another, but "satisfaction" changes its meaning. In addition, in the available comparative study the question on satisfaction came immediately after one on security, and this probably led people more often to respond in terms of financial criteria rather than of general satisfaction in life. Consequently, to check the reasonableness of using the question on satisfaction in life as an index of happiness, I compared the results (for Italy) of two different polls, one asking directly about happiness (described above), the other using the question on satisfaction from the available cross-national study. The structure of the answers was very similar (Table 3). On both questions, business and farm owners

TABLE 3. COMPARISON OF ITALIAN RESULTS ON QUESTIONS OF "HAPPINESS" AND "SATISFACTION WITH SITUATION" (PER CENT)

Occupation	"Dissatisfied" with present situation[a]	Occupation	"Unhappy" at this moment[b]
Business owners	31	Employers	10
Salaried managers	35	Managers	10
Farm owners	32	Farm owners	10
Artisans	43	Artisans	16
Clerks	55	Employees	14
Manual workers	64	Workers	26
Farm workers	63	Farm laborers	20

[a]From William Buchanan and Hadley Cantril, *How Nations See Each Other* (Urbana: University of Illinois Press, 1953), p. 176. The question was the same as that reported in Table 4 for nine countries including Italy.
[b]From *Doxa Bolletino,* No. 12 (April, 1948).

and managers reported themselves either dissatisfied or unhappy only half as often as did manual and farm workers, with clerks and artisans falling in between. The correlation was not perfect, but there was quite close association.

Allowing, then, for many necessary reservations, let us look at the responses to the question, "How satisfied are you with the way you are getting on now?" which was asked simultaneously in nine countries. The results (Table 4) are certainly less sharp and clear-cut than those obtained for job satisfaction.* There are numerous irregularities and ambiguities. For example, Germany produces not our familiar step pattern but a U-shaped curve, and Australia yields, if anything, an inverted U. These cases suggest what the table as a whole hints, namely, that the question is ambiguous and people respond to it in terms of different criteria. Nevertheless, there seems to be an underlying cross-national pattern. The higher non-manual positions hold at least rank 1 (lowest proportion dissatisfied), 2, or 3 in seven of nine countries, whereas the workers held so high a rank in no country and the farm laborers in one. The occupations were originally listed in a rough approximation of their standing in the hierarchy of power and rewards. It is interesting, therefore, that when we sum the rank orders for each occupation we emerge with a regular progression which follows the original ordering. Except for the owners, whose score of 27 is strongly affected by their extremely deviant response in Britain, there is a steady increase from manager (20), through professionals (24), white collar (33), artisans and skilled workers (45), and workers (50), to farm labor (53). That a comparable cross-national pattern emerges when either socioeconomic status or education is used as the independent variable strengthens our convic-

TABLE 4. PERCENTAGE DISSATISFIED WITH HOW THEY ARE "GETTING ON" BY COUNTRY AND OCCUPATION[a]

Country	OCCUPATION						
	Owners	Managers	Professionals	White collar	Artisans	Workers	Farm labor
Australia	11	18	15	22	31	17	17
Britain	41	21	14	36	40	36	26
France	38	29	55	56	56	67	63
Germany	46	39	50	35	37	48	52
Italy	31	35	46	55	43	64	63
Mexico	58	57	50	55	67	65	75
Netherlands	26	15	22	23	37	43	41
Norway	7	4	2	11	12	11	22
United States	20	22	26	24	28	31	39

[a]Adapted from data in Appendix D of Buchanan and Cantril, *op. cit.*, pp. 125-216.

* [Ed. note: See the full paper for details.]

tion that the underlying structure is real. The fact that the relationship holds more firmly when occupation or economic status rather than education are the independent variables suggests that, as we anticipated, the answers more strongly reflect satisfaction with economic than with spiritual welfare.

Whatever their weakness as a guide to the cross-national pattern we seek, these data also point to the usefulness of our procedure for identifying groups with special problems or distinctive responses to more general problems. It is striking, for example, that in Britain the owners formed the group whose members were *most* often dissatisfied with the way they were "getting on." But this was 1948, when they were threatened by the highest level reached by the wave of nationalization sentiment in England, and so the result is not surprising.

Some of the difficulty raised by the question on "satisfaction with getting on" could be avoided if the respondent were asked to disregard his financial condition. An international poll meeting this requirement is, unfortunately, not at hand. We should, however, examine an International Research Associate study in which the wording of the question and its location in the questionnaire may have somewhat reduced the role of economic referents. The question was: "Do you feel that you have gotten as far ahead as you should at this stage of your life, or are you dissatisfied with the progress you have made so far?" Here again, unfortunately, the question would probably be understood by many to mean mainly economic or material "getting ahead" or "progress." This assumption is greatly strengthened by the fact that the responses are more regular and the differences sharper when socioeconomic status rather than occupation is used (Table 5). Using socioeconomic status to

TABLE 5. PERCENTAGE SATISFIED WITH PROGRESS IN LIFE, BY COUNTRY AND STATUS[a]

| Country | Occupation | | | Socioeconomic group | | |
	Executive, professional	White collar	Wage earner	Upper	Middle	Lower
Australia	70	64	66	73	70	65
Austria	61	60	47	64	59	60
Belgium	37	36	21	43	41	34
Brazil[b]	74	60	63	81	71	54
Britain	79	66	70	73	68	71
Denmark	77	78	68	81	75	64
Germany	73	71	68	73	72	65
Japan	52	42	33	50	40	13
Netherlands	61	57	59	67	58	66
Norway	89	79	70	87	71	60
Sweden	71	58	67	80	67	60

[a]Tabulations from a study conducted by International Research Associates.
[b]Rio de Janeiro and Sao Paulo only.

classify the respondents, we find the step structure present in eight of eleven cases, markedly so in four. There is no instance in which the result is the complete reverse of our expectation, but in three countries the group classified as "middle" has the lowest proportion satisfied. Using occupation as the independent variable, we again have four strong cases and a fifth which is up to standard, but now six fail to qualify. In five of these instances the difficulty arises again from the fact that a higher proportion of the middle level of white-collar workers are dissatisfied than is the case among workers. If we compare the executive-professional and worker groups alone, the pattern is clear-cut in all eleven cases.[10]

In sum, no very "pure" measure of feelings of happiness or of spiritual or psychic (as against material) well-being, applied cross-nationally and fully reported, is at hand. Taking the available evidence together, however, we cannot entertain any other hypothesis but that the feeling of happiness or of psychic well-being is unevenly distributed in most, perhaps all, countries. Those who are economically well off, those with more education or whose jobs require more training and skill, more often report themselves happy, joyous, laughing, free of sorrow, satisfied with life's progress. Even though the pattern is weak or ambiguous in some cases, there has not been a single case of a *reversal* of the pattern, that is, a case where measures of happiness are inversely related to measures of status, in studies involving fifteen different countries — at least six of which were studied on two different occasions, through the use of somewhat different questions. There is, then, good reason to challenge the image of the "carefree but happy poor." As one angry man wrote to me, after he had read a news report of a speech I had made reporting the relation of laughter to social status: "And what the hell do you think the poor have to laugh about, anyway?"

Plausible as this contention may be on the surface, it is obviously not the end but only the beginning of a study. If those who are better placed and more fortunate more often report they are happy, can we test the validity of this report by such other measures as their rates of suicide, homicide, and mental illness?[11] If the proportion satisfied rises

[10] A twelfth case, France, was a strong instance of the expected relationship. Since socioeconomic status classifications were not available for France, it was excluded from Table 5 to make both parts strictly comparable.

[11] Suicide rates rise with socioeconomic status, but their absolute frequency is quite low in all groups. Homicides, many times more common than suicide, and psychopathic illness, which is incomparably more frequent, are both markedly commoner in the lower classes. Insofar as these rates, when combined, provide an index of misery, the pattern observed would be congruent with that already described.

with income, will better-paid workers in any country be happier than those less well paid at the same occupational level? Will raising the incomes of all increase the happiness of all, or does it require an unequal gain to bring happiness to some? What of the man who is well educated but poorly paid, or rich but poorly educated? Some questions of this kind can be answered by further cross-tabulation of the original IBM cards, which it is hoped will be possible at a later date.[12] Some will require new cross-national studies clearly focused on these issues. . . .

[12] The Roper Center for Public Opinion Research at Williams College plans to collect the IBM cards from studies conducted since World War II in some twenty countries. If this objective is achieved, it will open exceptional opportunities for comparative research. [Ed. note: This objective *was* achieved and these data are now available from the Roper Center, Williams College, Williamstown, Mass.]